The New International Economic Order

Westview Special Studies in International Economics

The New International Economic Order: Confrontation or Cooperation between North and South?
edited by Karl P. Sauvant and Hajo Hasenpflug

In the face of the continuing economic gap between the industrialized and the developing countries, the Third World began to demand a reorganization of the international economic system—its mechanisms, organizations, purposes—that would make the system responsive to the needs of all of its members. The United Nations' Sixth Special Session in 1974 made this demand a priority item on the international agenda, and since then, the establishment of the New International Economic Order (NIEO) has been pursued in a series of international conferences by increasingly organized and increasingly assertive Third World nations. In this book, Karl Sauvant and Hajo Hasenpflug have drawn together material relevant to the key areas of the NIEO, documenting the present structure of the international economic system in these areas and presenting the main proposals aimed at the establishment of the NIEO.

Karl P. Sauvant holds a Ph.D. in international relations from the University of Pennsylvania, where he also worked as a research associate in the Multinational Enterprise Unit of the Wharton School. He is currently transnational corporations affairs officer at the United Nations Centre on Transnational Corporations.

Hajo Hasenpflug studied economics at the University of Hamburg and is now head of the Department of Foreign Trade and Economic Integration of the HWWA-Institut für Wirtschaftsforschung—Hamburg, a major economics research institute in Germany. He has worked and written extensively in the areas of world trade and international economic cooperation.

Other Titles in This Series

Oil Money and the World Economy, Yoon S. Park

Controlling Multinational Enterprises: Problems, Strategies, Counterstrategies, edited by Karl P. Sauvant and Farid G. Lavipour

The New International Economic Order

Confrontation or Cooperation between North and South?

edited by
Karl P. Sauvant and Hajo Hasenpflug

Westview Press
Boulder, Colorado

Westview Special Studies in International Economics

Published 1977 in the United States of America by
Westview Press, Inc.
5500 Central Avenue
Boulder, Colorado 80301
Frederick A. Praeger, Publisher

Second printing, May 1978

Library of Congress Cataloging in Publication Data
Main entry under title:
The new international economic order.
(Westview special studies in international economics)
Bibliography: p.
Includes index.
1. International economic relations—Addresses, essays, lectures. I. Sauvant, Karl P. II. Hasenpflug, Hajo.
HF1411.N43 382.1 76-26623
ISBN 0-89158-139-1 (hardcover)
ISBN 0-89158-288-6 (paperback)

Printed and bound in the United States of America

To those I love—*K.P.S.*

To the memory of my grandfather, Johann Bösch,
with deep gratitude—*H.H.*

Contents

Tables

Chapter 7

Chapter 8

Chapter 10

Chapter 12

Chapter 13

Chapter 17

Chapter 18

Chapter 20

Chapter 22

Chapter 24

Preface

Between 1952 and 1972, the per capita real income in developed market economics increased from approximately $2,000 to $4,000 (at 1973 prices). During the same period, the per capita real income in developing countries rose from about $175 to a mere $300. Thus, in an era of unprecedented prosperity for the industrialized countries, the developing countries as a group did not improve their relative position; for many of them, in fact, it actually deteriorated. Acute poverty, chronic unemployment, and endemic undernourishment continued or even worsened in most Third World countries, while their economic dependence on the metropolitan countries increased and was even extended into new areas.

In the face of this situation, the developing countries could not but conclude that the present international economic system, in all its dimensions, is biased against them—that it is geared primarily toward increasing the comfort of the developed countries and not to the fulfillment of the basic needs of the developing ones. Obviously, the purposes, mechanisms, and structures of the present international economic system would have to be changed if they were to serve the interests of *all* its members. This is the objective of the New International Economic Order (NIEO).

The Sixth Special Session of the United Nations (UN) General Assembly (1974)—the first ever devoted exclusively to economic problems—marked the recognition of the need for change by the international community as a whole. The establishment of the New International Economic Order has since been vigorously pursued by increasingly organized and increasingly assertive Third World governments, as witnessed by the series of conferences that followed the Sixth Special Session.

The main objective of this volume is to review a number of important issues related to the New International Economic Order and, especially, to present, explore, and discuss various proposals and strategies aimed at its establishment. In the interest of facilitating an appreciation of the urgency of these proposals and strategies, and of the rationale underlying them, they will be related to the existing situation in the main areas of North-South relationship. If this book contributes to greater clarity in the discussion of the New International Economic Order, if it leads to a greater understanding of the position of the developing countries, and if it stimulates discussion of other measures aimed at improving the situation of the Third World, it will more than fulfill its purpose.

In the preparation of this volume we benefited greatly from the help and cooperation of a number of individuals and institutions. Special thanks are due to the authors whose contributions were specifically written for this book: Dieter Ernst, Peter J. Ginman, Catherine B. Gwin, Wolfgang Hager, Michael A. Morris, Tracy Murray, Charles Ries, Barbara Rogers, and Steven J. Warnecke. We very much appreciate the patience with which they took our comments and observed our deadlines. We are also very grateful to the United Nations, The UN Conference on Trade and Development (UNCTAD), The UN Industrial Development Organization (UNIDO), the World Bank for giving us permission to reprint their materials, and the Ministry of Economics of the Federal Republic of Germany for translating a speech of Minister of Economics Hans Friderichs into English. We are very much indebted to Mary McGee, without whose cheerful and untiring assistance the material for this study could not have been assembled so readily. We want to say thank you, too, to Vishwas Govitrikar for looking at various parts of the manuscript and to John Hale for his excellent copy-editing job. We owe a special debt of gratitude to Francisca F. Martinez, whose help in the preparation of the manuscript was invaluable. Finally, Lynne Rienner was responsible for the arduous task of transforming the manuscript into a book—and it was a great pleasure to work with her. Needless to say, the views expressed in this book do not necessarily represent those of the institutions with which the editors are currently affiliated.

Karl P. Sauvant
Hajo Hasenpflug
October 1976

Contributors

Dieter Ernst
Research Associate
Vereinigung Deutscher Wissenschaftler
Hamburg
Federal Republic of Germany

Hans Friderichs
Minister of Economics
Bonn
Federal Republic of Germany

Peter J. Ginman
Economic Affairs Officer
UNCTAD
Geneva
Switzerland

Catherine B. Gwin
Research Associate
Council on Foreign Relations
New York, New York

Wolfgang Hager
Senior Fellow
Forschungsinstitut der Deutschen
Gesellschaft für Auswärtige Politik
Bonn
Federal Republic of Germany

Mahbub ul Haq
Director
Policy Planning and Program
Review Department
World Bank
Washington, D.C.

Hajo Hasenpflug
Head, Department of Foreign Trade and
Economic Integration
HWWA—Institut für Wirtschaftsforschung
Hamburg
Federal Republic of Germany

Michael A. Morris
Assistant Professor
Department of Political Science
Clemson University
Clemson, South Carolina

Tracy Murray
Associate Professor
Graduate School of Business
Administration
New York University
New York, New York

Charles Ries
Assistant Director
Center for Multinational Studies
Washington, D.C.

Barbara Rogers
Research Fellow
School of Development Studies
University of East Anglia
Norwich
England

Karl P. Sauvant
Transnational Corporations
Affairs Officer
Centre on Transnational
Corporations
United Nations
New York, New York

Steven J. Warnecke
Associate Professor
Department of Political Science
City University of New York
New York, New York

Part 1

Introduction

1 *Toward the New International Economic Order*

Karl P. Sauvant

The foundations of the existing international economic institutions were laid during and immediately after World War II. They reflect the determination of the developed market economies (DMEs) to create favorable conditions for their speedy reconstruction after the war and the achievement of renewed and continued prosperity. The interests, needs, and special conditions of the developing countries (DCs), most of whom were still colonies in the immediate postwar years, were largely ignored in this process. As a result, and in spite of a few later changes, the system and its mechanisms did not improve the situation of most DCs to the extent desired. Acute poverty, chronic unemployment, and endemic undernourishment continued in most of them, or even worsened, and their economic dependence on the metropolitan countries was perpetuated and even extended into new areas. When these facts became well recognized and urgent issues for the Third World in the 1960s, it could not but conclude that a new economic order was necessary, an order that would explicitly recognize the needs and conditions of the developing countries. More specifically, the developing countries realized that the purposes of the existing international economic order would have to be broadened to include development. Furthermore, if these broadened purposes were to be effectively served, the mechanisms and structure of the old order would have to be appropriately altered.

These were the guiding principles of the two resolutions adopted in 1974 by the Sixth Special Session of the United Nations (UN) General Assembly and entitled "Declaration on the Establishment of a New International Economic Order" and "Programme of Action on the Establishment of a New International Economic Order." The objectives outlined in these documents were elaborated later in the year in the "Charter of Economic Rights and Duties of States" and further consolidated in a resolution on

---

The views expressed in this article do not necessarily reflect those of the institution with which the author is currently affiliated.

"Development and International Economic Co-operation," adopted in 1975 by the UN Seventh Special Session. With the adoption of these documents, the developing countries had succeeded in making development[1]—the establishment of the New International Economic Order (NIEO)[2]—the priority item on the international agenda.

Disappointments and Groping for a New Approach

Many observers of the international political scene in the 1950s and 1960s believed that many of the DCs' problems were largely a function of their political status. Once they achieved political independence, they would become full and equal members of the international community. Moreover, their participation in international economic interactions—whose benefits would quickly trickle down to them—coupled with a number of international and regional development efforts, would soon result in considerable improvements of their economic situation.

By the end of the 1960s, these hopes had been shattered. The First UN Development Decade—launched with great fanfare in 1961 and strongly supported by the Third World—fell short of its objectives; its extension in 1970 was viewed with dampened expectations. The Alliance for Progress, also launched in 1961 and accompanied with similar hopes, quietly faltered. Another regional effort, the First Yaoundé Convention of 1963, and its successors—the Second Yaoundé Convention and the Arusha Convention, both signed in 1969—shared the fate of the other efforts. A Non-Aligned Countries' Conference on Problems of Economic Development, held in Cairo in 1962, remained a straw in the wind. The initiatives of the UN Conference on Trade and Development (UNCTAD)—whose first meeting had produced the Group of 77—also amounted to very little. In fact, whatever the success of the development efforts of the 1960s, whatever the trickle-down effect, the gap between North and South did not become any narrower: while per capita real income (at 1973 prices) in the DMEs doubled from about $2,000 to $4,000 in the period from 1952 to 1972, in the DCs it rose by a mere $125—from $175 to $300. In other words, real income per head in the DCs amounted to approximately 9 percent of that in the DMEs in 1952 and to approximately 8 percent in 1972.[3] It appeared that the international and regional development efforts and related initiatives, or, more generally, the mechanisms of the international economic system, had failed to deliver what they had seemed to promise. In the words of UNCTAD:

> The fact that the developing countries did not share adequately in the prosperity of the developed countries when the latter were experiencing remarkably rapid expansion indicates the existence of basic weaknesses in the

> mechanisms which link the economies of the two groups of countries. . . . The weakness of this structure, the inadequacy of the mechanisms by which growth in the developed centres is transmitted to the third world, are manifested in each of the major areas of economic relations between developed and developing countries—in the trade in commodities and in manufactures, in the transfer of technology and in the provision of financial resources through the international monetary and financial system.[4]

Significantly, this recognition came at a time when it had become increasingly obvious that political independence is a mere chimera unless based on economic independence—unless the structures of economic dependence that characterize the relationships between developing and developed countries are transformed into structures of interdependence. Economic development thus came to be viewed with new urgency.

In their search for solutions to their problems, the DCs embraced the concept of individual and collective self-reliance. This concept was first enunciated by the Non-Aligned Countries—the political organization of the Third World—at their 1970 summit of heads of state or government in Lusaka.[5] It was further elaborated at their 1972 foreign ministers' conference in Georgetown,[6] and since then has been included in most major international economic documents. Self-reliance became all the more important since industrialization was often perceived to have turned into dependent industrialization, primarily through transnational enterprises (TNEs) and their foreign affiliates, thus reinforcing the existing structures and extending them into other areas.

Self-reliance is a program. It requires, in its collective dimension, that the political, economic, and sociocultural structures created to link colonies to metropolitan countries (in a status of dependence) be altered to link developing countries to one another (in a status of interdependence). In the political sphere, this process had commenced in the 1960s with the emancipation of the DCs from the political control of their former rulers and their organization in the nonaligned movement. The Lusaka summit marked the beginning of increased efforts to achieve economic emancipation. However, it soon became apparent that these efforts needed a broader and more comprehensive economic program in the framework of which self-reliance could be pursued and economic development could take place. Quite naturally, such a program had to deal with the external conditions of development and, more specifically, with the structure of the international economic system.

The formulation of this platform took place in the nonaligned movement, drawing on work done by the Group of 77, by UNCTAD, and by the UN (especially in connection with the development decades). As a result, the Non-Aligned Countries adopted, at their summit in Algiers in September 1973, an "Economic Declaration" and an "Action Programme for Economic Co-operation"[7] which called for a thorough reorganization of the international economic system. These documents, in turn, constituted one of the primary foundations (at times verbatim)[8] of the resolutions—the "Declaration on the Establishment of a New International Economic Order" and the "Programme of Action on the Establishment of a New International Economic Order"[9]—adopted eight months later at the Sixth Special Session of the UN General Assembly, the first special session to deal with economic issues. These resolutions, together with the "Charter of Economic Rights and Duties of State" (adopted in December 1974 by the regular Twenty-ninth Session of the General Assembly) and the resolution on "Development and International Economic Co-operation" (adopted September 1975 by the Seventh Special Session),[10] constitute the basic documents of the New International Economic Order.

New Objectives and a New Context

What distinguishes the Algiers and the Sixth Special Session resolutions from earlier international economic programs is not their comprehensiveness; in fact, such comprehensiveness had already been approached elsewhere, especially in the UN action program for the Second Development Decade and in various combinations of UNCTAD resolutions. Rather, what distinguishes these resolutions from their predecessors is their objective and the new environment in which they were formulated and advanced. The objective of these resolutions is no longer merely to improve the functioning of the existing international economic system, but rather to change its purposes, mechanisms, and structures.[11] As to the new environment, three factors in particular, all of them highly interrelated, are of key importance: (1) the emergence of the nonaligned movement as an international economic pressure group, (2) the politicization of the development issue, and (3) the growing assertiveness of the developing countries.

The Role of the Non-Aligned Countries

Several allusions to the role of the nonaligned movement have already been made in the preceding paragraphs. The movement had its origin in the bipolar world of the 1950s, when a group of DCs began attempts to exercise some independent influence in international relations.[12] Between the first summit in Belgrade in 1961 and the fourth summit in Algiers in 1973, membership increased from twenty-five to seventy-five. The Non-Aligned Countries, in other words, had been highly successful in persuading most of the DCs to join ranks with them. Moreover, since 1970, the members of the movement greatly intensified their interactions with one another, established closer lines of communication, and gave themselves a highly structured organizational framework. Finally, and most importantly for later developments, the nonaligned movement underwent a fundamental change in character. Before the 1970 Lusaka summit, the movement had concentrated on political matters. At Lusaka, economic questions, for the first time, received considerable attention with the enunciation of the concept of individual and collective self-reliance. And since Lusaka, the largest part of the concrete work of the movement has been concerned with self-reliance and development.[13] Three main reasons explain this change. Two of them—the disappointment in the development efforts of the 1960s and the growing recognition that political independence, to be viable, has to be based on economic independence—have already been mentioned. The third concerns the changing international political situation. Détente, political decolonization, and the stabilization of the East-West military situation made many of the original basic tenets of the nonaligned credo less urgent, and contributed to the substantive reorientation of the nonaligned movement. Thus, between Lusaka and Algiers, the movement had transformed itself from an informal gathering of like-minded leaders convened to discuss the world political situation into a highly organized international economic pressure group for the reorganization of the international economic system.

Politicization

This transformation had an important effect on the way in which international economic matters were presented and pursued. During the 1960s—and even at UNCTAD III (1972)—questions of economic development were essentially regarded as "low politics" left to the economics, financial, and planning ministries. Attempts at politicizing these issues—e.g., the Group of 77's Charter of Algiers (1967)—therefore failed. With the beginning of the 1970s, however, this attitude changed and development questions became "high politics": they were elevated from the level of heads of departments to the level of heads of state or government. This change found its first full expression when the Algiers summit of the Non-Aligned Countries—which was attended by more heads of state or government than any other international conference has ever been—embraced these questions for the first time at so high a level as major themes of its deliberations and actions. The resolutions adopted at Algiers represent the formal recognition by the policymakers of the DCs that their problems are not only a function of their political status but also of their economic status. Self-reliance and development, consequently, became highly politicized issues.[14]

Third World Assertiveness and Bargaining Power

Much of the bargaining power of the developing world consists of the power to disrupt the international economic system (and especially the sophisticated economies of the developed countries), to introduce uncertainties, and to foreclose possibilities—in other words, to increase the opportunity costs for developed countries. Disruptions and uncertainties might be created in such areas as the supply of natural resources,[15] the functioning of the financial system (mass debt defaults triggered by insolvency), or the operations of TNEs (a growing number of transnational enterprises receive a considerable share of their earnings from developing countries). Possibilities might be withheld in the area of market expansion. For instance, a Third World trading system—the establishment of which may be desirable in order to stimulate self-reliance—could limit the DMEs' access to the markets of the future, especially for products in which they are already approaching saturation. On the other hand, the potential of these markets is tremendous. A parallel might be drawn here to the treatment of the labor force in the industrial countries during the 19th century where business learned that workers are not only producers but also consumers. Over time, this realization led to a certain redistribution of income and greater prosperity for everyone. On the international level, the DCs are in many ways the workers of the developed countries, but their potential as consumers has scarcely yet been realized. Today, over two-thirds of the world population of about 4 billion lives in developing countries; by the year 2000, this proportion will have increased to four-fifths out of a total of over 6 billion. This population distribution raises not only market considerations but also the question of whether 15 percent of the world population can withdraw into a self-sufficient fortress and ignore the rest of the world—especially if likely military developments, including the spread of nuclear weapons to developing countries, are taken into consideration. The long-range risks and opportunity costs, in other words, may be much higher than the immediate costs of cooperating in the reorganization of the international economic system.

The main and most concrete assets of the DCs, however, are their natural resources.[16] With the growing awareness of the importance of economic matters, developing countries have also become increasingly cognizant of the bargaining power, however limited, which is represented by these resources. This recognition has come to be expressed in particular in the more assertive usage of the principle of permanent sovereignty over natural resources. In the 1960s, support of this principle used to be accompanied by references to international law for cases of dispute settlement. Concretely, this meant that in cases of nationalization the parent enterprise (and the home country) could refer to international law for prompt, effective, and adequate compensation. In the 1970s, the DCs discontinued these references to international law and, instead, insisted that disputes should be settled under national law. While this debate about principles probably did not effect much of a change in the behavior of host countries—as a rule, compensations continued to be paid in the relatively few cases of nationalization that occurred[17]—it still indicated a change of attitude. Developing countries increasingly sought to obtain control over their natural resources, or at least a greater share of the benefits associated with the exploitation of these resources, in order to use them as a stimulant for their own development. For the same reason, producers' associations were created. This change of attitude is illustrated by the Organization of Petroleum Exporting Countries (OPEC). Although OPEC was formed as early as 1961, it spent the whole decade of the 1960s bargaining about a new distribution of royalties that in the end brought additional revenues of $25 *million*. Between 1970 and 1974, on the other hand, OPEC's take from its natural resources increased by approximately $80 *billion*. In addition, virtually all crude-oil production facilities changed from foreign to (at least majority) national ownership. Not surprisingly, OPEC's performance stimulated a number of other producers' associations, most successful among them being the International Bauxite Association. Even if the Council of Producers' Associations established by the Non-Aligned Countries should become operational,[18] however, these other associations clearly do not reach or even approach the power of OPEC. But the proliferation of producers' associations and the insistence on national control over natural resources indicate that the DCs have become more assertive and are attempting to use their bargaining power as effectively as possible.

The success of one of these producers' associations—OPEC—was, in fact, instrumental in elevating the issue of development from a priority item on the agenda of the Non-Aligned Countries to a priority item on the agenda of the international community.[19] The word *instrumental* is important. With the Algiers summit, the DCs had reached such a degree of mobilization and organization, and the issue of development had acquired such salience, that it was only a question of time until these matters would be forcefully pursued on the international level. As a matter of fact, the Algiers summit had itself called for a special session of the UN General Assembly devoted to development—the later Seventh Special Session. However, the oil crisis changed this timetable. At the end of January 1974, President Houari Boumediene of Algeria, in his capacity as president-in-office of the Group of Non-Aligned Countries, requested a special session of the UN General Assembly to study the problems of raw materials and development[20]—the Sixth Special Session, held between 9 April and 2 May 1974. The events during and since that special session demonstrate that the efforts of the Non-

Aligned Countries had begun to pay off. They had created an organization that was capable of advancing the objectives of the Third World and that maintained the solidarity of the developing countries. In fact, the position of the Third World has been further strengthened because the Algiers summit and the Sixth Special Session led to a de facto merger of the Group of 77 with the nonaligned movement—if not in membership, at least in program and objectives. As a result, virtually all international conferences since Algiers and the Sixth Special Session have dealt with questions related to the establishment of the New International Economic Order.[21]

The NIEO Program: The Structure of This Volume

I observed earlier that the NIEO program distinguishes itself from earlier international economic programs by virtue of its objective.[22] Its objective is not merely to improve the functioning of the existing international economic system but rather to expand its purposes and to change its mechanisms and structures to suit the new purposes. The purpose to be added to the existing ones is development. Given the special situation of the DCs, the acceptance of this additional purpose involves the acceptance of a number of principles. They include greater control by DCs over their own economies, especially as expressed in the principle of permanent sovereignty of every state over its natural resources and all economic activities; greater participation of DCs in decision-making processes that affect their situation; international cooperation for development and active assistance to DCs; and preferential and nonreciprocal treatment for developing countries.

The problem is not so much the acceptance of these principles. Most developed countries have done this. The problem is their translation into changes in the mechanisms governing the interactions between North and South, changes that would eventually transform the structures that are the result of past and present patterns of interaction. The NIEO program is an attempt to set these changes in motion in areas of particular significance to the development process: trade and commodities, financial matters, science and technology, industrialization and transnational enterprises, and self-reliance.

The following chapters of this volume deal with the principal issues in each of the main areas just identified. In each case, an effort has been made to provide some background on the existing situation in order to facilitate the understanding of the urgency of the proposals of the NIEO program. A key document of this program—the resolution adopted at the Seventh Special Session—is reprinted as Chapter 2. The structure of this resolution—i.e., its division into several substantive areas—has served as the organizing principle of this book.

Before turning to the specific issues, however, the reader is introduced into the NIEO discussion. Part 2 deals with the position of the North and the South. Chapter 3, an UNCTAD document, contains a summary presentation of the key elements of the NIEO program. This is followed, in Chapter 4, by Charles Ries' review of the skeptics' arguments against the NIEO. A number of these arguments are part of the official policy of important developed states. This becomes apparent in Chapter 5, a speech by the Minister of Economics of the Federal Republic of Germany, Hans Friderichs, one of the most outspoken critics of the NIEO. In spite of such opposition on the part of a number of DMEs and their spokespersons, and in spite of efforts on the part of a number of DCs to pursue a policy aimed at the fastest possible implementation of the NIEO program, the atmosphere of confrontation that characterized the Sixth Special Session seemed to have given way to a new effort at collaboration during the Seventh Special Session. Catherine B. Gwin suggests, however, in Chapter 6, that this change may be one of form and not of substance; of tactics, not of strategies.

Parts 2-7, then, address themselves to the main areas of North-South economic interactions, each representing, as already indicated, one of the principal sections of the resolution adopted at the Seventh Special Session.[23] Part 3 deals with trade and commodity issues—issues that in the eyes of many DCs form the very heart of the North-South relationship. The part begins with an examination by Hajo Hasenpflug, in Chapter 7, of the deterioration of the position of the developing countries in world trade. Since this deterioration is largely a result of the primary-products structure of Third World exports, his analysis is followed, in Chapter 8, by an outline of UNCTAD's integrated program for commodities and the related issue of the indexation of prices. The integrated program is a comprehensive effort to establish new production and market structures for primary products; as such, many DCs consider it as the centerpiece of a new North-South relationship. Aspects of the integrated program are also the topic of Chapter 9, in which Wolfgang Hager reviews some of the benefits—including those for developed countries—of commodity agreements. A different approach to mastering part of the commodity problem, but an approach in some respect complementary to the integrated program, is examined by Hasenpflug in Chapter 10: the stabilization-of-export-earnings system currently being pioneered (on the basis of the Lomé Convention) by the European Community and its forty-six African, Pacific, and Caribbean country associates. In the next chapter, Chapter 11, Michael A. Morris deals with another aspect of the commodity issue—one of potentially important future consequences: the control and management of deep seabed nonliving natural resources through the application, within certain geographical limits, of the principle of permanent sovereignty over natural resources, and, beyond these limits, through an international seabed authority. This question has become one of the key issues of the Third Conference of the UN on the Law of the Sea, and Morris traces the relevance of the NIEO discussion for its emergence.

Immediate actions concerning commodities are important, since this sector plays a key role in many of the DCs' economies and since it is frequently the prime source of foreign exchange. The long-term objective of the Third World, however—and this is recognized as an integral part of the integrated program—is the transformation of the DCs from primary-product suppliers to processors and manufacturers. A principal obstacle for the achievement of this objective are the tariff and nontariff barriers of DMEs, which are the foremost export markets of the developing countries. One attempt to begin the elimination of these barriers has been made with the introduction of the Generalized System of Preferences (GSP). However, as Peter J. Ginman and Tracy Murray demonstrate in Chapter 12, the effectiveness of the GSP has so far been extremely limited. They conclude that a substantial liberalization of the system is necessary in order to stimulate Third World trade.

The development objective of the Third World requires substantial financial resources. Since exports alone will not be able to provide these resources (*inter alia* because of the conditions discussed in Part 3), other mechanisms have to be explored and utilized. Part 4 addresses itself to the transfer of real resources for development. Chapter 13, an excerpt from a document prepared for UNCTAD IV, outlines the present situation regarding financial cooperation between North and South, emphasizing in particular the relative decline of concessional flows to the Third World. Partly as a result of this decline, DCs had increasingly to rely on private capital markets with their less favorable conditions. This, in turn, has placed a new and rapidly growing burden on Third World states: external indebtedness and the servicing of this debt. From $9 billion at the end of 1956, the external debt of over eighty non-OPEC developing countries had reached $125 billion in 1974 and is expected to rise to around $150 billion by the end of 1975. This sum exceeds the 1974 value of total exports of these countries by one-third, and the annual servicing of these debts absorbs, on the average, over 10 percent of the total annual export earnings of the countries involved. This situation, and especially several proposals aimed at alleviating it, is the topic of Chapter 14 (excerpts from another document prepared for UNCTAD IV). It becomes obvious from these two documents that basic improvements in the present framework for international resource transfer are urgently required. Some possibilities are examined by Mahbub ul Haq in Chapter 15. These improvements have to go beyond the more narrow area of development assistance. They have to reach into the international monetary system, which, after all, constitutes the framework of the trade transactions and the development efforts of the Third World.

The grievances of the developing countries relating to the international monetary system and their main proposals for its improvement are concisely summarized in the communiqué—reprinted here as Chapter 16—issued by the Group of Twenty-Four after the January 1976 meeting of the International Monetary Fund (IMF) in Kingston.

The dependence of the developing on the developed countries is perhaps most pronounced in the area of science and technology—the subject matter of Part 5. Chapter 17—excerpts from a document prepared for UNCTAD IV—discusses the nature of technological dependence and its consequences for the Third World. The following chapter, Chapter 18, contains a set of UNCTAD proposals aimed at changing this dependence. One of these proposals, and a key one as far as present activities are concerned, relates to the formulation and implementation of a code of conduct for the transfer of technology. Dieter Ernst, in Chapter 19, critically evaluates the possible effectiveness of such a code and concludes that, in fact, it merely would codify the status quo.

The purpose of reorienting the international mechanisms and structures in the areas of trade, financial assistance, the international monetary system, and science and technology is to stimulate, if not to serve, industrialization and through it economic development. Industrialization, the topic of Part 6, remains the basic objective of the developing countries. Industrialization is expected to create employment, end undernourishment, eradicate mass poverty, and, in due course, secure a comfortable standard of living.

At the present time, DCs account for about two-thirds of the world's population, but they produce only about 9 percent (in 1972: $108 billion) of its total manufacturing output (of about $1,200 billion)—the rough equivalent of the manufacturing output of the Federal Republic of Germany. Chapter 20, a UN Industrial Development Organization (UNIDO) review of the present status of industrialization in developing countries, shows, furthermore, the great disparity of levels of industrialization among Third World nations. Four countries alone (India, Brazil, Argentina, and Mexico), for instance, account for more than one-half of the Third World's manufacturing output, while less than one-tenth of it is produced in Africa. In the face of this situation, it is a declared objective of the NIEO program to increase the DCs' share in world industrial output from the present 9 percent to at least 25 percent in the year 2000. Expressed in absolute figures, the target output is estimated to be $1,400 billion (in 1972 dollars), or somewhat higher than the manufacturing output of the entire world in 1972. Ambitious and arbitrary as this target may be, it is not necessarily impossible to achieve. According to UNCTAD's calculations, it assumes, for the period 1972-2000, average annual manufacturing-output growth rates of 5.1 percent for the developed countries (down 0.8 percentage points from the combined 1962-72 average rate of the DMEs and centrally planned economies), and of 9.6 percent for the DCs (up 3 percentage points from their average rate during 1960-72).[24] Nevertheless, it is unquestionable that major efforts have to be made to mobilize the resources and increase the international cooperation required to meet the target.

One of these efforts involves the gradual redeployment of appropriate industries from developed to developing countries. A similar effort is also one of the main objectives of the Lomé Convention. Steven J. Warnecke, in Chapter 21, examines the experience gained thus far and the difficulties associated with the implementation of the Convention's title dealing with industrial cooperation. He observes that in market economies the role of private business enterprises plays a crucial role in industrial cooperation and that these enterprises favor redeployment through the mechanism of foreign direct investment and, thus, through the establishment of foreign affiliates. In fact, and more generally speaking, the present development strategies of most DCs rely, to a varying degree, on the inflow of private foreign capital as made available by TNEs. The surge of foreign direct investment has, however, also given rise to the fear that industrialization has turned into dependent industrialization, benefiting, in the final analysis, more the home than the developing host countries. It is the prevalence of TNEs in the economic life of Third World states, and their relevance to all main areas of the NIEO program, that are at the root of the DCs' insistence on the principle of permanent sovereignty of every state over its natural resources and all its economic activities, and of their quest for greater control over TNEs. In Chapter 22, I review efforts at controlling TNEs at the national, regional, and international levels, giving special attention to the OECD Guidelines for Multinational Enterprises, the Foreign-Direct-Investment Statute of the Non-Aligned Countries, and the efforts of the UN to formulate an international code of conduct for TNEs. Also advanced is the idea of establishing at TNE headquarters Host Country Councils through which host countries could gain immediate influence on the decision-making processes of the main enterprises operating in their territory, thereby supplementing external control mechanisms by internal ones.

As noted above, the present development strategies of most DCs depend on financial inflows from abroad. But I also observed that the Third World's turn to the concept of individual and collective self-reliance signals the beginning of growing efforts to reduce this dependency through the increasing mobilization of its own resources. The achievement of self-reliance—the theme of Part 7, the final part of this volume—demands fundamental internal and external changes. In its external dimension, the implementation of (collective) self-reliance requires a change in the structures of vertical interactions between developing and developed countries in the direction of structures of horizontal interactions among developing countries. Trade among DCs, for instance, accounts for only one-fifth of their total trade, and this share has been declining. What is necessary, therefore, is increased economic cooperation among developing countries, and a whole set of relevant measures—ranging from the facilitation of intra-Third World interactions to direct collaboration efforts—is outlined in Chapter 23, excerpts from a document prepared for UNCTAD IV.

In its internal dimension, the implementation of the concept of (individual) self-reliance demands that conditions for the mobilization of the *entire* population and the realization of its potential for development are created. Among other things—like drastic changes in the class structure of individual countries aimed at allowing greater popular participation and sharing in the development process—this requires an acknowledgement of the important role of women in economic activities. Since women constitute a substantial percentage of the economically active population in many DCs (and especially in the rural sector, the most important one in the Third World), the conscious, complete, and equal integration of women in the development process is a precondition for the full realization of the entire potential of each developing country. As Barbara Rogers shows in Chapter 24, the final chapter of this volume, the NIEO discussion has contributed significantly to the appreciation of this issue (especially through the Mexico Conference on Women) and, thereby, has set in motion a train of events that can contribute to a strengthening of the forces of self-reliance.

For the developing countries, the NIEO program is the basis on which they can achieve independent development. It is an attempt to restructure the present international economic system in such a way as to make it responsive not only to the interests of the DMEs (who created the present system), but also to the interests and special conditions of the DCs (who inherited it). The issue is the establishment of a new order that more equitably serves the needs of *all* members of the international system. The transformation of the nonaligned movement into a highly organized international economic pressure group for the reorganization of the international economic system, the politicization of the development issues, and the growing assertiveness of the Third World have created a context within which this objective can—and will—be pursued more vigorously than in the past.

Notes

1. It should be noted that the NIEO program deals with one aspect of the total development process only—its external dimension, its international

framework. Another important—possibly even the most important—dimension concerns internal development and reforms. However, to the extent that a development approach (like the aid-by-trade concept) relies on foreign inputs or, more generally, on interaction with the rest of the world, the terms and conditions under which these inputs are made available—the ways in which these interactions are structured—strongly influence whether or not (domestic) development is encouraged and the direction in which it proceeds.

2. The DCs aim at the establishment of *the New International Economic Order*—an order that specifically acknowledges development as one of its main purposes and whose mechanisms and structures are changed to transform relations of dependence into relations of interdependence (especially through the implementation of the (undiluted) proposals outlined in the documents just cited). The DMEs, on the other hand, are willing to make certain improvements in the existing order, thereby moving to *a new international economic order.* The UN compromise settled on *a New International Economic Order*; thus, one can still generally place the sympathies of a speaker or writer according to her or his use of one of the noncompromise terms.

3. UNCTAD, *New Directions and New Structures for Trade and Development: Report by the Secretary-General of UNCTAD to the Conference* (TD/183), 14 April 1976, p. 4. Since earlier figures for DCs tend to have a high margin of error, the interpretation of trend data has to be very cautious. In addition, it should be noted that these figures conceal a wide range of conditions among DCs, ranging from a clear relative decline for some of them to above-average performance for others, and that they also reflect the differential increase of population in the countries concerned.

4. UNCTAD, *New Directions,* pp. 5-6.

5. Third Conference of Heads of State or Government of Non-Aligned Countries, "Declaration on Non-Alignment and Economic Progress," in Guyana, Ministry of Foreign Affairs, ed., *Main Documents Relating to Conferences of Non-Aligned Countries* (Georgetown: Ministry of Foreign Affairs, 1972).

6. Third Conference of Ministers of Foreign Affairs of Non-Aligned Countries, "The Action Programme for Economic Co-operation," in Guyana, *Main Documents.*

7. Fourth Conference of Heads of State or Government of Non-Aligned Countries, *Economic Declaration* and *Action Programme for Economic Co-operation* (UN document A/9330), 22 November 1973. For an analysis of the economic program of the nonaligned movement and the evolution of this movement into an international economic pressure group, see Odette Jankowitsch and Karl P. Sauvant, "The Evolution of the Non-Aligned Movement into a Pressure Group for the Establishment of the New International Economic Order" (paper presented at the Seventeenth Annual Convention of the

International Studies Association, Toronto, February 1976).

8. For a comparative analysis of the resolutions adopted at the 1973 summit of the Non-Aligned Countries and the Sixth Special Session, see Jankowitsch and Sauvant, "Evolution of the Non-Aligned Movement."

9. United Nations General Assembly resolutions 3201 (S-VI) and 3202 (S-VI), both adopted on 1 May 1974. Although the resolutions had been adopted without a vote, DMEs made a number of reservations; see United Nations documents A/PV.2229-2231.

10. United Nations General Assembly resolutions 3281 (XXIX), adopted 12 December 1974, and 3362 (S-VII), adopted 16 September 1975, respectively. The latter resolution is reprinted in the following chapter.

11. This change in orientation expressed itself, for instance, in the evaluation of the international monetary system. Whereas a 1971 Ministerial Meeting of the Non-Aligned Countries referred to "the monetary arrangements that have been carefully worked out since the Bretton Wood Conference," the Economic Declaration of the 1973 Algiers summit stated that "the monetary and financial system devised at Bretton Woods has served only the interests of some developed countries"; see, respectively, Ministerial Consultative Meeting of Non-Aligned Countries, "Communiqué Issued by the Ministerial Consultative Meeting of Non-Aligned Countries, New York, October 1971," in Guyana, *Main Documents*, p. 99; and Fourth Conference of Heads of State or Government of Non-Aligned Countries, UN document A/9330, p. 64.

12. The following is based on a more detailed discussion in Jankowitsch and Sauvant, "Evolution of the Non-Aligned Movement."

13. This is not to say that interest in "political" questions decreased. The dynamism of the movement, however, is now generated primarily by economic issues.

14. As indicated above, this process commenced in 1970 with the Lusaka summit of the Non-Aligned Countries. But that summit, as well as the subsequent Georgetown conference of foreign ministers, concentrated mainly on the issue of self-reliance and had not yet placed the situation of the DCs in the framework of the entire international economic system.

15. Hollis B. Chenery, for instance, estimated in 1975 that if efforts by the DMEs to limit their oil deficits would lead to a reduction of the normal 5 percent Organisation for Economic Co-operation and Development (OECD) growth rate to 3.5 percent, this "would wipe out some $300 billion in potential asset formation by 1980 and cause considerable unemployment" (see his "Restructuring the World Economy," *Foreign Affairs* 53 [January 1975]: 258).

16. On the question of natural resource diplomacy, see C. Fred Bergsten, "The Threat from the Third World," *Foreign Policy* 11 (Summer 1973): 102-124, and "The Threat is Real," *Foreign Policy* 14 (Spring 1974): 84-90; Stephen

D. Krasner, "Oil is the Exception," *Foreign Policy* 14 (Spring 1974): 68-84; Zuhayr Mikdashi, "Collusion could Work," *Foreign Policy* 14 (Spring 1974): 57-68; and Bension Varon and Kenji Takeuchi, "Developing Countries and Non-fuel Minerals," *Foreign Affairs* 52 (1974): 497-510.

17. A study prepared by the UN Secretariat reported only 875 cases of nationalization of foreign affiliates of parent enterprises of any nationality for the period 1960 to mid-1974 (in addition, in 10 percent of these cases, the affiliates were later returned to the foreign investor). See United Nations, Secretary-General, *Permanent Sovereignty over Natural Resources* (A/9716 and Add. 1), 20 September 1974. The total number of foreign affiliates is estimated to be about 50,000-70,000; approximately one-third of the book value that is represented by these affiliates is located in DCs.

18. See Chapter 22 below.

19. It is for this reason that the Sixth Special Session is more important than the Seventh. In addition, the Sixth Special Session put the subject matter into a North-South context.

20. This move by Algeria also diffused the threat to OPEC (perceived to result from the Washington Energy Conference which had been called for February 1974) by embedding the conflict over oil into the broader issue of raw materials and development (and thus into a more general North-South context), an area where the Non-Aligned Countries had just achieved a broad and solid consensus.

21. For further discussion of the background of the Sixth and Seventh Special Sessions, see Chapter 6 and Bratislav Gosovic and John Gerard Ruggie, "On the Creation of a New International Economic Order: Issue Linkage and the Seventh Special Session of the UN General Assembly," *International Organization* 30 (Spring 1976): esp. 310-319; this article (esp. pp. 323-345) also contains a detailed presentation of the positions of the Third World and of the DMEs during the negotiations of the Seventh Special Session, as well as the compromises achieved.

22. I am using "NIEO program" to refer to the proposals and measures contained in the various main documents (cited above) pertaining to the NIEO as well as the relevant UNCTAD documents related to these proposals and measures. Some of them are spelled out in detail; others have more the character of declarations of principles. Together with the philosophy underlying them (discussed in the text), they constitute what I refer to as the "NIEO program."

23. The NIEO program also includes measures concerning food, the least developed, land-locked and island developing countries, as well as the restructuring of the UN system. These issues will not be examined here, since they do not relate to the core of the North-South relationship; see, however, respectively, United Nations, *Assessment Present Food Situation and Dimensions and Causes of Hunger and Malnutrition in the World and Magnitude of the*

Food Problem in the Future and Possible Approaches to a Solution (E/Conf. 65/Prep/6), 8 May 1974; UNCTAD, *Least Developed among Developing Countries, Developing Island Countries and Developing Land-Locked Countries: Action on Special Measures in Favour of these Countries, Policy Issues and Recommendations. Report by the UNCTAD Secretariat* (TD/191), 6 January 1976; and United Nations, *A New United Nations Structure for Global Economic Co-operation: Report of the Group of Experts on the Structure of the United Nations System* (E/AC. 62/9), 28 May 1975. Moreover, most measures of the NIEO program contain special provisions for the least developed, island, and land-locked developing countries and frequently also for the most seriously affected countries; these provisions are not discussed here.

24. See UNCTAD, *Manufactures and Semi-manufactures: The Dimensions of the Required Restructuring of World Manufacturing Output and Trade in Order to Reach the Lima Target. Report by the UNCTAD Secretariat* (TD/185/Supp. 1) 12 April 1976.

2 *Development and International Economic Co-operation*

Seventh Special Session of the General Assembly of the United Nations

The General Assembly,

Determined to eliminate injustice and inequality which afflict vast sections of humanity and to accelerate the development of developing countries,

Recalling the Declaration and the Programme of Action on the Establishment of a New International Economic Order,[1] as well as the Charter of Economic Rights and Duties of States,[2] which lay down the foundations of the new international economic order,

Reaffirming the fundamental purposes of the above-mentioned documents and the rights and duties of all States to seek and participate in the solutions of the problems afflicting the world, in particular the imperative need of redressing the economic imbalance between developed and developing countries,

Recalling further the International Development Strategy for the Second United Nations Development Decade,[3] which should be reviewed in the light of the Programme of Action on the Establishment of a New International Economic Order, and determined to implement the targets and policy measures contained in the International Development Strategy,

Conscious that the accelerated development of developing countries would be a decisive element for the promotion of world peace and security,

Recognizing that greater co-operation among States in the fields of trade, industry, science and technology as well as in other fields of economic activities, based on the principles of the Declaration and the Programme of Action on the Establishment of a New International Economic Order and of the Charter of Economic Rights and Duties of States, would also contribute

---

Text of United Nations General Assembly resolution 3362 (S-VII), "Development and International Economic Co-operation," adopted 16 September 1975 by the Seventh Special Session of the General Assembly and reprinted with the permission of the United Nations.

to strengthening peace and security in the world,

Believing that the over-all objective of the new international economic order is to increase the capacity of developing countries, individually and collectively, to pursue their development,

Decides, to this end and in the context of the foregoing, to set in motion the following measures as the basis and framework for the work of the competent bodies and organizations of the United Nations system:

I. International Trade

1. Concerted efforts should be made in favour of the developing countries towards expanding and diversifying their trade, improving and diversifying their productive capacity, improving their productivity and increasing their export earnings, with a view to counteracting the adverse effects of inflation—thereby sustaining real incomes—and with a view to improving the terms of trade of the developing countries and in order to eliminate the economic imbalance between developed and developing countries.

2. Concerted action should be taken to accelerate the growth and diversification of the export trade of developing countries in manufactures and semi-manufactures and in processed and semi-processed products in order to increase their share in world industrial output and world trade within the framework of an expanding world economy

3. An important aim of the fourth session of the United Nations Conference on Trade and Development, in addition to work in progress elsewhere, should be to reach decisions on the improvement of market structures in the field of raw materials and commodities of export interest to the developing countries, including decisions with respect to an integrated programme and the applicability of elements thereof. In this connexion, taking into account the distinctive features of individual raw materials and commodities, the decisions should bear on the following:

a. Appropriate international stocking and other forms of market arrangements for securing stable, remunerative and equitable prices for commodities of export interest to developing countries and promoting equilibrium between supply and demand, including, where possible, long-term multilateral commitments;
b. Adequate international financing facilities for such stocking and market arrangements;
c. Where possible, promotion of long-term and medium-term contracts;
d. Substantial improvement of facilities for compensatory financing of export revenue fluctuations through the widening and enlarging of the existing facilities. Note has been taken of the various proposals regarding a comprehensive scheme for the stabilization of export

earnings of developing countries and for a development security facility as well as specific measures for the benefit of the developing countries most in need;

e. Promotion of processing of raw materials in producing developing countries and expansion and diversification of their exports, particularly to developed countries;

f. Effective opportunities to improve the share of developing countries in transport, marketing and distribution of their primary commodities and to encourage measures of world significance for the evolution of the infrastructure and secondary capacity of developing countries from the production of primary commodities to processing, transport and marketing, and to the production of finished manufactured goods, their transport, distribution and exchange, including advanced financial and exchange institutions for the remunerative management of trade transactions.

4. The Secretary-General of the United Nations Conference on Trade and Development should present a report to the Conference at its fourth session on the impact of an integrated programme on the imports of developing countries which are net importers of raw materials and commodities, including those lacking in natural resources, and recommend any remedial measures that may be necessary.

5. A number of options are open to the international community to preserve the purchasing power of developing countries. These need to be further studied on a priority basis. The Secretary-General of the United Nations Conference on Trade and Development should continue to study direct and indirect indexation schemes and other options with a view to making concrete proposals before the Conference at its fourth session.

6. The Secretary-General of the United Nations Conference on Trade and Development should prepare a preliminary study on the proportion between prices of raw materials and commodities exported by developing countries and the final consumer price, particularly in developed countries, and submit it, if possible, to the Conference at its fourth session.

7. Developed countries should fully implement agreed provisions on the principle of standstill as regards imports from developing countries, and any departure should be subjected to such measures as consultations and multilateral surveillance and compensation, in accordance with internationally agreed criteria and procedures.

8. Developed countries should take effective steps within the framework of multilateral trade negotiations for the reduction or removal, where feasible and appropriate, of non-tariff barriers affecting the products of export interest to developing countries on a differential and more favourable basis for developing countries. The generalized scheme of preferences

should not terminate at the end of the period of ten years originally envisaged and should be continuously improved through wider coverage, deeper cuts and other measures, bearing in mind the interests of those developing countries which enjoy special advantages and the need for finding ways and means for protecting their interests.

9. Countervailing duties should be applied only in conformity with internationally agreed obligations. Developed countries should exercise maximum restraint within the framework of international obligations in the imposition of countervailing duties on the imports of products from developing countries. The multilateral trade negotiations under way should take fully into account the particular interests of developing countries with a view to providing them differential and more favourable treatment in appropriate cases.

10. Restrictive business practices adversely affecting international trade, particularly that of developing countries, should be eliminated and efforts should be made at the national and international levels with the objective of negotiating a set of equitable principles and rules.

11. Special measures should be undertaken by developed countries and by developing countries in a position to do so to assist in the structural transformation of the economy of the least developed, land-locked and island developing countries.

12. Emergency measures as spelled out in section X of General Assembly resolution 3202 (S-VI) should be undertaken on a temporary basis to meet the specific problems of the most seriously affected countries as defined in Assembly resolutions 3201 (S-VI) and 3202 (S-VI) of 1 May 1974, without any detriment to the interests of the developing countries as a whole.

13. Further expansion of trade between the socialist countries of Eastern Europe and the developing countries should be intensified as is provided for in resolutions 15 (II) of 25 March 1968[4] and 53 (III) of 19 May 1972[5] of the United Nations Conference on Trade and Development. Additional measures and appropriate orientation to achieve this end are necessary.

II. Transfer of Real Resources for Financing the Development of Developing Countries and International Monetary Reforms

1. Concessional financial resources to developing countries need to be increased substantially, their terms and conditions ameliorated and their flow made predictable, continuous and increasingly assured so as to facilitate the implementation by developing countries of long-term programmes for economic and social development. Financial assistance should, as a general rule, be untied.

2. Developed countries confirm their continued commitment in respect of the targets relating to the transfer of resources, in particular the official

development assistance target of 0.7 percent of gross national product, as agreed in the International Development Strategy for the Second United Nations Development Decade, and adopt as their common aim an effective increase in official development assistance with a view to achieving these targets by the end of the decade. Developed countries which have not yet made a commitment in respect of these targets undertake to make their best efforts to reach these targets in the remaining part of this decade.

3. The establishment of a link between the special drawing rights and development assistance should form part of the consideration by the International Monetary Fund of the creation of new special drawing rights as and when they are created according to the needs of international liquidity. Agreement should be reached at an early date on the establishment of a trust fund, to be financed partly through the International Monetary Fund gold sales and partly through voluntary contributions and to be governed by an appropriate body, for the benefit of developing countries. Consideration of other means of transfer of real resources which are predictable, assured and continuous should be expedited in appropriate bodies.

4. Developed countries and international organizations should enhance the real value and volume of assistance to developing countries and ensure that the developing countries obtain the largest possible share in the procurement of equipment, consultants and consultancy services. Such assistance should be on softer terms and, as a general rule, untied.

5. In order to enlarge the pool of resources available for financing development, there is an urgent need to increase substantially the capital of the World Bank Group, in particular the resources of the International Development Association, to enable it to make additional capital available to the poorest countries on highly concessional terms.

6. The resources of the development institutions of the United Nations system, in particular the United Nations Development Programme, should also be increased. The funds at the disposal of the regional development banks should be augmented. These increases should be without prejudice to bilateral development assistance flows.

7. To the extent desirable, the World Bank Group is invited to consider new ways of supplementing its financing with private management, skills, technology and capital and also new approaches to increase financing of development in developing countries, in accordance with their national plans and priorities.

8. The burden of debt on developing countries is increasing to a point where the import capacity as well as reserves have come under serious strain. At its fourth session the United Nations Conference on Trade and Development shall consider the need for, and the possibility of, convening as soon as possible a conference of major donor, creditor and debtor countries

to devise ways and means to mitigate this burden, taking into account the development needs of developing countries, with special attention to the plight of the most seriously affected countries as defined in General Assembly resolutions 3201 (S-VI) and 3202 (S-VI).

9. Developing countries should be granted increased access on favourable terms to the capital markets of developed countries. To this end, the joint Development Committee of the International Monetary Fund and the International Bank for Reconstruction and Development should progress as rapidly as possible in its work. Appropriate United Nations bodies and other related intergovernmental agencies should be invited to examine ways and means of increasing the flow of public and private resources to developing countries, including proposals made at the current session to provide investment in private and public enterprises in the developing countries. Consideration should be given to the examination of an international investment trust and to the expansion of the International Finance Corporation capital without prejudice to the increase in resources of other intergovernmental financial and development institutions and bilateral assistance flows.

10. Developed and developing countries should further co-operate through investment of financial resources and supply of technology and equipment to developing countries by developed countries and by developing countries in a position to do so.

11. Developed countries, and developing countries in a position to do so are urged to make adequate contributions to the United Nations Special Fund with a view to an early implementation of a programme of lending, preferably in 1976.

12. Developed countries should improve terms and conditions of their assistance so as to include a preponderant grant element for the least developed, land-locked and island developing countries.

13. In providing additional resources for assisting the most seriously affected countries in helping them to meet their serious balance-of-payments deficits, all developed countries, and developing countries in a position to do so, and international organizations such as the International Bank for Reconstruction and Development and the International Monetary Fund, should undertake specific measures in their favour, including those provided in General Assembly resolutions 3201 (S-VI) and 3202 (S-VI).

14. Special attention should be given by the international community to the phenomena of natural disasters which frequently afflict many parts of the world, with far-reaching devastating economic, social and structural consequences, particularly in the least developed countries. To this end, the General Assembly at its thirtieth session, in considering this problem, should examine and adopt appropriate measures.

15. The role of national reserve currencies should be reduced and the

special drawing rights should become the central reserve asset of the international monetary system in order to provide for greater international control over the creation and equitable distribution of liquidity and in order to limit potential losses as a consequence of exchange rate fluctuations. Arrangements for gold should be consistent with the agreed objective of reducing the role of gold in the system and with equitable distribution of new international liquidity and should in particular take into consideration the needs of developing countries for increased liquidity.

16. The process of decision-making should be fair and responsive to change and should be most specially responsive to the emergence of a new economic influence on the part of developing countries. The participation of developing countries in the decision-making process in the competent organs of international finance and development institutions should be adequately increased and made more effective without adversely affecting the broad geographic representation of developing countries and in accordance with the existing and evolving rules.

17. The compensatory financing facility now available through the International Monetary Fund should be expanded and liberalized. In this connexion, early consideration should be given by the Fund and other appropriate United Nations bodies to various proposals made at the current session—including the examination of a new development security facility—which would mitigate export earnings shortfalls of developing countries, with special regard to the poorest countries, and thus provide greater assistance to their continued economic development. Early consideration should also be given by the International Monetary Fund to proposals to expand and liberalize its coverage of current transactions to include manufactures and services, to ensure that, whenever possible, compensation for export shortfalls takes place at the same time they occur, to take into account, in determining the quantum of compensation, movements in import prices and to lengthen the repayment period.

18. Drawing under the buffer stock financing facility of the International Monetary Fund should be accorded treatment with respect to floating alongside the gold tranche, similar to that under the compensatory financing facility, and the Fund should expedite its study of the possibility of an amendment of the Articles of Agreement, to be presented to the Interim Committee, if possible at its next meeting, that would permit the Fund to provide assistance directly to international buffer stocks of primary products.

III. Science and Technology

1. Developed and developing countries should co-operate in the establishment, strengthening and development of the scientific and technological

infrastructure of developing countries. Developed countries should also take appropriate measures, such as contribution to the establishment of an industrial technological information bank and consideration of the possibility of regional and sectoral banks, in order to make available a greater flow to developing countries of information permitting the selection of technologies, in particular advanced technologies. Consideration should also be given to the establishment of an international centre for the exchange of technological information for the sharing of research findings relevant to developing countries. For the above purposes institutional arrangements within the United Nations system should be examined by the General Assembly at its thirtieth session.

2. Developed countries should significantly expand their assistance to developing countries for direct support to their science and technology programmes, as well as increase substantially the proportion of their research and development devoted to specific problems of primary interest to developing countries, and to the creation of suitable indigenous technology, in accordance with feasible targets to be agreed upon. The General Assembly invites the Secretary-General to carry out a preliminary study and to report to the Assembly at its thirty-first session on the possibility of establishing, within the framework of the United Nations system, an international energy institute to assist all developing countries in energy resources research and development.

3. All States should co-operate in evolving an international code of conduct for the transfer of technology, corresponding, in particular, to the special needs of the developing countries. Work on such a code should therefore be continued within the United Nations Conference on Trade and Development and concluded in time for decisions to be reached at the fourth session of the Conference, including a decision on the legal character of such a code with the objective of the adoption of a code of conduct prior to the end of 1977. International conventions on patents and trade marks should be reviewed and revised to meet, in particular, the special needs of the developing countries, in order that these conventions may become more satisfactory instruments for aiding developing countries in the transfer and development of technology. National patent systems should, without delay, be brought into line with the international patent system in its revised form.

4. Developed countries should facilitate the access of developing countries on favourable terms and conditions, and on an urgent basis, to *informatique,* to relevant information on advanced and other technologies suited to their specific needs as well as on new uses of existing technology, new developments and possibilities of adapting them to local needs. Inasmuch as in market economies advanced technologies with respect to industrial production are most frequently developed by private institutions, developed countries should facilitate and encourage these institutions in

providing effective technologies in support of the priorities of developing countries.

5. Developed countries should give developing countries the freest and fullest possible access to technologies whose transfer is not subject to private decision.

6. Developed countries should improve the transparency of the industrial property market in order to facilitate the technological choices of developing countries. In this respect, relevant organizations of the United Nations system, with the collaboration of developed countries, should undertake projects in the fields of information, consultancy and training for the benefit of developing countries.

7. A United Nations Conference on Science and Technology for Development should be held in 1978 or 1979 with the main objectives of strengthening the technological capacity of developing countries to enable them to apply science and technology to their own development; adopting effective means for the utilization of scientific and technological potentials in the solution of development problems of regional and global significance, especially for the benefit of developing countries; and providing instruments of co-operation to developing countries in the utilization of science and technology for solving socioeconomic problems that cannot be solved by individual action, in accordance with national priorities, taking into account the recommendations made by the Intergovernmental Working Group of the Committee on Science and Technology for Development.

8. The United Nations system should play a major role, with appropriate financing, in achieving the above-stated objectives and in developing scientific and technological co-operation between all States in order to ensure the application of science and technology to development. The work of the relevant United Nations bodies, in particular that of the United Nations Conference on Trade and Development, the United Nations Industrial Development Organization, the International Labour Organisation, the United Nations Educational, Scientific and Cultural Organization, the Food and Agriculture Organization of the United Nations, the World Intellectual Property Organization and the United Nations Development Programme, to facilitate the transfer and diffusion of technology should be given urgent priority. The Secretary-General of the United Nations should take steps to ensure that the technology and experience available within the United Nations system is widely disseminated and readily available to the developing countries in need of it.

9. The World Health Organization and the competent organs of the United Nations system, in particular the United Nations Children's Fund, should intensify the international effort aimed at improving health conditions in developing countries by giving priority to prevention of disease and malnutrition and by providing primary health services to the communities,

including maternal and child health and family welfare.

10. Since the outflow of qualified personnel from developing to developed countries seriously hampers the development of the former, there is an urgent need to formulate national and international policies to avoid the "brain drain" and to obviate its adverse effects.

IV. Industrialization

1. The General Assembly endorses the Lima Declaration and Plan of Action on Industrial Development Co-operation[6] and requests all Governments to take individually and/or collectively the necessary measures and decisions required to implement effectively their undertakings in terms of the Lima Declaration and Plan of Action.

2. Developed countries should facilitate the development of new policies and strengthen existing policies, including labour market policies, which would encourage the redeployment of their industries which are less competitive internationally to developing countries, thus leading to structural adjustments in the former and a higher degree of utilization of natural and human resources in the latter. Such policies may take into account the economic structure and the economic, social and security objectives of the developed countries concerned and the need for such industries to move into more viable lines of production or into other sectors of the economy.

3. A system of consultations as provided for by the Lima Plan of Action should be established at the global, regional, interregional and sectoral levels within the United Nations Industrial Development Organization and within other appropriate international bodies, between developed and developing countries and among developing countries themselves, in order to facilitate the achievement of the goals set forth in the field of industrialization, including the redeployment of certain productive capacities existing in developed countries and the creation of new industrial facilities in developing countries. In this context, the United Nations Industrial Development Organization should serve as a forum for negotiation of agreements in the field of industry between developed and developing countries and among developing countries themselves, at the request of the countries concerned.

4. The Executive Director of the United Nations Industrial Development Organization should take immediate action to ensure the readiness of that organization to serve as a forum for consultations and negotiations of agreements in the field of industry. In reporting to the next session of the Industrial Development Board on actions taken in this respect, the Executive Director should also include proposals for the establishment of a system of consultations. The Industrial Development Board is invited to draw up, at an early date, the rules of procedure according to which this system would operate.

5. To promote co-operation between developed and developing countries, both should endeavour to disseminate appropriate information about their priority areas for industrial co-operation and the form they would like such co-operation to take. The efforts undertaken by the United Nations Conference on Trade and Development on tripartite co-operation between countries having different economic and social systems could lead to constructive proposals for the industrialization of developing countries.

6. Developed countries should, whenever possible, encourage their enterprises to participate in investment projects within the framework of the development plans and programmes of the developing countries which so desire; such participation should be carried out in accordance with the laws and regulations of the developing countries concerned.

7. A joint study should be undertaken by all Governments under the auspices of the United Nations Industrial Development Organization, in consultation with the Secretary-General of the United Nations Conference on Trade and Development, making full use of the knowledge, experience and capacity existing in the United Nations system of methods and mechanisms for diversified financial and technical co-operation which are geared to the special and changing requirements of international industrial co-operation, as well as of a general set of guidelines for bilateral industrial co-operation. A progress report on this study should be submitted to the General Assembly at its thirty-first session.

8. Special attention should be given to the particular problems in the industrialization of the least developed, land-locked and island developing countries—in order to put at their disposal those technical and financial resources as well as critical goods which need to be provided to them to enable them to overcome their specific problems and to play their due role in the world economy, warranted by their human and material resources.

9. The General Assembly endorses the recommendation of the Second General Conference of the United Nations Industrial Development Organization to convert that organization into a specialized agency and decides to establish a Committee on the Drafting of a Constitution for the United Nations Industrial Development Organization, which shall be an intergovernmental committee of the whole, including States which participated in the Second General Conference, to meet in Vienna to draw up a constitution for the United Nations Industrial Development Organization as a specialized agency, to be submitted to a conference of plenipotentiaries to be convened by the Secretary-General in the last quarter of 1976.

10. In view of the importance of the forthcoming Tripartite World Conference on Employment, Income Distribution, Social Progress and the International Division of Labour, Governments should undertake adequate preparations and consultations.

V. Food and Agriculture

1. The solution to world food problems lies primarily in rapidly increasing food production in the developing countries. To this end, urgent and necessary changes in the pattern of world food production should be introduced and trade policy measures should be implemented, in order to obtain a notable increase in agricultural production and the export earnings of developing countries.

2. To achieve these objectives, it is essential that developed countries, and developing countries in a position to do so, should substantially increase the volume of assistance to developing countries for agriculture and food production, and that developed countries should effectively facilitate access to their markets for food and agricultural products of export interest to developing countries, both in raw and processed form, and adopt adjustment measures, where necessary.

3. Developing countries should accord high priority to agricultural and fisheries development, increase investment accordingly and adopt policies which give adequate incentives to agricultural producers. It is a responsibility of each State concerned, in accordance with its sovereign judgement and development plans and policies, to promote interaction between expansion of food production and socioeconomic reforms, with a view to achieving an integrated rural development. The further reduction of post-harvest food losses in developing countries should be undertaken as a matter of priority, with a view to reaching at least a 50 percent reduction by 1985. All countries and competent international organizations should co-operate financially and technically in the effort to achieve this objective. Particular attention should be given to improvement in the systems of distribution of food-stuffs.

4. The Consultative Group on Food Production and Investment in Developing Countries should quickly identify developing countries having the potential for most rapid and efficient increase of food production, as well as the potential for rapid agricultural expansion in other developing countries, especially the countries with food deficits. Such an assessment would assist developed countries and the competent international organizations to concentrate resources for the rapid increase of agricultural production in the developing countries.

5. Developed countries should adopt policies aimed at ensuring a stable supply and sufficient quantity of fertilizers and other production inputs to developing countries at reasonable prices. They should also provide assistance to, and promote investments in, developing countries to improve the efficiency of their fertilizer and other agricultural input industries. Advantage should be taken of the mechanism provided by the International Fertilizer Supply Scheme.

6. In order to make additional resources available on concessional terms for agricultural development in developing countries, developed countries and developing countries in a position to do so should pledge, on a voluntary basis, substantial contributions to the proposed International Fund for Agricultural Development so as to enable it to come into being by the end of 1975, with initial resources of SDR 1,000 million. Thereafter, additional resources should be provided to the Fund on a continuing basis.

7. In view of the significant impact of basic and applied agricultural research on increasing the quantity and quality of food production, developed countries should support the expansion of the work of the existing international agricultural research centres. Through their bilateral programmes they should strengthen their links with these international research centres and with the national agricultural research centres in developing countries. With respect to the improvement of the productivity and competitiveness with synthetics of non-food agricultural and forestry products, research and technological assistance should be co-ordinated and financed through an appropriate mechanism.

8. In view of the importance of food aid as a transitional measure, all countries should accept both the principle of a minimum food aid target and the concept of forward planning of food aid. The target for the 1975-1976 season should be 10 million tons of food grains. They should also accept the principle that food aid should be channelled on the basis of objective assessment of requirements in the recipient countries. In this respect all countries are urged to participate in the Global Information and Early Warning System on Food and Agriculture.

9. Developed countries should increase the grant component of food aid, where food is not at present provided as grants, and should accept multilateral channelling of these resources at an expanding rate. In providing food grains and financing on soft terms to developing countries in need of such assistance, developed countries and the World Food Programme should take due account of the interests of the food-exporting developing countries and should ensure that such assistance includes, wherever possible, purchases of food from the food-exporting developing countries.

10. Developed countries, and developing countries in a position to do so, should provide food grains and financial assistance on most favourable terms to the most seriously affected countries, to enable them to meet their food and agricultural development requirements within the constraints of their balance-of-payments position. Donor countries should also provide aid on soft terms, in cash and in kind, through bilateral and multilateral channels, to enable the most seriously affected countries to obtain their estimated requirements of about 1 million tons of plant nutrients during 1975-1976.

11. Developed countries should carry out both their bilateral and multilateral food aid channelling in accordance with the procedures of the

Principles of Surplus Disposal of the Food and Agriculture Organization of the United Nations so as to avoid causing undue fluctuations in market prices or the disruption of commercial markets for exports of interest to exporting developing countries.

12. All countries should subscribe to the International Undertaking on World Food Security. They should build up and maintain world food-grain reserves, to be held nationally or regionally and strategically located in developed and developing, importing and exporting countries, large enough to cover foreseeable major production shortfalls. Intensive work should be continued on a priority basis in the World Food Council and other appropriate forums in order to determine, *inter alia,* the size of the required reserve, taking into account among other things the proposal made at the current session that the components of wheat and rice in the total reserve should be 30 million tons. The World Food Council should report to the General Assembly on this matter at its thirty-first session. Developed countries should assist developing countries in their efforts to build up and maintain their agreed shares of such reserves. Pending the establishment of the world food-grain reserve, developed countries and developing countries in a position to do so should earmark stocks and/or funds to be placed at the disposal of the World Food Programme as an emergency reserve to strengthen the capacity of the Programme to deal with crisis situations in developing countries. The aim should be a target of not less than 500,000 tons.

13. Members of the General Assembly reaffirm their full support for the resolutions of the World Food Conference and call upon the World Food Council to monitor the implementation of the provisions under section V of the present resolution and to report to the General Assembly at its thirty-first session.

VI. Co-operation Among Developing Countries

1. Developed countries and the United Nations system are urged to provide, as and when requested, support and assistance to developing countries in strengthening and enlarging their mutual co-operation at subregional, regional and interregional levels. In this regard, suitable institutional arrangements within the United Nations development system should be made and, when appropriate, strengthened, such as those within the United Nations Conference on Trade and Development, the United Nations Industrial Development Organization and the United Nations Development Programme.

2. The Secretary-General, together with the relevant organizations of the United Nations system, is requested to continue to provide support to ongoing projects and activities, and to commission further studies through

institutions in developing countries, which would take into account the material already available within the United Nations system, including in particular the regional commissions and the United Nations Conference on Trade and Development, and in accordance with existing subregional and regional arrangements. These further studies, which should be submitted to the General Assembly at its thirty-first session, should, as a first step, cover:

a. Utilization of know-how, skills, natural resources, technology and funds available within developing countries for promotion of investments in industry, agriculture, transport and communications;
b. Trade liberalization measures including payments and clearing arrangements, covering primary commodities, manufactured goods and services, such as banking, shipping, insurance and reinsurance;
c. Transfer of technology.

3. These studies on co-operation among developing countries, together with other initiatives, would contribute to the evolution towards a system for the economic development of developing countries.

VII. Restructuring of the Economic and Social Sectors of the United Nations System

1. With a view to initiating the process of restructuring the United Nations system so as to make it more fully capable of dealing with problems of international economic co-operation and development in a comprehensive and effective manner, in pursuance of General Assembly resolutions 3172 (XXVIII) of 17 December 1973 and 3343 (XXIX) of 17 December 1974, and to make it more responsive to the requirements of the provisions of the Declaration and the Programme of Action on the Establishment of a New International Economic Order as well as those of the Charter of Economic Rights and Duties of States, an *Ad Hoc* Committee on the Restructuring of the Economic and Social Sectors of the United Nations System, which shall be a committee of the whole of the General Assembly open to the participation of all States,[7] is hereby established to prepare detailed action proposals. The *Ad Hoc* Committee should start its work immediately and inform the General Assembly at its thirtieth session on the progress made, and submit its report to the Assembly at its thirty-first session, through the Economic and Social Council at its resumed session. The *Ad Hoc* Committee should take into account in its work, *inter alia,* the relevant proposals and documentation submitted in preparation for the seventh special session of the General Assembly pursuant to Assembly resolution 3343 (XXIX) and other relevant decisions, including the report of the Group of Experts on the Structure of the United Nations System entitled *A New United Nations*

Structure for Global Economic Co-operation,[8] the records of the relevant deliberations of the Economic and Social Council, the Trade and Development Board, the Governing Council of the United Nations Development Programme and the seventh special session of the General Assembly, as well as the results of the forthcoming deliberations on institutional arrangements of the United Nations Conference on Trade and Development at its fourth session and of the Governing Council of the United Nations Environment Programme at its fourth session. All United Nations organs, including the regional commissions, as well as the specialized agencies and the International Atomic Energy Agency, are invited to participate at the executive level in the work of the *Ad Hoc* Committee and to respond to requests that the Committee may make to them for information, data or views.

2. The Economic and Social Council should meanwhile continue the process of rationalization and reform which it has undertaken in accordance with Council resolution 1768 (LIV) of 18 May 1973 and General Assembly resolution 3341 (XXIX) of 17 December 1974, and should take into full consideration those recommendations of the *Ad Hoc* Committee that fall within the scope of these resolutions, at the latest at its resumed sixty-first session.

2349th plenary meeting
16 September 1976

Notes

1. Resolutions 3201 (S-VI) and 3202 (S-VI).
2. Resolution 3281 (XXIX).
3. Resolution 2626 (XXV).
4. *Proceedings of the United Nations Conference on Trade and Development, Second Session,* vol. I and Corr. 1 and 3 and Add. 1 and 2, *Report and Annexes* (United Nations publication, Sales No. E. 68. II. D. 14), p. 32.
5. See *Proceedings of the United Nations Conference on Trade and Development, Third Session,* vol. I, *Report and Annexes* (United Nations publication, Sales No. E. 73. II. D. 4), annex I. A.
6. See A/10112, chap. IV.
7. It is the understanding of the General Assembly that the "all States" formula will be applied in accordance with the established practice of the General Assembly.
8. E/AC. 62/9 (United Nations publication, Sales No. E. 75. II. A. 7).

Part 2

The Positions of North and South

3 The Elements of the New International Economic Order

UNCTAD

Recent resolutions adopted by the General Assembly—the Declaration and Programme of Action, the Charter of Economic Rights and Duties of States, and the resolution on Development and International Economic Co-operation—set out a large number of changes to be made in present international economic arrangements. Some of these changes would, in effect, constitute changes in the international institutional framework. Most of the changes envisaged, however, can be conceived as requiring modifications in the procedures or arrangements within the existing institutional structure.

Nonetheless, the concept of a new international economic order as one embodying institutional arrangements which promote the economic and social progress of the developing countries in the context of an expanding world economy must remain the central guide to international action. The achievement of all the structural changes necessary to overcome the major defects of the existing system of international economic relations should be conceived as a process over a period of time, its speed and effectiveness depending to a large extent on a complex of negotiations within and outside the United Nations (UN) system. But for such a new economic order to be meaningful in relation to the development objectives of the international community, these negotiations will need to aim eventually at achieving the structural changes required to overcome the defects of the existing system.

First, and most fundamental, measures will be needed to reduce, and eventually eliminate, the economic dependence of developing countries on developed country enterprises in the production and trade of developing countries, thus allowing these countries to exercise full control over their

---

Reprinted, with permission, from UNCTAD, *Trade and Development Issues in the Context of a New International Economic Order* (UNCTAD/OSG/104/Rev. 1), February 1976, pp. 8-33, with minor adaptations. The paper had been prepared as part of the documentation of the UNCTAD IV Seminar Programme.

natural resources. A second aim should be to promote the accelerated development of the economies of developing countries on the basis of the principle of self-reliance. Thirdly, appropriate institutional changes are required to introduce some measure of global management of resources in the long-term interests of mankind as a whole.

Any substantial reduction in the economic dependence of developing countries would involve the regulation of the operation of transnational corporations and other enterprises of developed countries so as to ensure that their operations support, rather than hinder, the development objectives of the Third World. The formulation and negotiation of an internationally acceptable code of conduct for the operations of transnational corporations—including rules governing the transfer of technology and the regulation of restrictive business practices—would thus constitute an essential element in the evolution of a new economic order.

Within the framework of such a code of conduct, developing countries will need to adopt measures to strengthen their bargaining power in their negotiations with the transnational corporations, to ensure that the terms and conditions of operation of these enterprises are such as to provide real benefits to the societies of the host countries. Such measures will comprise various forms of joint action by developing countries, ranging from the organization of information concerning alternative supplies of foreign technology and know-how, and strengthened scientific and technological co-operation among them, to the establishment of their own production, trading, and marketing networks in competition with those of the transnational corporations.

The elimination of the dependence of the economies of developing countries would not, however, by itself, achieve the development goals of the Third World. A simultaneous effort needs to be mounted by the developing countries themselves to build up their economies mainly on the basis of their own resources. Such a policy of self-reliance implies the full utilization of the domestic resources of the developing countries and close economic co-operation among them to achieve agreed objectives.

What is now required is the elaboration by the developing countries of a comprehensive strategy for strengthening their mutual co-operation in all aspects of their economic relations. Such a comprehensive strategy would include *inter alia* measures designed specifically to promote the flows of trade and finance among developing countries, to encourage joint ventures (as well as 'triangular' ventures, involving the technology and know-how of developed countries, both market economy and socialist), to build up an independent and viable scientific and technological base, and to take the first steps towards harmonizing their respective economic development programmes.

The fact that, for the first time, a group of developing countries, exporters of petroleum, now have command over a large volume of financial resources, could provide a unique opportunity for evolving a development strategy on the basis of collective self-reliance. The petroleum exporting countries have already shown their willingness to extend financial assistance to other developing countries. Indeed, in relation to real income, their aid programmes are considerably larger than those of developed market economy countries. A viable system of collective self-reliance would, however, need to go beyond arrangements for aid and provide new mechanisms designed to channel long-term investments in substantial amounts to capital-deficient developing countries.

A self-reliant approach to economic development could also lay the basis for a new orientation in development strategy, one that laid central emphasis on meeting the basic needs of the majority of the population of the Third World. This would imply an unprecedented expansion in the production of foodstuffs and of simple manufactured goods, using technology appropriate to the resource endowments of the developing countries themselves. Since the pattern of basic needs in developing countries is quite different from the pattern of import demand by developed countries, the adoption of a basic needs strategy of development would mean the emergence of a new pattern of industrialization in developing countries.

Moreover, such a new orientation in development strategy would also be accompanied by a new pattern of international trade, involving a substantially greater volume of trade among developing countries themselves. The expansion of production of simple manufactures in one set of developing countries would be matched by an expansion in demand for such manufactures in other developing countries. Moreover, a great potential exists for a general expansion in the mutual trade of the developing countries, particularly in view of the great diversity in their resource endowments, and in their scientific and technological capabilities, capital assets and acquired skills.

In many developing countries, the full mobilization of domestic resources, and the adoption of a basic needs strategy of development, will involve as a prerequisite the adoption of appropriate institutional changes conducive to the economic and social transformation which give 'development' a real meaning. Such institutional changes should also allow the majority of the population to participate to the full in the development of society.

A self-reliant development policy could give a much-needed impetus to the economies of Third World countries, and, in this sense, it could constitute the most dynamic element in the global strategy for development implied in the concept of a new international economic order. In this broader context, a policy of self-reliant development can be assisted by supporting measures, including financial and technical assistance, by developed countries and by relevant international organizations.

Finally, the introduction of the concept of global management of resources implies that the regulation of world market forces in the interests of the development process should become an essential element of a new international economic order. The normal operation of market forces has, over the years, been associated with excessive instability in many commodity markets, with recurrent shortages followed by surpluses, and with inadequate returns to developing countries. The working of market forces thus needs to be subject to regulation, so that world markets are less prone to uncertainty and instability and become rather a mechanism for the orderly development of production and trade. The concept of resource management can apply also to the rational utilization of the world's non-renewable resources—involving the elimination of their wasteful or extravagant use and the adoption of appropriate price and production policies—as well as to safeguarding all aspects of environmental health.

One step in this direction can be taken in the context of the integrated programme for commodities. That programme envisages a multidimensional approach to commodity market regulation and stabilization, which could include, where appropriate, both price and production policies, as well as long-term commitments on purchases and sales. In addition, more extensive economic co-operation among developing countries, and between developing countries and socialist countries, could be a means of introducing new elements of stability into international trade, insofar as such co-operation involved long-term agreements covering production and trade of specific products. In the longer run, effective global resource management would need to embrace more directly the harmonization of national development plans for natural resources. In a wider economic context, the application of the global management approach would also imply a thoroughgoing reform of the international monetary system to make it more supportive of the development of the Third World, as well as more conducive to an orderly adjustment process in the world economy.

The issues before the international community are essentially of two kinds. First, there are issues which relate to the more immediate problems facing developing countries, particularly the adverse effects on their trade and payments positions of economic recession and continued inflation in the developed market economy countries. A package of measures needs to be negotiated which would provide developing countries with adequate protection against such adverse effects, as an integral part of a global counter-cyclical policy. Second, there are the issues related to a longer-term restructuring of international economic relations, particularly as they affect the Third World. This restructuring will necessarily be a complex process and will involve detailed negotiations among all groups of countries over a period of time. These two sets of issues—the immediate need for a short-term economic security system and effective preparations for later negotiations in the context of a new international economic order—are discussed separately below.

An Economic Security System for Developing Countries

The economic crisis of the past two years has been accompanied by fundamental changes in the pattern and magnitude of trade and payments flows. The current account of the developed market economies as a group, which was in approximate balance in 1973, deteriorated by some $30 billion in 1974 to a deficit of unprecedented magnitude. However, a substantial recovery was achieved in 1975, the deficit for the year being estimated at only some $6 billion. This recovery was made possible by increased shipments to oil-exporting countries, together with an improvement in the terms of trade of the developed market economies with the rest of the Third World. The terms of trade swing in 1975 against the developing countries—which amounted in value terms to some $10 billion—reflected the impact of the recession in reducing the prices of their commodity exports and of the continuing high rates of inflation in the developed market economy countries in increasing the prices of their manufactured imports.

The obverse of this payments recovery by the developed market economy countries has been a sharp deterioration in the overall payments deficit of the non-oil exporting developing countries. Estimates now put this deficit at some $35-40 billion annually for 1975 and the following few years, as compared with only about $11 billion for 1973. It is quite evident that the existing institutional arrangements set up under the Bretton Woods system are hopelessly inadequate to deal with deficits of the present magnitude.

The Integrated Programme for Commodities

Such large deficits also reflect the fact that no comprehensive mechanism exists for protecting the prices of the primary commodity exports of developing countries from the adverse effects of economic instability in developed countries or for protecting the real value of their export earnings from erosion as a result of inflation in the outside world. Effective protection for developing countries in these respects is a major objective of the integrated programme for commodities. Indeed, had a comprehensive series of international buffer stocks for primary commodities—as envisaged in the integrated programme—been in operation over the past few years, developing countries would not have had to cope with an export price recession of major dimensions since the middle of 1974. Moreover, an effective buffer stock operation would also have brought benefits to developed countries by a substantial attenuation of the increase in the prices of their commodity imports in 1973 and the first half of 1974, an increase which was one element in the early phases of the recent inflationary upsurge.

The case for decisive action to establish agreed principles for commodity market stabilization, and a timetable for negotiations relating to individual commodity markets, is thus wider than the interests of developing countries alone. An effective system of market stabilization arrangements—based, as proposed in the integrated programme, on a series of buffer stocks financed from a central fund, and supported as appropriate by multilateral commitments on sales and purchases and by compensatory payments—would be a major step that the international community can take to strengthen the commodity sector of the economies of developing countries. Such a market stabilization system, by placing a "floor" under the commodity export prices of these countries, would protect them to a significant extent against the adverse consequences of economic recession in developed market economy countries. It would also, by reducing short-term instability in primary commodity markets, help to strengthen the competitive position of the exports of developing countries, particularly in relation to competing synthetic materials.

In a period of apparently endemic inflation, the negotiation of "floor" and "ceiling" prices in individual commodity agreements must aim to establish price levels which, in real terms, are not only acceptable to consumers but also provide incentives to producers to make adequate investments in commodity production. Appropriate provisions will therefore be required, in the framework of stabilization agreements for individual commodities, to revise as necessary the initially agreed price targets in the light of the rate of world inflation.

A comprehensive commodity market stabilization system would, as already indicated, bring benefits to developed importing countries. Such a system would be designed to prevent excessive commodity price increases during a boom or during a period of temporary commodity shortage. Moreover, the system could also provide for appropriate assurances of supply of essential commodities to developed importing countries at not more than agreed maximum prices during periods of shortage. This should avoid much of the inflationary stimulus, which sharp rises in commodity import prices have, in the past, given to the economies of developed countries.

The entire world commodity economy would benefit in the longer term also from the operation of such a stabilization system. The avoidance of excessive fluctuations in the major world markets for primary commodities would allow decisions on new investment to be taken on a rational basis in the context of reasonable assurance of the future growth in market demand. This, in turn, would help to prevent the emergence of shortages of productive capacity which have, in the past, been such a prominent feature of the economic cycle for many commodities. The integrated programme can thus be conceived as setting an institutional framework for the more orderly evolution of the world commodity economy.

Improved Compensatory Financing Facilities

The implementation of the integrated programme cannot, however, be expected to provide a full or comprehensive system of protection for developing countries against unforeseen adverse changes in the purchasing power of their primary commodity exports. For one thing, the series of international commodity agreements which are envisaged could not cover more than a certain number of individual commodities, either for technical or for other reasons. Second, these agreements operate to stabilize the world market for a commodity, while the exports of an individual developing country may be subject to fluctuation for local reasons, such as climatic variations, outside the control of the government concerned. Consequently, it is necessary to envisage some form of international arrangement to provide funds to compensate individual developing countries for shortfalls in the purchasing power of their aggregate commodity exports.

If the main thrust of international action is to establish a series of stabilization agreements, covering a wide range of primary commodities, then the associated compensatory financing required can reasonably be conceived as a subsidiary element, though one which is necessary to provide comprehensive short-term security for the export interests of developing countries.

The essential requirements of such an arrangement for compensating developing countries for shortfalls in the real earnings from their commodity exports could conceivably be met by appropriate improvements in the existing compensatory financing facility of the International Monetary Fund (IMF). However, the IMF facility is oriented towards assisting member countries to cope with temporary shortfalls in their aggregate export earnings rather than with shortfalls in the commodity sector alone. Moreover, since most of the socialist countries of Eastern Europe and all the socialist countries of Asia are not members of the IMF, no compensation arrangement operated by members of that organization can be universal in its scope.

Thus, if improvements to be made in the existing IMF facility do not, in the event, make specific allowance for the need to compensate for shortfalls in the commodity export sector, and/or if governments wish compensatory financing to be on a universal basis, new and separate institutional arrangements will be required to establish a compensatory financing facility to complement the series of international commodity market stabilization agreements which would form the core of the integrated programme.

The implementation of an integrated programme which included a compensatory financing arrangement for the residual fluctuations in the commodity export earnings of developing countries should result in a substantial limitation of the payments difficulties of the majority of non-oil-exporting developing countries. To that extent, also, the call on the IMF compensatory financing facility would be correspondingly reduced.

In any event, however, it has become increasingly urgent for this facility to be extended and the conditions of its use liberalized. The facility was established in a period when temporary balance of payments difficulties of individual developing countries tended to reflect the influence of poor crops due to climatic factors, or of inadequate domestic economic policies. The compensatory funds advanced were, thus, intended essentially to provide temporary balance of payments support while the borrowing country adopted appropriate internal adjustment policies. The recent expansion in the facility, while welcome, is relatively modest in character. The payments difficulties now being encountered, and likely to persist in the period ahead, are of a different character and of much greater dimension. They reflect changes of unprecedented magnitude taking place in the international economy, including in particular dramatic changes in relative prices and the worldwide impact of recession and continuing inflation in developed countries.

To meet such deficits, induced primarily by events outside the control of the developing countries, institutional arrangements are urgently required to channel financial support on a scale far larger than is currently available. Moreover, the terms and conditions should reflect the gravity of the economic situation of the large number of developing countries which will require such support. In particular, loans under an expanded facility should be made on a long-term basis rather than, as at present, be tied to a 3-5 year repayment period. There are two reasons for this. First, developing countries need long-term funds to assist them in readjusting their economies to meet their payments deficits on oil account. Secondly, the shortfalls in real export earnings resulting from the recession-cum-inflation in developed market economy countries need to be offset by long-term loans or grants if the burden of adjustment to these economic difficulties is to be minimized for the developing countries.

Debt Relief

Finally, a third element in an international system of economic security for developing countries could be the adoption of some broad principles for dealing with the burden of external indebtedness which has become a major constraint on the economic progress of a large number of developing countries. The present debt-servicing difficulties of developing countries reflect, in part, the serious payments disequilibrium that has emerged over the past two years resulting, as mentioned earlier, in a drastic deterioration in the current payments accounts of non-oil-exporting developing countries.

But these difficulties reflect, also, the malfunctioning of existing institutions through which long-term funds are channelled to developing countries. Inadequate official development assistance, both as regards its volume and its terms and conditions, has resulted in many developing countries seeking commercial loans on terms and conditions which have often been inappropriate and which have added significantly to the burden of debt service charges. The situation has been aggravated by the difficulties faced by developing countries in raising long-term loans on private capital markets, where funds have not always been available in terms of the interest rates and maturities suitable for their development needs.

There is, thus, a case for a dual attack on the debt service problem. First, in recognition of the widespread impact of maladjustments in the world economy on the external debts of developing countries, there is need to adopt a broad approach by considering the debt problems of individual countries in the framework of a set of agreed principles of debt relief in relation to their development requirements. These principles should, however, be flexible enough to distinguish between countries with distinct types of debt problems. In particular, special consideration needs to be given to the possibility of waiving interest payments on official development assistance loans to the least developed and the "most seriously affected" countries.

Secondly, new or revised institutional arrangements are needed to improve the access of developing countries to capital markets and to increase substantially the flow of official development assistance in the form of grants and low-interest loans, particularly to the more disadvantaged developing countries.

Decisive action to set in motion these three mutually supporting measures—the integrated programme for commodities, a greatly extended and liberalized compensatory financing facility, and measures for dealing with the debt problem—would constitute, by itself, a major breakthrough in international economic co-operation. It would, for the first time, put in place a comprehensive system to protect the external sectors of developing countries from the adverse consequences of economic instability in the developed market economy countries. Moreover, by injecting an important element of international regulation of the free play of market forces, it would help lay a basis for the longer-term structural changes in international economic relations that need to be negotiated in the years ahead.

Changing the Structure of International Economic Relations

The immediate programme of measures outlined above cannot be more than a first, albeit an important, step towards a new international economic order. Attention has also to be devoted to identifying the major areas in which negotiation on changes in the institutional structure of international economic relations should take place in the years ahead and to establish, so far as possible, the broad principles to govern such negotiations.

It was argued earlier that, for a meaningful new international economic order to emerge, negotiations should be envisaged in three principal areas: the reduction of the economic dependence of developing countries on developed country enterprises; the strengthening of trade and economic co-operation among the developing countries themselves; and the introduction of a significant measure of global management of resources.

Reducing the Economic Dependence of Developing Countries

Measures to regulate the operations of transnational corporations and other enterprises of developed countries need to be envisaged as part of a wider strategy of industrialization oriented to meet the elementary needs of the majority of the population of developing countries, and based on an increasingly independent technological capability.

The target set by the Lima Declaration—raising the share of developing countries in world industrial production from less than one-tenth at present to as much as one-quarter by the year 2000—will call for an unprecedented transformation of the economies of the Third World. New development strategies, based on a fuller mobilization of domestic resources, will be required. A more self-reliant industrialization policy, and an increased emphasis on meeting basic human needs, will result in significant shifts in the pattern of industrial production and in an increased use of indigenous technologies.

Moreover, both new opportunities and new requirements for greatly expanded trade among the developing countries themselves would be created by such an industrialization policy. A broadening of the range of goods produced and of the opportunities for specialization would increase the scope for the operation of genuine comparative advantage in the mutual trade of developing countries. A greatly expanded and more diversified industrial structure would also improve the ability of developing countries to export industrial products to the markets of developed countries.

However, an expansion of the trade of developing countries of the magnitude required is unlikely to come about of its own accord.[1] A comprehensive strategy to achieve this objective needs to be elaborated and implemented as an essential supporting element of efforts to reach the industrial growth target set out in the Lima Declaration.

A strategy for expanding trade in manufactures. A new trade strategy for expanding and diversifying the exports of manufactures from developing countries would need to include two main elements. First, measures will be necessary to remove existing constraints, at both the governmental and enterprise levels, to the expansion of trade in industrial products. At the governmental level, higher priority should be given by developed countries to the reduction of import barriers to the manufactured exports of developing countries—including a wider and enduring system of preferential access to their markets for such exports—as an integral part of the more general industrial policies which need to be implemented to assist the longer-term restructuring of the industries of developed countries. In this context, the Conference could consider adopting general principles designed greatly to improve the existing schemes of generalized preferences so that maximum benefit can be derived by the manufacturing industries of developing countries. A related principle which could be adopted would be that reductions in trade barriers agreed in the General Agreement on Tariffs and Trade (GATT) multilateral trade negotiations should be given advance implementation in favour of developing countries.

In the period ahead, positive measures—including adjustment assistance—to accelerate the process of structural change in the industries of developed countries should also form part of a global strategy to expand trade in manufactured goods. This will be especially important in relation to the Lima target which, as indicated earlier, will involve a commensurate expansion in manufactured exports from developing countries. However, without a complementary shift in the volume and pattern of demand for imports by the developed countries, the expansion in exports of manufactures from developing countries which is required is not likely to be attained. Such a shift in import demand by developed countries is likely to materialize only if these countries adopt adequate measures in good time to assist the process of structural adaptation in their own industrial sectors.

At the enterprise level, co-ordinated action by both developing and developed countries will be required to control restrictive business practices which adversely affect the growth of manufacturing production and trade of developing countries. While broad agreement has been reached on the desirability of control of such practices, little has so far been achieved to bring these practices under effective control. This is due, in part, to the fact that controls of restrictive business practices in developed countries are generally not concerned with the effects of such practices outside national boundaries. In addition, many developing countries are not yet fully aware of the nature and effects on their economies of restrictive business practices operated by enterprises of developed countries, and do not yet possess the necessary administrative and legal apparatus fully to control such practices.

An agreed strategy for the control of restrictive business practices as a common effort by both developed and developing countries has to be developed. The strategy could include the elaboration of a code of conduct, arrangements for the collection and exchange of information, and the establishment of consultation procedures whereby the adverse effects on their economies of restrictive business practices engaged in by a firm or firms of a developed country can be discussed by the host country with the developed country concerned with a view to taking agreed remedial action.

The removal of existing constraints to trade will not, however, be sufficient by itself to ensure an expansion in manufactured exports from developing countries on the scale implied in the Lima target. What is also required is the adoption by these countries of measures to improve their ability to export increased quantities of manufactures of the right type and on competitive terms.

As regards exports to developed market economy countries—which represent the predominant market for exports of manufactures by developing countries—such measures would include the elimination of fiscal and other policies which favour production for the domestic market and discriminate against exports. Incentives of various kinds might also be appropriate, in certain circumstances, to encourage the export effort. In addition, new or expanded institutional arrangements to facilitate export growth will be required, including adequate arrangements for the financing of export credits and for export insurance. Support by developed countries and by the international financial institutions will be needed to assist in the establishment of such new or expanded facilities.

These various measures would help to provide an economic environment in developing countries conducive to an expansion in manufactured exports. Within that environment, encouragement should be given to closer co-operation between productive enterprises in developing countries and marketing and distribution enterprises in developed countries to ensure the expanding market outlets that will be needed. In addition, developing countries should ensure that the activities of the transnational corporations which, with their affiliates, produce manufactures and semi-manufactures for export from those countries, result in an adequate return to the host country in terms of foreign exchange benefit, of value added, of skilled employment and of linkages with other industries and sectors of the economy.

The expansion and diversification of exports to developed market economy countries cannot, however, constitute a viable strategy by itself. It needs to be supplemented by measures to develop new channels of trade—to expand trade among developing countries themselves, as well as trade between developing countries and socialist countries. Such measures would provide new markets, and a new potential, for the growing manufacturing industries of developing countries. By the same token, they would reduce the existing excessive dependence of these countries on exports to the developed market economies. Measures to expand trade among developing countries are best considered as one element in a broader effort to strengthen economic co-operation among these countries, which is discussed in more detail below.

Trade and economic co-operation between developing countries and the socialist countries of Eastern Europe could also be very greatly expanded. This flow of trade is still largely confined to bilateral exchanges with a relatively small number of developing countries. A widening of geographical coverage and greater use of the multilateral payments facilities now available in trade with socialist countries of Eastern Europe could result in a substantial expansion in the mutual trade of the two groups of countries.

Such trade expansion should contribute to the industrialization and economic development programmes of the developing countries. The socialist countries of Eastern Europe could make a special contribution insofar as their own economic plans can be adapted to accommodate increased purchases of specific products from developing countries, as a counterpart to financial and technical assistance for specific industrial projects in those countries. Since economic management in the socialist countries is undertaken within a long-term planning framework, close co-ordination with the production and trade requirements of individual developing countries could introduce an important element of assurance of markets, as well as of capital inflows, for developing countries.

Closer economic links between developing countries and the socialist countries of Eastern Europe would require co-operation at the enterprise level also, including the establishment of joint projects in developing countries, covering the provision of technology, managerial and marketing expertise, research and finance from the socialist countries, combined with guarantees for the purchase of some agreed portion of the future output of the projects. In addition, triangular agreements could be elaborated, where appropriate, involving the supply of technology and know-how by enterprises of developed market economy countries, to supplement the resources of developing and socialist countries in specific projects.

The socialist countries of Eastern Europe could also consider additional measures to assist the restructuring of the institutional framework of international economic relations, as well as to provide special assistance to the countries most seriously affected by the current economic crisis. Such measures might include, for example, financial support for the common fund envisaged as part of the integrated programme for commodities, and technical support for, and co-operation with, regional transfer of technology centres when these are established. Additional credits on concessional terms to the most seriously affected countries might also be considered.

A new trade strategy for developing countries should thus be conceived as a multidimensional package of measures, encompassing measures by both developed and developing countries to remove existing constraints on trade, to improve the ability of developing countries to produce manufactured goods for export, and to open up new channels of trade. A further essential element in a viable strategy would be action by the international community, and by developing countries themselves, to create an adequate technological capability in these countries to support the vast expansion in industrial output that will be required.

Strengthening the technological base of developing countries. Hitherto, international efforts to promote the transfer of modern technology to developing countries, as part of a global development strategy, have concentrated almost entirely on the need for restructuring the existing legal and juridical system governing such technology transfer, so that this system may better serve the interests of developing countries. Consideration of the two main elements of a restructured international legal framework—a revised patent system and a code of conduct for technology transfer—has proceeded to the point when major decisions on these issues can be taken.

As regards the patent system, the pivot of a restructured legal framework must be a revision of the Paris Convention to meet the special needs of developing countries. This would open the way for corresponding revisions in national legislation and practices, so that the patent system as a whole can become an instrument of development policy. Discussions on alternative draft texts of a code of conduct for the transfer of technology have reached an advanced stage, there being general agreement among all groups of countries on the need for such a code.

The restructuring of the legal and juridical environment would help to create the permissive conditions for strengthening the technological capabilities of developing countries, thereby reducing their technological dependence. Such action, to be fully effective, must be supplemented by positive steps, at the national, regional and international levels, to strengthen the technological base of developing countries. If developing countries continue to be dependent on imported technology over the next 25 years to the same degree that they have in the past, the foreign exchange cost of such imported technology would rise by the year 2000 to some 20 to 35 times the present level, which would represent an unmanageable additional burden on the external payments position of these countries. The rapid industrialization of the Third World, on the scale envisaged by the Lima target, will not be feasible without a vastly expanded and strengthened technological capability in the developing countries themselves.

Marketing and distribution system for primary commodities. The economic dependence of developing countries is also manifested in the primary commodity sector of their economies, particularly insofar as transnational corporations control a substantial proportion of the foreign trade of developing countries in primary commodities. For many commodities, transnationals exercise considerable bargaining power, since they singly, or taken together, control the international marketing and distribution system, while they are typically faced with a large number of competing sellers of the commodity in Third World countries. In some cases, the transnationals or their affiliates have also become producers of primary commodities in developing countries, so that they are able to transfer goods to the parent company at internal book-keeping prices which maximise the global profit of the multinational operation as a whole.

Over a wide range of the commodity exports of developing countries, the degree of control exercised by the transnationals has been associated with a generally inadequate return to the producer in developing countries. While comprehensive statistics are not available, it would appear that the share of developing countries in the final price paid by consumers in developed countries is of the order of 10-15 percent for a number of commodities where transnational corporations play an important role in the marketing and distribution system. In many cases, too, the income of the estate worker, miner or peasant producer in the developing countries has remained at low levels, even in periods when final prices were relatively high on world markets.

A number of in-depth studies carried out in response to a resolution of the third session of UNCTAD indicate the need for developing countries to play a more active role to ensure that the marketing and distribution system for their primary commodity exports is more responsive to their needs and provides them with a more equitable share of the benefits of trade. In some cases, this objective may be attained by fiscal measures, such as an export tax imposed at a uniform rate by developing countries. In other cases, developing countries may have to consider some form of control over the transfer-pricing policies of transnational corporations.

A more independent role for developing countries in the marketing and distribution system will require, as a minimum, joint negotiation by these countries with the transnational corporations to secure more favourable returns to the producer, as well as the establishment of processing industries—where this would be viable—in the developing countries concerned. In certain cases, governments of developing countries may also have to consider participation in the ownership of the existing marketing and distribution facilities, or even the establishment of their own independent facilities.

An essential prerequisite of such measures, if they are to be effective, would be close policy co-ordination among the governments of the developing countries concerned. In this connexion, associations of producing countries can play an important role by injecting a degree of countervailing power in their negotiations with transnational corporations.

Strengthening Trade and Economic Co-operation Among Developing Countries

The failure of the existing international economic order to solve the problems of poverty and economic backwardness of the Third World has imparted a sense of urgency to the need for developing countries to reduce their dependence on the developed centres and to reorient their development strategy on the basis of their collective self-reliance.

The concept of accelerated economic development through closer links among developing countries is not a new one. Until recently, however, that concept found expression in integration schemes of a regional or sub-regional character, which currently embrace about one-half of the total number of developing countries. Within the framework of these integration schemes, considerable progress has been made in expanding the mutual trade of the member countries, in developing complementary industries, and in general harmonization of their development programmes. In certain sub-regional groupings, also, important initiatives have been taken to improve the bargaining power of the member countries in their dealings with transnational corporations and to regulate the operations of these corporations.

The new awareness on the part of developing countries of the need to strengthen their mutual economic relations, together with the new financial strength of the oil exporting countries, provides a unique opportunity for building a global system of economic co-operation among Third World countries on the valuable experience so far gained on a regional and sub-regional basis. Thus, closer economic co-operation among developing countries on a global basis would improve their bargaining power in their economic relations with developed countries and, more especially, with transnational corporations; it would also provide, to a much greater extent than hitherto, the means for accelerating their economic and social development through their own efforts.

The main elements of such a global system of Third World economic co-operation could be of two kinds: those which remove existing constraints and which generally facilitate the expansion of the mutual trade of developing countries and those of an active character, including joint planning of new productive investments.

The first category, of facilitating measures, would include new preferences on imports from other developing countries, covering both tariff and non-tariff barriers, and primary and processed commodities as well as manufactured goods and, to the extent possible, services such as banking, shipping and insurance. The purpose of such preferences would not be to reduce the existing degree of protection afforded to domestic production but rather to provide some incentive for importers in a developing country to buy from other developing countries rather than from their traditional suppliers in developed countries.

Such a global preference system could be built up from existing sub-regional preferential arrangements by adding regional preferences and, at a suitable date, preferences for developing countries in other regions. Special preferential concessions could be provided for the exports of the least developed countries in all regions. A number of aspects would require in-depth study including, in particular, the mechanisms to be employed to provide preferences in the operation of non-tariff barriers and to provide an equitable balance in the net advantages gained by participating countries.

Since the flow of trade among developing countries is generally impeded by payments difficulties, an expanded system of trade preference needs to be supported by payments arrangements specifically designed to facilitate trade among developing countries. In this connexion, immediate steps could be taken to strengthen the existing sub-regional clearing arrangements and to create linkages among them. As a longer-term goal, detailed consideration should be given to the establishment of payments arrangements for the Third World as a whole, which would provide credit to member countries for financing imports from other developing countries without immediate payment in convertible currency, while also allowing member countries to continue to earn convertible currency by exporting to traditional markets.

As indicated earlier, preferential trade and supporting payments arrangements are essentially facilitative measures, providing an institutional framework more conducive than that now existing to the expansion of trade among developing countries. An effective strategy for economic co-operation cannot, however, be confined to facilitating measures which, by themselves, may simply create opportunities for transnational corporations to rationalize their activities in developing countries.

An effective development strategy based on the collective self-reliance of Third World countries will require a series of mutually supporting measures of an active, rather than merely a facilitating, character. Such active measures need to be elaborated over the whole field of economic relations among developing countries. Special efforts should be devoted to the elaboration of joint production projects by two or more developing countries, since multinational co-operation of this kind could become a central instrument for expanding the productive capacity, technological capability and mutual trade of developing countries. It could also serve as a channel for mobilizing a part of the financial resources of oil exporting countries in a way which is not subject to control by transnational corporations and which does not require financial mediation by developed countries.

New institutional mechanisms will also be needed if the flow of long-term investment capital from oil exporting countries to other developing countries is to be very substantially increased. Such mechanisms should be designed to provide the investing countries with adequate security and reasonable rates of return, while providing the borrowing countries with capital on terms which they can afford. Feasibility studies of alternative mechanisms, such as investment guarantee schemes and interest subsidy arrangements, would appear to be urgently required.

A range of supporting measures will be essential if the industrialization objectives of the Third World are to be achieved. In particular, joint action by developing countries should be envisaged to strengthen their scientific and technological capability, including co-operation in research facilities and the development of indigenous technologies; co-operation to improve the economic and financial infrastructure affecting their mutual trade and payments flows; co-operation in the marketing of their exports in developed countries and in the purchase of their imports from those countries; and co-operation in improving their access to information on market conditions and on technology availability in order to strengthen their negotiating position vis-à-vis the transnational corporations.

The global system of economic co-operation among developing countries will necessarily be multidimensional and complex. The various elements will need careful elaboration and intensive consideration by Third World countries. Much preparatory work will be required, and alternative options must be assessed, before meaningful decisions can be taken. The immediate need would seem to be for governments of developing countries to take a decision in principle to set in motion the preparatory studies, so that the principal elements of an effective global system of economic co-operation among Third World countries can be established with the minimum of delay.

Global Management of Resources

A third broad element of institutional change in a meaningful movement towards a new international economic order would be the introduction of a significant measure of global management of resources. As indicated earlier, the concept of global management implies that the working of market forces should be subject to regulation so that they become a mechanism for the orderly evolution of production and trade, and operate to support the development objectives of the Third World.

International trading rules. There are three principal, interrelated, areas in which the international community could seek to apply the concept of global management by appropriate institutional changes. The first relates to the "rules of the game" governing international trade. These rules, as developed in the Havana Charter of 1948, and which were only partially embodied in the General Agreement on Tariffs and Trade, were designed essentially to provide an international legal framework conducive to the operations of trading enterprises in a freely competitive world market. The twin principles of non-discrimination and most-favoured-nation treatment, which are basic to the general agreement, are both necessary elements in the concept of a freely competitive trading system. Moreover, until the adoption of Part IV in 1964, action in the context of the General Agreement was governed by the principle of equal rights and obligations of all contracting parties.

Looking back over the period since the creation of GATT in the late 1940s, it would seem that the trading rules as then established do not adequately cover certain major developments in the world economy. First, the past several decades have witnessed a phenomenal growth in the economic power of transnational corporations, which now control or influence a substantial proportion of world trade. Decisions taken centrally by these corporations affect the geographical location of their production as well as the transactions between their subsidiaries and affiliates in different countries. Moreover, government actions, both in terms of national economic policies and in the framework of international agreements, have also become a powerful influence on the volume and pattern of international trade. The portion of trade which is genuinely subject to the "free play of market forces" has thus become significantly circumscribed.

A second factor has been the emergence of a large number of new nations from their previous colonial status and their need for rapid economic and social development. The "rules of the game," however, tend to operate in favour of the economies of developed countries, since their enterprises have the technical, financial and marketing strength to benefit from a freely competitive market where one exists. The principle of non-discrimination, in particular, cannot be expected to favour the infant manufacturing industries of developing countries.

Third, the GATT rules, being oriented towards a free market system, are not appropriate as principles governing the trade of socialist countries, which has tended to grow over the post-war period at a faster rate than other major flows of trade. A universally applicable set of trading rules would need special provisions to cover the policies and trading practices of these countries.

A thoroughgoing revision of the existing rules governing international trade would have to allow for these various changes in the structure of the world economy. In particular, a revised set of rules should aim to provide a legal framework conducive to a rapid expansion in the productive capacity and the foreign trade of the developing countries. This would imply the adoption of binding commitments by governments on some issues and of agreed guidelines or principles on others.

Of particular importance would be the adoption of binding commitments by developed countries to free entry to their markets for the export products of developing countries. Alternatively, if trade barriers of one kind or another are retained, the new trading rules should provide for some form of compensation to developing countries for the loss of market potential. For this purpose, "voluntary" export restraints agreed by developing countries to limit exports of particular products to developed countries should also be counted as involving loss of market potential. Further, the new "rules of the game" should recognize the need of developing countries to provide adequate incentives to encourage the exports of newly established industries, which should not be subject to anti-dumping or countervailing import duties in developed countries.

The new trading rules could also include guidelines or principles designed to regulate the use of restrictive business practices which adversely affect the trade of developing countries. Agreed principles should also be evolved for adjustment assistance programmes in developed countries, including related action to phase out import restrictions adversely affecting the trade of developing countries.

A new set of principles is also required in relation to trade preferences. Such preferences granted by developed countries to certain developing countries should not operate to the disadvantage of other developing countries. The rules should provide for appropriate compensation for such disadvantage if it occurs. Moreover, preferences granted by developed countries to developing countries should not be subject to discriminating conditions (for example, that the beneficiary countries should not be members of a producers' association). Furthermore, the right of developing countries to accord preferences on their mutual trade, without having to extend such preferences to developed countries, should become an integral part of a revised set of rules, rather than arising from a waiver, as at present.

These and other relevant principles will need detailed study and consideration by governments before any comprehensive revision of the general agreement, let alone the negotiation of a revised Havana Charter, becomes practicable.

International monetary reform. The second major area in which institutional changes should be envisaged is the working of the international monetary system. Indeed, because of the close interdependence of trade and monetary flows, such changes would be an essential support and complement to the revision of the international trading rules discussed above. It is unfortunately true that since the widespread adoption of floating exchange rates the momentum for the reform of the international monetary system has very largely been lost. Moreover, the adjustment process is, if anything, now operating less smoothly than before. Exchange rate determination, for example, is not following any definite pattern, international liquidity remains outside the effective control of the international community, while the flow of resources to developing countries is very substantially less than their needs in a period of continuing recession and world inflation.

There would seem to be general agreement that a reformed international monetary system would have to provide both a smoother and more flexible adjustment mechanism for the world economy as a whole and a greater flow of resources to developing countries on terms and conditions more appropriate to their needs than is the case at present. As regards the former objective, a reformed system should treat both surplus countries and deficit countries in a symmetrical fashion, rather than placing the onus of adjustment solely on the latter countries, as at present. Again, the treatment of the problems of reserve currency countries should not continue to be quite different from the rules applying to other countries. This consideration lends additional urgency to the need to phase in the Special Drawing Right (SDR) as the principal reserve unit of a reformed system.

As regards the flow of resources to developing countries, some major institutional changes will be needed. Over the past few years, only a marginal proportion of the new international reserves and liquidity has gone to the developing countries, though these countries have been faced, as mentioned earlier, with an unprecedented increase in their external payments difficulties. Under a reformed system, the developing countries should be enabled to receive the greater part of newly created international reserves and liquidity. Moreover, new mechanisms need to be evolved to ensure that the flow of financial resources to developing countries assumes a more automatic, or at least a more predictable, character.

This was the rationale behind the proposal to establish a link between SDR creation and additional development finance, but although the rationale is widely accepted, there is not as yet full agreement in favour of establishing the link. Recent developments, particularly the rapid expansion in international liquidity in the form of national currencies, seem to have weakened the case for further SDR creation in the near future. Nonetheless, the link could become an essential feature in a reformed international monetary system based on the SDR, and this should remain as a major objective of policy in this field.

The concept of making the flow of financial resources to developing countries more automatic or more predictable could be applied also to the official development assistance provided by developed market economy countries. It has been estimated that even if the latter countries resume a reasonable rate of economic growth, the non-oil-exporting developing countries will need an annual net capital inflow rising by 1980 to more than double the 1974 level, measured at constant prices, in order to achieve the economic growth target set by the International Development Strategy. A net capital inflow of this magnitude will not be feasible unless developed countries give high priority to achieve the 0.7 percent target for official development assistance. In view of the difficulties experienced by most of the donor countries in obtaining budgetary appropriations for increased aid to developing countries, serious consideration of new fiscal mechanisms is required. Of particular interest in this regard is the proposal for some form of international tax, with the proceeds earmarked for official development assistance. Suggestions have been put forward to levy such a tax on incomes in developed countries; alternatively, or additionally, a tax on the consumption of non-renewable natural resources or on the activities of environment polluting industries could be envisaged. Feasibility studies of such new fiscal mechanisms designed to expand the flow of development assistance could now usefully be made.

A complementary approach would be to use part of the total of official development assistance to subsidize the interest charges on loans raised by developing countries on private capital markets. The technique of interest subsidy is already embodied in the "third window" established by the World Bank and in the oil facility of the IMF. The extension of the interest subsidy principle to private capital markets would substantially increase the total flow of financial resources to developing countries and would significantly increase the range of developing countries able to borrow on these capital markets.

The various changes in the mechanisms of the international monetary and financing system discussed above are designed to make that system more responsive to the special needs of the developing countries within a smoother and more flexible global adjustment process. But it should not be forgotten that a major prerequisite for ensuring that the interests of developing countries are fully taken into account in a reform of the system is that the developing countries should be adequately represented in the decision-making bodies of all the international financial institutions.

Rational use of resources. A third area in which the concept of global management can be increasingly applied is in the use of natural resources, particularly the non-renewable resources of developing countries. Previous emphasis on overall income growth as the principal indicator of economic development has led to a wasteful use of the world's natural resources and to a multi-dimensional degradation of the environment. In developing countries the urgent need to increase their exports to developed countries has led in many cases to serious depletion of natural resources in forms such as deforestation, over-grazing of land, desertification, water and air pollution, and the depletion of mineral deposits at an excessive rate. Since most developing countries lack the resources adequately to combat these and similar adverse effects of the existing production cycle, economic growth has been accompanied by increasing environmental problems, not only of various forms of physical degradation, but also in human and social terms as, for example, in the growing urban poverty in many developing countries.

On the other hand, the rapid economic expansion of developed countries over the post-war period was based to a significant extent on the import of cheap fuel and raw materials from developing countries. There is now a widespread recognition that the availability of cheap materials and the pattern of technological advance has been one factor in inducing wasteful consumption and production patterns. There is increasing recognition by the international community of the critical pressures on resources and on the environment and of the need for a global management of resources which would ensure harmony between developmental needs and sustainability of ecological equilibrium.

Many of the problems of environmental degradation in developing countries can be met by the adoption of new development strategies by these countries themselves. Strategies aimed primarily at the reduction of poverty, a more equitable distribution of incomes, and a pattern of production designed to meet the elementary needs of the majority of the population would also help to avoid a wasteful use of resources and allow developing countries to be better placed to combat environmental degradation.

But in the longer term, internationally co-ordinated policies will be required to ensure that economic and social development is combined with effective environmental protection and improvement in both developed and developing countries. International policies will need to be specifically directed towards conservation and rational utilization of scarce raw materials and non-renewable resources, particularly by appropriate regulation of prices and, if necessary, of production levels. As indicated previously, the integrated programme for commodities would be a first step towards a rational management of the world's natural resources. Such specific policies, however, will be fully effective only if they are conceived and implemented within the broader institutional changes, discussed earlier, in the structure of international economic relations. These more fundamental structural changes, by providing the external conditions favourable to the rapid economic development of the Third World, will also provide developing countries with the means for combining economic growth with measures to combat environmental degradation, to relieve the burden of poverty and reduce existing income inequalities, and to improve the quality of life for the majority of their population.

Notes

1. To achieve the Lima target, developing countries will have to accelerate their rate of industrial growth sharply over the next quarter of a century—from 6½ percent a year during the 1960s and early 1970s to a rate in the region of 10 percent a year. On the basis of past experience, including that of

the present developed countries when they were at a relatively early stage of industrialization, the required rate of growth in exports of manufactures from developing countries is likely to exceed considerably 10 percent a year in real terms and could well be as high as 15 percent a year.

4 *The "New International Economic Order": The Skeptics' Views*

Charles Rics

Introduction

The establishment of a "New International Economic Order" (NIEO)[1] has become the objective of the developing countries, supported at least rhetorically by the major socialist nations. Several developed market economies such as those of the Scandinavian group and the Netherlands also politically support the concept. In the other industrialized countries, important segments of the foreign affairs elites support changes in the world economy aimed at improving the position and prospects of the developing world, although the question of the degree of change is, of course, a major point of discussion.

There are, however, important voices in the same industrial countries that question the basic idea of the NIEO, at least as described in the Declaration and Programme of Action of the United Nations (UN) Sixth Special Session, the Charter of Economic Rights and Duties of States, and the final resolution of the Seventh Special Session.

This paper examines the views expressed by the NIEO skeptics (especially in the United States) in order to clarify the several distinct bases upon which the developed countries are contesting elements of the NIEO. In addition, an effort will be made to explore how the developed countries may try to prevent—or at least contain—the implementation of the NIEO, should they choose to do so. How the developing countries and the industrialized world reconcile their practical and philosophic differences over the international economic system of the future will be in no small measure related to the response of the developing country "demandeurs" to the problems which the skeptics are seeing.

The views expressed here do not necessarily reflect those of the International Economic Policy Association and the Center for Multinational Studies with whom the author is currently affiliated.

Historical Perspective

The clarion call for the establishment of the NIEO, issued so dramatically at the Sixth Special Session of the UN General Assembly in 1974, took many in the developed world by surprise. Many of the component policies of the proposed economic order were certainly not novel, at least not to those in the foreign policy communities who concerned themselves with development issues. In fact, many of the arguments for the elements of the NIEO were made as early as the fifties and had been integrated earlier.[2] Rather, surprise stemmed from the sudden coalescence of virtually the entire developing world around a common position. The significance of this event was enhanced by the fact that, in order to secure the implementation of the NIEO, a complete change in the structure and mechanisms of international economic relationships was required, going far beyond the established development policies and institutions heretofore relied upon.

The immediate reactions to the NIEO program by the governments of the major developed countries—particularly the United States—cannot be separated from their responses to the Organization of Petroleum Exporting Countries' (OPEC's) actions during 1973 and 1974, i.e., the destination embargo on oil by its Arab subgroup and the quadrupling of the posted price for petroleum by OPEC members acting together.[3] These actions were seen as clear and present threats to the economic stability and national security of the major Organisation for Economic Co-operation and Development (OECD) nations, and each major industrialized country responded to the OPEC "challenge" in accordance with what it viewed as its own national interests.

The Sixth Special Session, convened in this atmosphere of crisis and economic threat, was quite naturally seen by the developed world as an attempt by the developing countries to build upon and duplicate OPEC's dramatic successes. The fears of this period were, for instance, reflected in a series of articles published under the heading, "One, Two, Many OPEC's . . .?" in the journal *Foreign Policy*[4] and in the crash review of the cartelization prospects for non-oil raw materials by government ministries and nongovernmental institutions.[5] The NIEO program in 1974 was seen by many in the developed world as synonymous with the Third World's drive for raw material cartels. The political responses, therefore, were largely conditioned by national policies toward these cartels and especially by the emerging perception of the spreading economic damage wrought by OPEC. In the U.S. case this initially combined outright opposition to the concept of commodity agreements, with vocal protest to the tyrannical majority that advocated them.

The broader challenge to the world's economic system by the NIEO program began to be more widely studied as the Group of 77, under the leadership of the nonaligned movement, demonstrated strength and resilience. The adoption by the UN General Assembly of the Charter of Economic Rights and Duties of States during the 29th regular session of the Assembly in December 1974 was an important watershed in this process. The Charter of Economic Rights and Duties codified the Group of 77's view of a system of international norms for economic relations. Many in the developed world remarked that the charter was all "rights" on the part of the developing world and all "duties" on the part of the developed. Its adoption, nevertheless, demonstrated the far-reaching systemic change required by the NIEO. Wider study leading to the adoption of a new developed-country strategy to "respond" to the NIEO began during 1975 and culminated in the new proposals at the Seventh Special Session in September.[6]

The final section of this paper will consider alternate courses of action open to the developed states for the delay or containment of the NIEO and the policies associated with these strategies. It is useful to begin, however, with a review of those skeptical to the philosophical basis of the NIEO, followed by a summary of the critics of the NIEO proposals on practical grounds.

The Skeptics on Principle

Most of those who are skeptical of the merits of the NIEO begin from the premise that such an order is not principally an economic program, but is rather a political offensive. For example, Irving Kristol has written:

> In truth, this 'new cold war' is not really about economics at all, but about politics. At bottom it is a conflict of political ideologies. What the Third World is saying is not that it needs our help but that their poverty is the fault of our capitalism. . . .[7]

From this standpoint, to accept the need for a NIEO, or to offer to discuss changes in the present economic structure, is to accept the moral responsibility for the poverty of the developing world and the terms of the debate set down by the Group of 77.

It is argued with considerable logic and factual background by the NIEO skeptics that the principal cause of the Third World's poverty is not external but internal. Daniel Moynihan made this argument eloquently in "The United States in Opposition," using the widespread evidence of governmental mismanagement, corruption, and inefficiency in developing countries to support it.[8] The drawback to adequate internal mobilization of resources for economic growth is said to be the political ideology of Fabian socialism. Governments in developing countries, having taken the domestic position that an equitable distribution of wealth and income is right and necessary, are described as turning to the international arena to fulfill their pledges.

Skeptics of the NIEO point to the conflict between, on the one hand, the rhetoric of developing country spokespersons—who inevitably describe their cause as just, imperative, and humane (frequently citing statistics on relative consumption of goods in the North and South, income levels, or food resources)—and, on the other, the widespread deprivation of human rights and economic oppression to which these new states subject their own people. This is a powerful argument, since in the North one of the most important motivations for the institution of special measures for the assistance of the developing countries (and the basis for sympathy for the NIEO program itself) is a basic concern for the material condition of the people of the Third World, not its governments.

This distinction was brought out by Robert Tucker in a recent *Commentary* article.[9] Tucker wrote that the developing country leaders demanding the NIEO are calling for special measures to improve the economic prospects and to assure the independence and sovereignty of their *states,* not their peoples. By contrast, those developed country elites, convinced of the need for changes, generally proceed from a new sensibility which leads them to believe that no people on earth should be deprived of the minimal basics of life. This humanitarian motive is described by Tucker as quite revolutionary, vesting people as people with rights in the international community quite aside from those derived from their allegiance to a state. Where the developing countries emphasize the state as the moral unit which deserves freedom, sovereign equality, and an equal chance for economic success, the developed countries are likely to see the poor and deprived Third World peasant as the object of special assistance.

This discrepancy in viewpoint can be expected to become increasingly evident. The U.S. Congress, for instance, while apparently willing to provide resources for development, has simultaneously been taking more and more of an "interventionist" line on the use of those resources. For example, the "New Directions" in aid embodied in the 1973 Foreign Assistance Act require the U.S. Agency for International Development (AID) to go much further in "direct assistance" to make sure resources reach the poorest, generally rural, people. AID is also required to obtain the "participation" of these poor in planning projects, not just to provide the resources to the developing nations' governments.[10] Similar trends are observable in the World Bank's concentration on the rural poor, the U.S. Congress' insistence on periodic reports on the condition of basic human rights in nations receiving military assistance, and in the objections raised to U.S. support for World Bank loans to Chile under both Presidents Allende and Pinochet (albeit on completely different grounds). Interventionism in foreign assistance is, of course, not new (witness the Alliance for Progress);

but in response to demands for "blank check" assistance, the case is being made that this approach would be a moral surrender to repressive regimes.

A second major philosophic basis for objection to the NIEO by industrialized country skeptics—led by the U.S. Treasury Department—has been that many of the Group of 77's proposals involve a limitation or even abolition of the primarily market-based system of international economic exchanges. The objections in the industrial countries to this move away from the "free market" concept are in turn based on the ideological contention that open markets are the best guarantors of human freedom and opportunity and the pragmatic calculation that free markets are the most efficient allocators of scarce resources. Of course, the arguments about a NIEO and free markets are rarely prefaced with the acknowledgment that what is at stake is really the relative intervention and management of markets: governments (through state-owned enterprises, tariffs, and quotas), as well as integrated private producers (through transfer pricing, internal stocking, and barriers to entry), tend to limit the free play of market forces. Yet, although large units with market power do tend to seek stability, raw materials markets are not yet widely managed in the sense that there is broad international cooperation to maximize the relative price.[11]

The U.S. Treasury Department's views on these issues were spelled out by Secretary William Simon at a recent foreign policy conference.[12] Simon stated the the United States, given the size and importance of its own economy, was "acutely aware" of its international responsibilities. Simon, however, attacked the "interventionist school" which detaches the producers more and more from "real market forces," making them dependent on artificial pricing mechanism for their welfare. The Department of the Treasury believed that its challenge was to expose "the false gods of many who seek a New International Economic Order." These gods—expropriation, indexation, and cartelization—"are not the answer for either the developing nations or the industrialized nations, and the sooner we all understand that, the sooner we can complete the building of more solid foundations for worldwide economic progress."[13] The basic philosophy, moreover, is that free markets are more than the most economically efficient allocators of resources: "We are firmly committed to the belief that the best model for economic prosperity is a system which unites freedom of commerce with freedom of the individual." This system is the "one that permits the developing countries to fulfill their desire for self determination."[14] Treasury Assistant Secretary Gerald Parsky has even related U.S. policies on the NIEO to the future of the U.S. system itself: "If for political reasons we agree now, or appear to agree, with demands for a new economic system, it will be impossible to justify on economic grounds our desire to preserve our system later."[15]

The concept of freedom linked to open economic systems was extended by William Safire in a *New York Times* article opposing U.S. agreement to the commissions set up by the Paris North-South Conference. Safire believed that "after a while, in the name of price stability and economic order, we will have acquiesced in the creation of a network of barriers, tariffs, special deals, reciprocal restraints, and income redistributions that will enmesh every American business decision in foreign policy, and—incidentally—*limit the bargaining freedom of United States workers*" [*emphasis supplied*].[16] This argument sometimes takes on elements of the Protestant work ethic, as in Safire's comment, "forget about hard work, forget about generations of development. The 'have not' nations want equality with the 'have' nations now, without going through the process of development."[17]

Others criticize the NIEO program for the procedure by which the developing countries have asserted their "rights," a procedure that, it is held, violates the principles of international law. Examples of this behavior are the OPEC nations' unilateral abrogation of earlier solemn contracts (such as the Tehran Agreement) and the emulation by others such as the Jamaican government (which unilaterally violated its contract with foreign bauxite producing companies, simultaneously withdrawing from the International Centre for Settlement of Investment Disputes, so as to deny its obligation to submit to international arbitration).[18] The cumulative effect of NIEO-inspired acts against international legal principles is substantially to destroy these principles as a basis for national action or responsiblity. It is fairly clear that the Organization of Arab Petroleum Exporting Countries' (OAPEC's) destination embargo on petroleum had the effect of halting the emerging international consensus on the proper use of economic power. This setback is clearly shown by the fact that, although the 1970 UN Declaration on Friendly Relations declared that "no state may use or encourage the use of economic, political, or any other type of measure to coerce another state in order to obtain from it the subordination of the exercise of its sovereign rights and to secure from it advantages of any kind," the Arab oil producers denied its applicability.[19] However, they apparently felt sufficiently embarrassed to push for its later modification. In the Charter of Economic Rights and Duties of States the phrase "and to secure from it advantages of any kind" was conveniently dropped.

Skeptics who suggest that the legal order provided by the NIEO will be considerably less than the structure it replaces argue that at least the existing system provides for certain minimum guarantees of "due process" which protect against politically motivated economic unilateralism. An exponent of this view is Timothy Stanley, who writes that the buffer of law (*juris*) between economics and politics is vital, and that whatever the short-term gains to some parties, "everyone loses in the long run if anarchy substitutes for the rule of law."[20] In other circumstances (as in a hypothetical future in which a commodity stabilization program has become a reality), the weak and poor will need to be protected against abrogation of contracts and other obligations (against cheating by fellow producers or against renegotiation of purchase obligations by consumers) even more than the economically strong. Furthermore, those developing countries that become net investors abroad (such as the oil producers) will be seeking "due process" safeguards for their assets. Stanley believes that the "prosperity of the West does not rest on technological, economic or military power alone. It owes a great deal to the development of the concepts of law and equity which guide its political and social systems."[21] It is the lack of a common politico-legal system for resolving conflict which, in Stanley's view, distinguishes the NIEO challenge from domestic labor union movements, with which it is often compared.

As noted above, the Charter of Economic Rights and Duties of States, thought by some to offer an alternative to traditional international law in this area, is seen by others as decidedly one-sided. Moynihan, for example, characterized the charter in this way.[22] Private investors were the group most directly denied protection—the Charter denies any espousal rights of an investor's home state in the case of nationalization. Corporate commentators have reacted to this provision with alarm.[23] It was a major reason for the negative votes on the charter by Belgium, Denmark, the Federal Republic of Germany, Luxembourg, the United Kingdom, and the United States in the General Assembly. The United States recently reiterated the position that even if its citizens accept a settlement for expropriated assets at "less than fair value," that action is not binding on their government, which "reserves its rights to maintain international claims for what it regards as adequate compensation under international law."[24]

One emerging theme in the response to the NIEO is to examine the reasons for the developed countries' sense of "guilt" toward the developing world and then proclaim the guilt either justified or unwarranted. One recent writer, P. T. Bauer, has examined the exploitation case of NIEO advocates (i.e., that Third World poverty and First World wealth are directly attributable to "exploitation" by developed countries) and rejected it.[25] Bauer observed that if this assumption were true, a high degree of participation in economic relations with the industrialized countries would bring corresponding levels of exploitation and relative poverty. He found that, in fact, the reverse is generally the case. Some of the poorest countries in the world, such as Burma, Nepal, Chad, and the Central African Republic are noteworthy precisely for their absence of relations with the industrial world.[26]

Bauer pointed out that there is little economic justification for a "guilt" feeling. He argued that national wealth is earned primarily through high productivity rather than by extraction from others; that debts represent resources transferred, often on highly favorable terms, rather than a "burden" gratuitously placed on the Third World; and that external economic relations are beneficial to development by opening up markets for exports and offering, on a competitive basis, technology and products from the developed countries. Bauer rejected the "demonstration effect" (whereby developed country consumer goods cause so-called cultural dependence), asserting that a greater choice of consumer goods actually serves as an incentive to higher productivity. Bauer also believed that Third World nations have not uncritically adopted Western ways but have, in fact, been quite selective.[27]

The most persuasive evidence for the guilt and responsibility thesis, of course, is the difference in standards of consumption between the industrial and the developing countries. The dramatic differences in consumption of food, energy, and all other goods are primarily responsible for the strong support for food, health, and other humanitarian aid programs of the developed countries; the vague feeling of guilt for having so much when others have so little is probably the basis of support for all development assistance. Bauer and others have objected to the difference in consumption being understood in this way. Bauer observed that "per capita production in America exceeds per capita production in India more than the difference in consumption, allowing it not only to pay for this difference in consumption, but also to finance domestic and foreign investment, as well as foreign aid."[28]

In a broader sense, of course, all of the commentators in developed countries discussed in this section have dealt with the "guilt" issue as they examine the moral charges of the proponents of change. Philosophic opponents argue either that the right and moral policies have been followed and should continue to be followed or that the changes proposed by the NIEO are unfair in themselves and will set dangerous precedents for the future. Either way, they are arguing that developed country guilt is misplaced.

The arguments presented so far generally dealt with the emotional and philosophic core of the NIEO claim. In the next section, the practical objections to NIEO components will be discussed. Although, politics being what it is, the rhetoric will frequently dwell on the philosophic (or the "guilt") issues, the actual outcome will frequently depend on the pragmatic analysis of national interest by all nations.

The Skeptics on Pragmatic Grounds

Most practical objections to the "Programme of Action for a New International Economic Order" (and the derivative proposals and ideas advanced in various forums since the Sixth Special Session) focus on the demands for an integrated program for commodity trade, including the indexation of commodity prices to world inflation levels, as proposed by the UN Conference on Trade and Development (UNCTAD).[29] These matters, together with some of the provisions pertaining to industrialization (including transnational enterprise issues, technology transfer, and restrictive business practices), the agreement to a date for the achievement of the 0.7 percent of GNP official development assistance (ODA) target, and the Special Drawing Right (SDR) development "link" prove the most difficult for the Western industrial nations to accept. Some analysts feel that the programs themselves are counterproductive, ill-advised, and inefficient from the standpoint of providing assistance to the developing countries, or that they will have serious consequences for future wealth, growth, and research in developed countries.

Many of the opponents to the integrated commodity program in the United States use the historical record of disappointments and failures in this field as a starting point. Other observers, of course, derive different lessons from the experience, but many in the developed world find the history of the coffee, cocoa, tin, sugar, and wheat agreements particularly discouraging. In his study of the history of these and other commodity agreements, Alton D. Law found difficulties in producer participation (nonuniversality of membership, and producers reluctant to shift resources to other industries), consumer participation (distrust of producer dominance and development of synthetics), and management (inadequate funds, and arbitrary determination of quotas).[30]

These are not trivial difficulties, and together the historical record serves as a strong practical argument against commodity agreements. The International Trade Commission (ITC), in a study of the U.S. commodity agreement experience at the request of the U.S. Senate Finance Committee, concluded that commodity agreements "often result in economic waste and misallocation of scarce productive resources, and historical experience has demonstrated their frequent failure to achieve their objectives."[31] Hendrik S. Houthakker, in a paper for the International Chamber of Commerce (ICC), stressed the problem of new producers as the critical cause of historical breakdown, "since in most commodities new producers will enter (or marginal producers expand) sooner or later when the price is relatively high, cartels have either broken down or have survived only by charging prices comparable to the market."[32] Other historical reviews focus on the lack of control over supplies reaching the market, i.e., the problem of adequate quotas.[33] The 1969 World Bank study of primary product stabilization attempts highlighted the problem of market forecasting, for inaccurate perceptions of market trends can wreak havoc on buffer stock transactions and quotas alike.[34]

Analyses of the historical experience with commodity agreements, however, are only of limited usefulness in responding to the UNCTAD integrated program. That program, by encompassing 18 commodities (as originally outlined, subsequently narrowed to an initial group of ten), international financing of buffer stocks, compensatory financing, long-term purchase agreements, and market access provisions, requires an enlarged frame of analysis. Its size alone (even in its smaller form, the size of the proposed buffer stock fund alone could total $6 billion[35]) has become an object of criticism, for a project on this scale would certainly not allow any opportunity for testing. Further, advocates of the integrated program, such as Gamani Corea, Secretary General of UNCTAD, are urging that the buffer stock fund be established first for its "catalytic impact," leaving specific commodity arrangements for later negotiation.[36] Thus, the advocates and the opponents of the "integrated program" must argue its practicality on the grounds of its predicted economic impact.

Besides the United States, an important international opponent of buffer stocks and other direct market intervention has been the government of the Federal Republic of Germany. Ministers of Chancellor Helmut Schmidt's government have criticized the commodity agreement approach on several occasions, with Economics Minister Hans Friderichs stating that the biggest danger in the long run lies in the production of chronic surpluses and a corresponding misallocation of resources.[37] Friderichs predicts that under such a program the producers, no longer having to bear the costs of overproduction, would not have an interest in adjusting output to demand. The result would be that the higher the production of commodities, the larger their income, with industrialization fading into the background.[38] Chancellor Schmidt also stated that, although the Federal Republic of Germany supports earnings stabilization without market intervention, "we are still opposed to commodity price cartels; we do not want any worldwide pile-up of raw materials."[39]

The U.S. government position on these issues (and the State-Treasury disputes over commodity policies) is, of course, well known, and the disputatious development of the Seventh Special Session position is discussed below.[40] The careful bureaucratic compromises involved in the U.S. position actually broke down briefly in January 1976 but were patched together. Assistant Secretary of the Treasury Parsky made a speech in San Francisco which was reported as taking "a strongly negative attitude toward international commodity agreements," stating that U.S. policy must not "sacrifice economic principles for the sake of political gains."[41] The following day, "sources" reported that the Parsky statement was "without authorization" and represented personal views.[42] The "true" U.S. policy was restated by an unusual joint State-Treasury press release that reaffirmed the case-by-case approach and stated that "we are prepared to consider measures that will improve the functioning of markets and will directly meet the problems of raw material producers and consumers." But the statement also declared: "We reject price-fixing arrangements that distort the market, restrict production, and waste resources. But this should not be the central issue."[43]

For the Third World, of course, price fixing (or more simply, price support) *is* the central issue, along with the protection of gains for the future (i.e. indexation). Earnings stabilization, on the other hand, is viewed as merely financial assistance to mitigate swings in prices around the same unsatisfactory trend. Hence the U.S. compromise, so painstakingly worked out between State and Treasury to meet the Treasury's objections, can only be considered as a mitigation of some of the commodity-related financial problems of the developing countries. Even these modest proposals may be subject to Congressional criticism and revision in the future, on the grounds that they are too generous at a time of domestic austerity. The House of Representatives is the serious roadblock here. Owing to the House's hostility to "bailouts," the International Development Association (IDA—the World Bank's "soft loan window") replenishment was soundly defeated by the House in January 1974 (only to be passed later in the year), and $50 million was deleted by the House from the U.S. contribution in 1976. Even the $25 billion "financial safety net" for other OECD nations (negotiated by the administration in 1974) has been held back from House consideration based on the general expectation that it too would be defeated.

However, even if the United States, the Federal Republic of Germany, and the other leading OECD nations can be persuaded on a "case-by-case basis" that commodity agreements can lend stability and predictability to the market, the United States and the Federal Republic of Germany remain adamantly against the associated proposals for "indexation" of commodity prices. Indexation is usually discussed as upholding the real value of commodity earnings by linking commodity prices to the movement of prices paid for manufactures. The West German government points out that indexation must lead to a distortion of conditions of competition, investment, and consumption, creating an "automatism for inflation."[44] Friderichs, the Economics Minister of the Federal Republic of Germany, has even suggested that such a scheme would be unfair to those developed countries with lower than average inflation rates, such as the Federal Republic of Germany or Switzerland, while rewarding those with high inflation rates.[45] The argument over the advantages of indexation, of course, presupposes that the creation of an acceptable index of manufactured goods is indeed possible. Developing countries suggest that their actual import price indices be used, but these measures do not adequately control for qualitative changes.

The indexation debate, while directly linked to the philosophic dispute over the virtues of "dirigisme," is also related to the long argument over the developing countries' "terms of trade." The developing countries have held that the market tends inexorably to erode the purchasing power of their export earnings. The developed countries' argument that there is no systematic bias one way or the other (and that, implicitly, no bias is desirable) received an important boost when an UNCTAD expert group reported its findings that there was no evidence of declining terms of trade for the developing countries.[46] Indexation, as perceived by developed countries, relates to the protection of the purchasing power of an *improved* price level for commodities; in the light of this new evidence, the developed nations are sure to try to convince the developing nations that their purchasing power has *not* been systematically eroded by the market.

Of all of the criticisms of the NIEO commodity plans, however, the most telling one is that the integrated program will not necessarily favor the majority of the Group of 77. Virtually all developed country analysts highlight the fact that reliance upon action in the commodity field has perverse distributional effects: it confers unavoidable "windfalls" and increases the power of several resource-rich developed countries (particularly the United States, Canada, and the Soviet Union). At the same time, it provides little benefit for, and may actually hurt, developing countries without significant raw material exports, a group which includes those "most seriously affected" by the oil price increases (commonly termed, in the impersonal language of international bureaucrats, the "MSAs"). Chancellor Schmidt urged that the MSAs—"those who live in the shadow of the international division of labor"[47]—not be forgotten in any general solution. Price indexing of raw materials to manufactured goods, or merely concerted market action to raise the relative prices of raw materials, would have the effect of injuring these poorest states, making their liberation from heavy aid inflows even more unrealistic. It would also tend to change the internal distribution of income within the countries that are producers, perhaps in politically troublesome ways.

One further objection not frequently made in public, yet strongly held in Europe and Japan, is that commodity price support would particularly increase the power and influence of the superpowers—the United States and the Soviet Union—to the disadvantage of the less well endowed industrial states.[48] The impact of the OPEC price increases, for example, illustrates the relative advantage accruing from the resource deposits of the superpowers. Thus, quite aside from the North-South issues, commodity price action would have important repercussions on the relationships of each superpower with its partners.

For many of these reasons, opinion in the industrialized countries has widely coalesced behind the concept of the stabilization of commodity export *earnings,* both as a way to blunt pressures for integrated multicommodity stabilization efforts with all their problems, and as a means of maintaining international financial stability. The two main earnings stabilization approaches are the "stabex" scheme of the European Community, and the "Development Security Fund" proposed by Kissinger at the Seventh Special Session. The "stabex" scheme is limited to a group of 29 raw and semiprocessed commodities and to the exports of the 46 African, Caribbean, and Pacific countries associated with the European Community.[49] The Development Security Fund as proposed by Kissinger, by contrast, would be broader, providing loans (and grants to the poorest) up to a total of $10 billion to finance externally caused shortfalls in export earnings of both commodities and manufactures.[50]

Indeed, in offering export earnings stabilization schemes, the developed countries have their own interests in view as much as those of the developing world. The developing countries have borrowed large sums in recent years from the private Eurodollar market, and financial stability has become a pressing concern. The risk of serious financial consequences to the developed world due to snowballing defaults caused by earnings shortfalls in the Third World, the so-called "economic domino" effect, is now feared by some. This is beginning to be examined in the United States in the context of the stability of the money center banks[51] and is being cited as a reason for additional financial support for Chile.[52] The Group of 77, taking a mirror-image view of the problem, has increased pressures for meaningful debt talks aimed at the negotiation of a "moratorium" for service payments for debts to governments.[53]

Compared to the broad area of commodities, the subject of industrialization has been only a slightly less controversial component of the NIEO program. The NIEO proposals in this area are most radically spelled out in the Lima Declaration adopted by the Second General Conference of the United Industrial Development Organization on 27 March 1975. The declaration, an exclusively NIEO document, calls for the achievement of a minimum 25 percent developing-country share of world industrial production by the year 2000 (the present share is 7 percent), to be achieved by a voluntary restructuring of industry in the developed countries. Developed countries were also asked to eliminate or reduce tariff barriers on products from developing countries; cooperate in ensuring that the activities of transnational enterprises conform to the economic and social aims of the host country; review and change the legal system for international protection of patents and trademarks; and cooperate in promulgating a code of conduct for the transfer of technology.

Faced with these demands, the United States took the opportunity to initiate the Moynihan "hard line," even before Ambassador Moynihan arrived at the United Nations.[54] The concept of restructuring the developed country economies for the purpose of transferring production to the developing world was flatly opposed for both practical and ideological grounds. The 25 percent of industrial production figure was rejected on practical grounds, with the United States arguing that it was "skeptical as to the utility of setting a formal target" because "there is no reliable, scientific basis upon which any particular figure can be set," and because "the setting of a global target will obscure the special needs of the most seriously affected countries." The real objections, however, were ideological, since the U.S. representative went on to say that "the U.S. Government is not in a position to guarantee that its private sector will perform in a way to meet any particular target. Our government does not have—nor does it wish to have—that type of control over our private sector."[55]

Included within the broad issue of industrialization are the thorny problems of the role, rights, and contributions of foreign direct investment, including the controversy over the transnational enterprise (TNE). The UN has been sponsoring special studies and research on the effects of TNEs since 1972, and many other international organizations have initiated parallel efforts. From the beginning, the difference in viewpoint between developed and developing countries has been apparent. It was, therefore, not surprising that the provisions of the Sixth Special Session Declaration and of the Charter of Economic Rights and Duties of States regarding foreign direct investment were termed unworkable by the industrial countries. The main differences stem from the opposing viewpoints on the role of international law in the settlement of investment disputes (especially as it relates to compensation), a difference in views that dates back to the Calvo Doctrine.[56]

The developing countries believe that nations have no obligations as to the fair treatment of investors under international law. The developed nations maintain that they do, and that rejection of legal standards will have wide-ranging and serious repercussions beyond the investment issue. At the Seventh Special Session, however, the developing and developed countries agreed not to deal with TNE issues in the final resolution. This compromise may be evidence that these issues are perceived to be less critical to the NIEO than others such as commodities, trade, the SDR link, etc. Or, more likely, it was due to the efforts of both sides to include only those issues where a reasonable degree of agreement was possible; and as the views of the developing and developed countries on TNEs seem irreconcilable, the tactical decision was made to ignore them in this document.

On the related debate over the transfer of technology, it is generally agreed that although the developing countries generally need more technology, they also need technology adapted to their needs. In the industrial countries, however, many believe that the UNCTAD code-of-conduct approach, a component of the NIEO, will not accomplish that end. This approach is seen to limit the returns to owners of technology both directly and indirectly and, therefore, may actually curtail the amount transferred.

Typical of this attitude is a recent editorial in *The Economist*. It suggested that the Third World "may yet achieve improvements in cost, quality, and terms only to find that the volume has fallen; because, in a world not yet run by governments, you cannot force the owners of know-how to part with it except on terms they too consider satisfactory."[57] The U.S. State Department has also objected publicly to political demands for technology without (or with little) payment for it. "Something for nothing, however, whatever the argument, will hardly transplant successfully. It suggests too easily the misconception that difficulties involved in the transaction are not a primary responsibility of the recipient. . . . Technology transfer to the LDCs . . . is the more likely to be maintained or increased if, in order to make the operation successful, they recognize that donor as well as recipient must derive fair advantage. . . ."[58]

Perhaps equally destabilizing to international financial relationships and, in the view of many developed states, counterproductive, is the NIEO adoption of the old proposal to establish a "link" between SDR creation and development assistance.[59] Experts, especially in the U.S. Treasury and Federal Reserve, as well as in the central banks of Europe, still react to this proposal with alarm, feeling that using the SDRs for anything other than the creation of international financial liquidity would be inflationary, especially if the industrial countries have no intention of transferring real resources to the developing countries in the same proportions. Gresham's Law[60] suggests that SDRs would circulate quickly, as each central bank sought to hold as few of them as possible. SDRs were created for the purpose of expanding the world's reserve assets beyond the limited supply of gold and in order to replace, at least to some extent, national currencies as international reserve assets. It has been difficult enough to maintain confidence in SDRs, skeptics maintain, and the idea that they can also be a method of redistributing resources appears to be dubious.[61]

Containing the Establishment of a New International Economic Order: Strategy and Tactics

The objections summarized in the preceding pages stem largely from those in the industrialized countries who oppose either the concept or the components of a NIEO. There are, of course, opposing views on both philosophical and pragmatic grounds. For example, some OECD nations, such as the Netherlands and Sweden, support the moral proposition that it is time for a NIEO. Other OECD nations pragmatically support progress toward commodity agreements, aid increases, and other NIEO objectives—perhaps because of their considerable dependence on raw material imports from the developing world. Japan and members of the European Community may be considered in this category. It is the United States which is most skeptical of the NIEO, and even the United States is proposing significant concessions to improve the prospects of the developing countries in many of the areas where the NIEO program calls for radical change. It must be emphasized, therefore, that none of the OECD countries, and few, if any, of the private commentators highlighted here, oppose the economic development of the developing world. In fact, many of those skeptical of the NIEO program believe that they have the Third World's "best interests" in mind.

If, however, the United States were willing to commit itself to delay, to derail, or to contain the implementation of the NIEO, several alternative strategies are available. For the purposes of exposition, three possible directions for the United States are explored. In the real world, of course, nations normally mix policies from different strategies, often without regard for consistency. Policy choice is also affected by the interests of allies. In the U.S. case, the greater vulnerability of its principal allies is likely to be a major constraint if it chooses to oppose a NIEO.

Possible U.S. Strategies Against the NIEO

Paradigm One: The unilateral strategy. The United States decides that the implementation of the NIEO is too costly in terms of future growth prospects and in terms of lost sovereign control over its own economic policy. The United States, therefore, pursues a policy of greater governmental control over foreign investment and technology, adopting tax measures to discourage its citizens from investing abroad; continues its policy of unilateral determination of aid totals and distribution in accordance with foreign policy objectives; maintains strict limits on trade preferences, freely utilizing quotas or removing preferences when domestic economic interests are imperiled; and pursues a policy of maximizing domestic production of minerals and other natural resources and the development of synthetic substitutes along the lines of Project Independence, including unilateral mining of the international seabed without regard to any UN-sponsored authority. This strategy leaves the principal OECD allies to their own interests, presumably resulting in the formation of protectionist economic blocs including, for example, Western Europe and parts of Africa or Japan and parts of Asia.

Paradigm Two: The alleviationist strategy. The United States, working closely with the European Community and Japan, makes a renewed and expanded effort to alleviate the effects of Third World economic deprivation, without the adoption of the economically inefficient "dirigist" policies of the NIEO program. In other words, concrete actions would be taken aimed at improvements of the situation of the developing countries, but no concessions would be made on the basic demands of these countries. This strategy would include the adoption and immediate implementation of the

Development Security Fund proposed by Kissinger at the Seventh Special Session (with liberal rules for development); the expansion of the resources of the International Finance Corporation (to provide equity finance to developing country institutions); the use of liberal adjustment assistance, perhaps including government-guaranteed employment to handle domestic injury complaints against imports under GSP provisions; the sympathetic consideration of producer-consumer commodity agreements for the purposes of market stabilization, but not for the transfer of resources; and the generous funding of regional technology banks which purchase appropriate technologies from industrial country owners for free or subsidized distribution to developing country enterprises.

Paradigm Three: The acquiescence but delay strategy. Based on an anticipation of the erosion of the solidarity of the Group of 77, the United States joins with other developed states in accepting major symbolic expressions of the NIEO. In other words, the NIEO is agreed to in principle, but concrete actions to improve the situation of the developing countries are avoided. Symbolic actions might include the acceptance of the Charter of Economic Rights and Duties of States; the adoption of a code of conduct for TNEs; the establishment of an international seabed resource authority with the power to develop the resources outside the 200-mile national control limit, either alone or in cooperation with private firms; and the acceptance of various future "targets" for developing country growth rates, proportions of GNP to be used for official development assistance, or proportions of industrial production to be carried out by developing countries.

The policies of paradigm three could have a large symbolic importance but limited practical significance. The duties imposed by the Charter are sufficiently broad that favorable interpretations can be made, at least in the short term, and in conceding exclusive sovereign control over foreign investment, the United States would only be acknowledging a *fait accompli.* The TNE code would still require (in an age of sovereign equality and independence) national implementation, and differences would affect investment flows, encouraging reasonable policies. The deep seabed minerals are far less important economically, now that a 200-mile limit seems to be assured; in any case, only developed countries possess the necessary technology for seabed mining, so that joint ventures for exploitation are inescapable. "Targets" are constantly set and not achieved, and there are always "exogenous" factors that can be blamed for failure. As the developed countries proclaim the "historic compromise," or the "planetary bargain," they can safely turn the concrete issues over to technicians, secure in the belief that many years of negotiation and compromise will protect the developed country interests, and bring out developing country differences, once the emotional issues are settled.

To these paradigms a fourth, totally hypothetical, option must be added—the forthright use of force (a "NIEO-imperialism?"). Brief discussion of this alternative ensued from the January 1975 publication of an article proposing the consideration of the use of force to break up OPEC.[62] But the present post-Vietnam American foreign policy makes the use of force an unacceptable option, especially in view of the diffused, hypothetical threat posed by the NIEO. Nonetheless, depending on Soviet responses, the capability exists, and therefore a policy to break the NIEO alliance by force is at least an academic option.

United States strategy to date must be considered a combination of paradigms one and two but without any clear long-range objectives. Despite rapid footwork in the post-OPEC negotiations of the oil sharing and financial safety net agreements, the establishment of the International Energy Agency and the proclamation of a "hard line," Congressional disagreement, and the reluctance to adopt any domestic production and conservation incentives contradict the international policy. In fact, the opposition to OPEC and the NIEO has been fitful and accompanied by enough conflicting signals (including the initiation of the Paris North-South Conference) to confuse those in the developing and developed countries alike. In my view, this vacillation is due as much to U.S. disagreement on objectives, Watergate paralysis, Constitutional debates over the proper role of Congress, and the post-Vietnam foreign policy drift as it is to any coherent "carrot and stick policy."

At the writing of this contribution, the probable U.S. policy mix for the medium term remains somewhere between the unilateral strategy and the alleviationist strategy. The recovery of the economy, especially the inflation performance, should determine the exact tactics used. A slow recovery, or an economic setback, would lead U.S. policy more towards unilateral alternatives; and a general belief that a sustained economic growth path has been attained once again would lead American policy in the alleviationist direction. As noted in the paradigm descriptions, the unilateral strategy would tend to lead to separate and probably mutually beneficial arrangements between regions of the developing world and the industrial regions of Western Europe and Japan, while the alleviationist strategy would tend to be pursued in close cooperation with the rest of the OECD.

Given the historic importance of principles to U.S. foreign policy and the arguments of NIEO skeptics on philosophical grounds reviewed in this paper, paradigm three, the acquiescence but delay strategy, seems unlikely to appeal to the United States. The duplicity required to pursue a policy of "agree but delay" does not seem possible in the open American system. The other OECD nations may, however, utilize some of the tactics of this strategy, conceding that there is a true need for a NIEO but offering specific proposals actually drawn from the alleviationist strategy.

The future, therefore, may see a gradual change in international economic relationships made possible by the return of OECD economic growth (perhaps *a* new international economic order, but certainly not *the* NIEO) accompanied, as always, by prophets of gloom, threats of conflict, and ringing blueprints for peaceful change. What seems most likely is that the reality of substantial interdependence will keep all policies of economic unilateralism to a tolerable level, although the proponents of unilateralism, be they protectionists, mercantilists, or autarkists, are currently stronger than at any time since World War II. Total satisfication of the philosophic advocates or opponents of the NIEO (or any other comprehensive "system" for the world's economy) will never be reached, because no real world economy ever fully complies with the ideology that is used to describe it, be it capitalist, marxist, or socialist.

Notes

1. See the introduction to this volume concerning the semantic dispute about the New International Economic Order.
2. See Raul Prebisch, *Change and Development: Latin America's Great Task* (Washington, D.C.: Inter-American Development Bank, 1970).
3. Nor, of course, can the striking unity and forcefulness with which the Group of 77 put forth the NIEO program in multilateral forums in 1974 and 1975 be separated from the demonstration effect of OPEC's actions.
4. See *Foreign Policy* 14 (Spring 1974): 57-90, including articles by Zuhayr Mikdashi, Stephen D. Krasner, and C. Fred Bergsten.
5. For example, the U.S. Council on International Economic Policy published a much shortened and carefully edited summary of its interagency "cartel" assessment as *Special Report: Critical Imported Materials* (Washington, D.C.: Government Printing Office, December 1974). Among nongovernmental institutions, the International Economic Policy Association, a private U.S. research group, published *U.S. Natural Resource Requirements and Foreign Economic Policy, Interim Report* (Washington, D.C.: International Economic Policy Association, 1974).
6. See Chapter 2 above.
7. Irving Kristol, "The 'New Cold War'," *Wall Street Journal,* 17 July 1975.
8. Daniel Moynihan, "The United States in Opposition," *Commentary* 59 (March 1975): 31-44.
9. Robert Tucker, "The New Egalitarianism and International Politics," *Commentary* 60 (September 1975): 27-40.
10. See Agency for International Development, *Implementation of "New Directions" in Development Assistance,* Report to Committee on International Relations, U.S. House of Representatives, 94th Congress, 1st Session.
11. See Harald B. Malmgren, "The Raw Material and Commodity Controversy," in *Contemporary Issues No. 1* (Washington, D.C.: International

Economic Studies Institute, 1975), pp. 10-14.
12. William E. Simon, "Address to Pacem in Terris IV," Washington, D.C., excerpted in *Treasury Papers* (January 1976), pp. 3-5.
13. Ibid., p. 4.
14. Ibid., p. 5.
15. Gerald Parsky, speech to San Francisco Council on World Affairs, 15 January 1976, in *Journal of Commerce* (19 January 1976). This speech was later described as "without authorization."
16. William Safire, " Brother, Can You Spare A Paradigm?" *New York Times,* 2 June 1975.
17. William Safire, "National Town Meeting," Transcript, Washington, D.C., 19 November 1975, p. 12.
18. "Bauxite Tax Testing Arbitration Unit," *New York Times,* 2 October 1975.
19. The Arab case is made by Ibrahim F. I. Shihata, "Destination Embargo of Arab Oil: Its Legality Under International Law," *American Journal of International Law* 68 (October 1974): 616-19. The argument that these principles do apply is forcefully made in Jordan J. Paust and Albert P. Blaustein, "The Arab Oil Weapon—A Threat to International Peace," *American Journal of International Law* 68 (July 1974): 418-23.
20. Timothy W. Stanley, "Some Politico-Legal Aspects of Resource Scarcity," *American University Law Review* 24 (Summer 1975): 1117.
21. Ibid., pp. 1120-21.
22. Moynihan, "The United States in Opposition," p. 38.
23. See U.S. Council of the International Chamber of Commerce, *A New Challenge to Private Enterprise* (New York: U.S. Council of the International Chamber of Commerce, April 1975) and "Who's Being Had? The Haves Aren't Exploiting the Have Nots," *Barrons,* 2 June 1975, p. 138.
24. *Department of State Bulletin* 74 (2 February 1976): 138.
25. P.T. Bauer, "Western Guilt and Third World Poverty," *Commentary* 59 (January 1976): 31-38.
26. Ibid., pp. 32-33. The same point is made by Philip Bowring, "The Irony of Blaming the Rich," *Far Eastern Economic Review*, 19 September 1975, p. 50; he advises those unhappy with commerce with the West to "fall back on self-reliance."
27. Bauer, "Western Guilt," pp. 34-35.
28. Ibid., p. 35.
29. United Nations Conference on Trade and Development, *An Integrated Programme for Commodities* (TD/B/C.1/166), 9 December 1974; See Chapter 8 below.
30. Alton D. Law, *International Commodity Agreements: Setting, Performance, and Prospect* (Lexington: D.C. Heath, 1975), p. 81.
31. U.S. International Trade Commission, *International Commodity Agree-*

ments, Report to Subcommittee on International Trade, U.S. Senate Finance Committee (Washington, D.C.: Government Printing Office, 1975), p. 3.
32. Hendrik S. Houthakker, *Global Resources in an Interdependent World* (Paris: International Chamber of Commerce, 1975), p. 11.
33. Chamber of Commerce of the United States, *World Trade in Commodities: Analysis and Policy Recommendations* (Washington, D.C.: Chamber of Commerce of the United States, 1975). See also Houthakker, *Global Resources,* p. 24.
34. Joint Staff Study, *The Problem of Stabilization of Primary Products* (Washington, D.C.: International Monetary Fund and International Bank for Reconstruction and Development, 1969), Part I, p. 95.
35. "UN Trade Panel Runs Into Snag," *New York Times,* 22 March 1976.
36. UNCTAD Information Service, Press Release (TAD/INF/781), Geneva, 8 December 1975, p. 2.
37. Hans Friderichs, Minister of Economics, Federal Republic of Germany, "Basic Problems of the World Economy," reprinted in this volume as Chapter 5.
38. Ibid.
39. Helmut Schmidt, "An Indivisible World Economy." Speech delivered in New York, 2 October 1976, *The Bulletin, Archive Supplement* (Bonn: Press and Information Office, Federal Republic of Germany, 14 October 1975).
40. See Chapter 6 below.
41. "Treasury Aide Cautions Against Commodity Pacts," *New York Times,* 16 January 1976.
42. "Government Softens Commodity Pact Attack," *Journal of Commerce,* 19 January 1976.
43. Joint State-Treasury Department Statement on Commodities, 16 January 1976, in *Department of State Bulletin* 74 (23 February 1976): 242.
44. Baron Rüdiger von Wechmar, "The Position of Developed Countries Regarding Key Elements of a New International Economic Order." Paper presented at the meeting of the International Studies Association, Toronto, Canada, mimeographed, 27 February 1976, p. 12.
45. Friderichs, "Basic Problems," p. 8.
46. "UN Study Finds Poor Nations Not Hit by Price Rises," *Washington Post,* 4 June 1975.
47. Schmidt, "An Indivisible World Economy."
48. See Friderichs, "Basic Problems."
49. See Chapter 10 below.
50. Henry A. Kissinger, "Global Consensus and Economic Development." Speech to UN General Assembly, 1 September 1975, *Department of State Bulletin* 73 (22 September 1975): 427-429.
51. See "Oil Land Deposits 5% at 6 Top Banks," *New York Times,* 12 March 1976. Based on Federal Reserve Board compilations made for the Senate

Foreign Relations Committee Subcommittee on Multinational Corporations, the six largest money center banks had, at end 1975, nearly $12 billion in loans outstanding to the developing countries, representing about 5 percent of total assets.

52. Jonathan Kandell, "Chile's Debts Worry Washington," *New York Times,* 15 March 1976. This concern, however, is reported as not influencing Western Europeans, and indeed it is difficult to see how another Chilean debt moratorium (President Allende proclaimed one in 1972) is likely to affect the credit of other developing nations.

53. "Poor Lands Seek Widening of Debt," *New York Times,* 17 February 1976.

54. Stephen F. Rosenfeld, "American, Without Apologies," *Washington Post,* 4 April 1975.

55. W. Tapley Bennett, "Statement to Second General Conference of the United Nations Industrial Development Organization, 18 March 1975," *Department of State Bulletin* 72 (21 April 1975): 520.

56. The Calvo Doctrine, as developed by the Latin American states, holds that a foreigner may be required to sign a contract with a clause stating that all disputes will be settled by local laws and tribunals. The developed countries hold that no citizen can sign away the rights of the home government.

57. *The Economist,* 29 November 1975, p. 79.

58. "Notes on Technology Transfer to LDC's and the U.S. Government's Role," *International Science Notes,* no. 34 (Washington, D.C.: Department of State, Bureau of Oceans and International Environmental and Scientific Affairs, June 1975), p. 5.

59. See "SDRs and Development, $10 Billion for Whom?," *Foreign Policy,* no. 8 (Fall 1972), pp. 102-128, containing articles on the merits of the SDR "link" by James Howe, Harry Johnson, and Imanuel Wexler.

60. Gresham's Law: an observation by economist Sir Thomas Gresham that when two coins are equal in debt paying value but unequal in intrinsic value, the one having the lower intrinsic value tends to remain in circulation, and the other hoarded.

61. Friderichs, "Basic Problems."

62. Robert W. Tucker, "Oil: The Issue of American Intervention," *Commentary* 59 (January 1975): 21-31.

5 *Basic Problems of the World Economy*

Hans Friderichs

Introduction

The economic system that emerged after World War II—relying, as it does, on market-economy principles—has formed the basis for unparalleled world economic growth. In the postwar period, it has brought almost uninterrupted economic growth to all countries and a high level of prosperity for a relatively large number of people. The difference between growth in all countries and prosperity for a relatively large number of people has to be noted. The highest growth rates have been achieved by the countries with liberal economic systems—mainly industrialized nations but also including some developing states like Brazil, Taiwan, and Singapore.

While the other developing countries have, to varying degrees, participated in this growth as well, on the other hand, I believe we should not overlook the fact that the prosperity gap between rich and poor—i.e., between rich and poor countries around the world—has become larger and not smaller. The developing nations' share in world trade has steadily declined, their income levels have lagged further and further behind the industrial countries, and their domestic employment problems have in some cases assumed alarming proportions. It is not surprising, therefore, that the developing countries are becoming more critical of the existing international division of labor. In their opinion, the present system is inequitable and not capable of solving development problems. The market mechanism, they assert, is an instrument of the powerful. Relying on a supposed historical right, they are now calling for "economic decolonization" as a corollary to political decolonization, to be achieved by a total recasting of economic relations. These demands have been encouraged by the actions of the oil-producing countries over the last two and one-half years. The success

---

This chapter is a translation of a speech delivered on 8 January 1976 in Mainz, Federal Republic of Germany.

of these actions is not to be denied. Following the example of the Organization of Petroleum Exporting Countries (OPEC), the developing nations would now like to have a say in determining the ground rules of the world economy.

One way they are trying to do this is by exploiting the distribution of votes in the United Nations (UN). In view of the new pattern of power relationships which this implies, the industrial countries of the world will, in the foreseeable future, have to adapt to a new polarity in world politics—namely, oil producers and developing nations on the one hand (paradoxical as this may appear) and traditional industrialized states on the other. To put it even more simply: the East-West problems that dominated our thinking in the twenty years after the war will continue, but these problems will be increasingly overshadowed by a split between North and South. It would be an oversimplification to relate all problems to this new polarity. Relations in the real world are conditioned by a more complex interweaving of interests than can be expressed in such a bipolar model. The fact remains, however, that the developing countries and the oil producers are calling for a new international economic order.

Demands of the South

The industrial countries were confronted with this design at the Sixth Special Session of the UN General Assembly, which—due to massive and, to some extent, political pressure from the developing world—adopted an action program to establish a new international economic order. The action program contains a wide-ranging list of demands and is aimed generally at a redistribution of wealth in favor of the developing nations. The lever to use, as the Third World sees it, is control of oil and raw materials. The demands include:

1. orientation of the international monetary system toward the interests of the developing world;
2. production cartels along the lines of OPEC;
3. commodity agreements to regulate prices and quantities;
4. linkage of export prices in the developing countries to the prices they have to pay for imports (under the general heading of "indexation");
5. extension of preferential treatment in trade;
6. recognition of developing countries' permanent sovereignty over their natural resources, covering also the issue of exploiting the ocean floor and the related question of territorial waters;
7. structural policies in the industrial countries to promote the industrial development of the developing nations; and
8. transfer of advanced technology to the developing countries, on

preferential terms—to some extent without a *quid pro quo* but with guarantees by governments.

Positions of the North

The industrial nations, including the Federal Republic of Germany (FRG), have indicated that they have major reservations about these extremely far-reaching demands. Meeting all of them would imply a dismantling of the market-based international economic system and its replacement by a largely dirigistic structure. A change of this kind would particularly affect two groups of countries adversely: the poorest of the developing nations, especially those without their own raw materials, and countries with extensive foreign economic involvement, such as the FRG. Other groups with large natural resources and smaller external economic involvements would definitely benefit—for instance, the Soviet Union and the United States, to mention only two. Both possess considerable reserves of oil and other raw materials and are less integrated in the world economy than the FRG. But criticisms and the expression of reservations will not be of much help; nor will simple references to the principle advantages of a marked-based system in coordinating the world economy.

We have to be frank and admit that market-economy principles have all too often been broken in the past by the industrial countries, and still are being broken, to the detriment of the developing world. Let me just repeat this for emphasis: they are being broken, not exploited. The industrial world should be taking up the challenge of the developing countries instead of answering them with professions of faith in theories and economic systems. In today's world, the industrial and developing countries are economically dependent on each other. We do not need only the oil and natural resources of the developing countries, and they do not need only our capital and technology. We both need each other as markets, without which we cannot make advances. Seeing that this is the case, neither side can be particularly interested in a confrontation; both sides should be keen to solve problems cooperatively. To put it another way, both are more or less in the same boat, and we should try to prevent the boat from capsizing. This means that we have to avoid creating new disequilibria while trying to eliminate those that undoubtedly exist between the industrial and developing countries. Our economic relations should be based, more than ever before, on the principle of comparative advantage.

This advantage will not be secured if the far-reaching demands of the developing countries are realized; instead, their implementation would certainly bring a worsening of the overall position. We therefore reject any complete recasting of the existing order, which, in the final analysis, has proven its value. The proper objective can only be sensible evolution—not a revolution that would destroy the present system. The proper solution can only lie in improving the mechanisms of the market—not in any escape into worldwide "dirigisme." What is needed is a realistic development and refinement of the international economic order, the elimination of shortcomings, as well as adjustments to what are certainly new and changed conditions. In the process, priority should be given to maintaining overall economic efficiency, the prerequisite for the improvement of living conditions in the poorest of the poor countries. Abuse of the market should be prevented, while the flexibility that the market provides under the present system should be retained. The importance of this factor is demonstrated by our adjustment to the explosion of oil prices, which has been dealt with more or less without serious breakdowns. Our general aim must, therefore, not be a new economic order, but, rather, structural improvements within the world economy that benefit the less developed nations. The implication for these countries is that they must recognize that confrontation will not get us any further. And, indeed, the atmosphere at the UN Seventh Special Session showed some signs of a willingness to be objective and to reconcile opposing interests.

The developing countries will, nevertheless, continue to pursue their goal of establishing a new international economic order. However, they are no longer bent on achieving this objective in one short, sharp effort, but rather via negotiations over a longer period of time. We should take advantage of this time to help reduce the stridency of the ideological debate, so that it gives way to realistic discussions and talks. We have to give our ideas greater substance and expound them to our partners. Talks have already begun at several levels: monetary issues are being dealt with in the International Monetary Fund (IMF), trade questions within the General Agreement on Tariffs and Trade (GATT), selected North-South problems within the organizations of the United Nations; and, finally, in December 1975, we saw the start of the main conference between oil producers, developing countries, and industrial states—this known as the Paris Dialogue. I would like to add here that we also hope economists will increasingly participate in these discussions. In particular, we expect help on the questions of what worldwide macro-economic costs would occur in realizing some elements of the new economic order and whether one can really expect that these costs will result in benefits for the needy countries. It would, after all, be foolish to introduce a new system without at least knowing beforehand whether it will finally profit those for whom it has been worked out. This holds especially true when tried-and-tested mechanisms are being called into question. Let me turn now to some of the demands that have been listed as contributing to the new international economic order and that go very much to the heart of the present system.

The Link

First, it must be remembered that resources sold to other countries cannot be distributed a second time. This simple and incontrovertible truth cannot be disguised by calling for indirect mechanisms of transfer, such as the so-called "link" between Special Drawing Rights (SDR) and development aid. For this reason, monetary policy should not be misused as a plaything at the mercy of the power interests of individual countries or degraded to being an instrument in the international competition for resources. Rather, the objective should be to orient the international monetary system along price-stability lines by taking into consideration the special interests of the developing countries. In this spirit, the FRG has supported the developing countries during the current talks within the IMF and has also made financial contributions—for example, in the design of various credit facilities, such as the oil facility, the trust fund, and the compensatory financing facility.

Commodity Cartels

Another way in which the developing countries consider they can force a transfer of real resources is by the formation of commodity cartels. The raw-materials producers—let us take copper as a classic example—would like to emulate the success of the OPEC states. In other words, they want to enlarge their foreign exchange earnings—and the real resources these provide—through the raising of commodity prices. This requires that the price elasticity of demand for raw materials over the long term should remain low and not exceed unity—that is, that the resultant drop in the level of demand from the industrial countries should be smaller in relative terms than the increase in prices. [For price elasticities of demand for different product categories, see Chapter 7, table 5.] Whether or not this is really the case over the longer term depends on:

1. the possibility of using other raw materials as substitutes;
2. the substitution of synthetics for raw materials;
3. the development of production techniques that help to cut down consumption of raw materials; and
4. the amount of raw materials extracted in countries that do not belong to a cartel.

The formation of cartels is particularly easy when the number of countries involved is small and when the countries actually have common political interests. Quite apart from the chances of whether or not a particular cartel will hold together, the potential "cartel partners" will have to ask themselves whether the conditions are as favorable as they are for oil cartels.

As has been shown, it is possible, to a large degree, to substitute one raw material for another in both the agricultural and mineral fields. Furthermore, the recycling of minerals is becoming increasingly important. When the price structure is right, the competitiveness of synthetic materials grows, and the inventive spirit is stimulated to develop methods of making more economic use of natural raw materials. In the long run, it is probable that the market mechanism will produce a reaction to commodity cartels that could well lead to a much lower level of trade with the developing nations. This would, in turn, mean that the cartel countries' foreign exchange earnings from sales of raw materials would sink below the previously reached level.

The Integrated Program for Commodities and Indexation

Not least of all because of these potential repercussions (as well as the permanent danger that the foundations on which such cartels are built might crumble from the beginning), many developing countries would like to see commodity agreements involving both producer and consumer countries. This approach culminates in the UN Conference on Trade and Development (UNCTAD) integrated program for commodities, which provides for a network of agreements covering all raw materials in which developing countries have an export interest. It is proposed that price ranges should be fixed and that they should be maintained by means of export quotas, compensatory market reserves (i.e., buffer stocks), or both, depending on the type of commodity involved. To finance these massive stocks, it is suggested that an international fund be set up with contributions from both sides—that is, consumers and producers—as a matter of basic principle. The idea is to establish high price levels and uphold the real value of earnings. This is to be done basically by combining the above approach with a system of indexation for raw materials prices, that is, by linking them to the movement of the prices paid by developing countries for their imports of manufactured goods. (Incidentally, countries like the FRG or Switzerland that have low rates of inflation would be harder hit by such a scheme than would countries with higher inflation rates, which would actually profit to some extent.)

There are major objections to an integrated commodity program of this kind, and I would like to outline them briefly. Seen in purely practical terms, such a system—particularly regarding indexation—would run into almost insurmountable difficulties if implemented on a worldwide scale. Most importantly, indexation in the form suggested by the developing countries would, in fact, have the direct result of terminating the market mechanism of price formation.

The biggest danger in the long term, however, lies in the production of surpluses and a corresponding misallocation of resources. The incentive to industrialize would be smaller, and once such a cartel or commodity agreement should break down, the problems would be proportionately larger. Since under such a scheme the producers would no longer have to assume the cost of removing surpluses through stockpiling, destruction, or consumption for extraneous purposes, they would no longer be interested in adjusting their commodity output to available demand. The result would be that the greater their initial production of commodities, the larger their income. The original aim of implementing a broad-based program of industrialization would recede into the background. If I may express myself a little more colloquially, there would soon be not only a Common Market "butter mountain" but international lead, zinc, and tin mountains as well, on a gigantic scale. I ought to add here that this is our Achilles heel: we object strongly to such commodity agreements, and in reply we are referred to the European agricultural policy. This hint should be sufficient to make it clear that there are issues here that cannot simply be swept under the carpet.

In financial terms, the scheme envisaged is likely to impose unprecedented strains on all concerned. In contrast to the case of regionally limited commodity agreements, an integrated program would lack the world market as a safety valve. Because surpluses would not be saleable on the world market at dumping prices, they would have to be destroyed, stockpiled, or used for other purposes than trading. All these alternatives imply further, large losses to national economics. I also think that such a system is totally unsuitable as a means for redistributing wealth between North and South—the original intention. The reason is that over half of the raw materials exported in the world come from the industrialized states. I will mention only a few of the most important exporters of commodities; they are the Soviet Union, the United States, Canada, the Republic of South Africa, and Australia. Measures to support prices would, therefore, largely (over 50 percent) benefit not the developing nations, but the commodity-producing industrial countries. I can also quote the relevant figure for the FRG: over 50 percent of the raw materials imported by this country come from industrial countries. On the other hand, price increases would not only affect adversely the industrialized nations, but, above all, the poorer developing countries—namely, those that have no raw-materials resources of their own. When we speak today of the Third and Fourth Worlds, we mean by the latter the countries that possess neither oil nor commodities. We would, in fact, see a replay on a larger scale of the scenario we have experienced (and are still experiencing) following the raising of oil prices.

Export-earnings Stabilization

The difficulties that the developing countries face when earnings from commodity exports fluctuate can be solved in a better way, at smaller cost, and without direct interference in the market. I believe, therefore, that the introduction of a system of export-earnings stabilization (and not commodity-price stabilization) would, in general, be better for the poorer developing countries. Declines in export earnings from raw materials in these countries should be bridged by credits at favorable conditions to be repaid when earnings go above the average. Such a system would have the advantage of providing selective aid to the particularly needy countries while minimizing the costs of the exercise. Also, the disadvantages of perpetuating existing structures would not arise.

In particular cases where it appears appropriate, we would not be totally against commodity agreements of the traditional kind—as long as the balance of costs and benefits is acceptable. The aim of these agreements, however, should always be to stabilize markets and not to serve as a vehicle for transferring funds. I consider that the prosperity gap between North and South can only be narrowed if the developing countries are integrated more closely into the world economy. In this context, the stabilization of commodity/export earnings can only be an aid to adjustment and provide a helping hand at the start. To support this, it is crucial that there be an "export-oriented" development strategy for the less developed countries. To me, this indicates that clear priority should be given to trade policies directed toward opening markets, so that access to the industrial and agricultural markets of the developed nations is made easier.

Access to Markets

The Tokyo Round, which began in autumn 1973, has opened up a new dimension in international economic relations. For the first time, nontariff barriers to trade—that is, the broad field of differing regulations and procedures that hinder the flow of goods—are being fully included in the discussions. These trade negotiations will also have to deal with the question of improving GATT or UNCTAD. Above all, this means working out whether a further reduction of trade barriers can be made easier by altering the present safeguard-clause arrangements.

In this connection a further point of crucial importance needs mentioning. It used to be the case that the exchange of tariff quotas benefited mainly the industrial countries. If we want to achieve an evolution of the present economic order, we must find ways of giving greater consideration to the interests of the nations of the Third World. This aim is served, among other ways, by the desire of the developing countries to see an improvement in the system of generalized tariff preferences and its extension beyond 1980. The FRG is prepared to do this. We will be using our influence within the European Community to help bring about further measures of liberalization, both in the current GATT negotiations and elsewhere. When I say "using our influence," I mean that the final responsibility is no longer ours, but lies with the Community. I think it will be necessary, in order to achieve further progress in liberalization, to dismantle existing mechanisms for the protection of particular group interests (I say this in full recognition of the implications), because, as a rule, they are not in accord with national economic interests, let alone international ones. This ought to apply to the agricultural system created by the Community as well as to the protection given to industrial producers here against competition from the developing countries—protection that is intended to keep these industries viable.

Of course, the necessary opening of markets cannot be carried out in an abrupt manner; otherwise, unwarranted social and economic problems would be caused. But unless we make a start toward reducing our own protectionist measures in critical areas, we expose ourselves to justified criticism from the developing countries. Only if we are prepared to eliminate all existing trade barriers affecting the developing nations will there be a real chance of narrowing the prosperity gap. It would then become apparent very quickly that administered world markets are irrelevant; the developing countries, too, will then realize that greater specialization in the production of raw materials is, on balance, more of a disadvantage to them.

Involving the developing countries to a greater degree in the world economy also depends on their ability to mobilize their productive forces and use them efficiently, thereby exploiting the competitive edge they have. Developing countries with no natural resources (or only very few) have, for the moment, only their reserves of labor as a decisive potential. The exploitation of this potential (remember these are countries without capital, know-how, or raw materials) and its integration into the international division of labor can be achieved more particularly by the relocation of processing industries that are relatively labor-intensive and that, for instance, only present minor transportation problems.

Structural Changes in Industrialized Countries

The greater involvement of these countries in the international exchange of goods is bound to have implications for the structures of the economies of the developed countries. The need for structural changes in the industrialized countries—a need which has become more evident than ever during the present recession—links up here with the desire of the developing countries to achieve larger shares in markets. It is clear to us that in the longer term the process of restructuring can only be promoted by an accelerated advance to higher levels of technology. To put it another way, with our higher educational level and our much higher social costs, we should be concentrating more and more on the manufacture of sophisticated products or, at least, on more sophisticated production techniques. This does not mean that we should work out the distribution of industries among various countries in political negotiations, as some developing countries have demanded. Experience in the state-planned economies shows that it is almost impossible to plan the pattern of industrial production because of its varied nature and the interdependencies among its parts. The result would be a squandering of scarce resources.

Let me state, therefore, my point quite clearly: in the future, as in the past, and worldwide, we must reject the idea of *ex ante* policies to steer industrial structures on a sectoral basis by means of administrative measures. On the contrary, policies of encouraging structural adjustments via the market mechanism and of supporting industrialization in the developing countries through various government incentives are the better approach. In the end, these policies are also likely to bring added growth for the developed countries by (a) encouraging a deliberate shift to more advanced technologies and more capital-intensive types of production (a shift, by the way, that need in no way imply a decline in the overall employment level) and (b) by the import of larger quantities of traditional products at much lower prices than are possible in the high-wage industrialized countries. This does not necessarily lead to a reduction in the industrial countries' ability to export. In fact, progressive industrialization of the developing countries—helped particularly by the transfer of technology—will, as a matter of course, create markets for high-quality goods and completely new technological products. It is a fact that most of the developed states' trade in industrial goods is not with the underdeveloped, but with the developed countries.

Foreign Direct Investment in Developing Countries

Exports can also be increased, and the international division of labor can be extended if the upstream sectors are suitably structured—in other words, by importing semi-manufactured goods and re-exporting goods that have been further processed. An active policy of industrialization, however, calls for a major transfer of capital to the developing countries over the coming years. Yet, the willingness of entrepreneurs to invest does not depend only on the establishment by governments of industrial states of instruments that encourage such investment. Companies will be more ready to commit themselves in the Third World if the conditions for foreign, direct investment in the host countries are right. If governments want foreign investors to introduce capital on acceptable terms, if they want them to reinvest profits in their countries instead of exporting them, and if they want them to regard commitments as long-term and generally to behave like nationals of the host country, then they must attempt to create an atmosphere of confidence.

This cannot be done by means of a resolution in the UN in which the developing countries claim the right to regulate foreign direct investment outside the framework of international law, solely under national laws that may be altered at any time. The necessary flow of capital to these countries will occur only if a code of practice can be established in the field of capital similar to that existing for trade under GATT. Even the GATT agreement was arrived at only after it had become clear to all concerned that trade wars were of benefit to no one. With regard to capital movements, this historical experience implies that we should prevent the breakout of an investment war. What is needed, instead, is a free zone for investments in which the developing countries would fully join. The international economic rules we have may well be partially out of date; they are also certainly open to improvement. But the system itself is not defective; it is just that we often apply it imperfectly. The basic point is that trade barriers should be further reduced and that a sensible scheme of compensatory financing should be set up. The efficiency of the world economy should be strengthed via the market mechanism, there should be more liberalization, more open markets, a better division of labor, and structural change; but not a change of the system. Economic events in the last two years have made it clear to everyone how quickly and disastrously the economic difficulties of individual countries can combine to trigger a sharp downswing throughout the Western world.

The socialist countries, by the way, have not remained unaffected by these events either. It has also become obvious that present problems, especially the narrowing of the prosperity gap between North and South, can be solved only jointly and with industrial countries that continue to be efficient. Only a growing economy can master the degree of structural change that is required to bring about the industrialization which is so necessary in the developing states. This is also one of the answers to those who ask, "What is the purpose of growth?"

The Need for Growth

Growth is not something to be pursued for its own sake, but without it we will not be able to deal with the problem facing us. The important thing today is to involve all countries in a common responsibility for the development of our world economy and, above all, to practice solidarity with the poorest of the developing nations. Even the oil-producing countries are beginning to realize this. As far as the industrialized countries are concerned, we must understand that we have not reacted quickly enough in the past to the sudden change in the structure of the world economy. We have been too little prepared to adjust our economies and have not invested sufficiently to meet future eventualities. In this context, the oil crisis has been—if I may put it this way—a healthy shock. It has sharpened the awareness of economic problems here and in all the other countries concerned. A hopeful element in the present situation (and one not present in 1930, by the way) is that all those involved now perceive the interrelatedness of the problems around the world. No one really thinks any more that difficulties can be solved in isolation, without paying regard to others. This is demonstrated by the uninterrupted series of international conferences that have taken place. Economic issues are being drawn more and more into the international, diplomatic arena and are being placed on the agenda of UN General Assembly sessions. We must hope that this awareness of the universality of the present world order will continue to grow.

Economic power has often been abused, and, in this, it is no different from political or military power. It should be the task of the UN to help prevent such abuses. Mr. Giscard d'Estaing, the President of France, recently said in an answer to a question about the international economic order: "A new world order must not become a victory of one set of countries over another, with transitory power relationships deciding the issue. It should instead be a victory of humanity over itself, since the problem involved is one of organizing mankind's economic life on a world scale." I share this view. We will be judged on whether or not we achieve this objective.

6 *The Seventh Special Session: Toward a New Phase of Relations Between the Developed and the Developing States?*

Catherine B. Gwin

On 16 September 1975, the Seventh Special Session of the United Nations (UN) General Assembly adopted a resolution calling for new initiatives on a broad range of development issues. While each of the proposed measures could, if implemented, mean real (though marginal) economic gains for developing states, the significance of the Seventh Special Session must be measured in political terms. As representatives to the session remarked at the time, in comparison to the Sixth Special Session sixteen months earlier, the Seventh Special Session was marked by a shift from "confrontation" to "conciliation."

In the short run, the shift from confrontation to conciliation will facilitate negotiations on concrete measures that are taking place in a number of different forums—e.g., the Paris Conference on International Economic Cooperation, the Geneva multilateral trade negotiations, and the Fourth UN Conference on Trade and Development (UNCTAD) session. From a longer-range perspective, the interesting question is whether the Seventh Special Session can be said to mark the beginnings of a new phase of relations between developed and developing states. In an attempt to answer that question, this essay will look briefly at the background of the Sixth and Seventh Special Sessions; the shift in tactics in the interim between the two conferences; the reasons for this shift; the outcome of the Seventh Special Session; and the implications of these developments for the future dialogue between North and South.

My thanks to Paul Hofmann for his help in gaining access to the Seventh Special Session.

Background to the Sixth and Seventh Special Sessions

Since the early postwar Geneva and Havana world trade conferences in 1947-48, the developing states have sought to impress upon the developed states the need to make the international economic system more responsive to their particular economic concerns. For instance, negotiations of international commodity agreements were urged at the Havana Trade Conference. Compensatory financing schemes, designed to mitigate problems of export-earning fluctuations, were recommended in UN reports in 1953 and again in 1961. Preferential treatment of developing states in multilateral trading arrangements were repeatedly stressed before and after the drafting of the General Agreement on Tariffs and Trade (GATT). These and other efforts met, however, with little support from the developed states in the 1950s and early 1960s. Such lack of support from the North, in addition to frustration over the slow progress of development in the South, led the developing states to alter their development strategies and to broaden their critique of the international economic system by the end of the 1960s.

Reflected in the change in orientation was a changing perception of the political dimensions of the resource problem and a reassessment of the nature of the problems of economic development. Shifts in the distribution of economic power in the world,[1] the emergence of new independent states, increasing First World reliance on Third World resources, heightened political sensitivity to patterns of economic interdependence,[2] the proliferation of enterprises doing business abroad, and shifts in the bargaining power of foreign investors in the raw material sectors vis-à-vis developing host countries altered the context of development. At the same time, the persistence of problems of unemployment, mass poverty and hunger, and foreign-exchange deficits in a context of rising rates of aggregate GNP growth raised doubts about early postwar growth priorities and development policies. The fundamental issue of achieving a better distribution of the gains from international economic transactions remained, but development policies were revised, and the means for achieving a redistribution of the world's economic opportunities were reassessed.

Together with a modification of import-substitution policies that tended to discriminate against export activities and domestic factors of production in favor of rapid industrialization based on capital-intensive investment, leading developing states began at the national level to seek control over the exploitation of their natural resources, to regulate the activities of foreign investment in their growing industrial sectors, and to improve the terms on which advanced technology was introduced. Internationally, they sought, *inter alia,* to gain preferential access to markets of developed countries for their manufactured and semimanufactured goods; they demanded increased decision-making power in international monetary institutions; they acted to affect international market conditions directly for their raw material exports; and they proposed multilateral aid mechanisms to make the transfer of real resources larger, more automatic and more concessionary. In essence, the Third World sought to alter the management of international economic interactions in their interest by gaining more direct influence over the market and the management processes.

To this end, they gradually evolved a strategy of collective action which involved (1) the formulation of a united Third World position in international economic negotiations with the developed states and (2) the translation of this united position, through the use of their "collective economic power," into political pressure.

The first of these endeavors began with the formation of a Third World caucus group—the Group of 77 (numbering over 100 today)—within the framework of the first UN Conference on Trade and Development. Since that conference in 1964, the procedure of working out a common Third World position prior to negotiations with the developed states has become a matter of practice in a widening range of international forums, such as the world conferences on the environment, population, food, and the law of the sea, as well as the special and regular sessions of the UN General Assembly and the UN Industrial Development Organization (UNIDO).

Initially, the adoption of a united negotiating position could be seen as a form of "pressure group" tactics, as distinct from "confrontational" tactics—the difference being largely one of whether or not decisional outcomes were based on compromise and consensus. The common front was, in other words, a means to focus negotiations around a series of concrete issues defined as important by the developing states and to impress on the developed states the importance of taking progressive actions on these issues. The inability of the developing states to make significant gains through negotiations with the developed states, carried out on a consensus basis, led, however, to a hardening of the Third World's common position; to the use of their majority voting strength in UN meetings; to a linking of issues as a method through which they collectively could exert pressure in support of their development demands (as in the linking of development assistance with negotiations on the law of the seas); and to a consolidation of their demands around a call for the establishment of the New International Economic Order (NIEO).

An early version of this call for a new order was expressed in the "Charter of Algiers"—a series of recommendations prepared by the Group of 77 in 1967 prior to UNCTAD II. This document (written well before the Organization of Arab Petroleum Exporting Countries (OAPEC) oil embargo, it should be noted) prefigured the Third World's formal demand for a fundamental transformation of those existing structures that maintained a persistent disparity of benefits.[3] Four years later, at the Group of 77's preparatory meeting for UNCTAD III, an expanded statement of the demand for a new order was issued in the form of the "Declaration and Principles of the Action Programme of Lima." And at the full UNCTAD session in April 1972, Mexico's President Luis Echeverria proposed the drafting of a UN "Charter of the Economic Rights and Duties of States." Among the key components of these documents, in terms of consolidation of Third World demands around the call for a new order, are the following: the claim of each state's full and permanent sovereignty over its own natural resources and economic activities; the right to regulate and exercise authority over foreign investment in accordance with domestic law and to expropriate foreign properties without guarantee of equitable compensation under international law; the right to organize producers' associations; the responsibility of all states to contribute to the development of international trade through the establishment of multilateral commodity agreements; the obligation of states to cooperate in achieving an adjustment in prices of exports of developing states in relation to prices of imports; the duty of states which have exercised coercive colonial or neocolonial policies to grant restitution and full compensation for exploitation and depletion of, and damages to, the natural resources, peoples, and territories of affected states; and the call for an improvement of the Generalized System of Preferences and promotion of increased net flows of real resources to developing states.

In a separate forum, the Fourth Conference of Heads of State or Government of Non-Aligned Countries (held in Algiers in September 1973) officially endorsed, *inter alia,* the call for a new and just international division of labor and a new monetary system, and reaffirmed the right of states to full exercise of national sovereignty over natural resources.[4] These and other demands of the Non-Aligned Countries, together with the work of the Group of 77, directly informed the formal *Declaration on the Establishment of a New International Economic Order* and the *Programme of Action on the Establishment of a New Internationl Economic Order*[5] adopted at the Sixth Special Session in 1974. The essence of this official demand for a new order is a call for the *redistribution* of the world's wealth and economic opportunities, *reparations* to foreign-dominated states, and *restructuring* of the international economic system and its institutions to guarantee that the interests of developing states are directly taken into account. The new order is to be based on the principles of "equity, sovereign equality, interdependence, common interest and co-operation among all States."[6]

The second endeavor of the developing states—the translation of their economic positions and leverage into economic influence and political leverage—took its most dramatic and compelling form with the embargo declared by the Arab oil-exporting states in October 1973. It should be noted however that in the Lima Declaration of 1971 and in the Algiers Declaration of 1973 the Group of 77 and the Non-Aligned Countries, respectively, had already recommended various forms of collective action. The Lima Declaration urged the establishment of united negotiating positions on resource exploitation and trading. And the Algiers Declaration strongly recommended the establishment and strengthening of producers' associations; urged that "all possible means" be used to achieve the objectives of Non-Aligned Countries; and outlined an action program for economic cooperation among developing states in an attempt to give form to the nonaligned movement's principle of "collective self-reliance."[7] Within six months after the embargo, moreover, the developing states as a group reemphasized, in the context of the Sixth Special Session, their united support for the actions of OPEC and their support for the establishment of the other OPECs—i.e., other producers' associations that would reorient the long-prevailing uneven distribution of gains from raw materials and trade.

These attempts by the Third World to exert collective commodity power, their solid support for OPEC, and their expressed readiness to use "all possible means" to achieve the objectives of the new order were condemned by the developed countries, especially the United States, and met with attempts at countervailing action designed largely to break the Southern states' solidarity. Of principal importance was the United States' effort in early 1974 to organize a coordinated Organisation for Economic Co-operation and Development (OECD) response to OPEC. This effort (which was opposed by France because of her concern that such action would only heighten North-South confrontation) was intended, according to Washington, to reduce the developed market economies' vulnerability to future oil-supply interruptions, but was viewed by the developing states as an effort to break up OPEC and to exert dissuasive force against other producers' associations. Specifically in response to the February 1974 Washington Energy Conference, President Houari Boumediene of Algeria, in his capacity as president-in-office of the Non-Aligned Countries, requested the convening of the UN Sixth Special Session. Thus, an atmosphere of confrontation set the scene for the Sixth Special Session. This atmosphere was heightened by the positions adopted by both sides at that session and continued to prevail in encounters between the United States and developing states until the collapse of preparatory meetings for producer-consumer talks in Paris in the spring of 1975.

The United States refused to participate in the preparations for the Sixth Special Session. In the course of the session, the developed states, particularly the United States, defended the existing international economic system as, in Secretary of State Henry Kissinger's words, "a common enterprise" in which none benefit "from basing progress on tests of strength"; played down the notion of redistributing wealth; and condemned producers' associations as instruments of economic pressure, warning that if a bloc of weak states was to resort to such pressure it would be at the risk of provoking a counter-bloc.[8] And they rejected the very notion that any one group of states owed reparations to another. While expressing a willingness to talk about economic cooperation within the framework of the existing system, the United States and various Western European states voiced formal objections to the adoption of resolutions that enjoyed majority but not unanimous support and made reservations regarding a number of key substantive points in those resolutions, including indexation, support of nationalization without reference to compensations under international law, restitution for exhausted resources, producers' associations, commodity marketing arrangements designed to fix prices, and allocation of a specific share of developed country markets for developing states' products. Later in the year, in response to the adoption of the "Charter of Economic Rights and Duties of States" (by a 120-to-6 vote in the regular Twenty-ninth General Assembly session), John A. Scali, the United States ambassador to the UN, sharply assailed the "tyranny of the majority."[9] And he announced that the United States would not participate in a Special Fund authorized by the Special Session to provide emergency relief and development aid to countries hardest hit by oil price increases and world inflation. This response was regarded by the Third World as an act of retaliation for the controversial majority decisions taken at the Sixth Special Session. It was, in their view, a confirmation of the American intent to break the solidarity of the petroleum-exporting and other developing states that had been forged in the aftermath of the 1973-74 oil embargo and price actions.

These suspicions were reinforced by the initial U.S. refusal to accede to the Third World's insistence that the energy producer-consumer talks promoted by the French government to take place in Paris consider not only petroleum but a broad range of other raw materials as well. This particular demand for an extension of the agenda was initiated by OPEC ministers at a meeting in Algiers in January 1975 and supported a month later in the context of the Dakar Conference of Developing Countries on Raw Materials. At that meeting, the 65 nonaligned and other developing states in attendance issued a declaration and program of action which gave expression to their determination "to change their traditional approach to negotiations with the developed countries and an appeal to their political goodwill which in reality was seldom forthcoming."[10] Buoyed by the dramatic actions of the OPEC nations, the Dakar documents urged, *inter alia,* that other producers' associations be formed and voiced support for the establishment of a "solidarity fund" for the financing of buffer stocks and related collective commodity action.

In the month of March 1975, following the Dakar Conference and preceding the collapse of the Paris Conference preparatory talks, the Second General Conference of the UN Industrial Development Organization

(UNIDO) was held in Lima. Called on the Third World's initiative to contribute to the establishment of the NIEO, the conference concluded with the adoption of resolutions that called for the establishment of an industrial development fund; recommended an increase in the developing states' share of total world production from the existing 7 percent to at least 25 percent by the end of the century; and expressed support for such principles as permanent sovereignty over natural resources, conservation of nonrenewable natural resources, and improved terms for licenses and equipment transferred from abroad. The final document as a whole was adopted by a roll-call vote of 82 for and a resounding "No" from the United States, with seven abstentions.

Over this whole period of mounting confrontation from late 1973 to early 1975, and especially at the peak of the world commodity boom in 1974, new raw material producers' associations were discussed and established for such raw materials as bauxite and iron ore; the renewal of the international coffee agreement was rejected by Third World coffee producers in favor of their own (short-lived) attempt to form a producers' association. In addition, a number of nationalizations of raw materials assets occurred, *inter alia,* in Venezuela, Guyana, and elsewhere, the impetus and origin of which had been a long time in developing, but whose occurrence in this period contributed to heightening tensions and an atmosphere of confrontation which reached a climax with the United States' refusal to accept the developing states' demands at the preparatory meetings for the Paris North-South Conference in April 1975.

The Shift from Confrontation to Conciliation

Then, following the demise of the Paris preparatory talks, a change occurred. Both the developed and the developing states indicated that they desired to see an improvement in the generally deteriorated set of North-South relations and that they viewed the scheduled Seventh Special Session as a possible setting within which to make such a change manifest. On 13 May 1975, in an address to the Kansas City International Relations Council, Kissinger stated that the U.S. was "prepared to engage in a constructive dialogue and to work cooperatively on the great economic issues" of mutual concern.[11] In a reversal of the U.S. position taken at the Paris preparatory talks only a month earlier, he committed the U.S. to a new round of combined energy and raw material dialogues and to the consideration of new commodity agreements. And he announced that the U.S. would propose new initiatives on trade within GATT, new financial arrangements within the International Monetary Fund (IMF), and a new system of international food reserves. These pledges were repeated later that month at ministerial-level meetings of the International Energy Agency and the OECD. In his address to the OECD, Kissinger stated that "our economic well-being depends on a structure of international cooperation in which the developing countries are, and perceive themselves to be, participants. The new problems of our era—ensuring adequate supplies of food, energy, and raw materials—require a world economy that accommodates the interests of developing as well as developed countries."[12] Then, in mid-July, after a flurry of interagency consultations in Washington, Kissinger revealed, in a speech to the Wisconsin Institute of World Affairs in Milwaukee, what would be the orientation of the U.S. at the UN Seventh Special Session. The participants of the Special Session, he suggested, could either flounder in rhetorical battles or move forward in a spirit of practical cooperation. "The United States has made its choice. We believe strongly in a cooperative approach . . . . We will approach the Special Session with determination to make progress; we intend to make concrete and constructive proposals for action across a broad spectrum of international economic activities such as trade and commodities, world food production, and international financial measures." Such action would be forthcoming, he implied, if the Third World abandoned its confrontation politics. Addressing the Third World directly, Kissinger said: "We have heard and have begun to understand your concerns. We want to be responsive. We are prepared to undertake joint efforts to alleviate your economic problems. Clearly this requires a posture of cooperation."[13]

Simultaneously, through the month of May, the United States, along with other OECD states, participated in preparatory meetings for the Seventh Special Session and, on the initiative of some of the more moderate Third World states, a series of informal working lunches were held at which representatives of the two groups of states sought to make their respective positions clear and to determine those points on which sufficient agreement existed in principle to allow for the implementation of concrete proposals.

Days before the opening of the Seventh Special Session in a separate, but not unrelated action, a major set of proposals was agreed to within the IMF. There was agreement to (1) abolish the official price for gold; (2) eliminate the obligation to use gold in transactions with the IMF; (3) sell one-sixth (25 million ounces) of IMF gold for the benefit of developing countries; (4) endorse studies concerning the establishment of a trust fund for developing countries as one way in which profits from the sale of gold could be used to benefit them; and (5) request the executive director to consider the possibility of improving the fund's existing policies on compensatory financing. Whether or not this meeting was scheduled to occur as a sort of preface to the Seventh Special Session, it contributed considerably to the atmosphere of conciliation between developed and developing states that was evoked on the very opening day of that conference.

On the opening day, the United States concluded a lengthy policy statement with this remark to the Third World states: "We have heard your voices. We embrace your hopes. We will join your efforts."[14] The full statement—which included several concrete proposals on such matters as trade, commodities, and financing—offered nothing that involved systematic and basic changes in the existing economic order, but made enough specific new proposals to create the impression of movement and to get delegates talking about the "new U.S. initiatives." This statement was followed by even more conciliatory speeches by several Western European ministers. The French Minister of Foreign Affairs Jean Sauvagnargues spoke of actions "essential for a new, more just and more equitable order." Britain's Foreign Secretary James Callaghan reaffirmed his government's support of "the view that the balance between rich and poor countries of the world is wrong and must be remedied." And the Canadian Secretary of State A. J. MacEachen, like the ministers of Austria and the Scandinavian countries, voiced recognition of "the need for changes in international economic relations in order to reduce the intolerable disparities between rich and poor nations."[15] These gestures toward conciliation, manifest in the changes in the diplomatic rhetoric and in the new attention to specific proposals, were matched by the moderate tone adopted by many representatives of the developing world in the spring preparatory meetings, in opening speeches, and later closed-door negotiations.

In the preparatory meetings, the developing states issued what was to stand as their position throughout the conference. The document, which reflected the moderates' view that no major international economic reform could take place without the active support of the United States, limited the issues to be pressed at the session to those considered to be the most urgent; directed attention to concrete proposals for action in areas where agreement seemed possible; and eliminated language that had been objected to by the U.S. in earlier Third World documents. Specifically, the Group of 77's position paper avoided direct mention of expropriation of foreign assets, reparations, and a set allocation of market shares for manufactured goods. Instead, the paper focused on a set of proposals for an "integrated programme for commodities" (drafted by a group of experts commissioned by UNCTAD), various issues related to the transfer of real resources, an array of familiar recommendations in scientific, technological, industrial and agricultural areas, and on the restructuring of the United Nations. The developing states were largely responsible, moreover, for an agreement worked out in advance on the mode of the session proceedings—a mode designed to minimize public-session speech-making and to maximize closed, committee negotiations. They also persuaded the developed states to appoint Jan Pronk, Minister for Development Cooperation of the Netherlands, to serve as the Ad Hoc Committee chairman in an attempt to put in place a representative of the developed states whom the developing states viewed as sympathetic to their cause.

Why the Change?

Why the change? Why, that is, was there a shift from confrontation to conciliation? A common theme in the speechmaking at the Seventh Special Session was that between the spring of 1974 and the fall of 1975 there had been a narrowing of differences in viewpoints between the rich and poor states. According to the British spokesperson, the developed states had come to recognize "the need for positive action" and the developing states to recognize "what's possible." And as proclaimed by the French, "despite, or perhaps because of, the deterioration in the world situation, ideas and attitudes have evolved. . . . Both sides now seem to avoid temptations to turn inward or to allow conflict between cartels of producers and consumers, tendencies which were such a threat at the end of 1973 and the beginning of 1974." Third World representatives, on the other hand, credited both the world economic situation and the pressures of Third World solidarity with having brought about closer convergence of viewpoints. According to the Venezuelan minister of International Economic Affairs, Manuel Perez Guerrero, the change in attitude stemmed from the developed states' "renewed sense of solidarity with the international community," and from the "firm position taken by the countries of the Third World supported by the existence and the actions of the OPEC countries."[16]

The problem with these explanations is that they overstate the degree to which there had been a narrowing of differences of viewpoints, and they confuse rhetoric with reality. The shift from "confrontation" to "conciliation" must be seen rather as a tactical shift that stemmed from perceptions of the limitations of continued confrontational politics. The objectives of neither the developing states as a group nor the United States would be advanced, it had come to be thought, by continued confrontation.[17]

The readiness of the Group of 77 to avoid further confrontation (which meant, in the end, compromise on almost every key point in their initial position paper) represented a pragmatic approach to negotiations. Such pragmatism, as one Third World ambassador explained in an interview, does not mean that the Group of 77 has abandoned its basic objective of establishing the NIEO nor given up its united front strategy. Rather, the willingness to negotiate a compromise reflected the ability of a group of moderate states to prevail upon the others to stand united behind an effort to get on with the implementation of concrete actions in those areas where such action seemed possible; and this reflected, moreover, the difficulties that the heterogeneous Third and Fourth World groupings faced in maintaining a unified posture in a time of world economic inflation and recession.

While the Sixth Special Session of the UN had been held in the final moments of a historic commodity boom and in the height of the resource scarcity "scare," the Seventh Special Session occurred after many commodity prices had dropped precipitously and after the effects of world inflation, recession, and higher oil prices on the less-developed states had become well documented. In a report presented to the Board of Governors of the World Bank on the same day as the opening of the Seventh Special Session, Robert McNamara warned, in fact, that the poorest nations of the world now faced a decade of economic stagnation. Their import prices were rising faster than their export prices. Per capita incomes of the poorest countries had declined by 0.5 percent in 1974 and were expected to decline further in 1975. Even in the middle-income developing countries there were signs of rising trade deficits and declining per capita incomes.[18]

Even with the decision of the rich OPEC states to continue to ally with the rest of the developing world, the Group of 77's deficit problems were unalleviated and their ability to influence international political and economic affairs remained limited by the general asymmetry of international economic and political power and by the group's lack of command over particular leverage points other than control over a large share of the world's known reserves and exports of oil.[19] Given the group's limited influence, diversity of capabilities and interests, and their continued individual dependence on the technologically more-advanced economies, to press for "fundamentals" at a time of economic crisis and at a time when at least some meaningful progress could be expected to be made would have risked the very solidarity which had given direction and momentum to their development demands. Thus, while some of the more radical Third World states, especially those who had been least seriously affected by the oil price increase (either because of low petroleum imports or receipt of Arab petro-aid), favored a continuation of a "hard-line," the Group of 77, as a whole, put forth a moderate position paper at the outset of the session and accepted a "compromise" resolution at the conclusion which fell far short of even their moderated demands.

For the United States, whose performance at the Seventh Special Session was key, the shift from confrontation to conciliation represented a tactical move that implied no more of a fundamental commitment to Third World development than the Third World's compromise implied retreat from the demand for equity and political status. Such a change in tactics was not motivated by a fear of threats from the Third World in the form of further producers' associations action, as various analysts have argued.[20] That explanation simply fails to hold up under scrutiny of the resource situation and under consideration of the strains on developing states of world inflation and recession. In fact, the U.S. government's perception of the supposed producer threat had been informed well before the United Nations meeting, by various analyses, including a report of the Council on International Economic Policy released in 1974, which concluded that neither the United States nor the rest of the industrialized world were likely to suffer serious supply shortages in the next few decades nor were they likely to be faced with a proliferation of producers' associations capable of embargoing supplies to increased price.[21]

According to an alternative explanation, the conciliatory gesture made by the United States at the Seventh Special Session was made merely as an attempt to take the wind out of the Third World's sails, to confuse and divert the conference from the developing states' proposals, and to play on time and the diversity within the Group of 77. In support of this explanation, one can point to passages in Secretary of State Kissinger's opening address which seemed designed to drive a wedge between the oil and non-oil states. Most notable is his remark on page two of the address: ". . . it is ironic also that the most devastating blow to economic development in this decade came not from 'imperialist rapacity' but from an arbitrary, monopolistic price increase by the cartel of oil exporters."

The problem with this explanation is, however, that it fails to anticipate the persistence with which the Third World states were intent on maintaining their solidarity—a solidarity maintained, as it turned out, at the expense of the acceptance of a compromise resolution. And had the United States only sought to subvert the session and divide the Third World, it would not have been necessary, one might add, to issue a comprehensive policy address which involved extensive intragovernmental consultation in the drafting stage. One has to look elsewhere for an explanation of the United States' shift from confrontation to conciliation, and in so doing one discovers the *limits* of the gesture made.

In essence, the U.S. initiatives at the Seventh Special Session reflect a recognition that the earlier attempt to "divide and conquer" had failed. To pursue it further would be counter-productive to the United States' basic objective of strengthening the efficiency of the world economy through improved international market mechanisms—an objective which the United States had come to view as requiring some accommodation with the developing states *within* the framework of reformed, but not transformed, international economic structures. Not only had OPEC not been shattered, but no developing state had openly turned against the association. The persistence of the Third World's solidarity was, in other words, one of the factors which influenced the U.S. shift in tactics. This does not mean, as developing states insist, that Third World cohesion compelled the developed states to alter their position; for, in fact, few positions were changed. Rather, what one sees is that with the Third World having demonstrated, by their linking of oil and other raw materials, that an open attempt to split them would only encourage a stronger sense of solidarity, the United States shifted to a readiness to talk about specific economic issues of concern to different countries with the hope that this would cause them to divide themselves. The direction of policy after the Paris preparatory talks became, in other words, one of discovering "communities of interest." This more positive appeal to distinct "communities of interest" was expected to allow encounters to go beyond the rhetoric of solidarity to discussion of substantive issues that were of concern to different developing states without, however, causing the United States to have to alter its position on the basic demands of the NIEO.

The offering of a set of U.S. initiatives at the Seventh Special Session, which pledged new measures of support for development consistent with a bolstering of the international commodity and capital markets and an improvement of the foreign investment climate, also served to allay potentially significant strains in the Atlantic Alliance. Such strains could have developed had the Western Europeans, individually or collectively, moved to make accommodations with the developing states, while the United States remained nonaccommodative. The possibility of such tension stems from the fact that many of the Western European states are more dependent on the Third World for energy and other natural resources than is the United States and that some have politically significant segments of their population genuinely more sympathetic to Third World demands for redistribution. In fact, the Western European states generally adopted a more conciliatory posture toward the Third World throughout 1974 and 1975. France boycotted the Washington Energy Conference after the United States refused its proposal to invite India, Brazil, and Zaire. The European Community, in February 1975, signed an aid and trade pact (the Lomé Convention) with 46 African, Caribbean, and Pacific (ACP) states which had been under consideration for several years and which included, among other things, an export earning stabilization scheme, duty-free access to the community's market for all ACP states' industrial products and for 96 percent of their agricultural products, a sugar purchase and supply guarantee, and a range of initiatives concerning industrial development without requiring any reverse preferences.[22]

Three months after the signing of the Lomé Convention, at a meeting of the Commonwealth heads of state, British Prime Minister Harold Wilson put forward a suggestion for a "general agreement on commodities." And at the conclusion of the Commonwealth meeting, a group of experts was appointed to draw up a "comprehensive and inter-related programme of practical measures directed at closing the gap between rich and poor countries."[23] An interim report of this group of experts was submitted to the Commonwealth in August 1975. It called not simply for a narrowing of the gap but for measures that would secure for all people a "minimum tolerable standard of existence."[24] As a part of those measures, the expert group voiced support for the UNCTAD integrated commodity program, producers' associations, indexation, concessional benefits to developing states in multilateral trade negotiations, improvements in the Generalized Scheme of Preferences, and an official aid target of 0.7 percent of GNP for all states with a per capita GNP of over $2,000.

These activities—along with some Western European states' attempts to reach bilateral accords with OPEC oil producers, some states' support for the link between SDRs and aid, and a generally more favorable response to commodity agreements—put a number of Western European states at odds with the United States. Without overstating the differences between the Western European states and the United States in their orientation toward the demand for the NIEO, the point can be made that Western European as well as Japanese willingness to make independent conciliatory gestures, and their expressions in private of an eagerness for the United States to assume a leading role in altering the deteriorated climate of North-South relations, had some bearing on the shift in the U.S. posture.

The key to the United States' shift from confrontation to conciliation was, however, the U.S. perception of a need to create conditions conducive to a strengthening of the existing order and compatible conditions supportive of international economic development. These conditions take the form, according to the views of officials of the U.S. administration, of an enhancement of "global efficiency." It is this concept of "global efficiency" that the U.S. administration seems to have in mind when it speaks of the "new interdependence" between developed and developing states and when it commits itself to "our common success"—i.e., common success in strengthening the existing order.

What follows from this vision of "global efficiency" is a recent concern that sustained Third World economic growth and raw material production will not be continued unless the present atmosphere of uncertainty in the raw materials market is altered, and that without new, additional foreign assistance in the majority of oil-poor developing states the growing foreign exchange deficits and debt-servicing problems will escalate. Related developments that have aroused U.S. concern include (1) the increased role of Third World governments in the raw materials production process; (2) the escalating costs in present and future raw material exploration and exploitation; (3) increasingly high financial risks involved in future resource exploration for both political and technological reasons; (4) the changing debt/equity ratio of foreign investment as private companies face greatly increased capital requirements and foreign investment regulations in the raw materials sectors; and (5) declining investments in agricultural sectors. Such developments undermine the capability of private enterprises to effectively control and thereby manage international raw material markets as they have done since World War II. They raise the possibility of widespread defaulting on debts and economic stagnation in the South (with their repercussions on the North), and they raise the unsightly specter of widespread famine in the developing world. They stimulate, in turn, the United States' interest in some new intergovernmental management efforts and some support for the food and raw material sectors in the developing states such as will contribute to the stability of the international trading and monetary systems. From a "global efficiency" perspective there has risen, in other words, a moderate concern over optimizing world raw material resources by doing more in those developing states where there are rich and accessible deposits of natural resources, an interest in stabilizing Third World export earnings through a liberalization of compensatory financing schemes, a willingness to discuss international assistance to public and private raw material investors, a new willingness to consider means of improving access to existing credit facilities to defray balance of payments crises, and interest in expanding foreign assistance burden-sharing responsibilities with a restructuring of roles in international organizations. *Other actions* that are called for by the developing states on the grounds of distributive justice, but which would mean price-fixing or other interventions in the market, substantial resource transfers, or a fundamentally new international division of labor, tend not to generate support, however, from such a global efficiency perspective. What this implies is that the U.S. shift from confrontation to conciliation was neither purely defensive nor wholly unsympathetic to the development problems of the Third World, but was a move that seems, nonetheless, to have done little other than contribute to the creation of a propitious moment in the North-South debate.

The Outcome of the Seventh Special Session

What emerged out of the complex of motives, interests, and perceptions was a *compromise* consensus resolution that outlined general policy goals and agenda issues to be pursued over the next several years in the seven substantive areas delineated in the original Third World position paper. This consensus was the outcome of round-the-clock negotiations on a point-by-point basis in which disagreement was handled by the use of ambiguous language. The compromise was struck by having the final document follow the *format* of the Third World position paper but depart little in general principle from the *substance* of the U.S. position as put forth in Kissinger's opening statement.[25]

In the three areas where most of the negotiating energies were directed—trade, transfer of real resources, and technology—the wording in the final resolution accorded with the basic U.S. position of supporting measures that would strengthen the existing system and bolster the international market, but rejected or relegated to further study any Third World proposal that aimed to fix prices, interfere in the market, or make transfers of real resources more automatic. Where, for instance, the Group of 77 had proposed that agreement "be reached at the fourth session of UNCTAD on an integrated programme for commodities which represent a large percentage of export earnings of developing countries," the final resolution called for "decisions on the improvement of market structures in the field of raw materials and commodities . . . including decision with respect to an integrated programme . . . taking into account the distinctive features of individual raw materials and commodities."[26] This went somewhat further than the U.S. proposal for a "coordinated approach" to raw material trading but represented a rendering fully consistent with the U.S. insistence on a case-by-case approach to commodities.

In addition, new steps were called for in the negotiation of nontariff trade barriers "on a differential and more favorable basis" for developing states, instead of the call being for "elimination of barriers of all kinds to the exports of developing countries, on a preferential and nonreciprocal basis." Liberalization of the Generalized System of Preferences (GSP) was supported, but not the developing states' demand that the GSP become a permanent feature of international trade.

Where agreements on other trade matters could not be reached, matters were relegated to "further study." Thus, a major Third World demand for indexation and insulation against the adverse effects of inflation was dealt with by agreement to further study "on a priority basis" direct and indirect schemes to "preserve the purchasing power" of developing economies.

In the area of transfer of real resources, the Group of 77's demand that financial flows be made more automatic was reduced to an agreement that the flows of concessional financial resources be "made predictable, continuous and increasingly assured." And the decision on the link between SDRs and development assistance, which the Group of 77 sought as one of a number of ways to make aid more automatic, was left to "form part of the consideration by the IMF" of the consideration of new SDRs "as and when they are established according to the needs of international liquidity."

More emphasis was placed in the final resolution than in the developing states' draft, however, on making improvements in access to capital markets for, and encouraging private capital flows into, the Third World—reflecting the U.S. emphasis on private capital initiatives and minimal government budgetary outlays. The particular U.S. contribution to this section of the final resolution included (1) a proposal to increase the capital of the World Bank Group; (2) encouragement of multilateral support for private management skills, technology, and capital; (3) a recommendation that developed economies grant increased access on favorable terms to their capital markets; and (4) a proposal for a development security facility to mitigate export earning shortfalls of developing states through IMF administered loans.

Similarly, in the part of the resolution which dealt with technology and science, a number of proposals were made that derived from a U.S. initiative and were not in the Group of 77's draft; at the same time, many of the points included fell far short of the original Third World demands. While the Group of 77 had urged that the developed states cooperate in the transfer of technology to developing states, the final resolution only called for cooperation between developed and developing states. While the Group of 77 called for a legally binding international code of conduct for technology transfers to be adopted no later than the end of 1977, the final resolution suggested that states cooperate simply "in evolving an international code of conduct," with no mention of a time-frame or the legal character of such a code. And, while the Group of 77 urged that developing states be granted preferential terms for access to technological information, the final resolution proposed that developed countries "facilitate access of developing countries on favourable terms and conditions."

As the final document reveals, in all major points of controversy the developing states retracted from their initial position for the sake of arriving at what could be called a "consensus" resolution, and the developed countries (particularly the United States) acceded to certain language and to the outline of an agenda of issues that went beyond their initial proposals without, however, committing themselves to any unacceptable action. Once the final document had been drafted, it was agreed that in order to avoid a display of any remaining dissension, reservations on the official resolution would be entered into the record of the verbatim report of the conference but not aired in open session. It should be noted, however, that despite this gesture, and despite the moderate, much compromised tone and content of the final resolution, the United States felt compelled to issue a rather lengthy list of reservations which are clearly indicative of how far apart it remained from the developing world. In its set of reservations, the United States indicated among other things that it cannot and does not accept any implication that the world is now embarked on the establishment of something called the New International Economic Order; that while it agreed to join others in the study of indexation it remained opposed to such a proposal; that it "does not like" the idea of specific ODA targets; that it does not support a link between SDRs and development assistance; and that it continues to believe that decision-making power in international financial institutions must take due account of relative economic positions.

Conclusion: A New Phase in North-South Relations?

In answer to the question of whether a significant new phase in North-South relations has yet begun, these observations suggest that what occurred was a *conciliation* without *reconciliation* of the basic issues and the fundamental principles at stake. To the developing states' demand for the more tightly managed NIEO in which collective decision-making directly takes into account problems of redistributing world economic opportunities, the developed states (led by the United States) have responded with some plans to reform and revitalize aspects of the existing international economic system, with principle attention to issues of efficiency and stability.

There continues, in other words, to be a lack of consensus between developed and developing countries on the question of the purposes and the management of the international economic order. Northern recognition of the South's problem of unstable export earnings has led to the U.S. proposal to *stabilize* overall export earnings, but not to stabilize prices and guarantee purchasing power. Trade reforms are urged, but actions needed to make the definition of a new international division of labor real are slow in coming. While the Third World Forum has explained that what the developing states seek in regard to transfers is "not massive redistributions of wealth" nor "equality of income" but rather "equality of economic opportunity,"[27] the United States attacks the redistributive principle and refuses to support the idea of new and automatic sources of aid.

Essentially, while the developing states are making a political and ethical claim for the restructuring of the world economic system, the developed states seem to be saying that there is a burden of proof which rests with the developing world that these claims will not raise unnecessary costs for the developed states. And in the absence of a broadly similar view of the problems, the U.S.-led approach of trying to identify and deal with specific "communities of interests" continues to appear to most developing states as a divisive and illegitimate tactic rather than as the constructive approach it could be in a context of broad consensus on goals. Such an approach, in the absence of a broad general commitment to, and consensus on, development threatens to break down rather than to reconstruct any sense of "community" among nations of the world. What is needed more fundamentally than (and prior to) piece-meal reform is an international commitment to the elimination of absolute poverty, a willingness on the part of developed countries to see shifts in industrial production, and willingness on the part of both developed and developing states to accept certain restraints on freedom of action.

Notes

1. From the vantage point of the developing states, the important change in the distribution of economic power in the postwar era has been the diversification of sources of overseas investment capital, technology transfers, expanded markets, and aid.

2. There is a large and growing literature on the development and the significance of economic interdependence in the postwar world. What seems important about the phenomenon of interdependence analyzed in this literature is not the increase in the actual quantity of interstate interaction or a change in quality (which has been much debated) but rather the increased political saliency of economic interdependence in a world in which national governments have become increasingly responsible for conditions of citizen welfare.
3. For a provocative analysis of the ethical questions raised by the developing states' call for the New International Economic Order, see two articles by Robert W. Tucker, "A New International Order?" and "Egalitarianism and International Politics," *Commentary* 59 (February 1975): 38-50; and 60 (September 1975): 27-40.
4. For an analysis of the role of Non-Aligned Countries, see Odette Jankowitsch and Karl P. Sauvant, "The Evolution of the Non-Aligned Movement into a Pressure Group for the Establishment of the New International Economic Order." Paper presented at the Seventeenth Annual Convention of the International Studies Association, Toronto, February 1976. Mimeographed.
5. United Nations General Assembly resolutions 3201 (S-VI) and 3202 (S-VI), respectively.
6. Quoted from the preamble of the *Declaration,* ibid.
7. See Fourth Conference of Heads of State or Government of Non-Aligned Countries, *Economic Declaration* (United Nations document A/9330), 22 November 1973.
8. Henry Kissinger, "Speech Delivered before the Sixth Special Session," *Vital Speeches* 40 (April 1974): 457.
9. *New York Times,* 13 December 1974.
10. *The Dakar Declaration Adopted at the Conference of Developing Countries on Raw Materials, Dakar, 3-8 February 1975* (United Nations document E/AC. 62/6), 15 April 1975, p. 8.
11. "Address by the Honorable Henry A. Kissinger, Secretary of State, before the Kansas City International Relations Council, Missouri, May 13, 1975," p. 241, reprinted in *Issues at the Special Session of the 1975 U.N. General Assembly,* for Hearings before the Subcommittee on International Organizations of the Committee on International Relations, House of Representatives (Washington: Government Printing Office, 1975), pp. 231-42.
12. "Address by the Honorable Henry A. Kissinger, Secretary of State, before the OECD Ministerial Council, Paris, May 28, 1975," reprinted in *Issues,* ibid., p. 252.
13. "Address by the Honorable Henry A. Kissinger, Secretary of State, before the Wisconsin Institute of World Affairs, Milwaukee, July 1975," (Washington: U.S. Department of State, Press Release, no. 370, 1975), pp.

7, 8.

14. "Address by the Honorable Henry A. Kissinger, Secretary of State, before the Seventh Special Session of the United Nations General Assembly, New York, September 1, 1975," Department of State, Press Release, no. 450, p. 27.

15. These citations are taken from United Nations, General Assembly, Seventh Special Session, *Provisional Verbatim Records,* A/PV. 2334, p. 37; A/PV. 2330, p. 46; and A/PV. 2331, p. 46.

16. Ibid., A/PV. 2337, pp. 96, 97.

17. Reference is made here to the United States alone, because the Western European states had already made efforts to reach accommodation with the developing states, as noted below, and because the United States' position at the Seventh Special Session was the key to the outcome of the Session.

18. Robert S. McNamara, "Poorest Nations Face Decade of Stagnation." Address to the Board of Governors of the International Bank for Reconstruction and Development, mimeographed (IBRD), 1 September 1975. See also IBRD, "Additional External Capital Requirements of Developing Countries," mimeographed (Washington: IBRD, 1974).

19. Distinct trends on the world energy scene helped create the context in which the OPEC action of 1973-74 could bear fruit. These trends, evident in the 1960s, include a substantial growth in overall energy consumption, a rising share of petroleum within that growing total, and, in turn, a steadily rising share (already high in the early sixties) of Persian Gulf and North African oil in accommodating that rise in oil consumption. For concise data on these trends, see J. Darmstadter and H. Landsberg, "The Economic Background," *Daedalus* 104 (Fall 1975): 15-38.

20. Much has now been written about "threats" from the Third World based on new found "commodity power." The leading U.S. proponent of this view is C. Fred Bergsten who argues that a number of new cartels can be expected in the 1970s. See his two articles: C. Fred Bergsten, "The Threat from the Third World, "*Foreign Policy* 11 (Summer 1973): 102-24; and "The New Era in World Commodity Markets," *Challenge,* September-October 1974, pp. 32-39. A rather different, highly interesting, interpretation of the impact of resource scarcity fears on development assistance politics is to be found in John P. Lewis, "Oil, Other Scarcities and the Poor Countries," *World Politics* 27 (October 1974): 63-86.

21. Council on International Economic Policy, *Special Report: Critical Imported Materials* (Washington: Government Printing Office, 1974). As the report noted, the vulnerability of the U.S. to price-gouging, supply interruptions, or other cartel action is limited by the fact that (1) the U.S. is relatively self-sufficient; (2) U.S. dependence on imports, where it exists, is highly concentrated on other developed countries; and (3) market forces are effective enough and cartels hard enough to organize to ease even the problems of

Western Europe and Japan, which are considerably more dependent on imported raw materials than the United States.

22. See Chapters 10 and 21 below.

23. "Excerpts of Commonwealth Summit Conference Communiqué," *Times* (London), 8 May 1975, p. 15.

24. *Towards a New International Economic Order* (United Nations document A/AC. 176/5), 8 September 1975, p. 11.

25. For a detailed analysis of the positions of the developed countries and those of the Group of 77, as well as their formulation in the final resolution, see Branislav Gosovic and John Gerard Ruggie, "On the Creation of a New International Economic Order: Issue Linkages and the Seventh Special Session of the United Nations General Assembly," *International Organization* 30 (Spring 1976): 309-345.

26. For the position of the developing countries, see Ad Hoc Committee of the Seventh Special Session, *Development and International Economic Co-operation: Informal Working Paper Submitted by the Chairman of the Group of 77 for Negotiation Purposes. Working Paper No 1* (4 September 1975), mimeographed; for the quotes from the final resolution, see United Nations General Assembly resolution 3362 (S-VII), "Development and International Economic Co-operation," reprinted as Chapter 2 above.

27. The Third World Forum, *Proposals for a New International Economic Order,* mimeographed (Mexico: The Third World Forum, 1975).

Part 3

International Trade and Commodities

7 *Developing Countries in World Trade*

Hajo Hasenpflug

One of the main reasons for the developing countries' demand for the New International Economic Order (NIEO), and especially for indexation, commodity agreements, buffer stocks, as well as for the removal of tariff and nontariff barriers against Third World products, is the failure of the traditional aid-by-trade concept. The overwhelming majority of the developing countries remains confronted with problems related to decreasing shares in world trade and deteriorating terms of trade.

In view of the developing countries' problems, politicians, economists, and officials of multilateral institutions have supported an intensification of the integration of the developing countries into the world economy and into international trade relations. This integration—or aid-by-trade idea—aims at increasing the exports of developing countries and, therefore, at increasing their foreign currency earnings; the transferral of ever growing amounts of real resources through direct aid measures by the industrialized countries would, thus, become less urgent. Growing exports were also expected to increase the rate of employment and enable small countries to build up larger industrial units that would be able to produce with economies of scale. The theoretical argumentation of the supporters of the aid-by-trade concept is based on nineteenth-century liberal economic concepts according to which free trade assures the optimal allocation of resources and every country participating in international trade will gain—including small and poor countries. Today, it has become clear that these concepts do not take account of the fact that although every country can gain from international trade, some countries, or groups of countries, gain more than others, thereby creating a widening gap between the welfare of trading nations. In fact, the industrialized countries benefited much more from international economic transactions than the developing ones. The main factors responsible for this development are the worsening position of the developing countries in world trade and their deteriorating terms of trade. In the following discussion, these factors will be treated in greater detail.

The Developing Countries' Share in World Trade

Until 1972, the share of the industrialized countries in world trade has increased steadily, whereas the developing countries' share has decreased, and that of the socialist countries has more or less stayed the same. Since 1973, the trend concerning the industrialized and developing countries has been reversed because of increased oil prices.

As table 1 shows, the industrialized countries raised their share in world trade between 1953 and 1972 from 64.9 to 71.5 percent. The Third World's share declined from 25.5 to 18.6 percent. The last figure includes an improved share of OPEC countries from 3.7 to 5.6 percent, leaving for the remaining developing countries, as a group, a share of 21.8 to 13.0 percent. The socialist countries maintained a share of between 9 and 12 percent. Due to the oil-price explosion,the situation changed drastically, as reflected in the following figures for 1974: industrialized countries 64.4 percent, developing countries 27.2 percent, developing countries excluding OPEC 14.2 percent, and socialist countries 8.4 percent.

Apart from the OPEC countries and a few others (like Hong Kong, Taiwan, or the Republic of South Korea) who have reached sufficient levels of industrialization and technology to supply developed countries with such consumer goods as textiles, and electrical and photographic products, the majority of the Third World has suffered under highly unfavorable trends in world trade for its exports. These countries' exports consist mainly of cash crops, semiprocessed foodstuffs, and raw materials, which experienced a steadily declining share in world trade. Between 1953 and 1974, the world trade share of these products (excluding fossil fuels) has fallen from 40.2 to 20.0 percent while the share of semifinished and finished goods has increased from 48.6 to 57.1 percent (see table 2).

Terms of Trade

The decline of the developing countries' world-trade position has been due mainly to unsatisfactory price trends in their principal export commodities. Between 85 and 90 percent of these exports consist of raw materials, and in many developing countries two or three commodities represent nearly all exports.[1] The export prices of these products have risen relatively little or not at all, while prices for manufactures have increased at a higher rate. The widening gap between prices of raw materials and manufactured goods and—because of the export structure of the respective country groups—between export prices of industrialized nations and developing countries can be clearly observed in the development of the terms of trade.

The United Nations Conference on Trade and Development (UNCTAD) Secretariat and the World Bank have published calculations

Table 1. Share of selected countries and regions in world trade, various years

(Percentage)

Country	Year				
	1953	1963	1972	1973	1974
Industrialized countries	64.9	67.4	71.5	70.7	64.4
EC Nine	27.9	33.7	37.0	36.5	32.6
France	4.9	5.2	6.2	6.2	5.4
Germany, Fed.Rep.	5.7	9.7	11.3	11.9	10.8
Italy	1.8	3.3	4.5	3.9	3.4
United Kingdom	8.7	7.2	5.8	5.3	4.6
Japan	1.5	3.5	6.9	6.4	6.6
United States	18.9	14.9	11.7	12.2	11.5
Developing countries	25.5	20.4	18.6	19.3	27.2
Brazil	1.9	0.9	1.0	1.1	0.9
Hong Kong	0.6	0.6	0.8	0.9	0.7
India	1.4	1.1	0.6	0.5	0.5
Iran	0.1	0.6	1.1	1.2	2.8
Kuwait	a/	0.7	0.7	0.7	1.3
Saudi Arabia	0.7	0.7	1.3	1.6	4.4
OPEC	3.7	4.1	5.6	6.1	13.0
Socialist countries	9.6	12.2	10.4	10.0	8.4
World total	100.0	100.0	100.0	100.0	100.0

Source: Calculated on the basis of figures from United Nations, Yearbook of International Trade Statistics, various vols. (New York: UN).

a/ Figure not available.

about commodity terms of trade. The figures of the World Bank have been calculated on the basis of 34 commodities, while UNCTAD's index consists of 28 commodities exported by developing countries. The 28 commodities chosen by UNCTAD represented 67.5 percent of the total value of all

Table 2. World trade in terms of regional and product structure, 1953 - 1974 (percentage of f.o.b. exports)

Region	Year	Product group					
		Food & drink[a]	Commodities excl. fuels[b]	Fossil fuels[c]	Total primary products[d]	Semifinished and finished goods[e]	Total exports of goods
Industrialized countries	1953	16.2	12.9	5.6	34.7	64.1	100
	1958	15.8	9.4	5.1	30.3	69.8	100
	1961	14.8	10.1	4.1	29.0	71.1	100
	1965	14.2	8.1	3.4	25.5	74.3	100
	1969	11.2	6.8	3.0	21.0	79.0	100
	1972	11.8	5.8	3.4	21.0	79.0	100
	1973	13.0	6.2	3.5	22.7	75.4	100
	1974	11.7	6.0	4.8	22.5	75.5	100
Developing countries	1953	37.5	29.0	22.1	88.6	11.1	100
	1958	37.0	23.7	26.7	87.4	12.5	100
	1961	32.9	22.8	29.3	85.0	15.0	100
	1965	34.0	18.9	31.2	84.1	18.2	100
	1969	26.1	16.3	32.8	75.2	24.8	100
	1972	22.9	13.1	38.6	74.6	25.5	100
	1973	20.8	13.0	39.3	73.1	25.4	100
	1974	f/	f/	f/	82.4	16.3	100

Socialist countries	1953 f/						
	1958	18.1	15.7	11.3	45.1	54.9	100
	1961	15.9	14.3	11.7	41.9	58.1	100
	1965	14.6	11.9	10.5	37.0	62.9	100
	1969	14.3	10.0	9.1	33.4	66.7	100
	1972	10.8	10.0	9.4	30.2	69.7	100
	1973	11.9	9.5	9.9	31.3	63.2	100
	1974	f/	f/	f/	34.5	59.9	100
World total	1953	22.3	17.9	10.2	50.4	48.6	100
	1958	21.7	13.9	11.5	47.1	52.8	100
	1961	19.5	14.3	10.2	44.0	56.0	100
	1965	18.4	11.5	9.8	39.7	60.5	100
	1969	14.8	9.6	9.1	33.5	66.5	100
	1972	14.3	8.1	10.4	32.8	67.2	100
	1973	14.9	8.5	11.0	34.4	63.4	100
	1974	12.6	7.4	20.9	40.9	57.1	100

Source: Calculated on the basis of figures from General Agreement on Tariffs and Trade (GATT), International Trade, various vols. (Geneva: GATT).

a/ SITC categories 0, 1, 4 and 22
b/ SITC category 2 excluding category 22
c/ SITC category 3
d/ SITC categories 0 - 4
e/ SITC categories 5 - 9
f/ Figures not available

Table 3. Comparison of World Bank and UNCTAD indices of terms of trade of primary commodities, 1953-1972

Year	Terms of trade	
	UNCTAD[a/]	World Bank
1953	126	122
1954	138	137
1955	133	130
1956	123	128
1957	116	118
1958	111	111
1959	107	110
1960	106	106
1961	101	98
1962	96	97
1963	100	100
1964	105	109
1965	100	109
1966	99	109
1967	95	100
1968	99	102
1969	100	104
1970	98	102
1971	86	89
1972	84	87

Source: Taken from UNCTAD, "Indexation: Report by the Secretary-General of UNCTAD," (TD/B/563), July 7, 1975, Table 3.

a/ Based on unit values of developing countries' exports of coffee, cocoa, tea, maize, rice, sugar, bananas, copra, coconut oil, groundnut oil, cotton, jute, sisal, natural rubber, wool, copper, tin, lead, zinc, bauxite, alumina, aluminum , iron ore, phosphate rock, manganese and on values of world exports of oranges (and tangerines) and tobacco. The index has been weighted by 1963 values of exports from developing countries. In 1963 the total export value of these selected commodities from developing countries represented 67.5 percent of the total value of all primary commodities (excluding petroleum) exported from developing countries.

primary products (excluding petroleum) exported by developing countries in the base year of 1963. Both time-series show that the terms of trade for the commodities covered declined between 1953 and 1972 at an annual average of about 2.2 percent. The UNCTAD index has fallen from 126 to 84 during this time period, and the World Bank index from 122 to 87 (see table 3). Since these figures have been deflated by the UN index of unit values of

Table 4. Development of world export volume between 196o and 1974 (196o = 1oo)

	Commodity group			
	All commodities	Agricultural prod.	Minerals[a/]	Manufactures
Year				
196o	1oo	1oo	1oo	1oo
1963	12o	111	12o	126
1968	178	136	172	2o5
1969	199	139	181	236
197o	215	15o	195	26o
1971	229	155	2o2	273
1972	249	164	214	3oo
1973	276	158	24o	351
1974[b/]	293	155	232	384

a/ Inclusive fuels and non-ferrous metals.

b/ Provisional.

Source: General Agreement on Tariffs and Trade (GATT). International Trade 1974/75 (Geneva: GATT,1975), p. 2.

manufactured goods exported by industrialized nations, they show the relative negative development in export prices of developing nations against those of industrialized ones.

Another major factor responsible for the negative development of the world-trade position of the Third World is the slow quantitative growth of the commodities exported by them. According to calculations made by the General Agreement on Tariffs and Trade (GATT) Secretariat, the world export volume of agricultural products and minerals has grown at a slower pace than that of manufactures. Taking 100 for 1960 as the basic year, world export volume had increased to 155 for agricultural products, to 232 for minerals, and to 384 for manufactures by 1974 (see table 4). Given that developing countries' exports consist mainly of agricultural products and minerals, this differential rate further contributed to their declining world trade share. Several factors explain this trend:

Table 5. Estimated income elasticities of demand
(Average for all countries of the world)

Product group	Elasticity
Food and beverages	o.5 - o.8
Agricultural raw materials	o.5 - o.6
Ores and metals	1.3 - 1.7
Fuels	1.o - 1.2
Capital goods	1.o and more
Consumer goods and other industry products	1.2 - 1.7

Source: Taken from Helmut Hesse, Strukturwandlungen im Welthandel 195o - 196o/61 (Tübingen: Verlag J. C. B. Mohr, 1967), p. 92.

1. In the raw material sector, consumption has declined because of the progressively falling proportion of raw materials used in production. Moreover, synthetics have provided increasingly stiff competition.

2. In the farm-produce sector, overall demand for foodstuffs has declined relatively. The major cause here is the low income elasticity of demand for agricultural goods (see table 5). Furthermore, the industrialized countries have increased their food self-sufficiency.

3. In the manufacture and farm-produce sector, developing countries encounter many tariff and nontariff obstacles from industrialized countries. Custom duties increase the prices consumers have to pay and, therefore, frequently prevent or hinder the entry of products by lessening considerably their competitiveness. Particularly noteworthy is that a higher duty rate is levelled on products with a higher degree of processing (see table 6). This, in addition, discourages the development of processing facilities in the developing countries and, therefore, the development of industries based on local raw materials.

Apart from the relatively high nominal customs duties, the effective tariff protection often prevents the imports of developing countries from reaching their markets, since effective protection rises the greater the degree of processing. Calculations made by Bela Balassa, W. M. Corden, and the UNCTAD Secretariat show that the effective tariff protection exceeds the nominal protection often by more than 100 percent (see table 7). Nevertheless, it has to be noted that the relative importance of tariff barriers has decreased while nontariff barriers have become more relevant. Developing

Table 6. Average nominal tariffs, by country and product group
(Percentage)

Country	Raw materials	Semi-manufactures	Manufactures
	Product group		
EC			
Arithmetic average a/	1.7	8.9	8.3
Weighted average b/	0.7	7.7	9.2
Japan			
Arithmetic average a/	2.2	9.6	11.3
Weighted average b/	6.0	9.6	11.5
US			
Arithmetic average a/	5.6	9.8	13.1
Weighted average b/	3.8	9.1	8.2

Source: Taken from General Agreement on Tariffs and Trade (GATT), Basis Documentation for the Tariff Study. Summary by Industrial Product Categories, Tariff 1973, Import 1970/71 (Geneva: GATT, 1974).

a/ Simple (unweighted) arithmetic average of all most-favored-nation duty rates applying to tariff lines within a commodity group.

b/ This average has been calculated in two steps. First, a simple (unweighted) arithmetic average of tariff lines was computed for each BTN (Brussels Tariff Nomenclature) heading. Then, each of these averages was weighted by the total combined imports of the eleven industrialized countries covered by the tariff study.

countries are justified in claiming that nontariff barriers impede their exports much more than those of industrialized nations. Measures like quantitative restrictions, discretionary licensing, variable levies, standards, and health and sanitary regulations especially hamper the export of developing countries' products when they are competing with "sensitive" products of developed countries. Processed agricultural goods, textiles, clothing, leather, and leather products, or electrical and mechanical appliances, deserve special mention since they are very often subject to protection.[2] They are normally considered sensitive products in industrialized areas, but, they are also products with which the industrialization process of developing countries begins. Import restrictions or "voluntary" export restrictions for developing countries have, therefore, a fundamental

Table 7. Comparison of nominal and effective rates of protection for agricultural products in the European Community, Japan, and the United States, 1971

(Percentages)

Product	European Community		Japan		United States	
	Nominal protection	Effective protection[a/]	Nominal protection	Effective protection[b/]	Nominal protection	Effective protection[b/]
Meat products	19.5	165.0	17.9	69.1	5.9	10.3
Preserved sea foods	21.5	52.6	13.6	34.7	6.0	15.6
Preserved fruit and vegetables	20.5	74.7	18.5	49.3	14.8	36.8
Grain and grain products						
Corn milling	12.0	82.1	25.6	68.7	4.3	0.0
Rice milling	16.0	105.9	15.0	49.0	36.2	327.6
Prepared foods	5.6	- 50.0	0.7	- 21.2	6.2	7.4
Flour and cereal preparations	20.1	94.7	23.8	75.4	10.9	34.8
Bakery products	12.0	0.0	20.9	17.3	1.9	0.0
Tobacco products	87.1	148.5	339.5	405.6	68.0	113.2
Prepared and processed food						
Pickles and dressings	20.1	25.9	21.9	59.8	9.4	- 26.9
Roasted coffee	15.2	35.7	35.0	137.1	0.0	0.0
Cocoa powder and butter	13.6	76.0	15.0	125.0	2.6	22.0
Misc. food products	12.0	6.7	28.6	58.2	2.7	0.2
Leather and products						
Leather	7.0	21.4	17.8	57.4	6.2	18.6
Footwear	9.4	12.0	22.4	32.5	10.5	15.4

Jute products						
Jute fabrics	21.1	57.8	20.0	54.8	3.0	7.4
Jute sacks and bags	15.3	9.8	34.3	75.2	4.1	11.6
Sisal and Henequen products						
Binder-bale twine	13.0	26.0	10.5	21.0	0.0	0.0
Sisal ropes and cables	13.0	26.0	10.5	21.0	13.2	26.4
Yarns, thread and fabrics						
Wool yarn and thread	5.4	16.0	5.0	13.3	30.7	62.2
Wool fabrics	14.0	32.9	14.7	35.1	46.9	90.8
Cotton yarn and thread	7.0	22.8	8.4	25.8	8.3	12.0
Cotton fabrics	13.6	29.7	7.2	4.9	15.6	30.7
Cotton clothing	14.0	17.6	14.7	27.3	20.0	33.6
Vegetable oils						
Coconut oil	11.5	132.9	9.0	49.2	9.4	16.3
Cottonseed oil	11.0	79.0	25.8	200.3	59.6	465.9
Groundnut oil	11.3	139.7	14.2	96.5	15.0	6.7
Soyabean oil	11.0	148.1	25.4	268.3	22.5	252.9
Rapeseed oil	9.0	57.2	15.1	22.3	20.8	60.9
Palm kernel oil	10.5	141.5	7.2	49.2	3.8	29.2
Lumber and paper products						
Plywood products	..	..	..	..	13.0	28.0
Paper and paper articles	..	..	..	..	5.0	13.0

Source: Taken from: UNCTAD, "An Integrated Programme for Commodities: Measures to Expand Processing of Primary Commodities in Developing Countries. Report by the UNCTAD Secretariat," (TD/B/C.1/197), October 23, Annex Table 1.

a/ Includes levies and other special charges.

b/ Effective tariff protection.

impact on their economies. For some countries, such restrictions affect their only major export items, thus causing wide-ranging effects on their balance-of-payments, employment, and economic growth.

Strategies for Improving the Third World's Position

As far as a further deterioration of the developing countries' terms of trade and their widely fluctuating export earnings are concerned, workable export-stabilization mechanisms have to be introduced for mineral and agricultural export products of developing countries. The experiences made with the export-earning stabilization system of the Lomé agreement between the European Community and her 46 associated countries could be used as a basis for implementing such a system on a worldwide basis.[3] In addition, commodity agreements and an international financing of buffer-stocks should be utilized for the same purposes.[4] But all these measures do not bring about the desired price increases.

What is necessary for the economies of the developing nations is a diversification of their export and production structure. The lopsided concentration on a few mineral or agricultural products causes economic vulnerability and instability. In countries that have minerals, mineral-processing industries have to be built up in order to raise the value-added in the countries where the exploitation is done. The same vertical diversification has to be achieved in the field of agricultural products. In countries where skilled and cheap labor forces are available, a speeded horizontal diversification is desirable. But such horizontal diversification raises the need for harmonized industrial policies. A danger exists that, in the absence of such harmonization, countries might diversify into products that are already in over-supply or that face other problems on the world market, such as competition from synthetics. But this is not an easy endeavour even in industrialized countries; even in the framework of regional integration schemes—where a special coordinating machinery exists—harmonization has never made much headway.

However, all these efforts are, to a great extent, in vain, if the developed countries maintain tariff and nontariff barriers in those sectors where the developing countries have a possibility to industrialize. What is necessary are effective structural policies in the industrialized countries in order to support the efforts undertaken in Third World countries. The problem, however, is that import liberalization and structural policies—or better, an anticipatory structural policy—are restricted by the rules and limits of parliamentary democracies, which virtually do not allow a structural policy that condemns certain sectors to be closed or to be transferred to developing countries. Realistically speaking, therefore, only those trade barriers are likely to be completely eliminated which have not been introduced with trade-distorting intentions. Standards, packing and labelling, or sanitary health regulations, as well as entry procedures and bureaucratic formalities, usually fall into this category. Industrialized countries can easily eliminate these barriers or support Third World countries, for instance through training courses, to better understand such regulations.

Overall, however, if the industrialized nations do not liberalize their import conditions vis-à-vis the Third World in a sufficient and satisfactory manner, the aid-by-trade concept is worthless and need not be discussed any longer.

Given the inflexible attitude of industrialized countries in the field of import liberalization, measures have to be explored and implemented that do not require the cooperation of industrialized countries. A strategy has to be supported that focuses on increasingly interdependent relations among developing countries and that reduces their collective and individual dependence on the industrialized nations. Consequently, all efforts have to be made to support regional economic integration schemes of developing countries with a high degree of common protection against products of industrialized countries.

The degree of such disintegration from trade with industrialized countries is, of course, a function of the economic strength and developing potential of any single country. The more developed a developing country is, the more it is on an equal level with industrialized countries and the more it can subject itself to strong competition in world trade. But for the great majority of the Third World, a protective strategy of collective and individual self-reliance appears to be more appropriate and advisable.

Notes

1. For some data, see Chapter 10 below.
2. For further details, see the discussion of the Generalized System of Preferences in Chapter 12 below.
3. For a discussion of this system, see Chapter 10 below.
4. See Chapters 8 and 9 below.

8 *An Integrated Programme for Commodities and Indexation of Prices*

UNCTAD

The Old and the New Approach

The international action required in the commodity sector needs to go beyond the approaches that have held sway since the post-war period—approaches whose basic elements were introduced in the Havana Charter. The Havana Charter did recognize the need for action in the field of commodities. But its guiding principles reflected the view that intervention in commodity markets by intergovernmental action should constitute the exception rather than the norm in commodity trade, that such action should be based on agreements to which both producers and consumers were parties, that equality of representation of producers and consumers should be reflected in individual commodity councils or organizations, and that the objective in terms of prices should be the control of fluctuations rather than the reversal or modification of long-term trends as determined by the forces of the market.

It has now to be recognized that this approach has failed to produce effective results even in terms of its own guiding philosophy. Over the whole post-war period there have been only five full-fledged international commodity agreements, covering wheat, sugar, tin, coffee, and cocoa. Of these, only the agreements for cocoa, tin and, more recently, for coffee have been successfully renegotiated. The negotiation of even the successful

---

Reprinted, with permission, from UNCTAD, *New Directions and New Structures for Trade and Development: Report by the Secretary-General of UNCTAD to the Conference* (TD/183), 14 April 1976, pp. 19-23; UNCTAD, *Commodities: Action on Commodities, Including Decisions on an Integrated Programme, in the Light of the Need for Change in the World Commodity Economy. Report by the UNCTAD Secretariat* (TD/184), 4 March 1976, pp. 6-15, 21-23, and 18-19; and UNCTAD, *The Indexation of Prices: Report by the Secretary-General of UNCTAD on the Findings of His Study* (TD/B/503), 6 August 1974, pp. 4-8, with minor adaptations.

agreements took many years of tortuous and frustrating effort. The International Cocoa Agreement, for instance, took 17 years to materialize. For the other commodities no lasting successful results have emerged so far, despite periodic confabulations between producers and consumers.[1] After the third session of the UN Conference on Trade and Development (UNCTAD) in 1972, "intensive intergovernmental consultations" were initiated for 13 commodities on a case-by-case basis, but though these served to elucidate problems, they failed to lead to the adoption of measures to relieve those problems. A host of factors underlie these failures. But predominant among them was a weakness in motivation on the part of consumers and a lack of capacity on the part of producers to command attention to their needs. For the consuming countries there was a strong disinclination to establish governmental intervention in "free" markets—a disinclination born of a system and an ideology which reflects the dominance of private interests. Although both consumers and producers may share a common interest in the avoidance of sharp price fluctuations, this interest can scarcely be an equal one, since commodities are a much smaller proportion of the total trade of the consuming than of the producing countries. Moreover, commodity negotiations on a case-by-case basis tend to focus sharply on the commercial interests of the consuming countries as buyers of a particular product, and do not allow sufficient scope for a consideration of issues in the wider perspective of the international development goals and policies of the consuming countries themselves. For this reason, difficulties on the more narrowly commercial questions tend to exercise an overriding influence on the final result.

On the side of the producer countries, there has hitherto not been sufficient capacity to exercise leverage through recourse to alternative actions. Not seldom, differences among themselves—sometimes reflecting a conflict of interest between new and established producers—stand in the way of consolidated negotiating positions. Case-by-case negotiations offer no scope for obtaining an attractive balance of advantage for an individual producer country by offsetting concessions that might be made by it in respect of one of its commodities by gains to be derived from others. A fragmented case-by-case approach could result in arrangements which succeed in strengthening prices of some commodities, to the neglect of others, and rebound to the disadvantage of developing countries which import the former and export the latter. This has, in fact, been the result of the limited coverage of commodity arrangements up to now. Moreover, such negotiations do not allow the developing countries to exercise pressure in common to ensure that the commodity question is dealt with as a major aspect of the overall development problem.

It is evident that any new approaches to the commodity problem would need to overcome these shortcomings. A recognition that the commodity problem is not one which concerns a few isolated commodities here and there but one that encompasses the basic structure of trade in primary commodities must be central to any new approach. In the quest for effective solutions it would, of course, be necessary to deal with the special problems of individual commodities. But such a treatment must fall within a framework of accepted principles, objectives and techniques which would bring to the negotiation of solutions for individual products the full weight of an international consensus which sees them as part of an interrelated attack on the commodity problem in general. The conditions for launching a new attack on the commodity problem are perhaps better now than at any time in the past. There is a growing recognition that this has been a field that has suffered relative neglect on the part of the international community, a neglect that has served, in the context of the current global recession, to severely aggravate the problems of the developing countries. But, even more important, the growing inclination and capacity of the developing countries to initiate action on their own (a development that had its strongest expression in the action of the countries members of the Organization of Petroleum Exporting Countries [OPEC]), a strengthening of the long-term market prospects for commodities that are potentially in short supply (the so-called non-renewable resources), the consequent concern of consuming countries with the adequacy and regularity of supplies, as with the need for investments in the producing area—all these have introduced new elements that could improve the prospects for effective action at the present time.

In order to meet the needs of the present time, the UNCTAD secretariat has presented the integrated programme for commodities, which aims at introducing a package of measures which, when taken together, will constitute an approach to the commodity problem that is more effective than anything attempted in the past.

The essence of the integrated programme is that, in contrast to previous approaches, it aims at dealing with the problem of commodities in a *comprehensive* and systematic way. It is not a mere appeal for starting a series of consultations, or even negotiations, on individual products in isolated fashion as was the case with such initiatives as the intensive intergovernmental consultations on commodities that followed the decisions of UNCTAD III in 1972. Nor is it an endeavour to provide only a broad framework of objectives and guiding principles that will influence and inspire the negotiations on individual products. It seeks, rather, to secure an international consensus to take action on a wide range of products through a set of specific measures which, to a greater or lesser extent, are applicable to each of these products. Certain of the instruments that the programme requires would, in fact, be employed to meet the needs of a number of commodities. The programme lays much stress on the comprehensive coverage of commodities. This is a reflection of the need to secure adequate balance in the treatment of different commodities. While no set of measures can benefit all developing countries equally, a comprehensive commodity coverage will go far towards safeguarding the position of most of them. The programme also places emphasis on a multidimensional approach to dealing with the problems of commodities, even when viewed as individual products. Export regulation was the instrument predominantly used in past agreements. The integrated programme, while recognizing the need for export regulation when the situation warrants it, seeks also to include a number of other mechanisms that have hitherto not been availed of to a significant degree but which could contribute much towards the attainment of the objectives for individual products.

Main Elements of the Integrated Programme

The integrated programme comprises five basic elements:

1. The establishment of internationally-owned stocks covering a wide range of commodities.
2. The establishment of a common financing fund that will make resources available for the acquisition of stocks.
3. The institution, in circumstances which justify it, of a system of medium- to long-term commitments to purchase and sell commodities at agreed prices.
4. The institution of more adequate measures than are at present available to provide compensatory financing to producers to cover shortfalls in export earnings.
5. The initiation of an extensive programme of measures to further the processing of commodities by the producing countries themselves.

These different elements of the programme need to be perceived as an interrelated whole; taken together, they seek to attack the critical problems of the commodity sector in the world economy. The mechanisms which are proposed in the programme are designed not only to mitigate the fluctuations in commodity prices, but also to stabilize the earnings of developing countries from their commodity exports at adequate levels and in real terms. The regulation of the commodity markets through individual commodity agreements made within the framework of the integrated programme will help to create the conditions for effective planning of production and investment in producing countries. It will enhance their capacity to adjust to structural changes and long-term trends, to undertake the progressive diversification of their economies and to expand the secondary stages of production based on the processing of commodities.

Commodity Coverage

The programme proposed would cover a sufficiently wide range of commodities of importance in the external trade of developing countries. To this end, a list of 17 commodities has been suggested. In total, these 17 commodities represent about three-quarters of the value of agricultural and mineral commodities, other than petroleum, exported from developing countries. Moreover, developed countries have a substantial trade interest in international market arrangements for these commodities. It may be noted that five of the commodities are covered by international agreements of one kind or another.

The list of commodities includes the ten "core" commodities on which attention has been focussed as storable products suitable for international stocking schemes, and on which the elaboration of the proposals for a common fund for financing stocks is based.[2] Of the ten "core" commodities—which together account for about 75 percent of the export value from developing countries of all 17 commodities—the trend in the real value of exports was practically zero or negative over the period 1953-1972 for seven commodities.[3] As regards the remaining three "core" commodities, the upward trend in the real value of exports was about 2 percent a year for sugar, while only for copper and tin did the growth rate in real exports exceed that rate (see table 1).

The ten "core" commodities also include many which exhibit excessive annual fluctuations in both prices and in export earnings of developing countries. Such fluctuations have been particularly prominent in the world markets for coffee, cocoa, sugar, rubber, jute, sisal, and copper.

The list shown in table 1 is not meant to be exclusive, and there are other commodities that merit international action. In any case, the decision on the list must remain the responsibility of governments. It should be stressed, however, that within the limitations of time, resources and past consideration of appropriate remedial action, it appears essential that the first phase of an integrated programme should concentrate on a selection of commodities for which early action would bring much-needed relief from the critical foreign exchange situation faced by many developing countries.

International Stocks

The establishment and operation of international stocks constitute a central feature of the proposals for an integrated programme. For each of the ten "core" commodities, it is proposed that the negotiation of international stocking arrangements should be undertaken, or existing stocking arrangements reviewed and, where necessary, strengthened. For some of these commodities, negotiations could lead to the immediate acquisition of

Table 1. Proposed commodity coverage of the integrated programme

	Exports from developing countries						
	Rates of growth 1953-1972			Indices of fluctuations 1953-1972 a/			Value in 1972
	Market prices	Value	Deflated value b/	Market prices	Value	Deflated value b/	
	(Per cent per annum)			(Per cent)			($ billion)
1. "Core" commodities							
Coffee	-1.6	1.0	-0.4	17.0	11.1	9.2	3.0
Cocoa	-1.3	1.7	0.2	23.0	13.4	12.6	0.7
Tea	-1.9	0.0	-1.5	6.2	5.5	6.0	0.6
Sugar	0.2	3.8	2.2	33.4	9.2	7.5	2.2
Cotton	-0.7	1.1	-0.4	8.2	9.1	7.9	1.8
Rubber	-3.2	-1.7	-3.1	13.2	14.7	14.4	0.9
Jute	1.9	0.7	-0.8	11.9	12.2	14.1	0.7 c/
Sisal	-1.2	-0.3	-1.8	18.0	26.3	28.6	0.1
Copper	4.0	7.8	6.2	21.5	17.1	17.5	2.4
Tin	4.0	5.2	3.6	7.9	18.8	10.4	0.6
2. Other commodities							
Wheat	..	-2.8	-4.2	4.7	28.6	31.1	0.2
Rice	0.5	0.3	-1.2	11.3	12.9	14.8	0.4
Bananas	-0.9	3.9	2.4	4.3	7.7	7.2	0.6
Beef and veal	6.9	12.0	10.3	20.8	15.4	15.1	1.4 d/
Wool	-2.0	-3.6	-5.0	11.4	10.2	12.5	0.2
Bauxite	2.6	8.1	6.5	4.7	8.8	10.8	0.5 e/
Iron ore	-2.4	9.3	7.7	8.3	10.8	12.3	1.0
Total	..	..	..	..	..	..	17.3

Sources: UNCTAD, *Monthly Commodity Price Bulletin* various vols., (Geneva: UNCTAD); FAO, *Trade Yearbook*: various vols. (Rome: FAO); national statistics.

a/ The fluctuation index is the average over the period of differences between annual observations and calculated trend values (irrespective of sign) expressed as percentages of the trend value.

b/ Export value deflated by UN unit value index for world exports of manufactured goods.

c/ Including jute manufactures.

d/ Including cattle.

e/ "Prices" are export unit values; value in 1972 includes alumina.

stocks in order to support agreed minimum price levels; for others, new schemes could be established, or existing ones strengthened, to deal with downward price movements and excessive supplies when these emerged.

International stocking policies are desirable for a number of other commodities in addition to the ten "core" commodities. The most important of these is the group of food grains, for which action to ensure adequate global reserves and more stable prices has been under intensive international examination since the food crisis of 1972/1973. A comprehensive policy to improve the food supplies of developing countries would need to include stocking provisions which gave developing countries assurance of supplies at reasonable prices and without disruption of food aid.

For each commodity, the size of an international stock would need to be carefully assessed with a view to providing assurance of adequate supplies at all times, preventing excessive price fluctuations, and providing assurance of disposal of production undertaken on the basis of a realistic assessment of demand. For most, or all, of the arrangements for individual commodities involving provisions for the establishment of international stocks, the stock mechanism would need to be combined with other market regulation techniques, as appropriate. In particular, for commodities facing unsatisfactory price trends, the stock mechanism will need support by some form of supply management, such as an export or production regulation arrangement, in order to achieve a remunerative level of prices for the producers.

Common Fund

Rationale. Hitherto, the establishment of an international stock negotiated in the framework of a commodity agreement has been dependent upon ad hoc financing arrangements. These arrangements have generally placed the burden of finance on the producers, while the amount of finance made available has tended to be inadequate. Moreover, proposals for the establishment of international stocks have sometimes not received serious consideration because of their financial implications. On the basis of past experience, it would seem that the effort to establish a series of international stocks for major traded commodities, as envisaged in the integrated programme, will be seriously constrained unless an adequate and assured source of finance is readily available.

The proposal to set up a common fund is intended to remove this constraint. The existence of such a fund would allow the negotiation of international stocking schemes to go forward unhampered by the particular financial difficulties of individual participating countries under ad hoc systems of financing. The availability of finance would exercise a catalytic role in stimulating new commodity stocking arrangements, and would thereby give a much-needed stimulus to the early completion of the round of individual commodity negotiations envisaged in the integrated programme.

The establishment of a common fund would constitute a major improvement in the existing international institutional arrangements relating to primary commodity markets. As an operational instrument which could take an overall view of the problems of the world commodity economy, the common fund could inject a new dynamism into international commodity policy. If it disposed of adequate funds, it could take needed action, as governments may agree, to support weak commodity markets, encouraging remedial measures to achieve balance between supply and demand. The establishment of the fund would provide an opportunity to create decision-making machinery which would provide developing, as well as developed, countries with an appropriate share of responsibility in the formulation of operational policies.

Mode of operation. The primary function of the common fund would be to lend to individual commodity organizations operating international stocks, under appropriate conditions. It is these organizations which would trade in individual commodities by buying and selling, and which would own and dispose of the international stocks. The fund would lend to the commodity organizations as they need finance to buy stocks, and would be repaid as the organizations acquire funds from stock disposals.

The exact financial relationship between the common fund and individual commodity organizations would be a matter for negotiation between the fund and the organization concerned, taking into account the specific needs of the particular commodity scheme. Moreover, the future of self-financing arrangements, where these existed, would need to be considered in the light of the advantages mentioned in the following paragraph.

By acting as a central source of finance for all the various commodity organizations, the common fund would be in a position to obtain better terms of borrowing on capital markets than would the individual commodity organizations, as it would pool and reduce the risks and its bargaining strength would be greater. Moreover, the common fund required to operate a given number of separate stocking schemes would be smaller than the aggregate of the funds required by individually financed commodity stocks, since a common fund could take advantage of the different phasing of financial flows into and out of individual stocking accounts. In addition, a system of common financing would require the schemes to hold less liquid funds on average over time than would be necessary for ad hoc financing.

Cost of establishing a common fund. An examination of the probable cost of initial acquisitions of stocks for the ten "core" commodities, together with an allowance for other commodities (except grains) for which international stocks would be suitable, indicates that an aggregate capital fund of $3 billion would be required. Of this total, $1 billion could be provided as paid-up risk capital and $2 billion as loans. It is also proposed that governments should undertake a further commitment of $3 billion—again with $1 billion in the form of paid-up capital and $2 billion as loans—to be on call if and when needed. Thus, it is envisaged that the major portion of the capital for the common fund would be loans carrying interest charges, since the operation is regarded as essentially self-financing.

It is envisaged that the call-up of capital would be linked to the negotiation and operational requirements of the various international stocks to be set up. Thus, the commitment of capital to the common fund would not involve governments setting aside large financial resources before the negotiations of individual commodity schemes were completed, any more than it would in the case of direct contributions under ad hoc financing of such schemes.

Sources of funds. It is proposed that the paid-up capital of the common fund should be subscribed by countries which are importers or exporters of the commodities to be covered by the integrated programme, while it is envisaged that countries—such as certain petroleum exporters—in balance of payments surplus would extend long-term loans to the fund.

Thus countries which export or import the commodities in question, and which stand to benefit from the integrated programme—as a result of reduced market instability, a smoother flow of supplies, or more remunerative prices—would be expected to contribute, the basis of contribution being subject to negotiation. However, special measures in favour of "least developed" and "most seriously affected" developing countries which are exporters or importers of the commodities covered by international arrangements established under the integrated programme should be an accepted feature of such arrangements. Such measures might include exemption from the obligation to contribute to the capital of the common fund, and specially favourable treatment in the allocation of export quotas should an export regulation scheme be adopted.

It is anticipated that the long-term loans to the capital of the common fund that could be made by a number of petroleum-exporting countries would be encouraged, since investment in international stocks would be backed by attractive collateral with reasonable rates of return.

Other Measures in Commodity Agreements

The operation of international stocks will generally need to be supported by other measures in commodity agreements. In the case of non-storable commodities, reliance would have to be placed on measures other than stock operation.

Among these measures would be supply management by producers and, wherever feasible, multilateral trade commitments by both consumers and producers. These two techniques, applied in conjunction with stocks as appropriate, would be the principal means of achieving long-term equilibrium of demand and supply at prices which, in real terms, are remunerative to producers and equitable to consumers. For the management of supply, export quotas might be necessary, but techniques such as uniform *ad valorem* export taxes or minimum export price schemes, and co-ordination of diversification and investment plans could also be considered. Multilateral commitments would be particularly useful for facilitating longer-term planning of resource use and investment and for providing greater assurance of trade volume and export income.

By means of stocking, supply management or trade commitments, or by combinations of these measures, it should be possible, for some commodities at least, to achieve the objective of maintaining prices at adequate levels in real terms. Price targets in commodity arrangements would have to be flexible, however, to enable account to be taken of structural changes in supply or demand, though in some cases it might not be possible to prevent a deterioration in the trend of price in real terms, especially if world inflation continues to be relatively rapid.

In such cases, therefore, alternative means would have to be sought to achieve orderly adjustment in supply while maintaining the import purchasing power of developing countries exporting the commodities concerned. In some cases provision might be made within commodity arrangements for short-term financial assistance to developing exporters, linked perhaps to diversification or other measures of adjustment.

For primary commodities produced under protection, such as cereals, sugar and meat, improvements in access to markets should be provided for within the framework of international arrangements. Furthermore, arrangements for a number of commodities should provide for the reduction of barriers to imports of the processed forms of the commodities with which they are concerned.

Various additional measures will be required to meet the particular circumstances of individual commodity markets. Such measures would range from promotion of consumption to activities designed to define principles of international behaviour that can be monitored and elaborated through an international arrangement, for example, with regard to codes of conduct on trade restriction or discrimination, and to the treatment of processed products in trade. In addition, for a wide group of commodities, co-ordinated efforts to stimulate research and development of natural products facing competition with synthetics would be valuable, so that developing country producers in general would be able to take full advantage of the more stable and expansionary conditions of trade encouraged by the economic provisions of commodity agreements.

Negotiated price ranges. In the present period of continuing high rates of inflation—a period likely to persist for some years ahead—any price range initially fixed in money terms will become significantly eroded in real terms after a relatively brief period. To safeguard the real earnings of the commodity exports of developing countries, therefore, the agreements setting up the market regulatory mechanisms envisaged in the integrated programme should have provisions for periodic review and adjustment of the initial price ranges agreed upon to allow for the effects of inflation. Such provisions would constitute an application of the concept of indexation within the framework of internationally agreed techniques of regulation of primary commodity markets. Without such indexation provisions, any agreement on price ranges would rapidly lose its meaning.[4]

Commodity-by-commodity negotiations. The agreements for the individual commodities to be covered by the integrated programme will have to be separately negotiated in view of the wide differences in their conditions of supply and demand, in the degree of price instability, in the trend of prices and in the nature of the institutional structures involved. It should be emphasized, however, that the undertaking of such commodity-by-commodity negotiations within the framework of an integrated programme would constitute a marked break with the traditional practice of negotiating in isolation arrangements for individual commodities.

On the basis of past experience, it is evident that this traditional approach has had only very limited success, and suffers from a number of major weaknesses. First, it has resulted in market regulation agreements for only a few commodities, to the neglect of the majority. Thus, the benefits of market regulation have accrued to certain countries, and not to others. Second, a commodity negotiation taken in isolation inevitably gives undue prominence to narrow commercial and short-term national interests at the expense of the longer-term interests of the world commodity economy, and of the need to strengthen the commodity sectors of developing countries. Third, the traditional approach provides no opportunity for individual countries to strike a balance of advantage over a whole range of commodity negotiations.

By its comprehensive coverage of a wide range of commodities of trading interest to a large number of countries, both developed and developing, and by the proposed organization of individual negotiations within the framework of an agreed time scale and common principles and procedures, the integrated approach can be expected to overcome the various weaknesses of the traditional commodity-by-commodity approach.

Compensatory Financing of Export Fluctuations

The price and earnings stabilization that can be achieved through international commodity arrangements will need to be supplemented by a strengthened system of compensatory financing of export fluctuations, in order to deal with the circumstances of individual countries. For example, stable world market prices may not stabilize earnings for an individual country if its exports are adversely affected by poor crops. Improved compensatory financing would therefore be an essential component of the integrated programme, to offset residual fluctuations in the earnings of individual developing countries from their commodity exports as a whole.

An adequate system of compensatory financing in the context of the integrated programme for commodities would require considerable improvements in the existing International Monetary Fund (IMF) facility or the creation of a new facility. The IMF facility, as operated up to the end of

1975, proved inadequate in several major respects. An expanded and liberalized IMF facility came into operation from the beginning of 1976, which is expected to lead to increased use of the facility to about $1 billion in the current year.[5]

However, drawing on past experience of the IMF facility, and taking account of its recent enlargement, as well as the principles underlying the STABEX scheme operating under the Lomé Convention,[6] it would appear that a number of major improvements are still required for the facility to become fully adequate as a component of the integrated programme. First, the special difficulties in commodity sectors of developing country exports point to the need to compensate for shortfalls either on the basis of the total commodity exports of the country or on the basis of all merchandise exports, whichever shortfall is the larger. Secondly, shortfalls in real export earnings should be the basis for compensation, aiming at the smoothing of the trend in the purchasing power of exports. Thirdly, the problems that give rise to the need for compensatory financing warrant provision for more liberal terms of financial assistance than is provided on the ordinary lending terms of the IMF. This can appropriately be achieved by introducing a grant element into compensatory financing and linking repayment of compensatory loans to recovery in export earnings over a longer period than the medium-term financing currently available, such easing of terms and conditions to apply particularly for the poorest developing countries. Fourthly, the solution of difficulties caused by export fluctuations should not be made conditional on the immediate balance of payments situation, and thus on the requirement of a narrowly-defined balance of payments test.

The question of the need for entirely new arrangements for offsetting residual fluctuations in the commodity export earnings of developing countries would depend on whether governments find it possible to amend the IMF facility to the necessary extent, as well as on their attitude towards wider participation on compensatory financing arrangements.

Related Issues

Marketing and Distribution Systems

The institutional arrangements for the marketing and distribution of the primary commodity exports of developing countries have an important bearing on the benefit which these countries derive from their export trade, as well as on their degree of control over the exploitation of their natural resources. The technical characteristics of the marketing and distribution systems vary considerably among the various primary commodity markets. For some, sales at auctions are a central feature, while for others much of the trade is handled under medium- or long-term contracts, or consists of "captive" trade within the same firm or financial entity.

A major feature of the post-war development of the marketing and distribution of the primary commodity exports of developing countries has been the growing influence of the large transnational corporations based in developed countries. These corporations now control, in one form or another, a substantial proportion of the foreign trade of developing countries. In some cases, the transnationals or their affiliates have also become producers of primary commodities in developing countries, so that they are able to transfer commodities to the parent company at internal book-keeping prices which maximize the global profit of the multinational operation as a whole.

The transnational corporations involved in the commodity trade of developing countries can generally exercise considerable bargaining power since they singly or taken together control the international marketing and distribution network, while they are typically faced with a large number of competing sellers of the commodity in developing countries. Where transnational corporations are substantially involved in the export trade of developing countries, the return to the individual producer has been generally inadequate in real terms. For a range of such commodities for which data are available, the share of developing countries in the final consumer price is of the order of 10-15 percent, indicating that the greater part of the value added in the production and distribution of food and raw materials accrues to firms, often vertically integrated, domiciled in developed countries.

For many commodity markets dominated by transnational corporations, the situation is characterized by competition in the final product market combined with a monopsonistic position of each corporation as buyer of the commodity from developing country producers. As a result, prices are kept at competitive levels in consumer countries, while the need of the transnational corporation to maximize its global profit provides the incentive for it to use its superior bargaining power to keep the remuneration of the producers in developing countries at a relatively low level.

The geographical diversification of the production and trading interests of the transnational corporations over the past decade has provided these firms with greater flexibility in most global operations. The ability to switch to alternative sources of supply confers great bargaining power on a transnational corporation buying in a given developing country. The development of effective countervailing power on the part of the producers cannot therefore be based on action by individual countries alone.

In recent years, there have been a number of cases of co-operative action taken by groups of producing countries to increase their bargaining power in their economic relations with transnational corporations, and to enhance their degree of participation in the international marketing and distribution of their commodity exports. In some cases, increased participation may be gained by joint ventures with the transnational corporations concerned. In other cases, a more equitable share of the benefits of trade may be derived by uniformly applied fiscal policies by governments of producing countries. In some situations, a more radical approach would involve the purchase, either in full or to an extent sufficient to provide policy control, of existing foreign enterprises which market the commodity exports of developing countries.

Producers' Associations

Increasing co-operation among commodity producing countries, both unilaterally and in conjunction with consuming countries, will be needed to bring the integrated programme to fruition. The producers have a potentially key role because most of the instruments envisaged in the programme are capable of activation by the producers themselves. Export quotas under existing international agreements have been operated essentially under agreement among producers, the role of consuming countries being to "police" their implementation. Again, the international buffer stocks so far established have been financed almost entirely by the producing countries themselves.

More effective and more comprehensive regulation of primary commodity markets will require closer co-ordination of the interests of the producing countries. The establishment of producers' associations is essentially a recognition of this need. Such associations (some of which include developed, as well as developing, producing countries) exist for a range of important commodities of export interest to developing countries. By the formulation and implementation of common policies, the activities of producers' associations can introduce an element of countervailing power to the market strength currently exercised by transnational corporations in a number of primary commodity markets. Thus, a better balance of market forces should emerge, one which allows developing producing countries to retain a more equitable share of the benefits of international commodity trade than is the case at present.

In addition, producers' associations could play a central role in the formulation of a suitable package of measures to be applied in the regulation of the commodity markets with which they are concerned. Such preparatory work would facilitate the series of negotiations on individual commodities among all interested trading countries, both producers and consumers, and would materially contribute to a speedy conclusion of such negotiations.

Indexation of Prices

Safeguarding the purchasing power of developing countries. The integrated programme for commodities can be conceived as a central element in a wider effort by the international community to restructure the world community economy so as to accelerate the development of the Third World. In this context, an important complement to the integrated programme would be the establishment of additional mechanisms designed to safeguard the purchasing power of the aggregate exports of individual developing countries.

Though the International Development Strategy for the 1970s embodied a target rate of growth of 7 percent a year for the real export earnings[7] of developing countries, actual performance so far in the present decade has fallen far short of this target for a large number of developing countries. Over the period from 1970 to 1974, almost 40 countries, accounting for half the total population of the Third World, experienced an annual rate of increase of less than 7 percent in the purchasing power of their export earnings over manufactured imports. Of these, 16 countries suffered absolute declines in real export earnings, while for a further eight countries the corresponding growth rates were below 4 percent a year. Present indications are that the position deteriorated sharply in 1975, with many more countries suffering substantial deterioration in the real value of their exports.

Trends in the purchasing power of exports are a result of the corresponding trends in export volume and in the terms of trade of the exporting country concerned. No single developing country, as a rule, has the power to influence either of these elements by its own policies. The volume of exports of many primary commodities is constrained to an important extent by agricultural protectionism in developed countries as well as by relatively low income and price elasticities of demand. Where, however, these constraints are not important, as for minerals and metals, notable increases in the volume of exports have been achieved. For manufactures, too, there are widespread tariff and non-tariff barriers to developing country exports to the markets of developed countries.

The terms of trade of developing countries are heavily influenced by economic conditions in the developed market economy countries. Recession in the latter countries, by reducing demand for consumption and stock accumulation, tends to result in price falls for primary commodities, whereas inflation in developed countries results in increased prices of essential industrial products purchased by developing countries. The combination of recession and inflation in the developed market economies has been a major factor in the sharp deterioration in both the merchandise trade balance and the purchasing power of exports of a large number of developing countries since the end of 1973.

It has already been suggested that market regulation agreements for individual commodities should include provisions for periodic review and adjustment of the price ranges initially agreed, in the light of the effects of inflation on the prices of manufactured goods imported by producing countries. Such adjustment, which may be termed "direct indexation," could make a substantial contribution to the objective of safeguarding the real earnings of developing countries from their primary commodity exports. Essentially, it would involve provisions, within the framework of an international commodity agreement, for the adjustment of aggregate supply in relation to demand, so as to maintain the price within an agreed range in terms of its purchasing power over manufactured goods. Supply regulation could be supported in some cases, where bilateral or multilateral contracts between governments or private firms cover an important part of world trade in a commodity, by appropriate provision for adjustment of the contract price to allow for inflation.

Direct indexation of commodity prices would, however, be feasible only for those commodities for which effective market control is established in the framework of international agreements, such control being exercised by means of supply regulation in addition to other techniques such as buffer stocks. Moreover, the degree of success in indexation by supply regulation would vary from commodity to commodity.

Consequently, since direct indexation by market regulation cannot be expected to cover effectively more than a certain range of commodities, consideration needs to be given to complementary measures to achieve the indexation objective. Such complementary measures could consist of an arrangement under which exporting developing countries would receive financial compensation for any shortfall of the market price of specific commodity exports below an indexed reference price.

Indexation-techniques. For those commodities for which direct indexation on a commodity-by-commodity basis could be effected, it would be necessary to link[8] prices of the exports of developing countries to some indicator of the purchasing power of these exports. This indicator might take any of several forms, each of which would lead to a quite distinct version of indexation. Thus, the indicator might be costs of production of the exported commodities, world prices of manufactured products incorporating these commodities, or prices of imports into the developing countries.[9] The last-mentioned form seems to be the most appropriate if indexation is viewed as having universal application. It would affect more directly than any of the other commodity-by-commodity variants the terms of trade of the developing countries, and the indexation formula could be adjusted to cover imports into all or only particular groups of developing countries (e.g., those exporting a given commodity), and from all or only particular groups of developed countries. The other versions mentioned above may be suitable in certain instances where, for example, the primary commodity requires relatively standardized techniques of production, so that costs of production can be readily identified, or when the primary commodity is used in producing a single major product.[10]

For the year (or quarter or month) in which indexation commenced (the reference period), there would be established a reference price for the commodity to be indexed. This initial level of the reference price should be one considered appropriate in relation to the level of prices of imported goods at the time the scheme began. It could be based upon some agreed "normal" terms of trade ratio for the commodity concerned, derived from historical values of that ratio, or it could be an estimate of the true equilibrium level of the price or of a "fair" or "remunerative" price in existing market circumstances. These would be matters for negotiation in the initial phase of any indexation scheme. Provision would have to be made to review these reference levels in the light of changed market conditions, at periodic intervals or whenever an agreed number of parties to the scheme so requested.

Whatever the method employed for determining the initial level of the reference price, however, its future level would be determined automatically by a simple formula relating movements in the reference price proportionately to movements in the price index of imported goods, with intervention by the appropriate bodies to ensure that the market price was kept throughout as close as possible to the reference price.[11]

Commodity coverage. The commodities for which direct indexation might be attempted are those whose supply could be effectively controlled. Such control might be based *inter alia* on buffer stocks, production regulation, export quotas or uniform export taxes; the suitability of these different forms of control would vary from one commodity to another. Whatever the mechanism, the scope for price control, through supply regulation, would clearly be greatest for those commodities facing relatively price-inelastic demand; for other commodities the effects of price changes introduced via direct indexation might induce more-than-offsetting changes in the volume of the commodity exported.

Supply control might be achieved within the framework of international commodity agreements. For the two commodities for which international agreements incorporating market regulation already exist—cocoa and tin—it would in principle be possible to negotiate pricing provisions which embraced the objectives of indexation. As both producing and consuming countries participate in these agreements, both parties would have to accept such provisions. Indexation clauses might also be written into any further international commodity agreements which might be negotiated in the future.

Where international commodity agreements prove impossible to achieve, indexation might be effected by co-operation among exporting countries. In the cases of bananas,[12] bauxite, coffee, copper, phosphates and tea, in addition to the obvious case of petroleum, the bulk of exports is from developing countries. For commodities like iron ore, manganese ore and sugar, which are exported to a substantial extent by developed as well as developing countries, the co-operation of the former countries would be essential in the regulation of supplies for the purpose of indexation.

There remain a number of commodities facing inelastic demand conditions for which supply regulation would be difficult to achieve, either because the commodities are perishable (such as fruits), and so cannot be stored, or because they are produced by a large number of independent producers (as in the case of oilseeds and oils). Direct indexation for such commodities would be feasible if a single body could be established by producing and consuming countries which would act as both buyer and seller of all such produce entering the world market. Consequently, in these cases, indirect indexation, linked to price (and possibly quantity) norms, would appear to be more suitable than direct indexation.

In the case of commodities such as cotton, wool, rubber and hard fibres, which are subject to competition from synthetic substitutes, the prices of the substitutes set upper limits to the prices that can be obtained for the natural commodities. The prices of synthetics, however, are themselves likely to be subject to upward pressures in conditions of inflation. Hence, provided supplies of the natural commodities can be effectively regulated (for example, by means of buffer stocks) it should be possible at least to keep their prices in line with those of the competing synthetics.

The income transfer effects of indirect indexation on a commodity-by-commodity basis would be different from those of indirect indexation on a country-by-country basis. Under the latter approach, the transfer payments would be calculated, on the basis of the shortfall of the total export earnings of a country, in real terms, from an agreed norm;[13] above-norm earnings on some export items would be offset against below-norm earnings on others.[14] Under the commodity-by-commodity approach, however, there would be no such offsetting, since payments to exporting countries would be related to the shortfalls of market prices of individual commodities from their price norms, with no account taken of commodities whose prices exceeded their norms. In order to avoid open-ended commitments, however, quantity norms for each commodity and each country would also probably be set, and shortfall payments would not be made for quantities exported above these limits.

Economic consequences of indexation. Direct or indirect indexation of primary commodity prices could be an effective means of protecting developing countries from a deterioration in their commodity terms of trade caused by the spread of inflation among the developed market economy countries, a matter over which the developing countries have no control. It would also provide a stimulus to developed market economy countries to reduce their rates of domestic inflation, in so far as the rate of increase of the prices of their primary commodity imports would decline *pari passu* with reductions in the rate of increase of the prices of their export good due to inflation.

The evidence adduced in the study suggests that indexation would increase only marginally the rate of international inflation.[15] Moreover, indexation would not itself be a generator of inflation, since it would merely be a response to inflation generated within the industrialized countries as a group, independently of events and policies in the developing countries.

Of more importance would be the possible effect of indexation in increasing the pressures currently felt on their balances of payments by some industrialized countries heavily dependent upon food and raw materials imports. The international repercussions of these national balance-of-payments pressures would depend upon the policies adopted for dealing with them. If the policies included reductions in direct aid flows to the developing countries, they would tend to cancel out the advantages of indexation to the developing countries as a whole, although their impact on individual developing countries would probably be uneven. Moreover, as some developing countries are themselves substantial importers of primary commodities, measures would be necessary to offset or avoid any deterioration of these countries' balances of payments which might be caused by indexation.

Direct indexation, by requiring the regulation of commodity prices, would lead to a certain rigidity of the commodity price structure as well as of the relationship between prices of commodities and manufactured goods and thus to a different allocation of resources in developing countries than would otherwise obtain. The price structure resulting from indexation should therefore be kept under review in order to prevent any misallocation of resources, which would lead, for example, to overproduction, and to take account of changing demand conditions, such as shifts in consumer tastes.

At the same time, by reducing the short-term instability of commodity prices and thus creating conditions for a more stable supply of indexed commodities, indexation could lead to an improved international allocation of resources. Moreover, depending upon the initial levels of the reference prices, it might lead to a more economical use of non-renewable resources, with consequent longer-term benefits for the world community. Finally, indexation, by maintaining the purchasing power of developing countries, which are an important market for the exports of the developed countries, could counteract any tendency to a contraction of world trade.

Notes

1. Regular consultations between producers and consumers have taken place for many years both in the Food and Agricultural Organization (FAO)

and UNCTAD, and in various autonomous commodity bodies, for a number of commodities not subject to formal international agreements. Such consultations have taken place in producer-consumer forums covering tea, jute, rubber, cotton, wool, hard fibres, rice, vegetable oils and oilseeds, and bananas, among agricultural commodities, and lead, zinc and tungsten among minerals.

2. These ten "core" commodities are cocoa, coffee, copper, cotton, jute, rubber, sisal, sugar, tea, and tin.
3. Coffee, cocoa, tea, cotton, rubber, jute, and sisal.
4. For further discussion of the indexation issue see pp. 147-152.
5. The expanded IMF facility provides for a larger amount of loans than under the previous facility, the calculation of shortfalls for compensation will be based on trends that give weight to past growth in exports, while more flexible procedures are introduced in the processing of requests for assistance. However, the IMF has made stricter the rules for early repayment, and has maintained the 3-5 year limits on final repayment.
6. For a detailed discussion of the STABEX scheme, see Chapter 10 below. Footnote added by the editors.
7. The term "real export earnings" is used interchangeably with "purchasing power of export."
8. The aim of indexation might be to stabilize the terms of trade of each exported commodity or merely to defend a floor level of the terms of trade for the commodity. The latter (price support) objectives would normally involve only upward adjustment in the export prices of commodities, whereas the stabilization objective might require downward adjustments from time to time, if the purchasing power indicator were to decline. In this report it is assumed that the objective is stabilization, unless otherwise specified.
9. The last-mentioned indicator would require the use of one index or a combination of import price indices which are readily available, but such indices are of imperfect quality. The construction of a new index more suited to the purposes of indexation is desirable. The wide dispersion of measured price changes according to the various existing import price indices, however, suggests the need for a careful evaluation of the most appropriate index to use, including an index of generalized inflation. One possibility for this last type of index might be a simplified standard index relating to prices of a selected number of the more essential manufactured goods of import interest to all developing countries.

There are, moreover, a number of problems associated with export price series for commodities. A significant flow of trade in many commodities is not carried out through long-term contracts and through internal transfers within transnational enterprises. Thus, the prices quoted on the residual free markets may apply only to a small share of trade in some commodities, and

this factor must be taken into account in determining the export price which is to be indexed. For example, the "major producers' price," at which most zinc is traded outside North America, is but one-half of the London Metal Exchange price: the US producers' price for copper is about 20 percent less than the corresponding London Metal Exchange price; and so on. For further examples see OECD, *Economic Outlook* (Paris: OECD, 1974), p. 32.
10. Jamaica has recently linked its taxation of bauxite producers to the price of aluminium ingot.
11. In the case of a price support version of direct indexation intervention would be confined to preventing the market price from falling below the reference price.
12. It should be noted that the substitution elasticity for bananas is relatively high, and hence any producer agreement aimed at raising prices would have to be implemented with caution.
13. The norm for total earnings would be calculated on the basis of an agreed quantity, multiplied by the (indexed) reference price, of each of the country's export items. It would thus automatically increase as the purchasing power indicator referred to on page 149.
14. The compensatory financing facility of the IMF, which is not based upon the concept of indexation, reflects the country-by-country approach in which above-norm earnings offset below-norm earnings. Furthermore, this facility provides only short-term relief in the form of repayable, interest-bearing loans, and is conditional upon the borrowing country's agreeing to follow internal policies approved by the Fund.
15. The OECD secretariat has estimated that in 1974, after the full effects of the commodity price boom are accounted for, the aggregate impact of the rises in the import unit values of commodities, other than oil, including non-ferrous metals, will merely be to "add another 1 percent to the Total Domestic Expenditure price deflator of the OECD area as a whole." See OECD, *Economic Outlook* (Paris, OECD, 1974), pp. 29 and 37.

9 *Administered Commodity Markets: The Search for Stability*

Wolfgang Hager

Commodity Markets

Any producer seeks to maximize returns and to stabilize the conditions under which products are marketed. The producer of manufactures can adjust price and output in response to short-term accurate information. A good part of the adjustment is borne by others: the public purse pays for idled labor while suppliers of raw and intermediate inputs lose markets. Moreover, manufacturers can achieve a built-in stability of demand for their products through product differentiation, oligopolistic price and market-sharing agreements, and long-term supply contracts which are commonly practised by large corporations.

In the past, when production was largely in the hands of private firms, some of these mechanisms even worked in the field of raw materials. Integrated enterprises all but solved the problem of price and market stability. Where this was not the case, producer manipulation of international prices via the metal exchanges—e.g., the lead and zinc producers bidding for their own product on the London Metal Exchange and stockpiling metal in the London Metal Exchange warehouses, and oligopolistic price discipline prevented prices falling to uneconomic levels, as well as rising to levels that would jeopardize the market share of one metal relative to others.

By contrast, given the multitude of producers in the field of agricultural raw materials—tin represents an analogue among the minerals—stabilization (where it was attempted at all) has here almost always involved governments.[1] This stabilization could take the form of production controls (U.S. wheat), national marketing boards (Australian wool), or both (Brazilian coffee). In most cases, stockpiles were a necessary adjunct to stabilization. As soon as a significant noncolonial trade in commodities developed in the twentieth century, the advantages of cooperative market stabilization by several producers led to attempts at international commodity stabilization. One of the most successful of such attempts was the rubber cartel run by the British and Dutch enterprises in the interwar years—until price gouging triggered the development of synthetic rubber in the U.S., depriving the natural product of two-thirds of its market.

The depression of the 1930s caused a dramatic decline in raw material prices and led to the proliferation of generally unsuccessful schemes of price setting and export restraints by producers' associations. With the 1937 International Sugar Agreement, consumers began to participate, in a limited way, in market stabilization. Such attempts were expanded in the postwar years. Virtually the only role, so far, played by consuming countries in support for stabilization schemes was to help police export quotas negotiated with and among the producing countries, i.e., to help a weak cartel to prevent cheating by its members. The most notable example was the Third International Coffee Agreement (1962-1972), through which the consuming countries may have transferred $600 million to the producing countries.[2]

What the consuming countries have failed to do, so far, is to participate in the financial burden of market stabilization: the cost of stockpiling needed when production exceeds export quotas continues to fall entirely on the producing countries. This also applies to the one commodity agreement with a jointly administered buffer stock, the International Tin Agreement, although the renegotiated agreement of 1975 envisages voluntary contributions to buffer-stock finance by France and the Netherlands.

This is not the place for a comprehensive assessment of past attempts to stabilize commodity markets. Most analysts agree that a high degree of economic sophistication, sufficient discipline by the participants, and substantial buffer stocks are preconditions. These conditions have not been present in past schemes.

Economic sophistication among the participating countries is not unrelated to the discipline required for successful market management. The great stress that producers' associations like IBA (bauxite), CIPEC (copper) or OIEC (iron ore) place on the exchange of information points to this relationship. The chances for discipline are also enhanced through regional suborganizations in charge of commodity policy which are being set up in many parts of the Third World and which create broad political linkages. Third World solidarity as such, on the other hand, is unlikely to contribute significantly to restraint by producers—witness the unwillingness of East African tea producers to forego plans to expand production to the detriment of the established Indian producers.

While it is open to question whether the objective conditions for successful commodity agreements have improved, there can be little doubt that the need for them has grown substantially in recent years. The refusal by the developing countries and other raw material producers to bear, by themselves, the full economic risks and costs associated with interdependence will be the most effective political force pushing toward administered commodity markets in the future. It is worth pointing out that the U.S.—the world's greatest commodity exporter—refuses to bear the cost of market instability (inflation) and stabilization (buffer stocks) by herself: she is busily negotiating an international grain reserve system with strong participation by consuming countries, and she has concluded long-term purchasing agreements with the Soviet Union and Japan which bear a striking resemblance to the purchase commitment approach suggested in the UN Conference on Trade and Development's (UNCTAD's) integrated program.[3]

The Interest of the Consumer Countries

What is less clearly recognized is the objective interest of consuming countries to contribute toward commodity market stabilization. To make this point, a short digression on the current situation in the field of resource investment is necessary.

In the early 1970s, a number of economic and political factors combined to produce a potentially grave threat to the availability of mineral raw materials by the end of the decade: investment in the exploration and development of new resources showed a relative decline. Generally speaking, the problem arises from the fact that virtually no raw-material-producing country, developed or developing, can generate sufficient capital to develop its own deposits. Hence, outside capital and outside technology must be brought in.

In the past, this presented few problems, at least not in market economies. Direct private investment from consumer to producer countries made up for the deficiency. In the last decade, however, the world's entire minerals sector has been taken out of the rules of the game summed up in the term "liberal world economy." Instead, governments have been, or are now, taking over a large part of the economic decision making and even the managerial tasks formerly left to private enterprise. Yet, private companies remain essential. The result is a systemic clash that is highly dysfunctional to the orderly development of future supplies.

To start with the simplest consequence, it now takes much longer to negotiate exploration and production contracts. This causes delays of several years. Such contracts now cover such items as production obligations, the ratio of reinvested and repatriated profits, state participation, and the degree of processing to be done locally in addition to the tax and royalty provisions that have always been part of such agreements. Furthermore, there is an increasingly wide gap between governments and companies in the perception of the profitability of a given deposit. This gap is not only due to the capacity of enterprises to make superprofits on some deposits to balance out their marginal operations elsewhere. A government, understandably, looks at the domestic cost picture and tries to pocket the possible economic rent in the form of taxes and royalties. However, given the greater contacts among producer governments and the public nature of the contracts (because of their importance to domestic politics), the most favorable contract quickly becomes the norm for all new contracts concluded. It also becomes the basis for the renegotiation of old contracts, even where economic conditions are less favorable.

At the same time, in order to be attracted by new investment opportunities, enterprises now require a much higher level of profitability than in the past. This is primarily due to the uncertainty regarding future ownership and/or the degree of autonomy in the exploitation of deposits. Whereas companies used to assess profitability against the total lifetime of a deposit, e.g., fifteen or twenty years, they now want to see their money back within five years of starting full-scale production (which means at least ten years after the first outlay). Even that period is long compared to the speed with which political change takes place in most countries.

Furthermore, the scale of new investment projects is rising steeply. As mining companies are forced into increasingly distant and inhospitable parts of the globe, only very large projects justify the extensive infrastructure development required (transport, electricity generation, etc.). Lower-grade deposits require more expensive machinery. These larger investments also extend the period between the initial investment and the first commercial delivery of ore. In the past, investment by mining enterprises was largely self-financed. Now companies are increasingly forced to go to a sceptical capital market for new funds. Uncertainty over future market prices adds further to uncertainty.

In 1972-73, the consequences of these difficulties became apparent. While in earlier boom periods investment had always increased, it now was failing to do so, in spite of raw material prices that were a multiple of normal prices. Canada is one example. In Australia, exploration expenditures fell by 33 percent in dollar terms between 1970-71 and 1973-74. The development of huge new copper deposits in Panama and Bougainville (Papua, New Guinea) has been delayed for years due to protracted negotiations. Yet, if the future world demand of copper is to be met, two new "Bougainvilles" a year are required.

One of the greatest threats—directly and indirectly—to investments for an expandmng raw material supply is the chronic instability of markets. The direct impact is twofold. During recurrent periods of low prices, the cash flow of enterprises deteriorates dramatically (especially now that high, fixed fiscal charges by governments are becoming the rule), thus reducing their capacity to invest. Secondly, forecasting profitability of new deposits becomes mere guesswork when prices can fluctuate by a factor of three or four within the space of two years.

Price instability also works indirectly by influencing host-government policies toward enterprises and consumers. When prices are high, governments step up their fiscal and parafiscal demands, thus reducing superprofits to a "reasonable level." These fiscal charges then become permanently locked into the cost structure, severely depressing profitability in bad years. On the other hand, developing countries' resentment—understandable in countries earning up to 90 percent of their foreign exchange through raw material exports—becomes explosive when prices decline for a year or two, leading to an increase in radicalism toward the industrialized countries in general and the exploiting enterprises in particular.

It is a vital interest of the raw material consuming countries to shift the struggle over the equitable distribution of benefits derived from the international division of labor from the micro-economic level—where it smothers economic activity—to the macro-economic level—where broad and mutually satisfactory bargains can be struck. Within the context of commodity agreements, participation by the consuming countries in the cost of market stabilization can be traded off against a predictable and stable investment environment. Even where such bargains cannot be struck explicitly, a general process of "détente" in North-South relations implicit in a joint management of commodity markets would reduce much of the political and economic pressure on private foreign direct investment

A further consumer interest in stabilization arises from the negative impact of commodity-price fluctuations on conjunctural management. This issue has become much more urgent for two reasons. First, the emergence of a world conjunctural cycle since the late 1960s has greatly magnified price fluctuations: the commodity boom of 1973-74 and the drastic fall in the price of many commodities in 1975-76 are examples.

Second, the dangers of speculation are now far greater than in the past. Speculation has always played a large and often perverse role in commodity markets. Since most supplies are under intracompany, commercial, or intergovernmental contract, the physical quantities traded on commodity exchanges are usually quite small. Yet, they have to bear the full weight of total supply-demand imbalances. Furthermore, speculators (including user industries) amplify rather than reduce market imbalances: they buy when prices rise (in anticipation of further rises) and sell when prices fall, thus depressing the market still further.

In recent years, a further element has increased speculative activity. Monetary instability, weak stock markets, and inflation have given commodities a quasi-monetary role. In 1973 alone, forward trading in the United States increased by almost $100 billion to $135 billion.[4] Increasingly, funds move in and out of commodity markets, not because of intrinsic market trends, but in response to exchange rate expectations, interest rates on commercial paper, and the ups and downs of the stock market.

The effect of violent price fluctuations on the economies of the developing countries is widely recognized. What is less generally understood is the impact on the economic management of Western European countries and Japan. Increases in commodity prices tend to occur at the beginning of an economic upswing, starting the inflationary spiral and worsening the balance of payments beyond the usual level associated with reflation. During a (world) economic downswing, raw material prices decline. As receipts by raw material producers fall, so does their capacity to import. Thus, demand for the exports of the industrialized countries falls when it is most needed to stimulate the economy. In other words, unstable commodity markets are highly pro-cyclical. Any serious cost-benefit analysis of commodity agreements by governments must, therefore, take into account the welfare losses associated with the decreased ability to conduct an effective conjunctural management.

Stabilizing Earnings

Since the self-interest of consuming countries in market stabilization is not generally recognized, the industrialized countries respond to the narrower purposes of Third World demands, namely to achieve greater stability of export earnings by various schemes designed to bridge earning shortfalls by loans or grants. This has the advantage of replacing a highly complex intervention in the market place by a relatively simple banking operation. For many products, such schemes may indeed be a useful adjunct to, or substitute for, commodity agreements. While for most mineral and agricultural industrial raw materials, variations in price are due to a conjunctural shift in demand in developed countries, for many tropical food products the variations are due to changes on the *supply* side. A stable price during periods of oversupply would leave countries with huge unsold stocks that could otherwise be disposed of in the market at lower prices. Greater quantities, at a lower price, can mean constant or increased export earnings.

In the past, the only means available for stabilizing export earnings was a special International Monetary Fund (IMF) compensatory finance facility which provided low-interest swing credits in bad years, to be repaid in good years. At the September 1975 Special Session of the United Nations, Secretary of State Henry A. Kissinger proposed a much more ambitious version of this scheme, a development security facility to be established by the IMF. Its purpose would be to stabilize *all* export earnings of developing countries by annual loans up to $10 billion, with a provision that loans be converted to grants under certain conditions.

A less ambitious scheme, covering fewer countries and fewer products (commodities only), and with a stabilization fund whose size is one-twenty-fifth of Kissinger's proposals, is the export earnings stabilization scheme concluded in the Lomé Convention between the European Community and its forty-six associates. This scheme is being discussed elsewhere in this volume in greater detail.[5]

Full Commodity Agreements

The stabilization of export earnings is, however, not a substitute for full commodity agreements. A full commodity agreement is one incorporating buffer stocks and export and/or production limitations with the aim of stabilizing prices within a narrow range. The purposes of such arrangements are (a) income stabilization for producers and (b) stable supplies for consumers under predictable conditions in both the short and the long term. Unlike schemes that only stabilize earnings, commodity agreements can give greater security not only to countries, but also to private firms engaged in the production and consumption (processing) of raw materials. Commodity agreements, especially those for industrial, nonperishable raw materials, are therefore of particular interest to industrialized countries. The disadvantages include the difficulty of negotiating such agreements, especially as regards the price range that is to be the basis for stabilization, and the difficulty of amending such agreements once they are concluded. Much opposition comes from consumer governments that fear the high cost of purchasing the initial buffer stock. Finance ministers in all developed countries, using the somewhat narrow time perspective of the annual budget, see expenditure on buffer stocks as a net outflow, not as an investment.

The cost of buffer stocks—of their initial purchase and capital cost, and the storage costs—thus represents an important barrier to the conclusion of commodity agreements. UNCTAD estimated the cost of setting up an eighteen-commodity scheme at $10.7 billion. Later revisions, which left out cereals, put the figure at $6 billion. This amount represents about 2.7 percent of total world monetary reserves of Special Drawing Rights—SDR 183 billion (April 1975)—and less than 5 percent of the reserves of the industrialized countries. Since most countries now need smaller reserves than before (because floating exchange rates minimize the amounts needed for central bank intervention), a subscription by the industrialized countries and the oil producers (whose reserves stand at SDR 43 billion) of about 3 percent of their reserves to the IMF would raise enough capital to finance substantial buffer stocks.[6]

But the figure of $6 billion is a "worst case" figure, since it assumes simultaneously intervention buying to the limit of the buffer stock for each commodity. The annual storage cost is about 3 percent for the "core commodities" selected by UNCTAD (e.g., excluding grain and iron ore), while the interest rate of the present limited buffer-stock facility of the IMF is 5 percent. If the margin between buying and selling is 10 percent, and stocks are held no longer than eighteen months, the buffer stock would make a profit if prices were indexed. These profits would increase the shorter the periods of price swings.

Indexation

No single issue in the field of international trade is approached with so much confusion, passion, and ignorance as the Third World's demand to index the price of raw materials to a standard of inflation that maintains the real purchasing power of commodities in terms of manufactured imports. Three politically and economically distinct demands have been muddled in the debate: first, indexation is used as a legitimizing formula by the oil producers to make up, through nominal price increases, for the considerable erosion of the prices imposed in 1973-74. The bitter resistance of major developed consumer countries to this demand confuses the continued debate of the cartel price as such, and the grounds for adjusting that price which would be reasonable if the price itself were an internationally agreed one.

The second reason for confusion must be laid squarely at the door of the Third World countries themselves, who link the demand for indexation alternatively with a demand for the *maintenance* of purchasing power and for *improved* terms of trade. Spokespersons of the developed countries tend to take the second demand—which is analytically and politically very different from the first—as the core of the demand for indexation. The confusion is compounded by the money illusion: stable real prices *do* mean increasing nominal prices.

The third reason for the instinctive, if muddled, opposition to indexation stems from the fear that an acceptance of the principle would entail a world of administered commodity markets. Again, this issue is a separate and weighty problem in itself. Only when and where administered commodity markets are, in fact, agreed upon by the international community can the question of indexation be posed at all.[7]

Yet, if one wants to enter into commodity agreements, it would be absurd, dishonest, and counterproductive to fix floor and ceiling prices in nominal terms at a time when a 5-10 percent inflation will remain in the world norm. Absurd, because it is difficult to accept the logic that an equilibrium price range, once negotiated, should fall by perhaps 10 percent annually in real terms. Dishonest, because the commitment to stabilize entered into by the industrial countries would be quickly eroded to the point of irrelevancy. And counterproductive, in a literal sense, because one of the functions of commodity agreements, i.e., to stabilize expectations of investors and therefore to contribute to an orderly expansion of production, would be undermined.

Several objections are usually raised. The first is the impossibility of finding an appropriate standard of reference against which to index world inflation: Organisation for Economic Co-operation and Development (OECD) inflation, OECD export prices (if so, how to account for qualitative improvements reflected in higher unit prices?), etc. It is, therefore, considered more practical to institute periodic reviews of negotiated price ranges. This solution was adopted for the 1975 Cocoa Agreement. This argument is a clear case of too much sophistication applied to a relatively crude mechanism. If the developed countries agreed to a conservative measure of inflation (e.g., domestic OECD inflation) by which to adjust the price ranges of commodity agreements, there would be a substantially higher probability that these ranges move in the right direction. As pointed out earlier, a *fall* in the equilibrium price by an annual 5-10 percent is the least likely economic hypothesis. Periodic reviews of price ranges would still be necessary. But they would not have to start from the presumption of fundamental disequilibria wrought by past inflation. Much North-South bitterness could thus be avoided in future reviews.

A second objection relates to commodities whose price, in a free market situation, would fall in real terms due to improved technology or other reasons. Again, this concern brings too much sophistication to a crude price setting exercise: within the life span of the usual commodity agreement, say five years, such secular declines in real production costs would be well within the margins of intervention prices within which supply and demand forces could select the most efficient producers, stimulate greater use, etc. Again, an assumption of zero variation in real prices has a far greater chance of being right than the built-in bias for a decline of the equilibrium price several times that of anything observable in the real world, which is implicit in nominal price ranges.

It is, furthermore, argued that indexation would help the developed countries who, after all, furnish a large proportion of the world's raw materials. Again, this objection assumes that indexing involves real increases in prices, i.e., a transfer of resources, something that should be strictly reserved for *bona fide* developing countries. But if one accepts the argument that world-wide stability of raw materials markets is essential for rich consuming countries—since they benefit both in terms of conjunctural management and through greater economic and political security for raw-material investment—then the fact that Australia and Canada are part of such stabilization is no longer a valid criticism.

Lastly it is argued, especially in the Federal Republic of Germany, that indexation unfairly harms countries with low inflation rates in that they would be forced to pay the "higher" prices triggered by the inflation rates of their less fortunate partners. This argument leaves out of account—

among other things—that revaluations (through floating or re-pegging of SDR-parties) bestow a more than compensurate terms-of-trade gain. Inflation is also a concern in another criticism of indexation: the fear that inflation becomes "locked-in" the system. This argument can only be made if one expects the real terms of trade of commodities to decrease substantially in the future: the opposite expectation seems more reasonable. On the other hand, the really devastating inflationary effects stem from the pro-cyclical short-term fluctuations of commodity prices which, as argued above, would be dampened by an effective stabilization policy of which indexation is an element.

In essence, therefore, the problem of indexation does not arise and cannot be discussed without at the same time raising the issue of commodity agreements as such. Bad commodity agreements, most experts would agree, are both economically and politically destabilizing rather than stabilizing. Without sufficient financial resources, buffer stocks can only buck short-term market trends for a brief period, after which even more violent price fluctuations follow. Without realistic price ranges for intervention, the agreement quickly breaks down and producers seek alternative means of protecting their interests. In the final analysis, non-indexed price ranges are an institutionalized expression of bad faith of consumers.

Notes

1. One exception is that part of the world banana trade dominated by U.S. "integrated" enterprises.
2. Alton D. Law, *International Commodity Agreements* (Lexington: D.C. Heath, 1974), p. 45.
3. See Chapter 8, above.
4. "The Raw Material Prices Time Bomb," *Financial Times,* 26 March 1975.
5. See Chapter 10, below.
6. This would get around the legal constraints that may prevent central banks from engaging in commodity purchases directly. In practice, the sums required will be much smaller, since the producer countries, who at present carry the full burden of stockpiling, will wish to contribute in the future, if only to enjoy a greater say over the operation of the fund.
7. As the example of the Organization of Petroleum Exporting Countries (OPEC) shows, indexation could also become an issue within successful unilateral price cartels. However, such cartels would adjust prices as unilaterally as they set them, with or without agreement from consumers. Again, it is the setting of prices, rather than the adjustment, that lies behind the debate.

10 The Stabilization of Export Earnings in the Lomé Convention: A Model Case?

Hajo Hasenpflug

The Convention of Lomé—signed on 28 February 1975 by the European Community (EC) and by 46 states in Africa, the Caribbean and the Pacific (the ACP states)—was eulogized as "a historical event," "a gleam of common sense in this world," "a new model," and "the beginning of new economic relations between industrial and non-industrial countries." This praise based itself particularly on the Convention's Title II, "Export Earnings from Commodities," and its Chapter 1, "Stabilization of Export Earnings." This paper will briefly review the pros and cons of the export-stabilization system—the so-called STABEX mechanism—and it will discuss whether this mechanism marks a milestone in the relations between North and South.

Indexation, Price Stabilization, and Export-earnings Stabilization

In view of the marked dependence of the majority of developing countries on their earnings from exports of a few commodities (see tables 1 and 2), the states which were associated with the EC through the two Conventions of Yaoundé and the Arusha Agreement had repeatedly presented demands for the stabilization of their producer prices. When the EC was enlarged, the EC states in principle recognized the validity of these demands by Protocol 22 of the Act of Accession[1] so as to conform with the interests of the sugar and raw material exporting countries of the Associated African States and Madagascar as well as the Commonwealth countries.

Starting from maximal positions, the ACP states in the negotiations demanded that a guarantee of the purchasing power of their major export products should form part of the stabilization system for their export earnings. The EC, on the other hand, did not want such an indexation of export and import prices. Apart from difficulties of a statistical nature, which, in the eyes of the EC, would probably have defied solution, the

Table 1. Shares of STABEX products in total exports of some ACP states, 1973

Countries	Product and percentage in total export
Botswana	Raw hides, skins and leather 9
Burundi	Coffee 86, cotton 3, raw hides, skins and leather 6
Central African Republic	Coffee 23, wood 21, cotton 18
Chad	Cotton 69
Congo, People's Republic of	Wood 42
Dahomey	Palm products 34
Ethiopia	Coffee 38, raw hides, skins and leather 13
Fiji	Coconut oil 5
Gabon	Wood 32
Gambia	Groundnuts, groundnut oil and oilcake 94
Ghana	Cocoa 61, wood 19
Ivory Coast	Cocoa 15, coffee 23, wood 29
Kenya	Coffee 22, tea 11
Liberia	Iron ore 71
Madagascar	Coffee 3o, sisal 3
Malawi	Tea 17, groundnuts 7
Mali	Cotton 39, groundnuts 7
Mauritania	Iron ore 73
Niger	Groundnuts 15, groundnut oil 9
Rwanda	Coffee 61, raw hides and skins 4
Senegal	Groundnuts and groundnut oil 35
Sierra Leone	Iron ore 1o, palm nuts and kernels 5
Somalia	Bananas 26
Sudan	Cotton 56, groundnuts 9
Togo	Cocoa beans 26, coffee 13
Tonga	Copra 5o
Uganda	Coffee 66, cotton 15, tea 5
United Republic of Cameroon	Cocoa 23, coffee 26, wood 12
United Republic of Tanzania	Coffee 19, cotton 13, sisal 9
Upper Volta	Groundnuts and groundnut oil 8, cotton 22
Western Samoa	Copra 45, cocoa 28

Source: IMF, International Financial Statistics (Washington: IMF, 1974), and various national statistics.

Commission of the EC doubted whether indexation would really be of benefit to all, or even only some, of the associated states, since, as it was noted, trade not only takes place between industrialized and developing countries but also among developing countries. Moreover, such interference with the market mechanism was thought to give rise to ruinous surpluses (as experienced with the common agricultural policy of the EC).

The Commission of the EC also did not want to stabilize the price of major ACP export products because an analysis of factors contributing to

Table 2. Important export products of selected ACP countries not covered by the STABEX scheme: proportion of total exports

(Percentages)

Country	Product	Country	Product
Central African Republic	Diamonds 44	Senegal	Cereals 17.4 Phosphates 8.5
Congo	Diamonds 14.8	Sierra Leone	Diamonds 71
Gabon	Wood 36.8	Somalia	Live cattle 5o.1
Guyana	Bauxite 47.9	Togo	Phosphates 29.2
Jamaica	Bauxite 22.7 Aluminium 34.2	United Republic of Cameroon	Aluminium 9.5
Malawi	Tobacco 34.6		
Mali	Live cattle 48.2 Fish 14.1	United Republic of Tanzania	Diamonds 1o.7 Vegetables and fruit 9.2
Niger	Live cattle 14.3	Upper Volta	Live cattle 36.9
Nigeria	Tin 4.4	Zaire	Diamonds 5.3
Rwanda	Tin 31.1		

Source: UNCTAD, "Commodities: Preservation of the Purchasing Power of Developing Countries' Exports. Report by the UNCTAD-Secretariat" (TD/184/Supp. 2), March 5, 1976, Annex II, p. 6.

the instability of the developing countries' export earnings revealed to officials of the EC that a fluctuation in commodity prices is not the only phenomenon involved. The Commission came to this opinion after it had conducted a study of variations in export quantities, prices, and earnings for fourteen main commodities exported by the developing countries. Forty-four cases of variation were established in this way, and their analysis produced the following findings:

1. If price fluctuations and variations in quantities are compared, it was found that in 28 cases, quantities fluctuated more sharply than prices; in 16 of these cases, fluctuations in quantities were less than 20 percent; in a further 6 cases, they were between 20 and 30 percent; and in the remaining 6 cases they were greater than 30 percent. In 16 cases, price fluctuations were greater than variations in quantities. These findings showed (for the first

time) that quantities fluctuate relatively more sharply than prices. Quantity fluctuations were generally caused by one, or a combination, of the following factors:

a. Price fluctuations following changes in the economic trend in the industrialized countries.
b. Climatic conditions in the exporting developing countries.
c. Other factors such as decreases in production due to strikes, accidents, wars, etc.

2. If variations in quantities were compared with fluctuations in export earnings, it was found that in 18 cases, fluctuations in earnings were approximately equal to those in quantities; consequently, variations in quantities more or less offset price fluctuations, or vice versa. Of these 18 cases, the two variables fluctuated by less than 10 percent in 6 cases, by between 10 and 20 percent in 8 cases, and by more than 20 percent in 4 cases. Where quantities and prices varied inversely, the smallest variation—in this case that of prices—was cancelled out. But in 26 cases, variations in prices and those in quantities had a cumulative effect, thereby increasing considerably the instability of export earnings.[2] Partly as a result of these findings, the EC decided finally to agree to a stabilization of export earnings instead of focusing on export prices.

The Stabilization System

The STABEX mechanism is limited to product-earnings from those ACP exports that affect employment and induce a deterioration in the overall terms of trade. The selection criteria take into account (a) that receipts derived from any ACP raw material are by tradition unstable (owing to fluctuations in prices and/or quantities), (b) that the economies of the ACP countries are dependent upon these products, and, finally, (c) that these products are important for creating and sustaining employment in the exporting countries. The selection criteria furthermore take into account the effect of a fluctuation in export earnings of a commodity on a country's terms of trade with the EC and also the different levels of development of the ACP countries (giving special preferences to the least-developed, landlocked, and island-developing states).

In accordance with these criteria, eleven major (with seventeen subsidiary) products of export interest to the ACP states qualified for the provisions of the mechanism, with a twelfth major product, iron ore, accepted by inclusion by the EC only under protest.[3] Special provisions were made concerning sugar.[4]

The list of commodities covered by the STABEX mechanism is not necessarily closed with the twelve commodities mentioned in the convention. The list is expandable. The convention allows an expansion of product coverage by a decision of the highest organ of the convention, the Council of Ministers. Such a decision, however, cannot be taken sooner than twelve months after the entry into force of the convention; furthermore, it requires that within this period the products in question are of considerable importance for the economies of one or more ACP states and that they have been affected by sharp fluctuations in export earnings. This provision would appear to lend some flexibility to the STABEX scheme, except that the usefulness of it is limited by the provision that an expansion of the list does not affect the financial resources available for the overall operation of the scheme.

The financial resources for the STABEX mechanism have been limited to 375 million units of account for the duration of the convention, divided into five annual tranches of 75 million units of account. Provision have, however, been made that the installment of any one year may be exceeded by up to 20 percent[5] and that residual amounts may be carried forward to the following years. In principle, the financial transfers take the form of loans.

To prevent the system from degenerating into a "bottomless pit," the EC states have stipulated (and the other countries have accepted) that the recipients of interest-free transfers shall, as a rule, contribute to a re-augmentation of the stabilization fund when their earnings situation has improved; 24 poorer countries have, however, been exempted from these obligatory re-payments.[6]

Whether and when the mechanism of the stabilization system is brought into operation for any of the listed commodities is determined by reference to a dependence threshold and a release threshold. The dependence threshold limits the mechanism to countries that derived a certain minimum percentage share of their total export earnings in the preceding year from the particular commodity concerned. As a rule, the minimum rate is 7.5 percent (for sisal 5 percent); for 34 least-developed, landlocked or island-developing countries, however, the dependence threshold is 2.5 percent.[7] The significance of the release threshold is that it limits the operation of the scheme to situations in which proceeds from exports of a commodity to the EC are at least 7.5 percent below a reference level at which the EC obtained its supplies in the four preceding years; for the 34 poorest countries, the release threshold is 2.5 percent. The reference level established by the release threshold is the average of the export earnings (reference quantities multiplied by the reference unit value) for the four years preceding each year of application of each ACP state's earnings from its exports of a particular product to the community. The reference level for 1975, for example, is calculated on the basis of the results from 1972 to 1975, and so on.

The ACP countries concerned are entitled to request compensatory financial transfers when both these indicators—the dependence and the release threshold—apply. The difference between the reference level and actual earnings constitutes the basis for the transfer. The loans must be repaid in the five years following the disbursement if the unit value of the exports of a specific product is higher than the reference unit value *and* if the quantity actually exported to the community is at least equal to the reference quantity. In this case, the recipient state is required to pay back into the system (within the limit of the transfers it has received) an amount equal to the reference quantity multiplied by the *difference* between the reference unit value and the actual unit value.

The following examples from the EC Commission illustrate the mechanism.[8] In them, the reference value is assumed to be 10,000 (obtained by multiplying a reference unit value of 100 by a reference quantity of 100), and the country in question will be assumed to have received a transfer amounting to 1,000 during the preceding year.

Case 1. The actual unit value is 120, and the actual quantities are 80, so that actual earnings are 9,600. Although compared to the reference unit value the actual unit values have risen, the country not only does not have to pay anything back into the fund, but may apply for a transfer of 400.

Case 2. The actual unit value is 105; actual quantities are 100. In this case, actual earnings amount to 10,500, and the country has to pay back 500.

Case 3. The actual unit value is 120, the actual quantities 100, amounting to total actual earnings of 12,000. Because the country has received a transfer of 1,000, it has to pay back this sum, but can keep the additional 1,000.

Case 4. The actual unit value is 100, the actual quantities are 110. Although actual earnings are 11,000, the country is not required to pay back anything, since the actual unit value does not exceed the reference unit value.

Evaluation of the STABEX Mechanism

In the discussions about the pros and cons of the STABEX mechanism, two arguments in particular have been advanced. The first one holds that a stabilization of export earnings may tend to solidify the economic structure of the ACP states and tend to delay or impede the diversification of their exports; this argumentation of "free-traders" cannot be accepted, because the EC could add to the products covered—if necessary—semifinished products in order to create incentives to build up processing industries within the Third World.

The second argument is based on the fear that the financial resources of the STABEX fund may not be adequate for the attainment of the desired objectives. This argument is based on the following reflections:

1. The reference level of the average export earnings for the four preceding years will be very high for some time to come, because the commodity boom of 1973-74 will continue to form a part of the reference period. As a result, almost all states can be expected to apply for compensatory transfer payments for virtually all the products listed and the ceiling will be reached soon. For the same reason, it is to be expected that no repayments will be made in the near future. In the event of a gradual decline of world market prices (but their stabilization at a high average level), it must be expected that payments will only be made to ACP states. Even if after the current depression in the commodity markets prices were to rise sharply, repayments would not commence until the years 1973 and 1974 have been left behind in the reference level calculations. Until 1978, in other words, disbursements are, on balance, likely to exceed any repayments, with the result that the STABEX mechanism will suffer severe financial strains in the first five years of its existence and probably will quickly reach its ceiling.
2. The ACP states could increase their outputs and offer larger quantities. If in that case the price were to fall (price elasticity larger than 1), financial transfers would be required to compensate for the declining price ("minimum price effect").
3. The special arrangement made for the 34 less-developed ACP states and the tendencies indicated here make it unlikely that repayments would be forthcoming. The revolving loan principle of the STABEX mechanism thus may be negated.

The expectations that the fund of 375 million units of accounts will soon be exhausted because of the above-mentioned reasons could indeed become a reality. But this is nevertheless no strong argument against STABEX. It only means that a fund of that size for 29 products of 46 countries for a time-period of five years may be too small.

To sum up, an evaluation of the Lomé export-earnings stabilization system must lead to the conclusion that the concept of an equalization fund to offset fluctuations in the export earnings of developing countries can serve as a model for future improvements of development-aid policies. In view of the fact that the exports of primary commodities provide most ACP states with their principal source of foreign currencies and, thus, perform a key function in the development of these countries, the new system may constitute the basis for more secure long-term financing of economic projects and programs that are essential for growth and economic development. The only qualification to be made is that the system inherently contains temptations that may lead to a solidification of existing structures.

Another qualification, concerning the disturbance of free market processes through STABEX, cannot be taken seriously. Most commodity markets are either oligopolistic or monopolistic in nature. The issue, therefore, is not to replace a laissez-faire market system by a state-organized market, but rather to replace control by transnational enterprises with control by producer and consumer states. On balance, therefore, the stabilization system has to be viewed positively, although one has to keep in mind that this system does not deal with the problem of the developing countries' deteriorating terms of trade. Thus, the STABEX mechanism is a model case for stabilizing export earnings on a worldwide basis, but not for stabilizing these earnings at an adequate level.

If a global export-earnings system analogous to the STABEX scheme (but also dealing with the terms of trade) should be implemented, the following conditions have to be fulfilled:

1. The reference level of earnings should take the form of a target or norm to be subject to periodic revision in the light of changing market conditions but remaining in force for a fixed period of not less than three to five years.
2. The list of beneficiary countries obviously would have to include more developing countries and especially the least-developed, the most seriously affected, the island, and the landlocked developing countries.
3. The participating importing countries would have to include most of the principal commodity importing countries, be they developed market economies, centrally planned economies, or OPEC countries.

Notes

1. ". . . the Community will make it its business to safeguard the interest of all the countries (AAMS and Commonwealth countries in Africa, the Indian and Pacific Oceans, and the Caribbean) the economy of which depends to a large extent on the export of basic products, especially sugar. The case of sugar shall be dealt with in this light and bearing in mind the importance of sugar exports to a number of these countries, more especially Commonwealth countries." See European Communities, *Treaties Establishing the European Communities* (Luxemburg: EC, 1973), pp. 1411-1415.
2. Commission of the European Communities, "The Lomé Convention: The Stabilization of Export Earnings," *Information Development and Cooperation,* no. 94 (1975), pp. 2-3.
3. The original list proposed by the EC comprised groundnuts, cocoa, coffee, cotton, coconut products, and bananas. Hard bargaining by the ACP

resulted in the extension of the list to cover the following 12 main products with their 17 derived products: (1) groundnut products—(a) groundnuts shelled or not, (b) groundnut oil, and (c) groundnut oilcake; (2) cocoa products—(a) cocoa beans, (b) cocoa paste, and (c) cocoa butter; (3) coffee products—(a) raw or roasted coffee, and (b) extracts, essences or concentrates of coffee; (4) cotton products—(a) cotton, not carded or combed, and (b) cotton linters; (5) coconut products—(a) coconuts, (b) copra, (c) coconut oil, and (d) coconut oilcake; (6) palm, palm nut and kernel products—(a) palm oil, (b) palm nut and kernel oil, (c) palm nut and kernel oilcake, and (d) palm nuts and kernels; (7) raw hides, skins and leather—(a) raw hides and skins, (b) bovine cattle leather, (c) sheep and lamb skin leather, and (d) goat and kid skin leather; (8) wood products—(a) wood in the rough, (b) wood roughly squared or half-squared, but not further manufactured, and (c) wood sawn lengthwise, but not further prepared; (9) fresh bananas; (10) tea; (11) raw sisal; and (12) iron ore and concentrates and roasted iron pyrites.

4. In the provisions for sugar, the EC has gone a step further. It has undertaken to absorb an amount of cane sugar equivalent to 1.28 million tons of white sugar annually for an indefinite period at a price not lower than the EC intervention price. The ACP states have agreed to supply such a quantity. To the extent of the purchase guarantee, the imported sugar is treated like the domestic product for which the benefits of the sugar market order can be claimed. For the first 18 months of the agreement, the EC has accepted a higher guaranteed price: 2,553 units of account per metric ton for cane sugar and 3,172 units for white sugar. The guarantee price will be renegotiated each year; it will be between the standard price and the intervention price. Concerning the costs, it has to be mentioned that the financial burden on the EC will be heavier the further the differential between the low world-market price and the higher intervention-price widens and the less successful the efforts are to keep the self-supply ratio in the EC below 100 percent.

5. The maximum amount STABEX can disburse in one year is thus 75 million units of account plus 15 million units of account: 90 million units of account.

6. Botswana, Burundi, Central African Republic, Chad, Dahomey, Ethiopia, the Gambia, Guinea, Guinea-Bissau, Lesotho, Malawi, Mali, Mauritania, Niger, Rwanda, Somalia, Sudan, Swaziland, Togo, Uganda, United Republic of Tanzania, Upper-Volta, and West Samoa.

7. These countries are the Bahamas, Barbados, Botswana, Burundi, Central African Republic, Chad, Dahomey, Equatorial Guinea, Ethiopia, Fiji, the Gambia, Grenada, Guinea, Guinea-Bissau, Jamaica, Lesotho, Madagascar, Malawi, Mali, Mauritania, Mauritius, Niger, Rwanda, Somalia, Sudan, Swaziland, United Republic of Tanzania, Togo, Tonga, Trinidad and Tobago, Uganda, Upper Volta, Western Samoa, and Zambia. For several of

these countries—Burundi, Ethiopia, Guinea-Bissau, Rwanda and Swaziland—the system operates in regard to all exports irrespective of destination.

8. Commission of the European Communities, "Stabilisation of Export Receipts," *The Courier: European Community/Africa, Caribbean, Pacific,* no. 31 (March 1975), p. 27.

11 *The New International Economic Order and the New Law of the Sea*

Michael A. Morris

Demands for changes in the structure of the international system by developing states have gradually mounted in the postwar period. They involve a desire for general systemic reform as well as revisions in specific functional areas. The New International Economic Order (NIEO) and the New Law of the Sea (NLOS) represent two such efforts, the first of a general, and the second of a specific, functional nature. Efforts for a NLOS have been under way for many years. Since the Sixth Special Session of the General Assembly of the United Nations (UN), the NLOS has become increasingly related to the more comprehensive yet recent quest for the NIEO. After a brief review of the chronology and basic issues of the NLOS, the relationship between the NLOS and the NIEO will be examined. Specifically, this chapter will show that the developing countries aim for a law of the sea that reflects their perceived interests. The strongest linkage between the NIEO and the NLOS has emerged in the area of natural resources. The issue involves the control and management of deep seabed nonliving natural resources: through the application, within certain geographical limits, of the principle of permanent sovereignty over natural resources, and, beyond these limits, through an international seabed authority. The scope and powers of the international authority, in turn, have become major NLOS issues separating developed and developing states. They constitute, therefore, a significant test case for the implementation of the NIEO.

The New Law of the Sea

The 1958 and 1960 Geneva conferences (the First and Second UN Law of the Sea Conferences) codified the existing customary law of the sea and

---

The author wishes to thank Ann Hollick and Renate Platzöder for their helpful comments.

introduced the principle of the continental shelf. Developing countries, however, and in particular those from Latin America, continued to demand revisions in the law of the sea. These demands crystallized, in 1967, in a call by Ambassador Arvid Pardo of Malta for a seabed treaty to prevent the unilateral expansion of coastal state jurisdiction and, at the same time, to allow the international development of the resources of the seabed for the sole benefit of the developing countries. A series of events helped to mobilize diffuse support for a NLOS among developing states. An Ad Hoc Committee of developing and developed states, later succeeded by a permanent Seabed Committee, was set up in 1968 to study the seabed issue. By 1970, sufficient interest had been awakened among developing states to obtain the adoption of a UN resolution calling for a moratorium on seabed exploitation, a Declaration of Principles establishing the seabed beyond national jurisdiction as the common heritage of mankind, and a resolution calling for the Third Conference of the UN on the Law of the Sea (CLOS).[1] These resolutions together placed the need for a new law of the sea, including a deep seabed regime, squarely before the developed states.

Most developed states, at first, did not favor the movement to convene the CLOS, most did not want a strong international seabed authority, and all (including some other states) were interested in preventing the establishment of a 200-mile territorial sea. Maritime powers, especially the U.S. and the USSR, particularly felt that developing states' claims for a 200-mile territorial sea and for a strong international seabed authority (whose competence could also include pollution control and scientific research) would undermine the traditional freedom-of-the-high-seas concept.

Since developed states were neither able to head off the CLOS nor convoke it merely to ratify their interests, they began to bring their influence to bear on limiting revisions in particularly sensitive areas of the law of the sea. For several reasons, a 200-mile economic zone was more palatable than a strong international deep seabed regime. The great maritime powers, after all, would gain disproportionately through an extension of national jurisdiction. Landlocked, shelf-locked and strait-locked countries would gain little or nothing, while the United States, with its two long coastlines and the Hawaiian, Micronesian, and Alaskan archipelagos, would acquire more resources than any other state, including the USSR. The interests of transnational enterprises of developed states (most of them based in the United States) would consequently not be damaged that much by 200-mile economic zones, zones that would encompass about one-third of the total ocean space. The interests of these enterprises would be damaged, however, by a strong international regime that might limit or severely regulate their access to the deep seabed.

The United States, for example, made much more significant concessions (without, however, giving anything up) in the national jurisdiction area (a

200-mile zone) than in the international area (where it continued to press for a weak international regime). By the early 1970s, the United States had accepted the principle of broad coastal state economic jurisdiction for an unspecified distance beyond a 12-mile territorial sea as part of a satisfactory overall settlement on the law of the sea. In the 1974 Caracas session of the CLOS, the first substantive round after an earlier procedural session in New York City, the United States made the more explicit concession that the economic zone could be 200 miles, again with the qualification that it be part of a satisfactory overall settlement. This proposal coincided in large part with most developing states' proposals for economic and resource jurisdiction over a 200-mile zone, but fell short of some other developing states' much more extensive 200-mile territorial sea claim of full sovereignty over the area. Domestically, offshore fishing interests, too, pressed effectively for U.S. adoption of a 200-mile fishing zone.

As for deep seabed mining responsibility, the 1970 U.S. seabed proposal placed heavy reliance on transnational enterprises and no reliance on an international authority. The proposal did provide that in a trusteeship area between the 200-meter depth limit and the international zone (managed by coastal states) the international authority would receive a substantial portion of fees and payments collected from mining operations, particularly for economic assistance to developing countries. Even this concession to the developing states on the seabed issue was subsequently eliminated as U.S. economic interests (petroleum and hard minerals industries and offshore fishing) began to mobilize politically in favor of a broad national economic zone and a weak international seabed authority, which might only have some revenue-collection power beyond the 200-mile limit.[2] As long as the deep seabed was regarded as a source of fantastic wealth, including as a source of finance for development, the hardening of the revenue-sharing provisions of U.S. seabed policy within the 200-mile limit was regarded as of secondary importance. Recent studies, however, have recognized that the revenue sharing potential of the deep seabed is much more modest than once believed and, therefore, recommend sharing of oil revenues within the 200-mile limit, or, better still, from the continental margin to the 12-mile limit.[3]

On the developing states' side, claims for a 200-mile territorial sea or zone and for a strong international seabed authority had the fundamental aims of securing exclusive control over certain natural resources (living as well as mineral ones), of guaranteeing control over the utilization of the remaining deep-sea resources through some juridical regime and of ensuring their participation in the distribution of benefits associated with seabed mining through some automatic percentage formula. The poorer states tended to regard these demands as defensive measures to offset the technological superiority of developed states and to control the effects of deep seabed mining on their own raw material exports. In addition, an international regime was increasingly regarded as an independent source of development finances.[4]

With the United States and other developed states basically continuing to favor a weak international regime for the management of deep seabed resources—and the developing states a strong one—the U.S. official report on the Caracas session concluded that the seabed authority had emerged as the most important issue separating the two groups.[5]

Certain conclusions emerge about the background of the NIEO-NLOS relationship. The developing states' movement to assert control over, and to guarantee free and equal access to, natural resources directly influenced their thinking about ocean resources. This thinking, together with a general distrust of transnational enterprises, received strong impetus from the resolutions adopted by the Sixth and Seventh Special Sessions of the General Assembly of the UN. The spirit of assertiveness underlying these resolutions began to infuse the CLOS and especially the quest for satisfactory control and management of the deep seabed. At stake was the control of natural resources—a fundamental principle of the developing countries—and the effects of exploitation of seabed resources for the mineral exports of a number of developing countries. Furthermore, in the context of the demands for more—and increasingly automatic—financial development assistance, at stake was also the distribution of the gains associated with the exploitation of the deep seabed. The nature and scope of the international deep seabed authority, therefore, became key issues, especially as a compromise solution seemed to be emerging for a 200-mile economic zone, if not for a 200-mile territorial sea. Here, the NIEO-NLOS linkage has been most intense as the NIEO influenced thinking about the international authority and incorporated this issue-area into its broader design.

Links Between the New International Economic Order and the New Law of the Sea

The resolutions of the Sixth Special Session entrusted all specialized UN conferences as well as other UN bodies with the implementation of the NIEO.[6] For reasons of substance and timing, this strategy for implementation of the NIEO through specialized, functional conferences, as well as through other bodies, was especially appropriate for the law of the sea area. With regard to substance, the question of the distribution of benefits from raw material exploitation was central to both the NIEO and the NLOS; and the question of exploring "other means of transfer of real resources which are predictable, assured and continuous"[7]—e.g., the distribution of the earnings of the international authority—loomed in the background. As for the tactical advantages of timing, the first substantive session of the CLOS followed just six weeks after the Sixth Special Session had closed. And preparations for the Seventh Special Session overlapped the second CLOS substantive session in Geneva, while the Seventh Special Session itself preceded the third CLOS substantive round (held in New York City in March-May 1976) by a mere six months. So, the timing of the NIEO Special Sessions permitted an opportunity for an immediate and direct impact on the CLOS sessions, an opportunity that indeed was seized.

Infusion of the spirit and ideology of the NIEO into the CLOS sessions, especially the international authority issue, can be illustrated more specifically. In the opening meeting of the 1974 Caracas session, for example, the Secretary General of the UN, Kurt Waldheim, explicitly recognized the common aims of the Sixth Special Session and the CLOS in promoting the orderly use of natural resources. He concluded that the quick succession of these conferences in 1974 "clearly showed the international community was ready to adopt an approach which gave importance to each issue while not losing sight of their interconnexion." In effect, he reminded delegates that the NIEO-NLOS link had led to the law of the sea conference:

> Finally, and most important in bringing about the Conference, had been the mounting pressure on world resources and the awareness that the sea-bed and the oceans contained some of the largest unexploited reserves available to man. The Conference had been convened because of the realization that those resources must be developed in an orderly manner fov the benefit of all and must contribute to a more equitable and workable global economic system.[8]

Halfway through the Caracas session, Mexico's President Luis Echeverria again elevated the NIEO-NLOS linkage to the highest political level. In introducing President Echeverria to the special meeting convened to hear his address, the president of the conference, H.S. Amerasinghe of Sri Lanka, called attention to the Mexican president's initiative and role in promoting the "Charter of Economic Rights and Duties of States." Amerasinghe himself endorsed the NIEO concepts in noting that "the new international legal order governing the use of the oceans and their resources which the Conference was expected to formulate should, if it satisfied the principles of justice and equity, be a stimulus and an inspiration in the framing of that charter."[9] For his part, President Echeverria claimed that a (weak) international scabed authority—one merely granting exploitation concessions and licences to transnational enterprises—would give rise to a new form of colonialism. Instead, he urged that the NLOS should be an important instrument to help implement the NIEO:

> The law of the sea formulated by the Conference could be a powerful instrument which would enable the third world to achieve permanent and

> effective sovereignty over all its natural resources, and which indirectly would make for a more democratic and juster international division of labour.
>
> It was the purpose of the charter of economic rights and duties of States, being prepared by a working group of the United Nations, to enunciate principles encouraging more equitable economic relations among States.[10]

All accounts indicate that President Echeverria, the only head of state to address the Caracas session other than the president of the host state, made a profound impact on delegates from the developing states.

A survey of general statements delivered by delegations from developing states at the CLOS likewise reveals pervasive reliance on what has been referred to here as NIEO concepts. Explicit references to a NIEO-NLOS linkage occurred with some frequency, as well as explicit references to the Sixth Special Session as the general framework to guide specific law of the sea negotiations.[11] Similarly, many statements at the general debate during the Seventh Special Session referred explicitly to the on-going law-of-the-sea negotiations (usually demanding a strong international seabed authority) as an important part of the drive for the New International Economic Order.[12]

An organic link exists, moreover, between the NIEO and the NLOS through the Group of 77 and its political organization, the nonaligned movement. The Group of 77 in effect has been the UN caucus of developing states in economic matters, and, under the leadership of the Non-Aligned Countries,[13] also became the focal point for Third World proposals and cooperation at the Special Sessions and the law of the sea conference. The "Resolution Concerning the Law of the Sea" of the Fourth Summit Conference of the Non-Aligned Countries at Algiers (1973), for example, recalled how past nonaligned conferences had influenced preparations for the CLOS and called for a strong international authority to distribute benefits from deep seabed exploration equitably, with particular attention to the special needs and interests of developing states.[14] The Group of 77 was subsequently so active at the Caracas session that to some it "turned out to be the heart of the conference."[15]

Rough similarities in the general strategies of the Group of 77 at the Special Sessions and the CLOS are evident as well. The Sixth Special Session was noted for the aggressive, uncompromising role played by the Group of 77 and for the confrontation between the developing and developed states. Following in quick succession, the Caracas session was not able to resolve the standoff between the developed and developing states' positions on the international authority and was largely limited to a clarification of positions and issues. After Caracas, the two groups' positions began to become more conciliatory, apparently since the developing states increasingly recognized that effective consensus was required for action, while the developed states learned that Third World solidarity on CLOS issues was not transitory. This new spirit of accommodation became evident during the preparatory meetings for the Seventh Special Session (March–August 1975);[16] the Seventh Special Session itself (September 1975) was noted for constructive negotiations between the developing and developed states. Serious negotiations began also at the CLOS's Geneva session (17 March–9 May, 1975), where an "Informal Single Negotiating Text" was prepared for subsequent consideration at the fourth session in New York City (15 March–7 May, 1976).

Apart from such general trends and similarities, the NIEO discussions also influenced the CLOS in more specific, procedural ways. Negotiating style at the CLOS, for example, has tended to reflect Group of 77 practices developed in the General Assembly: "The Conference suffers from the carryover of a negotiating style more suitable for General Assembly recommendations or negotiation of abstract issues than for texts intended to become widely accepted as treaty obligations affecting immediate interests of states in a dynamic situation."[17] Only a limited number of developing states was represented at the 1958 and 1960 Geneva law of the sea conferences, after all, and conference preparations and negotiations were of a technical-legal character; at the present CLOS, on the other hand, developing countries constitute a majority and generally favor radical change in the existing law. At Geneva, too, "classical" conference procedures generally permitted problems to be isolated and to be resolved one by one, while the deep political divisions of the CLOS prevented agreement on a basic negotiating text in the preparatory sessions and required a "gentlemen's agreement" to defer voting until all efforts to reach consensus had failed. In this politicized context, all parties were reluctant to accept less than a comprehensive "package deal" encompassing major issues.[18] A case in point, mentioned previously, is the U.S. acceptance of a 200-mile economic zone contingent on a satisfactory overall settlement, including particularly also the straits and international authority issues.

If a politicized negotiating style complicates conclusions of a treaty, the politicization of the CLOS does reflect greater determination on the part of developing states to press their demands. As the demands of the NIEO have increasingly infused the debate about the international authority, the international seabed regime has become the decisive element in negotiating a package deal between the developed and developing states. The next section of this chapter examines the Group of 77's proposals at the CLOS about the international regime and how they relate to basic NIEO concepts developed by the same groupings.

The International Seabed Authority

Nearly a dozen seabed proposals were submitted from 1970 through 1973 to Subcommittee I of the Seabed Committee as part of the preparation for the CLOS.[19] Basically, these proposals can be divided into those of developing states favoring a strong international authority and those of developed states favoring a weak authority. But the Group of 77, as such, did not make a seabed proposal during this period; the developing states were, in fact, divided on a number of specific issues. Writing just before the Sixth Special Session and a few months before the Caracas session, one observer noted "the disunity of the 'Group of 77' in its response to maritime problems."[20] While a strong authority was favored by developing states, there was disagreement about the extent to which the authority itself should try to undertake exploration and exploitation and how much stress should be placed on a licensing system or on a system of negotiated service contracts and joint ventures. Diverging views also existed concerning measures to be taken in cases where seabed mineral production were to adversely affect prices of land-based producers. Some states proposed assistance or compensation, others advocated price and production controls, and still others had simply not made up their minds about what to do. Divisions between landlocked and coastal developing states and patrimonialist and territorialist factions also undermined Third World maritime unity prior to the CLOS.

Subcommittee I of the Seabed Committee did bequeath twenty-one alternative draft articles (several versions of each of the twenty-one articles) to its successor, the First Committee of the CLOS, about the general powers of the authority without, however, going into the details of rules and regulations for deep seabed mining. Fifty-two additional alternative draft articles prepared by the subcommittee did deal with the status, scope, functions, and powers of the international machinery to be established for the exploration and exploitation of the seabed area, but were not objects of negotiations at Caracas.[21]

The Special Sessions tended to politicize both sides of this debate about principles. The United States, on the one hand, was extremely reluctant to accept open-ended proposals which said "little if anything about how the mining system would in fact work" and gave "no guarantee" that its interests would be respected, especially in light of "the political power of the land-based producers within the Group of 77 in this negotiation, and the absence of more vigorous and widespread assertion of consumer interests at the Special Session of the UN General Assembly in the spring of 1974."[22] On the other hand, the Group of 77 was able to benefit from the growth in Third World unity stimulated by the Sixth Special Session and succeeded in forging a common seabed proposal about some important general principles. It agreed on a common text for the key article 9 of the draft on the overall power of the authority and general conditions of access to deep seabed resources, and it elaborated this article into a seabed proposal on the same subjects near the end of the Caracas session.[23]

While the developing states now presented a united front in the First Committee, the door to a compromise was left open. The Group of 77 version of article 9 contained a very important concession to the developed states about the role of transnational enterprises in deep seabed mining. The authority would carry out mining activities directly, but it could also "confer certain tasks to juridical or natural persons, through service contracts, or association or through any other means" over which it would maintain "direct and effective control."[24] The Group of 77 proposal contained another conciliatory article, moreover, referring to the security of tenure of contractors. While the authority would retain financial control through majority share and administrative control of any such undertaking (paragraph 9) and could require a share of the production and proceeds from associations with transnational enterprises (paragraph 14), the effort of some to exclude these enterprises from deep seabed mining altogether had been dropped. Discussion in the First Committee at Caracas subsequently focussed on the Group of 77's revised version of article 9, which has been described as "the turning point" in the negotiations on the article.[25] Developed states at Caracas still favored a version of Article 9 that would preclude any direct mining by the authority itself, but at least a compromise was reached to continue discussing the general powers of the authority and conditions of access to the international area while deferring discussion of specific conditions of exploration and exploitation, unless relevant to the general discussion.

The continuing evolution of the debate between the Group of 77 and the developed states indicates that an accommodation might be worked out about the general system of exploration and exploitation. The United States began to modify its insistence on a weak authority at Caracas[26] and, on 11 August 1975, shortly after the Geneva session, advanced a new compromise proposal to meet the demands of the developing states. The proposal accepted some key planks of the earlier Group of 77 proposal at Caracas: the authority could directly carry out seabed mining operations for the benefit of the developing states; states and enterprises that would carry out seabed mining would pay an agreed (but still unspecified) portion of their income to the authority for the benefit of developing states; and means of a transfer of seabed mining technology to developing states would be explored. At the Geneva session, the United States, in response to continued Group of 77 pressure to discourage any unilateral exploitation of the seabed prior to a general treaty, again reaffirmed its opposition to unilateral action.[27] At the subsequent New York City session, Secretary of State Kissinger did warn that the United States would have to explore and mine on its own, unless agreement was reached soon on an ocean treaty, but sweetened the threat with an offer of a temporary limit on seabed mineral production that would be fixed in the treaty.[28]

Agreement over the specific conditions of exploration and exploitation continued to elude the negotiators, since Kissinger's latest offer was at best a temporary expedient. Broad consensus had nevertheless been building up among the developing states regarding specific conditions of exploration and exploitation, especially price and production controls and a compensation mechanism to offset any adverse effects of seabed mining for land-based producers. UN and UNCTAD reports prior to the Caracas session had called attention to these potentially adverse effects and had suggested production and price controls, compensation arrangements, and revenue gathering mechanisms for the authority to prevent or remedy falling prices of land-based minerals.[29] These and similar projected studies were described as part of the Sixth Special Session's comprehensive approach to commodities of export interest to developing countries.[30] A follow-up study, completed shortly before the Geneva session, outlined in greater detail a three-pronged strategy of production and price controls, commodity arrangements, and compensation. This strategy was in consonance with the resolutions of the Sixth Special Session, it was noted, since "the exploitation of the deep sea-bed resources, the common heritage of mankind, most obviously form one of the cornerstones of the immense co-operative effort envisaged in the new international economic order."[31]

Such detailed studies clearly influenced the thinking and the proposals of the Group of 77 at the Caracas session.[32] The group of 77, after all, grew out of UNCTAD in 1964 and shares its determination to reshape international economic relations. At Geneva, the Group of 77 continued to regard "the conference as the opening wedge in their drive to achieve a 'new international economic order'."[33] In doing so, it began to orient the debate toward more specific questions than it had done at Caracas. Discussions began about the structure, powers, and functions of the international machinery, and the Working Group of the First Committee developed a unified text on a contractual joint-venture system based on the Group of 77's proposal at Caracas. The "single negotiating text" of the First Committee[34] attempted to harmonize and synthesize the approaches of all groups, but still contained specific measures central to Group of 77 strategy, such as ease of access of developing states to patented and nonpatented seabed technology (article 11.1.a), preferential access of developing states to production of seabed minerals (article 28.xi), undetermined but "equitable" sharing of benefits and revenues for developing states (articles 26.2.x and 45), production controls (article 30.b), and price controls (annex I, part B.4.ii). The developed states continued to object to such specific measures as production and price controls and to all but a weak compensation mechanism. Nevertheless, the unity of the Group of 77 managed to seize the negotiating initiative at the Caracas and Geneva sessions, as well as during negotiations over a revised negotiating text at the New York City session.

Conclusions

Should the efforts for the new law of the sea continue to evolve from rhetoric and confrontation toward specific proposals and a spirit of compromise, the prospect for a mutually acceptable international seabed authority will remain favorable. The developing countries already appear to have obtained partial acceptance of their two key principles relating to the subject matter: participation in the control of the exploitation of deep seabed natural resources and creation of a new source (even if only of limited size) for the automatic transfer of financial resources for development. But the developing states' concern with extending national control to 200 miles has had unfortunate effects on the international authority. The revenue potential for development of deep seabed resources is not as abundant as once believed, and substantial revenue-sharing arrangements within the 200-mile limit are no longer politically feasible. Political unity, stimulated and guided by the NIEO program, had gained much in the prolonged CLOS political debate. But it still remains to be seen how extensive these gains can be translated into control over natural resources and the transfer of real resources.[35]

Notes

1. United Nations General Assembly resolutions 2574D (XXIV), 2749 (XXV) and 2750C (XXV), respectively.
2. Ann Hollick and Robert E. Osgood, *New Era in Ocean Politics* (Baltimore: The Johns Hopkins University Press, 1974), esp. pp. 1-73.
3. A proposal of the Trilateral Commission; see Richard N. Gardner, "Offshore Oil and the Law of the Seas," *New York Times*, 14 March 1976, p. 14. One of the studies summarized in this article estimates that even a 50 percent sharing of profits from the mining of manganese nodules in the international area would yield only $76-118 million a year for international development by 1980, while a 2 percent royalty on the value of the oil production from the 12-mile limit out to the 200 meter depth limit could add about $800 million a year by 1986, and a 10 percent royalty on the value of oil produced between the 200-meter depth mark and the edge of the continental margin could yield $1 billion annually for international development by 1980.
4. This brief description of developing states' ocean policies and concerns is analyzed in greater detail, with specific reference to Brazil and Latin

America, in a larger study of the author supported by the Organization of American States and the Conjunto Universitario Candido Mendes, Rio de Janeiro, Brazil. Preliminary conclusions were reported in "Trends in U.S.-Brazilian Maritime Relations," *Inter-American Economic Affairs* 17 (Winter, 1973): 3-24. Subsequent field research was carried out during much of 1974 and 1975, including interviews with nearly all of the members of the Brazilian delegation to the Caracas round of the CLOS. See also a forthcoming article by this author, "The Domestic Context of Brazilian Maritime Policy," in *Ocean Development and International Law: The Journal of Marine Affairs.*

5. U.S., Department of State, Office of Media Services, *Special Report,* no. 8 (1974), p. 5. Testimony by John R. Stevenson, Special Representative of the President and chairman of the U.S. delegation to the CLOS, before the Senate Foreign Relations Committee on September 5, 1974.

6. Article IX(2) and (4) of the "Programme of Action on the Establishment of a New International Economic Order." Resolution 3202 (S-VI) adopted by the General Assembly during its Sixth Special Session.

7. United Nations General Assembly resolution 3362 (S-VII), "Development and International Economic Co-operation," Article II(3). See Chapter 2 above.

8. United Nations, Official Records, *Third United Nations Conference on the Law of the Sea* (New York: United Nations, 1975), vol. I, pp. 37-38.

9. Ibid., p. 195.

10. Ibid., pp. 197-198. The "Charter of Economic Rights and Duties of States" was approved a few months after the Caracas CLOS session, and article 29 indeed called for the establishment of an international regime, which would ensure equitable distribution of benefits from seabed mining, taking into account the particular interests and needs of developing states.

11. Ibid., e.g., Algeria, p. 167; China, p. 80; Congo, p. 107; Honduras, p. 81; Madagascar, p. 106; Morocco, p. 178; Nepal, p. 170; Pakistan, p. 146; Paraguay, p. 161; Republic of Vietnam, p. 66; the UNCTAD representative, p. 183; Venezuela, t. 189, etc.

12. "108 Delegations Participate in General Debate on New Economic Order," *UN Monthly Chronicle* 12 (September, 1975): e.g., introductory statement by Abdelaziz Bouteflika, President of the Seventh Special Session (p. 15); Afghanistan (p. 20); Bhutan (p. 24); Guatemala (p. 38); Kuwait (p. 46); Zaire (p. 70); etc.

13. See Odette Jankowitsch and Karl P. Sauvant, "The Evolution of the Non-Aligned Movement into a Pressure Group for the Establishment of the New International Economic Order." Paper presented at the Seventeenth Annual Convention of the International Studies Association, Toronto, 25-29 February 1976.

14. Reprinted in United Nations document A/9330, 22 November 1973, pp.

52-54.
15. Elisabeth Mann-Borgese, "Report from Caracas: The Law of the Sea," *The Center Magazine* 7 (November-December, 1974): 33.
16. "Preparations for the Seventh Special Session of the United Nations General Assembly," *Department of State Bulletin* 72 (23 June 1975): 871, 874. In separate testimony before the Subcommittee on International Organizations of the House Committee on International Relations, Paul Boeker (Deputy Assistant Secretary for Economic and Business Affairs) and Clarence Ferguson, Jr. (U.S. Representative on the UN Economic and Social Council) concurred that the Group of 77 had demonstrated a new spirit of compromise during the early stages of the preparatory meetings.
17. John R. Stevenson and Bernard H. Oxman, "The Third United Nations Conference on the Law of the Sea: The 1974 Caracas Session," *American Journal of International Law* 69 (1975): 1.
18. For discussions of the politicization of the CLOS, see Constantin A. Stavropous, "Problemas de Procedimiento de la Tercera Conferencia Sobre El Derecho del Mar," in *Las Naciones Unidas y El Mar,* ed. H.S. Amerasinghe et al. (Mexico: Secretaria de Relaciones Exteriores, 1974), pp. 46, 49; and Robert L. Friedheim, "A Law of the Sea Conference—Who Needs It?," in *International Relations and the Future of Ocean Space,* ed. Robert G. Wirsing (Colombia, South Carolina: University of South Carolina Press, 1974), esp. the section on "The Politics of the Law of the Sea," pp. 46ff.
19. John R. Stevenson and Bernard H. Oxman, "The Preparations for the Law of the Sea Conference," *American Journal of International Law* 68 (1974): esp. pp. 4-8.
20. René-Jean Dupuy, "The Law of the Sea Conference: A Bid to Resolve Contradictions," *International Perspectives,* March-April, 1974, p. 71.
21. UN, General Assembly Official Records, *Report of the Committee on the Peaceful Uses of the Sea-Bed and the Ocean Floor Beyond the Limits of National Jurisdiction* (New York: United Nations, 1973), vol. II, pp. 51-165.
22. All quotes from Stevenson and Oxman, "The Third United Nations Conference on the Law of the Sea," p. 9.
23. Third Conference on the Law of the Sea, *Text on Conditions of Exploration and Exploitation Prepared by the Group of Seventy-Seven* (A/CONF.62/C.1/L.7), 16 August 1974.
24. Third Conference on the Law of the Sea, *Draft Articles Considered by Committee at Its Informal Meeting* (*Articles 1-21*) (A/CONF. 62/C.1/L.3), 5 August 1974.
25. C. F. Amerasinghe, "Basic Principles Relating to the International Regime of the Oceans at the Caracas Session of the U.N. Law of the Sea Conference," *Journal of Maritime Law and Commerce* 6 (January, 1975): 218, 224; and A. O. Adede, "The System for Exploitation of the 'Common Heritage of Mankind' at the Caracas Conference," *American Journal of*

International Law 69 (1975): 39ff.
26. Adede, "The System for Exploitation," p. 45.
27. United Nations, Official Records, *Third United Nations Conference on the Law of the Sea* (New York: United Nations, 1975), vol. IV, pp. 53-55.
28. Kathleen Teltsch, "U.S. Seabed Proposals Set Off Debate," *New York Times,* 11 April 1976, p. 10.
29. See conference document *Reports submitted by the United Nations Conference on Trade and Development* (A/CONF./62/26), 6 June 1974.
30. United Nations, Official Records, *Third United Nations Conference on the Law of the Sea* (New York: United Nations, 1975), vol. I, p. 183. Statement by G.D. Arsenis of the United Nations Conference on Trade and Development. United Nations Conference document *Economic Implications of Sea-Bed Mineral Development in the International Area: Report of the Secretary-General* (A/CONF./62/25), 22 May 1974, pp. 45-81.
31. United Nations Conference document, *Economic Implications of Sea-Bed Mining in the International Area: Report of the Secretary-General* (A/CONF./62/37), 18 February 1975, pp. 1, 10, 14.
32. The role and importance of the United Nations and UNCTAD studies at Caracas and plans for the follow-up study before the Geneva session are discussed by Kenneth O. Rattray, Rapporteur-General of the CLOS, in Annex I, "Statement of Activities of the First Committee," of a UN CLOS document, *Statement of Activities of the Conference During Its First and Second Sessions* (A/CONF./62/L.8/Rev.1), October 1974, pp. 3, 5.
33. Report on the Geneva session by Ronald Schiller, "The Grab for the Oceans: Part II," *Reader's Digest,* December 1975, pp. 105-106.
34. Third Conference on the Law of the Sea, *Informal Single Negotiating Text* (CONF. 62/WP.8/Part I), 7 May 1975.
35. Since completion of this paper in early 1976, two articles have appeared which via different routes collaborate the conclusions reached here. The first article, on the basis of an extremely complex model for content analysis, concludes that the major impact of the NIEO on the CLOS was in the area of the international seabed authority. See Robert L. Friedheim and William J. Durch, "The International Seabed Resources Agency Negotiation and the New International Economic Order." Paper delivered at the 1976 Annual Meeting of the American Political Science Association, Chicago, Illinois, September 3, 1976. Indeed, the fifth round of the CLOS closed in September, 1976, in a deadlock over the international seabed authority, with a number of states in the Group of 77 insisting on a dominant role for the authority in mining. The second article explicitly links "new international economic order diplomacy" to 12 major issues. A NIEO-NLOS linkage is asserted as well, but is neither examined in detail nor documented as was done above. See Branislav Gosovic and John Gerard Ruggio, "On the Creation of a New International Economic Order: Issue

Linkage and the Seventh Special Session of the UN General Assembly," *International Organization* 30 (Spring 1976): 335, 344.

12 *The Generalized System of Preferences: A Review and Appraisal*

Peter J. Ginman and Tracy Murray

Commencing in 1971, the long awaited Generalized System of Preferences (GSP) was introduced by a number of industrial nations including Australia, Austria, Canada, the European Community (EC—Belgium, Denmark, France, Federal Republic of Germany, Ireland, Italy, Luxembourg, Netherlands, and the United Kingdom),[1] Finland, Japan, New Zealand, Norway, Sweden, Switzerland, and the United States.[2] Under the GSP, tariffs charged on imports of manufactured and semimanufactured products from the developing countries are granted preferential reductions with the most-favored-nation (MFN) duties charged on imports from other sources.

The idea for such a system was introduced at the first UN Conference on Trade and Development (UNCTAD) held in Geneva in 1964.[3] The goal of this conference was to establish a new international trade policy that would contribute to raising the material wealth of the developing countries through trade rather than aid. The basic desire was to reduce the developing countries' excessive dependence on commodity exports for foreign exchange earnings by creating international trade incentives to stimulate their exportation of industrial goods. It was recognized that the developing countries find it very difficult to produce and sell manufactured goods in the industrial countries when competing for market-access on an equal basis with producers in industrial nations. Being unequal producers, they should not be expected to compete effectively on an equal basis. Instead, their

---

P. J. Ginman was on leave with the UNCTAD Secretariat when this paper was first drafted; the opinions expressed, however, do not necessarily reflect those of the UNCTAD Secretariat. The research for this paper was financially supported, in part, by a summer research grant from the New York University and the New York University project on the "Multinational Corporation in the U.S. and World Economy." We would like to thank Ingo Walter for helpful comments on early drafts of this paper.

exports should receive preferential treatment; thus, the GSP was proposed.

During the interim period from 1964 to 1971, numerous international negotiations on the GSP took place in the UNCTAD Special Committee on Preferences and finally culminated in an initial system. As might be expected, the outcome of this dramatically new policy involving over 100 independent nations was not completely satisfactory to all. Since 1971, additional negotiations have taken place—with limited success—to discuss ways of improving the GSP. The GSP is also considered to be an important part of the negotiations on the establishment of the New International Economic Order (NIEO) as contained in the resolutions of the Sixth and Seventh Special Sessions of the United Nations General Assembly.[4]

The GSP was never considered as a panacea for solving all of the complex problems of economic development. Nevertheless, it was offered by the developed countries as an important new step toward helping the developing countries help themselves. Given this spirit of cooperation, it is surprising that the GSP as introduced has been so severely criticized. While it is currently too early to concretely conclude that the GSP will fail, the evidence gained to date strongly suggests that the GSP of today is unlikely to live up to its expectations. The major shortcomings are that (1) many important products of export interest of the developing countries have been excluded from the GSP; (2) the safeguard measures often result in preferential treatment being denied; (3) the "rules of origin," which guarantee that the benefits of the GSP actually accrue to the exporting developing country, are too restrictive; and (4) the administrative procedures are sometimes too difficult for the developing countries to be effectively implemented. If the GSP is to become as important as was promised, substantial improvements must be made in answer to these criticisms; these improvements must be coupled with developing country initiatives to take advantage of their opportunities under the GSP. Thus, the future success of the GSP requires a joint effort by the developed and the developing countries.

The purpose of this contribution is to document the existing shortcomings in the GSP in the spirit of constructive criticism. We then indicate the kinds of improvements that are needed if the GSP is to generate the maximum trade benefits that the developing countries are likely to obtain from a purely tariff-based policy. Any additional benefits must come from developing country initiatives or other aspects of the NIEO.

Evolution of Generalized Preferences

The present structure of world trade is, in part, one of the legacies of colonialism and its dependence-oriented trading relationships. Since World War II, the trade policies of the developed countries have evolved along self-interest lines. Any trade liberalization introduced by one country is offered in return for a concession gained from another; that is to say, tariff reductions were negotiated in General Agreement on Tariffs and Trade (GATT) on the basis of reciprocity. Since the concessions desired were export oriented, requiring improved market access, and since the developing countries had no market to speak of, the developing countries' trading interests have, by and large, been overlooked by the numerous GATT negotiations which have taken place during the post-World War II period.

Thus, when the developing countries began to emerge as active participants in the world economy, their efforts to expand trade were frustrated from the outset by this established international environment governing trade relations. A by-product of this developed-country dominance was the evolution of a world tariff structure which, despite successive rounds of multilateral tariff negotiations, was decidely biased against the interests of the developing countries. The typical profile of tariffs faced by developing countries was that of a pyramid, i.e., zero or very low tariffs on their traditional commodity exports, gradually escalating tariffs on nontraditional exports of semimanufactured and manufactured products of a higher order of processing, and very high duties on labor-intensive products whose international comparative advantage had shifted from the developed countries. This vertical ordering of tariffs acted as a further barrier to industrialization by discouraging even the processing of local raw materials.

Obviously, the developing countries were in need of a drastically new international trade policy, a policy that was not based on reciprocity. Thus, when the idea of a *nonreciprocal* GSP was offered by UNCTAD, the developing countries pressured for it with all of their combined influence. The idea was that preferential tariffs would result in developing country exports displacing exports from other sources, thus leading to a substantial increase in the world demand for developing country exports.

But this concept of trade diversion led to another problem. If only one or two industrial nations were to grant preferential treatment on one or more special products of export interest to the developing countries, these developed countries could experience increases in their imports via the diversion of trade destined for other industrial countries. Such trade diversion could result in substantial import displacement of domestic production for specific developed nations even when developing country exports of such products to the developed countries as a whole grow only moderately. To minimize this problem, the GSP was envisaged to be a system in which all developed countries would grant preferential tariff treatment on *all* manufactured products, i.e., a *generalized* system. Unfortunately, the developed countries were unable to agree on a common system covering all such products. Instead, each developed country introduced its own GSP "scheme," and the GSP was destined to become a set of different national (or regional for the EC) preference schemes rather than a generalized system.

Who Benefits?

The over 100 countries now belonging to the Group of 77 have become the common denominator in most GSP schemes, with individual developed countries reserving the right to decline to grant preferential tariff status to any developing country on grounds "which they hold compelling." This clause opened a loophole for overt discrimination among the developing countries in what was envisaged to be a *nondiscriminatory* generalized system of preferences; the primary invokers of this loophole are the EC and the U.S.

The EC recognizes a wide range of developing countries and territories as beneficiaries; however, certain of them are discriminated against and denied GSP treatment on certain products. For instance, as a prerequisite for GSP treatment on most textile products, beneficiaries must abide by the "voluntary" export restrictions embodied in the GATT "Arrangement Regarding International Trade in Textiles"; only 16 developing countries meet this prerequisite. For textile products not covered by the GATT arrangement and for footwear, the EC does not grant GSP treatment to developing territories; this clause excluded Hong Kong, the major developing supplier, from GSP treatment on these products.[5]

Another problem involves those developing countries that have special trading relationships with the EC, initially under the Second Yaoundé Convention and the Arusha Agreement. These agreements have recently been renegotiated under the Lomé Convention, and now cover 46 developing countries in Africa, the Caribbean, and the Pacific: the 22 Yaoundé and Arusha countries plus 24 ex-Commonwealth developing countries which gained associate status as a result of the United Kingdom's accession to the EC. The Lomé countries have access to EC markets under a regime that is more favorable than the access accorded under the GSP—the product coverage is broader, the access is not limited by ceilings, and the origin rules are more liberal (these aspects are discussed in the following three sections). For all practical purposes, the 46 developing countries are not "real" GSP beneficiaries as far as the EC is concerned. In fact, they have acted as an anti-GSP lobby, pressuring the EC to design GSP provisions that safeguard the trade advantages of the associates.

The U.S. is the only country to designate eligible beneficiary developing countries on the basis of political criteria. The U.S. specifically excludes communist developing countries (except Romania and Yugoslavia), members of the Organization of Petroleum Exporting Countries (OPEC) and potentially members of any other producers' association, countries which grant "reverse" preferences, and countries which nationalize or expropriate U.S. investments without adequate compensation. All of these criteria violate the nonreciprocity principle of the GSP, explicitly or implicitly (in that they attempt to obtain economic or political concessions). The two which are of most significance deal with OPEC and "reverse" preferences.

The OPEC clause prohibits GSP treatment to all members of the organization. The U.S. president has attempted to obtain a congressional waiver for those OPEC members who did not participate in the 1973 oil embargo; the congressional refusal to grant such a waiver reflects the strong U.S. opposition to OPEC. The "reverse" preference clause was inserted to combat the EC association policy whereby the developing country associates granted special access to EC exports to the disadvantage of U.S. exports. Partly as a result of this U.S. pressure, the Lomé Convention is a one way preference street—the EC grants preferential access but does not receive such access from the associates. The major "reverse" preference issue today involves the EC Mediterranean policy, consisting of special preferential trade agreements between the EC and countries of the Mediterranean. Of the countries which have such agreements, Greece and Spain have been denied GSP treatment; however, beneficiary treatment is accorded to Algeria, Cyprus, Egypt, Israel, Lebanon, Malta, Morocco, Tunisia, and Turkey. These latter countries receive GSP status under a waiver covering "reverse" preferences that do not have a significant adverse impact on U.S. exports. (Morocco grants "reverse" preferences to all trading partners on an MFN basis.)

The unfortunate aspect of the U.S. criterion for beneficiary status is that the day-to-day political behavior of beneficiaries will be used by the U.S. to determine whether particular developing countries are to continue to enjoy GSP treatment. Of particular concern are the issues of future producers' associations and nationalization or expropriation.

None of the other industrial countries introduced GSP schemes that discriminate among developing countries. This does not mean that they were unconcerned about excessive import competition as a result of GSP treatment. They solved such problems in other ways. Instead of discriminating among developing countries, they simply excluded "import-sensitive" products from their GSP schemes; but so did the discriminatory schemes of the EC, Japan, and the U.S.

Product Coverage and Limitations

As already noted, the primary objective of the GSP is to expand export earnings of the developing countries by stimulating developed country imports of manufactured and semimanufactured products, the incentive being provided by preferential tariffs. Hence, the GSP will only assist the developing countries in exporting those manufacture goods that are, in fact, subject to duty. Goods already admitted duty-free by the developed countries—primarily agricultural commodities and industrial raw materials—by definition fall outside the scope of the GSP or, for that matter, any preferential tariff program.

Based on current trade patterns, nearly three-fifths (58 percent in 1970) of the exports of the beneficiaries to the developed countries are duty-free on an MFN basis. These duty-free items are heavily concentrated in primary commodities and in other products historically exported by the developing countries during the colonial and postcolonial period. In addition, the concept of preferences on manufactured and semimanufactured goods has been generally interpreted by the developed countries to be manufactured *industrial* goods, and not processed agricultural and fishery products. Hence, most dutiable products in the agricultural sectors also fall outside the scope of the GSP. Such products account for another one-seventh (14 percent in 1970) of beneficiary trade with the developed countries. After excluding beneficiary exports admitted duty-free as well as exports of dutiable agricultural products, we find that developing country exports of manufactured goods potentially eligible for GSP tariff treatment account for roughly one-fourth of their trade with the developed countries. Clearly, this greatly limits the relevance of the GSP and severely curtails the contribution which the GSP can make toward industrializing the developing countries.

Moreover, in negotiating the GSP it was agreed that the developed countries could take whatever safeguard measures they deemed necessary to protect their domestic markets from undue disruption that might be caused by preferential imports from the developing countries (see the next section for a detailed discussion of these safeguard measures). By including a unilaterally administered safeguard system, the developed countries introduced additional limitations into their GSP schemes and a higher degree of uncertainty. Each developed country has taken advantage of this clause to protect domestic producers of such "sensitive" products as textiles, leather, and petroleum-based products, i.e., products that account for the bulk of developing country dutiable trade in industrial goods. Most developed countries excluded these products *a priori* from preferential treatment. The EC excluded all industrial raw materials to accommodate the trade interests of the African Associates (and textiles via discriminatory beneficiary lists). The U.S. has the most extensive list of excluded products, including textiles, shoes, petroleum products, electronics, glass, selected steel items, and a few others of lesser importance. Japan followed suit by excluding textiles, leather, and petroleum-based products, as well as a few additional products. The products excluded by the EC account for one-third of its dutiable imports of industrial products from the beneficiaries; the U.S. excludes just

Table 1. Industrial country imports from developing countries, 1970[a/] (1970 in millions of dollars)

Importer	Total imports	Dutiable imports	Covered by GSP	GSP as percentage of total imports	GSP as percentage of dutiable imports
EC: All products	18,175	5,479	1,447	8	26
Agricultural	4,683	3,850	357	8	9
Industrial	13,492	1,629	1,090	8	67
U.S.: All products	7,846	4,539	1,712	22	38
Agricultural	3,421	1,387	809	24	53
Industrial	4,425	3,152	903	20	29
Japan: All products	6,906	3,984	772	11	19
Agricultural	1,059	640	29	3	5
Industrial	5,847	3,344	743	13	22
Others: All products[b/]	2,852	1,058	522	18	49
Agricultural	997	567	104	10	18
Industrial	1,855	491	418	23	85
TOTAL: All products	35,779	15,060	4,453	12	30
Agricultural	10,160	6,444	1,299	13	20
Industrial	25,619	8,616	3,154	12	37

Source: Based on UNCTAD, "Second General Report on the Implementation of the Generalized System of Preferences: Study of the UNCTAD Secretariat" (TD/BC.5/22 and Corr. 1), 17 April 1974, and UNCTAD, "Scheme of Generalized Preferences of the United States of America" (TD/B/C.5/38), 6 November 1975.

a/ For the EC, Lomé Convention countries are not included. The U.S. figures exclude the newly designated beneficiaries: Cyprus, Hong Kong, Israel, Romania, Somalia, and Turkey.

b/ Includes Austria, Canada, Finland, New Zealand, Norway, Sweden, and Switzerland.

under three-fourths and Japan excludes four-fifths of such trade. The data in table 1 quantify these exclusions. And the value of what remains is revealed by the summary of the data contained in table 2.

This summary reveals that only 12 percent of developing countries' exports are, in fact, covered by the GSP. In fact, as will be shown below, if exclusions due to ceiling-type safeguards are taken into account, the effective coverage is only approximately 4 percent of developing country exports. And how costly is this to the developed countries? The answer would depend on how one measures cost. In terms of tariff revenue forgone by the developed countries, the GSP costs are estimated to be in the range of $400-500 million annually, based on 1970 trade flows. This cost is inconsequential when compared with the $6.2 billion in "official and multilateral"

Table 2. Product coverage of the GSP, 197o

Product group	Value of developing countries' exports (Million dollars)	Percentage[a/]
All products	35,779	1oo
less duty-free	-2o,719	58
less dutiable agricultural and fishery items not covered by GSP	- 5,145	14
less dutiable petroleum items not covered by GSP	- 3,o65	9
less other dutiable industrial items not covered by GSP		
--textiles and footwear	- 637	2
--industrial raw materials excluded by EC	- 591	2
--import-sensitive electronic items excluded by U.S.	- 557	2
--miscellaneous other exclusions	- 612	2
GSP product coverage	4,453	12

Source: Same as Table 1.

a/ Shares do not add to 1oo due to rounding.

development aid granted by these same countries in 1970.[6] The production effect due to increased GSP imports has been estimated at roughly $400 million annually—again inconsequential for countries whose gross domestic production is measured in the billions and trillions of U.S. dollars annually Or if employment displacement is of concern, the estimate is of the order of 25,000 jobs—again inconsequential when compared with the normal annual change in employment in these developed countries of approximately 2.3 million jobs.[7]

Nevertheless, it would be too much to conclude that the GSP offers no potential. A multitude of factors have contributed to the creation of the current pattern of trade. The structure of tariff rates is only one of them. Thus, changes in the structure of tariff rates potentially can lead to changes in trade patterns. It is not unreasonable to anticipate that at least some reallocation of production favoring the developing countries and some expansion of their manufacturing exports will take place.Since the industrial country markets for manufactured goods have been growing rapidly, it has been argued that by emphasizing these goods, the historical dependence on exports of primary products could be reduced, and badly needed foreign exchange could be earned. Even for resource-rich developing countries, industrial diversification is an important prerequisite for economic advancement. The preferential reduction of tariff rates should make the prospects for exporting industrial goods more attractive to the developing countries and, consequently, should stimulate greater investment in the productive capacity of export items. Whether or not this hoped-for development will be realized is as yet uncertain, as it takes time for these incentives to be translated into action. Moreover, these incentives are hampered by additional restrictions placed on GSP under the guise of safeguard measures.

Safeguard Measures

In addition to the restricted product coverage, the developed countries included a safeguard system to protect themselves against a potential flood of imports from the developing countries. Many GSP schemes included a traditional GATT-type escape clause whereby the country reserves the unilateral right to withdraw preferential tariff treatment on specific products if preferential imports increase sufficiently to injure domestic producers. In practice, this escape-clause safeguard has not been a serious problem for the developing countries; it has been invoked only once—by the U.K., which restored its MFN duty on imports of leather from Argentina, Brazil, Colombia, and Uruguay.

In addition to such safeguards, some preference-giving countries have built into their schemes further limitations on the amounts of certain "sensitive" items that may receive preferential treatment. The three principal schemes embodying such limitations are those of the EC, Japan, and the U.S. The approaches used by these three countries deserve attention, because, together, they account for 88 percent of GSP covered imports (see table 1).

The EC and Japan provide their domestic producers with additional protection through systems of ceilings that at first glance appear reasonable. Preferential tariffs apply on imports up to a ceiling; MFN duties are charged on imports in excess of this ceiling. Thus, the ceilings do not limit imports but instead determine the tariff rate to be applied. This seems like a justifiable safeguard in that domestic producers are protected only by MFN tariffs, and then only when imports from the developing countries grow too rapidly, i.e., exceed the ceilings which are administered on a product by product basis. Of course, the key to whether or not this is restrictive depends on the magnitude of the ceilings.

The basic formula for calculating the ceilings—base year imports from the beneficiaries plus a growth factor related to the level of imports from third countries—seems reasonable. In the case of products for which the developing countries are already major suppliers and where they have demonstrated an ability to compete in world markets and, therefore, do not need preferential treatment, the ceilings are relatively restrictive; this does not present a major problem since exports from the developing countries in excess of the ceiling are permitted under normal duties. On the other hand, in the case of products for which the developing countries are noncompetitive and account for only a minor share of world exports, the growth factor used for calculating the ceiling is large. Moreover, in such instances the expected increase in developing countries' exports should not pose much of a problem to the developed-country producers, as there is substantial room for this trade to simply displace imports from other (nonpreferred) sources.

However, when the actual practices and experiences under the ceiling systems of the EC and Japan are examined, it becomes clear that their effects on developing country exports run counter to the rationale underlying the ceiling concept. Ceiling calculations are normally based on trade data which lag the current year by at least two years. As a result, such reference years lead to import ceilings which fail to reflect the actual growth patterns in developing country exports. In fact, for many important products the ceilings fall far short of the normal level of trade that would have occurred even in the absence of any GSP stimulus. Thus, in order for preferential tariff rates to contribute to an expansion of trade, they must apply on expanded *levels* of trade. Otherwise, they offer no net incentive to importers to increase their orders, and the GSP incentives for "trade expansion" cannot function.

A related problem which compounds the restrictive effect of the ceiling system involves the definitions of product groups used in administering the ceiling limitations. Products that are exported successfully by developing countries are usually very narrowly defined so that these countries will account for a large share of the developed country's imports; as a result, the ceilings will be highly restrictive. In contrast, noncompetitive products tend to be broadly defined, resulting in rather large growth factors. Thus, the full benefits of preferential treatment will apply only on products which developing countries export in minor volumes—if at all.

Since the ceilings apply to imports from all beneficiaries combined, it might be possible for any particular developing country to generate a significant increase in preferential trade *even within* the confines of an overall restrictive ceiling. This, however, is prevented in the cases of the EC and Japan under the rationale of spreading the benefits of the GSP by reserving a portion of the ceiling for the less competitive developing countries. *Maximum-amount* constraints have been formulated that limit preferential treatment of imports under the GSP from individual beneficiaries to 20 percent, 30 percent or 50 percent of the ceiling, depending on the product group involved. Thus, no single beneficiary can receive preferential treatment on exports exceeding one-half of the ceiling (in many cases one-fifth). This maximum-amount limitation might be reasonable under conditions of great import diversification. However, in actual practice, imports from the beneficiaries are highly concentrated. For any given manufactured product there are generally less than five major suppliers; most often there are only one or two. With such an uneven distribution of trade, this maximum-amount provision simply cuts off the major supplier, reserving a significant portion of the ceiling for minor suppliers that are unable to take advantage of the situation. As a result, a large part of the ceilings can be expected to remain needlessly unutilized. Recent evidence supports this view.[8]

In addition, for products considered "sensitive," the EC allocates the ceiling among its member states according to a fixed formula: 10.5 percent of the ceiling for Benelux, 5 percent for Denmark, 27.5 percent for the Federal Republic of Germany, 19 percent for France, 1 percent for Ireland, 15 percent for Italy, and 22 percent for the U.K., with slight departures from these percentages for textile products. This procedure transforms each EC ceiling into seven separate country ceilings. Of course, actual EC imports from developing countries are not distributed among the member states according to these same shares for every product. Consequently, some country quotas will be exceeded by developing country exports and others underutilized. And those GSP imports in excess of a given country's allotment cannot gain preferential treatment to another EC country. This has led to a portion of beneficiary trade becoming sterilized, thereby, losing its preferential status.

The experience under Japan's system of ceilings parallels in many ways that of the EC, particularly regarding the restrictiveness of the ceiling and maximum-amount limitations. However, in 1973 Japan did introduce a policy of "flexible administration" which allows imports to continue receiving preferential treatment after the ceilings and maximum amounts have been reached. Only when such imports are likely to adversely affect domestic producers will they cease to gain GSP benefits. This liberalized approach, however, excludes a number of product groups of major interest to the developing countries.

Another aspect of the ceiling system is that it creates uncertainty for importers who, because of the ceilings, cannot know in advance whether or not GSP preferences will be received when their goods are cleared through customs. Consequently, importers are likely to be reluctant to contract for goods at prices reflecting preferential tariff rates. Additionally, and more importantly, this uncertainty is likely to dampen the investment incentive for new productive capacity for GSP products in developing countries. This is not to say that such investment will not take place. Rather, the GSP advantages are likely to be heavily discounted by investors. Thus, the GSP is unlikely to provide the stimulus anticipated by the developing countries when they originally negotiated the introduction of the new system.

The U.S. GSP scheme also embodies a framework for limiting preferential treatment which, at first glance, seems reasonable—as did the ceiling systems of the EC and Japan. The major safeguard provision in the U.S. variant is the traditional GATT-type escape clause. But in addition, the U.S. has specified "competitive need" criteria which provide that preferential treatment will not be granted (instead MFN duties are charged) in those cases where normal U.S. imports of a given product from a single beneficiary developing country exceed (1) $25 million annually[9] or (2) 50 percent by value of total U.S. imports of the product. Other beneficiary developing countries will continue to enjoy preferential treatment on the product and the affected beneficiary will continue to enjoy preferential treatment on other products. The rationale underlying these criteria is to provide for a withdrawal, or phasing-out, of preferential treatment in those cases where it can no longer be justified on the grounds of promoting the development of a particular industry in the developing country concerned. In addition, this provision provides some advantage for the less competitive developing countries by giving them preferential treatment over the major beneficiary suppliers affected by the criteria. On the other hand, in cases where U.S. imports are small and primarily originate in a single developing country, the 50 percent limit will preclude preferential treatment on a modest flow of trade. Unlike the ceiling systems of the EC and Japan, these "competitive need" criteria are of an "all or nothing" type: once either limit is exceeded, preferential treatment ceases and is not renewed at the beginning of the following year.

An UNCTAD analysis of these criteria indicates that they will severely limit the advantages of the U.S. scheme. Based on 1970 trade flows, about half of developing country exports of eligible products would be excluded from GSP treatment. Due to these criteria falling primarily on semimanufactured products rather than more sophisticated items, it indiscriminately harms the least developed as well as the more advanced developing countries—a contradiction with the underlying rationale for these competitive need criteria. The $25 million limitation would have affected 18 articles and 12 countries in 1970, but in value terms these exclusions amount to 49 percent of the total trade covered by the scheme. Even though it might be conceded that the $25 million limit is a reasonable definition of an internationally competitive industry, the 50 percent limit certainly is not. This latter restriction, had it applied in 1970, would have been invoked in 211 cases, only 32 of which involve import flows of more than $3 million annually; these 211 cases represent 7 percent of the trade eligible for GSP treatment. Certainly, these are not cases in which particular developing countries have demonstrated an ability to compete in world markets. Instead these are simply cases in which the product happens to be very narrowly defined in the U.S. tariff codes.

Up to this point, we have only discussed the negative aspects of the ceiling-type limitations from the viewpoint of the developing countries. On the other hand, the EC and Japan introduced ceilings to safeguard the interests of domestic producers. Yet, given the low share of imports originating in the developing countries and the serious supply limitations, it is unlikely that GSP imports will suddenly grow to the extent of seriously disrupting developed countries' markets. Furthermore, any increase in developing country exports can be expected to largely displace imports from nonpreferred sources.

Although it is possible that preferential trade could pose a problem for domestic producers of particular products, the automatic ceiling mechanism which limits preferential treatment without any direct tie to injury to domestic producers is much more restrictive than necessary to protect domestic producers.[10] In order to safeguard injured sectors without unduly limiting preferential trade, a more flexible safeguard based on a causal tie between injury and increased preferential trade is needed.

Rules of Origin

One of the initial aims of the GSP was to stimulate production and employment in the export sectors of beneficiary countries. However, preferential tariff rates as a stimulus might bring about an unintended result, namely a deflection of international trade among industrial countries. Instead of one industrial nation exporting goods directly to another and facing MFN tariffs, the exporter might send the goods first to a beneficiary developing country for importation and then immediately re-export them to the initially-intended industrial nation, thereby gaining entry at the GSP preferential tariff rate. In this way, the GSP could initiate a system of diverting trade through beneficiary countries, stimulating the creation of "trading houses" rather than industrial production. To prevent such a deflection of trade, "rules of origin" were established. These rules constitute a set of requirements designed to prevent the beneficiaries from simply re-exporting goods produced elsewhere without substantial processing. The rules of origin do not, however, inhibit transnational enterprises from gaining advantages under the GSP. By shifting production of inputs to beneficiary countries, these enterprises can "export" to plants in a developed country and, by meeting the processing criterion, take advantage of preferential treatment for the exports of their foreign affiliates.

In general, the rules of origin specify three conditions that must be met before an exported good qualifies for GSP treatment: (1) the goods must be shipped directly from the beneficiary developing country to the preference-giving country without intermediate processing or trading; (2) the goods must undergo minimum processing in the beneficiary country; and (3) the goods must be accompanied by appropriate documentation which certifies that they qualify for GSP treatment.

The minimum processing criterion varies from country to country with two general definitions: the "process criterion" and the "value-added criterion." Under the process criterion—used by the Western European developed countries and Japan—the exported good must be classified under a different Brussels Nomenclature tariff heading than any of the imported materials or components used in its production. However, certain exceptions to this general rule occur in which a product undergoes a change of tariff heading after only superficial transformation. On the other hand, there are a number of cases in which substantial transformation has occurred without a change in tariff heading. Since these exceptions could not be agreed upon by all preference-giving countries using the process criterion, each country elaborated a set of exceptions to the general rule. These rules are overwhelming in their complexity. For example, the exceptions list of the EC involves some 85 pages of technical specifications. The developing countries have encountered tremendous difficulty in understanding, let alone administering, these rules.

The value-added criterion implemented by the U.S., Canada, and New Zealand simply specifies that the value of imported materials and components must not exceed a certain percentage of the value of the exported good, i.e., 50 percent. Although this principle is straightforward, serious difficulties arise in determining the value of the final good or the imported materials and components.

In addition to adding complexity, the rules of origin also contain a number of clauses that further reduce the scope of the GSP. Various goods have been *de facto* excluded from preferential treatment because the minimum transformation requirements under the process criterion are too difficult to meet. For example, transistor radios do not qualify for GSP treatment in the EC if they are made with imported transistors, which few developing countries can domestically produce. Thus, for all practical purposes, the EC does not grant preferences on transistor radios. The U.S. limits imported materials and components to 35 percent of the domestic processing cost, which excludes such cost items as executive salaries, local transportation, royalties and license fees, profits, etc. This lowers the base for determining the maximum allowable import content for GSP goods to a figure far below the implied 65 percent; it often falls as low as 10 or 15 percent.

The difficulties associated with the rules of origin have been recognized in many international forums and efforts are under way to simplify and harmonize them. For example, the anomalies between substantial transformation requirements and procession realities, as well as the particular problems of landlocked countries in meeting direct transportation rules, have been recognized and measures to take such factors into account are gradually being implemented. Unfortunately, progress has been slow to date; there is still a long way to go.

Supply Capabilities

Most examinations of the GSP have been appropriately critical of the schemes in operation with little attention being given to the "consumers" of the GSP. It must be recognized that the GSP is a trade policy aimed at stimulating industrialization via export expansion. The benefits of such a policy will be allocated on the basis of an ability to export products covered by the schemes, i.e., primarily manufactured and semimanufactured industrial products. Consequently, the benefits will be concentrated among the few more advanced developing countries with very little going to the other more than 100 developing countries.

The extent of this uneven distribution of GSP trade is indicated by the data presented in table 3. The nine countries listed account for over two-thirds of the GSP product coverage. The second column under each scheme—effective coverage—indicates the trade benefits which remain after the restrictive impact of the ceiling-type safeguards have been subtracted; *the average effective coverage is only one-third of the GSP product coverage or only 4 percent of total developing country exports to the preference-giving countries* (recall table 1).

Even though an uneven distribution of trade was anticipated, the actual degree of concentration is more than expected. Taiwan alone accounts for almost 20 percent of the "effective" coverage even though it is not a beneficiary under the EC scheme. Over half of the "effective" GSP trade is accounted for by only four developing countries. Still, the vast majority of products defined in the tariff schedules of the developed countries are included in the preference schemes. While some of these products are highly sophisticated and beyond the present production capabilities of most developing countries, many could in the future become viable exports. Thus, while actual trade volume covered by the GSP is low, product coverage is wide, leaving substantial opportunity for the developing countries to develop exports under the GSP provisions.

Appraisal and Prospects

The overriding conclusion of this evaluation of the GSP is rather depressing. To summarize, it is a tariff program that effectively covers only 4 percent of developing country exports to the preference-giving countries because (1) much of developing country exports (agricultural commodities and industrial raw materials) already receive duty-free access under MFN treatment; (2) the GSP excludes most other agricultural products; (3) many manufactured and semimanufactured products for which the developing countries have a comparative advantage have been excluded, e.g., textile, leather, and petroleum products; and (4) over two-thirds of the trade covered by the GSP does not receive preferential tariff treatment because of the ceiling-type safeguards imposed by the EC, Japan, and the U.S. or because of rigid processing and administration requirements specified in the rules of origin. Finally, rather than a program to help all developing countries, the vast majority of the GSP trade benefits will accrue to only a dozen or so of the more advanced developing countries. The others have little capacity to benefit from any tariff policy, let alone the very restrictive GSP.

This rather depressing conclusion is further enhanced by two other observations. First, the analysis ignores the impact of the numerous nontariff barriers to trade that are completely unrelated to the GSP—such nontariff restrictions as contained in health standards, packaging regulations, market controls, subsidies to import-competitors, the EC variable levy system, the voluntary export restrictions against trade in textiles, etc. The GSP provides for a reduction in tariffs, but not for the relaxation of any other regulation governing international trade. There can be little doubt that EC preferences for textile products are completely frustrated by the voluntary export restrictions imposed against such trade. And EC preferences on agricultural products covered by the Common Agricultural Policy are of minimal value, since the variable levy which operates to protect domestic producers is left intact. These examples drawn for the EC indicate that for some products nontariff barriers pose a more serious barrier to trade than MFN tariff rates. Undoubtedly, the developing country exporters will face similar problems in exporting under the GSP provisions of other schemes as well.

Equally as threatening as existing nontariff barriers is the current trend in the international community toward greater resort to other protective measures; witness the recent U.S. decision to impose new controls on speciality steel imports, or the recent designation of electronics as import-sensitive for purposes of the U.S. GSP. If the developing countries do develop export potential under the GSP, what assurances do they have that new barriers will not be erected against such trade?

The second threat to the future of the GSP relates to recent events in Western Europe. As an aftermath of the EC enlargement, negotiations occurred which led to the formation of a Western Europe free trade area in

Table 3. Effective GSP coverage and major suppliers of industrial products, 197o (Millions of dollars)

Beneficiary supplier	U. S. scheme[a/] product coverage		E C scheme[b/] product coverage		Japan scheme product coverage		Total product coverage	
	GSP	Effective	GSP	Effective	GSP	Effective	GSP	Effective
Taiwan	492	219	--	--	73	23	565	242
Mexico	4oo	175	21	15	11	9	432	199
Yugoslavia	42	4o	356	111	1	1	399	152
South Korea	229	96	48	15	52	19	329	13o
Hong Kong[c/]	--	--	254	23	--	--	254	23
Brazil	9o	83	85	36	15	11	19o	13o
Singapore	127	5o	34	12	7	3	168	65
India	45	37	38	18	61	9	144	64

Iran	--	--	1o4	22	0	0	1o4	22
SUB-TOTAL	1,425	7oo	94o	252	22o	75	2,585	1,o27
Other Benef.	218	134	15o	1o1	523	4	891	239
TOTAL	1 643	834	1 c9o	353	743	79	3,476	1,266

Source: Based on UNCTAD "Operation and Effects of the Generalized System of Preferences (New York: United Nations, 1974) (E.73II.D16), "Scheme of Generalized Preferences," and "Operation and Effects of the Scheme of Generalized Preferences of the European Economic Community Study of the Operation of the Scheme in 1972: Study of the UNCTAD Secretariat" (TD/B/C.5/34/Add.1), 17 November 1975.

a/ Calculated from 1973 data and deflated to 197o trade levels. At the time these calculations were made, the final product coverage was not known; these figures include import-sensitive electronic and glass articles as well as a few other items subsequently removed from the U.S. GSP. The estimated product coverage, incorporating these new deletions, is $9o3 million. The "effective" product coverage would be $548 million. The effect of these deletions on each country could not be determinded from existing data. This accounts for the apparent discrepancy with the figures provided in Table 1.

b/ Calculated from 1972 data and deflated to 197o trade levels.

c/ Hong Kong has since been added to the U.S. beneficiary list. Hong Kong is subject to special exclusions under the scheme of Japan.

Note: --indicates that the developing country is not a beneficiary under the GSP scheme.

manufactured products—including, unlike the GSP, most processed agricultural and fishery products. As long as Western Europe was divided into two trading blocs, the EC and the European Free Trade Association (EFTA), preferences granted to the developing countries by any Western European nation placed the beneficiary exporters in a preferred position vis-à-vis exporters in the other bloc, as well as other nonbeneficiaries—primarily the U.S., Japan, Canada, and Eastern European nations. But the expansion of the EC and the formation of a free trade area removes all Western European producers from the nonbeneficiary class and places them in a "more preferred" position. Because of the aforementioned limiting features of the GSP schemes, Western European exports have access to the regional market that is more favorable than the GSP access enjoyed by the developing countries. The beneficiaries, in effect, have become preferred sources of Western European importers only over the non-Western European nonbeneficiaries. In essence, the value of preferences granted by all of the Western European countries has been seriously diluted by the creation of this Western European free trade area.

And the future of preferences granted by the U.S., Japan, Canada, Australia, and New Zealand? Only time will tell. The GSP was initially established for a ten-year period and made subject to extension if experience with the system warrants it. Prolongation and improvement of the GSP depends not only on its performance, but also on the scope remaining for tariff preferences to be an effective stimulus for expanding the exports of the developing countries. This remaining scope is subject to further erosion as the developed countries have launched a new round of multilateral trade negotiations (MTN) under the auspices of GATT. It is too early to predict the outcome of these negotiations, but the objective of significant reductions in tariff levels is a plausible result. Substantial MFN tariff cuts would necessarily reduce the GSP preferential tariff margins, thereby further eroding the trade advantages under the GSP. Consequently, the developing countries view these negotiations with considerable concern.

Since the developing countries have sought nonreciprocity and nondiscrimination in the MTN—principles that have largely been acknowledged by the developed countries—their bargaining position differs from that of the other participants. However, despite this lack of reciprocity, the developing countries are not impotent given the increased awareness of their united strength as a result of their successful organization in the nonaligned movement and the Group of 77, the current worldwide energy crisis, and the emerging raw materials trends. In view of this change in their political and economic stature, and the limited opportunities for real concessions within the scope of the GSP, they may be well advised to seek alternative measures to assist their economic development. Such an opportunity for meaningful concessions does exist within the UN negotiations for the establishment of the NIEO initiated in the Sixth Special Session of the General Assembly. In fact, the GSP received serious attention during the Fourth UN Conference on Trade and Development (which met during May of 1976). It was agreed that it should be extended beyond its initial ten years' duration and adapted "to respond better to developing countries' needs." The conference also recommended that consideration be given to "binding in GATT of preferential tariff margins."[11]

Notes

1. When the GSP was first introduced, Denmark, Ireland and the U.K. were not members of the EC; instead, these three countries introduced separate GSP schemes. As of 1 January 1974, the nine members of the enlarged Community were participating in a common GSP scheme.
2. The U.S. was the last major country to introduce its preferential tariff scheme; it became effective on 1 January 1976.
3. Raul Prebisch, *Towards a New Trade Policy for Development* (United Nations: New York, 1964)
4. See General Assembly resolutions 3201 (S-VI) para. 4(n), 3202 (S-VI) para. I(3) and General Assembly resolution 3362 (S-VII) para. I(8).
5. Japan was also concerned about the supply capabilities of Hong Kong; consequently, Hong Kong is denied GSP treatment for a list of specially chosen products.
6. Organisation for Economic Co-operation and Development, *Development Assistance* (OECD: Paris, 1971).
7. For these production and employment estimates see Tracy Murray, *Trade Preferences for Developing Countries* (London: Macmillan, forthcoming), Chapter 7.
8. The following products are EC examples: lead oxides, leather, travel goods, protective gloves, veneer basketwork, umbrellas, wigs, glassware, imitation jewelry, copper bars, locks, lamps, radio receivers, bicycle parts, watch cases, chairs, dolls, certain toys, and carnival items. For these products, the "reserved" parts of the ceilings exceed combined minor supplier exports by more than 350 percent. See UNCTAD, *Operation and Effects of the Generalized Preferences Granted by the European Economic Community: Study by the UNCTAD Secretariat* (TD/B/C.5/3), 11 January 1973.
9. This $25 million figure is adjusted annually in proportion to the growth in U.S. gross national production.
10. These safeguards reduce the GSP product coverage by 68 percent for the EC, 89 percent for Japan and 35 percent for the U.S. See UNCTAD, documents cited in table 1 above.
11. See UNCTAD, Press Release (TAD/INF/824-825), 1 June 1976.

Part 4

Transfer of Real Resources

13 *Financial Resources for Development*

UNCTAD

Capital Requirements and Capital Availabilities: The Consistency between Flow and Growth Targets during the Second Half of the Development Decade

Studies prepared at the beginning of the Second Development Decade indicated that there would be broad technical consistency between the volume of flows implied by fulfilment of the flow targets and the external financing required by the growth targets contained in the International Development Strategy.[1] This consistency held, roughly speaking, during the first half of the Decade. There is evidence, however, that the capital requirements associated with the rates of growth stipulated in the Strategy will be higher in the second half of the Decade than they were in the first half. Thus, projections of the capital requirements in 1980 of non-oil exporting developing countries indicate that these requirements will grow quite rapidly during the remainder of the decade.[2] As may be seen from Table 1, the level of net capital inflows required to achieve the income growth target of the Second Development Decade is projected to reach in 1980 $119 billion at current prices, corresponding to $78 billion at 1974 prices. These projected capital requirements are equivalent to 1.7 percent of the projected GNP of Organisation for Economic Co-operation and Development (OECD) countries in that year and to 1.5 percent of the projected combined GNP of OECD countries and of the socialist countries of Eastern Europe. The official development assistance (ODA) component of the capital requirements in 1980 is assumed to be equivalent to 0.7 percent of the projected GNP of OECD countries in that year.

Reprinted, with permission, from UNCTAD, *International Financial Co-operation for Development: Report by the UNCTAD Secretariat* (TD/188/Supp.1 and Corr.1), 13 February 1976, pp. 6-19. Annex Tables 1 and 2 are from UNCTAD, *International Financial Co-operation for Development: Report by the UNCTAD Secretariat. Addendum* (TD/188/Supp.1/Add.1), 20 February 1976, pp. 3, 6.

Table 1. Balance of payments in 1973-1975 and projections for 1980 for non-oil-exporting developing countries

($ billion)

	1973	1974 (preliminary)	1975 (estimate)	1980 (projected)
Exports, f.o.b. a/	65.3	90.1	88.3	157.3
Imports, c.i.f.	78.3	124.2	129.9	244.3
Trade balance	- 13.0	- 34.1	- 41.6	- 87.0
Non-factor services, net	4.0	4.8	2.7	3.5
Investment income payments, net	- 6.1	- 7.5	- 9.7	- 33.9
Private transfers	2.9	3.3	3.4	5.6
Current account balance b/	- 12.2	- 33.5	- 45.2	-111.8
Net capital inflow (current prices) c/	20.3	35.9	44.0	118.6
Net capital inflow (1974 prices) c/	-	-	-	77.9

Source: UNCTAD secretariat, based on data from the Statistical Office of the United Nations and IMF and projections derived from the LINK system (for explanation of methodology see, UNCTAD, "Trade Prospects and Capital Needs of Developing Countries".)

a/ Assumes an annual growth rate of OECD countries of 4.8 per cent for the period 1975-1980 and of 6 per cent for the socialist countries of Eastern Europe.

b/ Excluding official transfers.

c/ For the projection period these figures represent the net capital requirements and are computed as the current account balance plus an allowance for reserve increases required to maintain a constant reserves-to-import ratio.

Table 2. Non-oil-exporting developing countries: Change in net capital requirements for given changes in assumptions
($ billion)

Changes in assumptions	Change in capital requirements 1980
1. Alternative growth targets of developing countries	
a. Target growth rate of non-oil-exporting developing countries is reduced from 6.2 per cent to 5.4 per cent per year	- 15.4
b. Target growth rate is reduced from 6.2 per cent to 4.4 per cent per year	- 35.8
2. Alternative OECD growth assumptions	
a. OECD growth rate for the remainder of the decade is increased from 4.8 per cent to 5.8 per cent per year	- 8.7
b. OECD growth rate for the remainder of the decade is decreased from 4.8 per cent to 3.8 per cent per year	+ 12.3
3. Alternative assumptions about intra-trade of developing countries	
a. The share of non-oil-exporting developing countries in the OPEC market is maintained at its 1971-1972 level	- 5.2
b. Rate of growth of export volume to other non-oil-exporting developing countries is increased from 6.7 per cent to 7.7 per cent per year	- 2.1
4. Alternative assumptions about other trade policies	
a. The rate of growth of exports of manufactures is increased from 20 per cent per year to 22 per cent per year	- 10.5
b. Growth rate of the volume of exports to socialist countries rises from 6.8 per cent to 8.3 per cent per year	- 1.5

Source: UNCTAD secretariat estimates.

The capital requirements of the non-oil-exporting developing countries in 1980 have been projected on a number of assumptions regarding the course of events in the world economy. The sensitivity of the results to changes in those assumptions is set out in Table 2. As may be seen from that table, if the annual average growth rate of OECD countries were to increase by 1.0 percentage point from the projected rate of 4.8 percent, the annual capital requirements of the non-oil-exporting developing countries would be reduced by less than $10 billion in 1980. Conversely, if the growth of OECD countries were to fall by 1.0 percentage point per annum from the projected rate, capital needs would increase by slightly more than $12 billion by 1980. This asymmetry results from the fact that the projected deterioration in the terms of trade of developing countries in the case of a slowdown in the rate of growth of OECD countries is proportionately larger than the projected improvement in those terms of trade in the case of an acceleration in the rate of growth of OECD countries.

It is also worth noting that in the same way that the rate of growth of OECD countries affects the capital requirements of developing countries, the extent to which the OECD countries meet the capital requirements will also have a bearing on the rate of growth of OECD countries themselves. Thus, it has been estimated that capital flows from OECD countries of the order implied in the flow and aid targets of the International Development Strategy would raise the annual growth rates of GNP of those countries by 0.7 percentage points above those that would occur if the performance of OECD countries under the targets were to continue as in the past.[3] This estimate serves to highlight the significance of acceleration of the pace of development of developing countries for the growth of developed countries themselves. Viewed in this context, increased transfer of resources to developing countries serves to accelerate the growth of both donor and recipient countries.

Failure to meet the flow targets would have a seriously adverse effect on the development of developing countries. Indeed, for a large number of developing countries, failure to move towards the 0.7 percent target would lead to severe constraints on imports and development expenditures which, in turn, would result in substantially lower growth rates than those experienced in the past. For example, projections indicate that under these conditions the *per capita* income of the most seriously affected (MSA) countries in 1980 may not be appreciably higher than the levels obtained in 1973, with many of these countries even experiencing declines in *per capita* income.

The situation for other developing countries would be equally grave; although these countries may succeed in maintaining modest advances in *per capita* income, they would experience a decline in growth rates even greater, in relative terms, than for the MSA countries.

To be sure, the probable constraint with regard to the availability of development finance is the scarcity of concessional funds. It is therefore possible that, in the absence of sufficient concessional finance, several countries might attempt to maintain growth rates by financing their increased payments deficits by loans from private capital markets. The feasibility of this course of action, however, may be called into doubt. For example, it is estimated that, if loans from private markets were to make good the shortfalls in official flows, gross borrowing from private capital markets would have to increase by 34 percent per annum, reaching an annual level of $124 billion in 1980. For developing countries as a whole the substitution of private capital for official development assistance on such a scale would result in an increase in the proportion of debt service to exports of goods from 13 percent in 1975 to about 50 percent in 1980.

Financial Co-operation: The Lessons from the Past

In the preceding section it was argued that shortfalls in the attainment of the financial flow targets appear likely to have particularly grave consequences for developing countries during the remainder of the present decade. The failure of developed countries during the first half of the decade to meet the flow targets set out in the International Development Strategy have already had consequences for the growth of developing countries, and have had an important influence on the external financial position, and in particular, the debt-servicing situation, with which they must face the future. In retrospect, it seems clear that the primary shortcomings of international financial co-operation has been the failure of developed countries to move toward, let alone achieve, the 0.7 percent ODA target. As a consequence, concessional and non-concessional flows did not become available in the proportions envisaged in the Strategy, and non-concessional flows came to play an important role as the source of growth in external financing. Yet the character of these flows, together with some of the policies undertaken with regard to them, have prevented them from making good, to the greatest extent possible, the shortfall of ODA.

Development Assistance up to 1974: The Principal Characteristics

The shortfall of official development assistance from the levels targeted in the International Development Strategy has been a major deficiency in the structure of international co-operation for development.[4] In nominal terms, total net disbursements of ODA by Development Assistance Committee of the OECD (DAC) member countries[5] grew, on average, at an annual rate of around 5 percent from 1961 to 1974. In real terms, however, ODA failed to advance: indeed, its 1974 level stood below that for 1963 (see Table 3). On the other hand, income growth in the developed market-economy countries was rapid: their combined GNP rose by over three-fourths during the 1960s. Consequently, ODA expressed as a proportion of GNP declined sharply: whereas it had stood at a level of 0.52 percent in 1961-1962, by 1969 it had dropped to 0.34 percent and stood at 0.33 percent in 1974. This decline occurred notwithstanding the fact that the ODA of certain developed countries rose steeply. A number of smaller donors increased their ODA disbursements substantially, registering significantly higher ODA/GNP ratios. The disappointing aggregate figures are thus to be explained by the performance of some of the larger donor countries.[6]

Behind the flagging aid effort of the major donors is the fact that aid

Table 3. Net financial flows from DAC member countries to developing countries and multilateral agencies, 1961-1974 a/

($ million)

Year	ODA		Non-concessional flows (current prices and exchange rates)			Total flows	
	At current prices and exchange rates	At 1970 prices and exchange rates	Bilateral official (OOF)	Bilateral private	via multilateral institutions	Valued at current prices and exchange rates	Valued at 1970 prices and exchange rates
1961	5 150	6 190	719	3 016	320	9 205	11 131
1962	5 402	6 385	527	2 214	254	8 396	10 008
1963	5 728	6 676	240	2 590	-36	8 521	10 108
1964	5 902	6 685	-41	3 268	454	9 583	11 118
1965	5 873	6 659	300	3 865	252	10 289	11 800
1966	5 961	6 509	392	3 768	228	10 350	11 500
1967	6 511	7 024	477	3 881	487	11 356	12 493
1968	6 282	6 662	740	5 683	757	13 461	14 521
1969	6 550	6 809	577	6 148	404	13 680	14 415

197o	6 791	6 791	868	6 4o1	745	14 8o4	14 8o4
1971	7 661	7 187	986	7 195	1 o37	16 878	15 923
1972	8 538	7 3o4	1 16o	7 9o6	1 o53	18 657	16 28o
1973	9 378	6 526	2 o73	11 192	647	23 29o	17 316
1974	11 316	6 488	2 199	12 9o1	-85	26 331	16 334
1961-1974 (per cent) b/	5.2	o.3*	17.8	13.6	13.1 c/	9.3	4.8

Sources: UNCTAD secretariat, based on OECD, Development Co-operation, 1975 Review (Paris: OECD, 1975); OECD, Flow of Resources to Developing Countries (Paris: OECD, 1973).

a/ Including flows to southern European recipient countries and territories.

b/ Average annual rate of growth, calculated by fitting a log-linear regression equation to the relevant time series. An asterisk indicates that the calculated rate of growth is not significantly different from zero at the lo per cent confidence level.

c/ 1961-1973.

programmes do not spring from a single-minded commitment to support the development process, but are motivated by a multiplicity of objectives. The promotion of development, to be sure, is one major consideration, but others—such as the furtherance of the political, strategic, commercial and cultural influence of the donor country—also tend to be present. This has raised a number of problems. Aid, in any event, could not have succeeded in fulfilling simultaneously all the different roles assigned to it, particularly by the largest donors. Moreover, experience has shown that the capacity of aid to further the political and military interests of its donors has often been quite limited. At the same time, the contribution that aid can make to development has sometimes been exaggerated, so that the impact of aid has tended to fall short of expectations. This was partly due to the mistaken assumption that aid to developing countries could foster development as quickly as aid to the European countries had brought about their recovery from the ravages of the Second World War—a view that neglected to take due account of the length of time needed to overcome the structural impediments to economic growth in developing regions. Hence, groups in the major donor countries that had been strongly in favour of aid became less enthusiastic in its support. This "aid fatigue" in donor countries was not relieved by the fact that the general public was presented with an inflated picture of the sacrifice entailed by the assistance programmes: performance under the 1 percent target was frequently taken as a measure of the aid effort, even though a large component of such flows involved no burden at all for the creditor country; and tied aid and food aid were depicted as exclusively international transfers, with their role in generating internal transfers among sectors of the national economy being overlooked. Thus, excessive and sometimes incompatible expectations from aid, on the one hand, and inflated estimates of its costs, on the other, served to bring about a virtual paralysis of the aid effort in the traditional donor countries.

Non-concessional Flows

If ODA flows stagnated during the 1960s and early 1970s, other sources of funds displayed considerable dynamism. As may be seen from Table 3, net non-concessional flows from DAC member countries to multilateral institutions grew rapidly between 1961 and 1974. This flow of funds from private capital markets to multilateral institutions allowed the latter to expand their regular lending programmes: net receipts by developing countries of loans from multilateral institutions at market-related interest rates rose from an average level of $170 million in 1961-1962 to $613 million in 1972-1973—an average annual growth rate of 13 percent.[7] This expansion was accompanied by diversification of the channels through which funds were disbursed. The share of the regional banks in total "hard" lending by the multilateral agencies, which had been 1 percent in 1961, reached 27 percent in 1973, while that of the World Bank Group fell from 99 percent to 72 percent (the residual being accounted for by the European Investment Bank).

Non-concessional flows directed toward developing countries through bilateral channels also exhibited rapid growth during the 1960s and early 1970s. As shown in Table 3, bilateral OOF expanded at an average annual rate of nearly 18 percent during the period 1961-1974 (although most of the growth occurred during the latter half of the period), while private bilateral flows grew at an average annual rate of 14 percent. Because of the dynamism of non-concessional flows, the growth rate of the total net flow from DAC member countries during the period (at current prices and exchange rates) was almost double that of ODA. Bilateral financial transactions of a non-concessional character have, however, grown in a spasmodic manner (see Table 4). For example, in 1965 they advanced by almost one-third, mainly on the strength of a rapid increase in net private direct investment. In 1968, non-concessional flows jumped by nearly one-half, owing to rapid growth in net disbursements of official and private export credits in addition to a sharp increase in private direct investment. The most remarkable spurt occurred during 1971-1973, which witnessed the emergence of the Euro-currency market as an important source of funds for developing countries. Bilateral portfolio investment, however, also showed a sharp increase in 1972, but export credits registered a marked deceleration, apparently because of a tendency on the part of those developing countries that could do so to borrow in the Euro-currency market rather than take up export credits. The ability of these developing countries to do so was of considerable benefit to them, inasmuch as they were thereby able to choose suppliers on the basis of quality and price rather than of the credit terms being offered. On the other hand, the interest costs of Euro-currency loans have generally been higher than those available for export credits.

The dynamic expansion of non-concessional flows, and in particular of private flows, has been instrumental in ensuring that the total flow of financial resources to developing countries expanded steadily in a period of lagging ODA. But the two categories of flows are only partial substitutes for each other. The characteristics of non-concessional flows, and their contributions to the development process, are quite different from those of ODA: being governed essentially by criteria of creditworthiness, they are directed to a relatively small number of developing countries. Indeed, the distribution of non-concessional lending shows a high degree of concentration. For example, during the period 1970-1973 seven countries, accounting for around one-fifth of the GNP of the developing world, received two-thirds of the funds raised by bond issues,[8] while six countries, with around one-quarter of total GNP, accounted for two-thirds of publicized Euro-

Table 4. Non-concessional flows from DAC member countries to developing countries and territories,[a] 1961-1974

(Millions of dollars)

Year	Export credits[b]				Net bilateral OOF c/	Net bilateral portfolio investment and other	Net private direct investment	Total (net) (8) =(2)+(4)+(5) + (6)+(7)	Euro-currency credits d/	Total (10) =(8)+(9)
	Official		Private							
	Gross (1)	Net (2)	Gross (3)	Net (4)	(5)	(6)	(7)		(9)	
1961	893	636	-	573	83	610	1 834	3 736		3 736
1962	698	458	352	572	68	147	1 495	2 829		2 829
1963	480	190	398	660	49	327	1 603	2 830		2 830
1964	421	-123	584	859	82	837	1 572	3 227		3 227
1965	666	198	464	751	102	655	2 459	4 165		4 165
1966	777	259	627	1 124	155	470	2 174	4 182		4 182
1967	927	392	921	1 007	85	770	2 103	4 357		4 357
1968	1 267	646	1 033	1 597	93	940	3 146	6 422		6 422
1969	1 234	502	4 553	2 047	75	180	2 921	5 725		5 725
1970	1 497	578	5 217	2 142	290	716	3 543	7 269		7 269
1971	1 763	573	6 508	2 831	412	733	3 632	8 181	1 000	9 181
1972	2 066	724	6 063	1 448	436	1 984	4 474	9 066	3 917	12 983
1973	2 486	1 117	6 938	1 196	956	3 286	6 711	13 266	9 271	22 537
1974	2 587	691	8 697	2 482	1 508	3 795	6 626	15 102	9 608	24 710

Sources: OECD, Flow of resources to developing countries and Development Co-operation, 1975 Review.

a/ Including flows to Southern European recipient countries and territories.

b/ Credits with an original maturity of one year or more.

c/ Other than official export credits.

d/ Estimates by the UNCTAD secretariat.

currency credits. Likewise, during the period 1969-1973, nine countries, accounting for 32 percent of the combined GNP of developing countries, received two-thirds of private direct investment flows, while ten countries, accounting for 31 percent of combined GNP, received two-thirds of official and private export credit disbursements.

Paradoxically, perhaps, the multilateral development financing agencies also concentrated their regular lending on a relatively small number of countries. Nine countries, with 36 percent of the total GNP of development countries, received over two-thirds of net disbursements of World Bank lending in the period 1969-1973; what is more, seven of these nine countries appear in one or more of the lists of principal recipients referred to in the preceding paragraph. Thus, while the multilateral lending institutions undoubtedly did succeed in making capital available to countries which were not in a position to tap sources of private capital, it would appear that their main function was to improve the terms of borrowing for those countries that already had access to such sources.

The Question of Distribution

The distribution of financial flows among developing countries is determined by a combination of policy measures taken by individual donor agencies and market forces. At present, there are relatively few international norms serving to guide decisions of various donor agencies,[9] and those that do exist are partial and incomplete.

One practice that has emerged in recent years for dealing with the problem of co-ordinating donor activities is the organization of aid consortia and consultative groups. In these groups, donors jointly examine the aid needs of a particular recipient country and consider their joint and individual capacity to meet those needs. Although such international mechanisms ensure some measure of consistency in the treatment of a particular recipient country, they do not provide the basis for an overview of the needs of that recipient relative to those of other developing countries.

Tentative and inconclusive steps toward meeting the latter problem were taken with the international designation of groups of developing countries having certain common characteristics, such as the least developed among the developing countries and the most seriously affected developing countries. Although the international evaluation of relative need that lies behind these groupings has no doubt been a useful process, the designation of these groups themselves is not without danger. The difficulty here lies not so much with the groups themselves, but with the tendency of some donors to adopt the view that because the needs of some recipients for concessional assistance are particularly urgent, the needs of other recipients have become less urgent. This attitude, although no doubt unintended, is perhaps the inevitable result of the technique of dividing developing countries into groups, rather than establishing measures and guidelines for relative need that apply uniformly to all developing countries.

In any event, the lack of comprehensive criteria in this area has led to a wide variety of practices, with the distribution of concessional assistance sometimes depending on historical, cultural, or commercial ties, rather than on relative poverty or need. The variety of outcomes is illustrated by the fact that, in 1974, 85 percent of Norway's bilateral ODA was directed toward recipients with a *per capita* GNP of less than $200, and only 0.3 percent toward those with a *per capita* GNP of $1,000 or more. By contrast, in the same year, 27 percent of France's bilateral ODA was directed toward recipients with a *per capita* GNP of less than $200, and 35 percent toward those with a *per capita* GNP of $1,000 or more.[10]

In general, however, the failure of ODA to expand rapidly to meet the capital needs of developing countries, together with the perceived needs of the poorest countries and the increased access of some other developing countries to private capital, has led to a situation in which ODA is being diverted from some developing countries to others. As may be seen from Table 5, bilateral ODA to developing countries and territories with a *per capita* GNP of less than $300 expanded in nominal terms; the share of these countries in total bilateral ODA flows rose from 64 percent in 1969-1970 to 69 percent in 1974. When account is taken of changes in prices, these bilateral ODA flows to this group of countries were 20 percent lower in 1974 than in 1969-1970. Countries in the *per capita* GNP range of $300-$800, on the other hand, experienced, in the aggregate, a slight decline in bilateral ODA receipts in absolute terms: if the increase in prices over this period is taken into account, the value of ODA flows to these countries in 1974 was only about one-half that received in 1969-1970.

It is against this background that a number of relatively more advanced developing countries have had recourse to private sources of capital, engaging essentially in the financing of development programmes by means of medium-term credits. This situation generally led these countries to pursue a strategy of export-led growth, since a rapid advance in the purchasing power of export earnings, which minimizes any potential conflict between meeting debt-service payments and meeting the import requirements associated with rising output and standards of living, was viewed as a primary indicator of a country's creditworthiness. This pattern of development, and the viability of the external financial position of a developing country following it, therefore depends on a continual rapid expansion of the external purchasing power of exports and on continual availability of private capital flows.

Table 5. Distribution among groups of developing countries and territories of bilateral official development assistance of DAC member countries

Countries or territories with GNP *per capita* a/ in 1972 of:	1969 - 1970		1972 - 1973		1974	
	$ million	Percentage of total	$ million	Percentage of total	$ million	Percentage of total
$149 and below	2 055	42.8	2 245	39.9	2 687	41.7
$150-$299	1 041	21.7	1 421	25.2	1 733	26.9
$300-$449	885	18.4	939	16.7	848	13.2
$450-$599	242	5.0	171	3.0	247	3.8
$600-$799	68	1.4	62	1.1	71	1.1
$800-$999	183	3.8	198	3.5	212	3.3
$1000 and above	332	6.9	595	10.6	641	10.0
Total	4 806	100.0	5 631	100.0	6 439	100.0

Source: OECD, *Development Co-operation, 1975 Review* and data supplied by the OECD secretariat.

a/ $149 or less: Afghanistan; Bangladesh; Benin; Burma; Burundi; Chad; Democratic Yemen; Ethiopia; Gambia; Guinea; Haiti; India; Indonesia; Laos; Madagascar; Malawi; Maldives; Mali; Nepal; Niger; Nigeria; Pakistan; Rwanda; Somalia; Sri Lanka; Sudan; Timor; United Republic of Tanzania; Upper Volta; Yemen. $150-$299: Bolivia; Cape Verde; Central African Republic; Comoros; Egypt; Equatorial Guinea; Guinea Bissau; Jordan; Kenya; Liberia; Macao; Mauritania; Morocco; Papua New Guinea; Philippines; Republic of South Viet-Nam; Senegal; Sierra Leone; Thailand; Togo; Uganda; United Republic of Cameroon; Western Samoa. $300-$449: Algeria; Angola; Colombia; Congo; Ecuador; El Salvador; Ghana; Guatemala; Guyana; Honduras; Iraq; Ivory Coast; Malaysia; Mauritius; Mozambique; Paraguay; Republic of Korea, Sao Tomé and Principe; Seychelles; Syria; Arab Republic; Tonga; Tunisia; Zambia. $450-$599: Brazil; Dominican Republic; Fiji; Iran; New Hebrides; Nicaragua; Oman; Peru; Saudi Arabia. $600-$799: Territories of the Afars and Issas; Bahrain; Belize; Costa Rica; Lebanon; Mexico; Uruguay. $800-$999: Barbados; Chile; Gabon; Guadeloupe; Hong Kong; Jamaica; Panama; Surinam; Trinidad and Tobago. $1.000 and above: Argentina; Bahamas; Bermuda; Brunei; French Guiana; French Polynesia; Israel; Kuwait; Libyan Arab Republic; Martinique; Netherlands Antilles; New Caledonia; Qatar; Reunion; Singapore; United Arab Emirates; Venezuela.

Annex Table 1. **Performance under the 1 per cent target[a] of DAC member countries**

1962-1974

(percentage of GNP)

Country	1962	1963	1964	1965	1966	1967	1968	1969	1970	1971	1972	1973	1974	Total flows ($ million)	
														1973	1974
Australia	0.43	0.51	0.57	0.64	0.63	0.74	0.73	0.74	1.10	1.33	0.94	0.51	0.65	332.2	506.2
Austria	0.36	0.07	0.19	0.49	0.35	0.38	0.62	0.49	0.42	0.46	0.18	0.56	0.45	152.8	147.2
Belgium	0.92	1.25	1.05	1.28	0.97	0.83	1.15	0.99	1.09	1.02	1.15	0.98	1.00	448.7	532.0
Canada	0.27	0.31	0.30	0.33	0.47	0.44	0.45	0.49	0.68	0.91	0.89	0.82	1.10	978.0	1 567.3
Denmark	0.20	0.13	0.36	0.15	0.19	0.20	0.67	0.82	0.51	0.82	0.54	0.61	0.55	168.6	167.7
Finland	...	...	...	...	...	...	...	...	0.24	0.27	0.36	0.15	0.30	25.5	61.4
France	1.88	1.49	1.46	1.30	1.21	1.14	1.32	1.17	1.11	0.90	0.95	1.08	1.09	2 750.6	2 991.5
Germany, Federal Republic of	0.65	0.60	0.65	0.60	0.61	0.89	1.17	1.00	0.61	0.67	0.48	0.40	0.68	1 382.6	2 601.5
Italy	0.82	0.56	0.40	0.42	0.95	0.37	0.71	0.95	0.71	0.74	0.53	0.34	0.30	467.0	447.7
Japan	0.49	0.39	0.36	0.55	0.61	0.66	0.71	0.72	0.88	0.92	0.92	1.40	0.65	5 682.6	2 920.2
Netherlands	0.86	0.92	0.69	1.23	1.20	0.98	0.70	1.29	1.31	1.15	1.55	0.90	1.24	534.4	858.0
New Zealand	...	...	...	...	0.21	0.21	0.26	0.32	0.36	0.33	0.33	0.28	0.36	31.0	44.3
Norway	0.13	0.37	0.36	0.54	0.22	0.36	0.64	0.45	0.57	0.49	0.34	0.45	0.77	89.5	176.9
Sweden	0.24	0.32	0.35	0.35	0.48	0.50	0.50	0.73	0.59	0.58	0.57	0.64	1.06	319.0	587.1
Switzerland	1.51	1.74	0.86	1.38	0.71	0.85	1.38	0.55	0.55	0.89	0.49	0.62	0.53	256.6	245.2
United Kingdom	0.89	0.80	0.96	0.99	0.82	0.70	0.78	0.95	0.92	0.85	0.84	0.79	1.17	1 395.0	2 234.3
United States	0.69	0.70	0.78	0.73	0.61	0.69	0.67	0.49	0.54	0.58	0.57	0.54	0.62	7 044.0	8 645.0
DAC average	0.75	0.72	0.76	0.75	0.68	0.71	0.77	0.68	0.69	0.71	0.68	0.71	0.72	22 058.1	24 733.5

Source: OECD, Development Assistance (Paris: OECD, various issues); OECD, Development Co-operation, 1975 Review (Paris: OECD, 1975); and information supplied by the OECD Secretariat.

a/ Net flows of financial resources to developing countries in Africa, Asia, Latin America and multilateral institutions as a percentage of GNP at market prices.

Annex Table 2. Performance of DAC member countries under the ODA (0.7 per cent) target (percentage of GNP at market prices)

Country a/	1961-1962 average b/	1969	1970	1971	1972	1973	1974	1969-1974 average
France	1.31	0.65	0.64	0.65	0.66	0.58	0.59	0.62
Netherlands	0.47	0.49	0.61	0.58	0.67	0.52	0.63	0.59
Australia	0.43	0.56	0.59	0.53	0.59	0.44	0.37	0.53
Sweden	0.09	0.43	0.37	0.43	0.48	0.56	0.72	0.52
Belgium	0.64	0.49	0.46	0.50	0.55	0.51	0.50	0.50
Denmark	0.11	0.38	0.37	0.42	0.45	0.48	0.55	0.46
Canada	0.12	0.33	0.42	0.42	0.47	0.43	0.50	0.44
Norway	0.14	0.30	0.32	0.33	0.43	0.44	0.57	0.42
United Kingdom	0.56	0.37	0.34	0.39	0.37	0.33	0.38	0.36
Germany, Fed. Rep. of	0.45	0.33	0.30	0.33	0.30	0.28	0.34	0.31
United States	0.56	0.32	0.30	0.31	0.28	0.23	0.25	0.28
New Zealand	...	0.22	0.22	0.23	0.25	0.27	0.31	0.26
Japan	0.17	0.26	0.23	0.23	0.21	0.24	0.24	0.24
Switzerland	0.06	0.16	0.15	0.12	0.21	0.16	0.14	0.16
Finland	...	...	0.07	0.12	0.15	0.16	0.18	0.15
Italy	0.17	0.09	0.16	0.15	0.08	0.11	0.16	0.13
Austria	0.04	0.10	0.07	0.08	0.08	0.15	0.18	0.12
DAC average	0.52	0.34	0.33	0.34	0.32	0.30	0.33	0.32

Source: OECD, Development Co-operation, 1975 Review and data supplied by the OECD secretariat.

a/ In descending order of average performance in 1969-1974.

b/ Including flows to southern European recipient countries and territories, i.e. Cyprus, Gibraltar, Greece, Malta, Spain, Turkey and Yugoslavia.

Notes

1. See UNCTAD, *Trade Prospects and Capital Needs of Developing Countries During the Second United Nations Development Decade* (New York: United Nations, 1972), sales no. E. 72. II. D. 11.
2. For a detailed analysis of capital requirements of developing countries, see UNCTAD, *Trade Prospects and Capital Needs of Developing Countries, 1976-1980: Report by the UNCTAD Secretariat* (TD/B/C.3/134), 15 April 1976.
3. This effect is discussed at length by the UNCTAD secretariat in *Trade Prospects and Capital Needs of Developing Countries.*
4. For detailed information on the topics covered in this section, see annex I of UNCTAD, *International Financial Co-operation for Development: Report by UNCTAD Secretariat. Addendum* (TD/188/Supp.1/Add.1), 20 February 1976.
5. The socialist countries of Eastern Europe have not agreed to commit themselves to the flow targets.
6. See Annex Tables 1 and 2 for the performance of DAC member countries under the 1 percent and the 0.7 percent target. Footnote added by the editors.
7. See annex table I-11 of UNCTAD, *International Financial Co-operation* for

annual data, 1969-1975. In 1974, multilateral lending institutions turned heavily toward non-DAC sources for their borrowing at market interest rates. Consequently, flows of private funds from DAC member countries to multilateral institutions dropped precipitously. The lending activities of multilateral institutions also expanded sharply in 1974.
8. Excluding Israeli bonds, which are a special case.
9. Internal guidelines no doubt exist in most donor agencies. The precise nature of these guidelines is rarely open to public scrutiny, however.
10. See OECD, *Development Co-operation, 1975 Review,* statistical annex, table 31.

14 *Debt and Debt Service*

UNCTAD

Background

Debt and debt service have an important bearing on the net transfer of resources to developing countries and, therefore, on the efficacy of donor programmes in the area of international financial co-operation. The effect of debt-service payments on net transfers varies according to the class of transaction involved. Because developing countries make use, to different degrees, of various categories of transactions, these differences also lead to a varied influence of debt on net transfer for various categories of countries.

In the tables and paragraphs which follow, use has been made of information compiled by the World Bank in its Debtor Reporting System. The Debtor Reporting System provides data on the external public debt of developing countries, which is defined as "debt repayable to external creditors in foreign currency, goods or services, with an original or extended maturity of more than one year, which is a direct obligation of, or has repayment guaranteed by, a public body in the borrowing country."[1] The information collected by the World Bank thus does not cover private transactions which take place without benefit of a public guarantee in the debtor country, or transactions giving rise to short-term debt.

Gross disbursements to 86 developing countries grew at an average annual rate of 13 percent during the period 1965-1973 and amounted to $24 billion in the latter year.[2] However, in the same period debt-service payments grew by 16 percent annually, reaching $11 billion.[3] The consequences of these differential rates of growth was that the net transfer of resources advanced by only 10 percent annually during the period, amounting to $13 billion in 1973, or a little more than one-half the amount of new disbursements. When

---

Reprinted, with permission, from UNCTAD, *International FinancialCo-operation and Development: Report by the UNCTAD Secretariat* (TD/188/Supp.1), 13 February 1976, pp. 31-46 with adaptations. Annex table 1 is from UNCTAD, *International Financial Co-operation for Development: Report by the UNCTAD Secretariat. Addendum* (TD/188/Supp.1/Add.1), 20 February 1976, pp. 14-16.

account is taken of price increases for goods and services made available to developing countries, the annual growth of the transfer was of the order of 3 percent. Over the same period, outstanding debt, including debt undisbursed, grew at an average annual rate of 15 percent, reaching $119 billion by the end of 1973.

Detailed data on debt service and disbursements are available for a smaller sample of countries. As may be seen from Table 1, the rates of growth of disbursements and debt service for 67 non-oil-exporting developing countries varied considerably for different types of transactions. Disbursements of official loans and grants grew at an average annual rate of 8 percent from 1965 to 1973, while debt-service payments resulting from official loans grew at an average annual rate of 15 percent. Consequently, the net transfer was at the modest growth rate of 5.5 percent per annum, rising from $2.9 billion in 1965 to $4.5 billion in 1973. Disbursements of private loans grew considerably more rapidly over the period than did other types of transaction. Disbursements by private banks rose particularly sharply, and outpaced the rate of growth of debt service associated with such loans. Consequently, the net transfer associated with this type of transaction rose sharply, reaching $2.8 billion in 1973. It should be noted, however, that the rapid expansion of bank lending to developing countries is of a relatively recent origin: the average annual rate of expansion was 53 percent from 1970 to 1973. Given the maturity of such credits, the growth of such disbursements in the period under review has resulted in a roughly equivalent rise in net transfer. In subsequent years, as repayments fall due, the rate of advance of net transfer may be expected to fall, even if gross disbursements were to grow at recent rates.

Not all developing countries have the same access to the different types of flows mentioned above, nor do all countries with equal access to certain types of funds necessarily receive equivalent amounts of those funds. Consequently, the growth of disbursements, debt service and net transfer varies considerably among groups of countries. As may be seen from Table 2, countries with a *per capita* GNP of $201-$300 experienced a particularly rapid advance in debt-service payments from 1965 to 1973, leading to a virtual stagnation in the level of net transfer. Countries with a *per capita* GNP in the $301-$400 range also experienced a rapid increase in debt service, which kept the rate of growth of net transfer to modest levels. Countries with a *per capita* GNP of $401 and above, which have been the major beneficiaries of the expanded flow of private lending, experienced rapid increases in debt service, leading to significant growth of net transfers. As a result, over one-half of the recorded net transfer in 1973 was directed toward those countries.

In addition to their effect on net transfer, debt-service payments also have a bearing on the short-run balance-of-payments position of debtor coun-

Table 1. Gross disbursements, debt service and net transfer by type of transaction for 67 non-oil-exporting developing countries, 1965 and 1973

($ million)

Type of transaction	Disbursements		Debt service		Net transfer	
	1965	1973	1965	1973	1965	1973
Total	5 726	16 281	2 227	7 751	3 499	8 530
of which:						
Official bilateral	3 620	6 786	719	2 301	2 901	4 485
of which:						
DAC	3 451	5 311	626	2 004	2 825	4 307
Multilateral	728	2 057	331	977	397	1 080
Private: suppliers' credits	571	1 312	587	1 417	-16	-105
private banks	546	4 849	417	2 081	129	2 768
other private	255	1 201	173	813	82	388

Source: UNCTAD, "International Financial Co-operation," Annex II.

Table 2. Gross disbursements, debt service and net transfer for 67 non-oil-exporting developing countries according to income group, 1965 and 1973
($ million)

	Disbursements		Debt service		Net transfer	
	1965	1973	1965	1973	1965	1973
Total (67 countries)	5 726	16 281	2 227	7 751	3 499	8 530
Countries with *per capita* GNP in 1972 of:						
$100 or below	287	1 422	8	156	279	1 266
$101-$200	1 672	2 437	422	1 034	1 250	1 403
$201-$300	618	1 019	119	503	499	516
$301-$400	591	1 480	186	687	406	793
$401-$800	1 209	4 235	360	1 948	849	2 287
$801 and above	1 350	5 689	1 134	3 424	216	2 265

Source: Same as Table 1.

tries. Debt-service payments constitute a sizeable element in the external payments of developing countries. Moreover, such payments are determined according to a fixed schedule, which does not take into account changes in a country's balance-of-payments situation. Consequently, given present policies on debt and debt service, debt-service payments cannot play a role in adjusting a country's balance-of-payments deficit.

This characteristic of debt-service payments has become particularly significant in the current situation. Developing countries as a whole had a current-account deficit in 1974 of some $33.5 billion, and one of their major preoccupations since has been to secure the means of financing in the future a deficit of this size. Inflexibility in the scheduling of debt-service payments has meant that this category of transaction had to be excluded when considering the means by which the increased deficits might be financed.[4]

The significance of debt-service payments in relation to the increased current-account deficits of non-oil-exporting developing countries may be seen from Table 3, which indicates that for a sample of 55 such countries debt-service payments in 1974 corresponded to 41 percent of the increase in their combined current-account deficit. To be sure, the figure of 41 percent represents the maximum by which flexibility in the timing of debt-service payments could have contributed to financing the increment in the current-account deficit. Even then, it would have been necessary for all debt-service payments due in 1974 to be postponed; likewise, it also assumes that such postponement would have no effect on the inflow of new capital. Nevertheless, the figures in Table 3 do provide a rough indication of the possibilities that existed for financing the increase in the current-account deficit of developing countries in 1974 by providing for flexibility in the timing of debt-service payments.

In the event, such flexibility was not forthcoming. Only 28 percent of the external deficit of non-oil-exporting developing countries in 1974 could be covered by bilateral ODA and concessional flows from multilateral institutions. Consequently, a substantial part of the $33.5 billion deficit was financed either by direct investment or by recourse to credits bearing commercial interest rates, and as already mentioned, the financing of the 1975 deficit from private sources appears to have been even greater.

These developments in 1974 and 1975 have serious implications for the external solvency of non-oil-exporting developing countries in 1976 and 1977. Current projections indicate that there may be some slight reduction in their current-account deficit in 1976. This deficit nonetheless appears likely to fall in the range of $35-$40 billion, an order of magnitude that was until recently without precedent. Projections for 1977 indicate a deficit of similar size. Moreover, the acceleration of short- and medium-term borrowing that occurred in the early 1970s will lead to an even sharper acceleration of debt-service payments. It thus seems likely that for non-oil-

Table 3. Current-account balances and debt-service payments for 55 non-oil-exporting developing countries, 1973 estimates for 1974 ($ million)

	Exports	Imports	Trade balance	Current-account balance[a]	Debt-service payments[b]	Ratio of debt-service payments in 1974 to increase in current account deficit (percent)
Africa[c]						
1973	6 650	7 185	-535	-876	572	
1974	9 407	11 273	-1 866	-1 755	796	91
East Asia[c]						
1973	13 231	15 714	-2 483	-374	725	
1974	19 642	25 959	-6 317	-3 696	867	26
South Asia[c]						
1973	4 265	4 611	-346	-740	871	
1974	5 559	7 466	-1 907	-2 717	1 167	59
Middle East[c]						
1973	1 949	5 458	-3 509	-1 231	482	
1974	2 500	7 222	-4 722	-2 578	612	45
Southern Europe[c]						
1973	10 994	19 079	-8 085	739	1 122	
1974	14 603	29 372	-14 769	-5 924	1 248	19

Latin America[c]						
1973	19 162	20 937	-1 775	-2 837	3 752	
1974	25 943	35 754	-9 811	-11 048	4 592	56
Total (55 countries)						
1973	56 424	73 435	-17 011	-5 397	7 532	
1974	77 312	117 453	-39 641	-27 808	9 289	41

Source: UNCTAD secretariat, based on information supplied by the World Bank and IMF.

a/ Excluding interest payments on public and publicly guaranteed debt.

b/ Payments on public and publicly guaranteed debt, as reported by the World Bank.

c/ Africa: Central African Republic, Ethiopia, Ghana, Ivory Coast, Kenya, Madagascar, Malawi, Mali, Mauritius, Morocco, Senegal, Sierra Leone, Somalia, Sudan, Togo, Tunisia, Uganda, United Republic of Tanzania, Upper Volta and Zaire.

East Asia: Republic of Korea, Malaysia, Philippines, Singapore and Thailand.

South Asia: India, Pakistan and Sri Lanka.

Middle East: Israel and Lebanon.

Southern Europe: Cyprus, Greece, Malta, Spain, Turkey and Yugoslavia.

Latin America: Argentina, Bolivia, Brazil, Chile, Colombia, Costa Rica, Dominican Republic, El Salvador, Guatemala, Guayana, Haiti, Honduras, Jamaica, Mexico, Nicaragua, Panama, Paraguay, Peru and Uruguay.

exporting developing countries as a whole the ratio of debt service on public and publicly-guaranteed debt to the export of goods will rise from a level of 11 percent in 1974 to 18 percent in 1976 and 21 percent in 1977. Moreover, when rough account is taken of estimated debt service on credits not covered by the World Bank's reporting system, it would appear that these ratios will reach 26 percent and 29 percent respectively.

The events of 1974 and 1975, and the outlook for 1976 and 1977, affect individual developing countries in varying degrees. It is clear, however, that the external financial position of a large number of developing countries has been worsened by these events and that difficulties in servicing external debt have become acute and will become even more acute in the future. The question therefore arises whether international measures are required on a large scale to deal with a common problem afflicting a large number of developing countries.

Proposals for a Broad Approach to Debt Problems in the Current Situation

Proposals Relating to Private Debt

It has been proposed that an international fund be established that will have the function of refinancing for a certain period of time the service payments on the commercial debt of developing countries having an original maturity of from one to ten years. The refinancing would take place at commercial rates of interest and would not involve concessional funds.

The refinancing of service payments on commercial debt in this way would have a two-fold effect on the external financial situation of developing countries. First, it would alleviate their immediate balance-of-payments situation by reducing the amount of debt-service payments that had to be made during the period that the scheme was in operation. Second, it would widen the maturity structure of commercial debt outstanding, thereby improving the structure of external indebtedness in general of developing countries.

Suppliers' credits provided by financial institutions in developed countries and loans from private banks are the two major sources of private credits with medium-term maturities. The consequence of a scheme to refinance debt-service payments arising from these two categories of loans are indicated in Table 4. As may be seen from that table, the refinancing during the three-year period 1974-1976 of debt-service arising from these two categories of loans would have consolidated payments amounting to $14.4 billion. This sum represents 47 percent of the total projected debt-service payments during that three-year period and an annual basis corresponds to approximately one-fifth of the increment in the current-account

Table 4. Projected debt-service payments on debt outstanding at end-1973 for 67 non-oil-exporting developing countries (\$ billion)

	Period	
	1974-1976 (3 years)	1974-1978 (5 years)
Suppliers' credits: debt-service payments	5.2	7.7
of which:		
amortization payments	4.1	6.0
Private banks: debt-service payments	9.2	15.3
of which:		
amortization payments	5.4	9.3
Suppliers' credits + private banks: debt-service payments	14.4	23.0
of which:		
countries with *per capita* GNP in 1972 of		
\$376 and above	11.1	17.9
\$375 and below	3.3	5.1
of which:		
under \$200	1.2	1.8
MSA countries	1.1	1.8
least developed countries	0.1	0.4
Suppliers' credits + private banks: amortization payments	9.5	15.3
of which:		
countries with *per capita* GNP in 1972 of		
\$376 and above	7.0	11.4
\$375 and below	2.5	3.9
of which:		
under \$200	0.9	1.5
MSA countries	0.9	1.4
least developed countries	0.2	0.2

Source: UNCTAD secretariat, based on information supplied by the World Bank.

deficit of developing countries in 1974. The projected amortization payments on these two categories of debt equal \$9.5 billion, or roughly 11 percent of the total outstanding debt of developing countries in 1973. However, as much as 40 percent of the outstanding debt arising from suppliers' credits and private bank loans would have been funded into loans bearing decidedly longer maturities. As may be seen from Table 4, a refinancing scheme operating for a five-year period would have even more pronounced effects on the external situation of developing countries.

Table 4 also shows that the main effects of the scheme to refinance debt service arising from these two categories of transactions would be felt by countries with a *per capita* GNP of \$376 and above. The benefits to these countries of such a scheme would be \$11.1 billion, or 77 percent of the total refinancing available to developing countries.

The figures set out in Table 4 also provide financial estimates of the financial requirements of such a scheme. In considering these requirements, it should be noted that the techniques of refinancing debt payments allow considerable scope for flexibility. Thus, it would be possible to envisage a scheme in which only a certain proportion of debt-service payments due on certain categories of debt was refinanced. If, for example, it were decided to refinance one-half of the amortization or debt-service payments owed on account of suppliers' credits and private bank loans the cost of the scheme would be one-half the amounts shown in the table.

The purpose of a refinancing scheme is not to increase the total flow of resources to developing countries over the longer term but rather to adjust the annual pattern of the flow. Consequently, refinancing will have the effect of lowering debt-service payments during the period of operation of the scheme, at the cost of raising them during the subsequent period. Table 5 shows the projected annual debt-service payments for the period 1974–1980, after hypothetical refinancing, as a percentage of the annual payments that would have been due without refinancing. It was assumed that amortization payments on suppliers' credits and private bank loans would be refinanced during the period 1974–1976 by new loans having terms of 9 percent interest, three years grace period and 15 years maturity. As may be seen from the table, assuming such refinancing, total annual debt-service payments on debt outstanding when the scheme was initiated are reduced by roughly 25 percent during the period in which the scheme operates, and raised by about 15 percent during the subsequent period.

Proposals Relating to Official Debt

It has been proposed that debt-service payments on official loans to MSA [most seriously affected] countries should be waived for the remainder of the decade and that consideration should be given to the possibility of converting ODA debt owed by the least developed countries into grants.

It has also been suggested that debt-service payments on official loans to all countries might be waived for the remainder of the decade.

For a sample of 67 developing countries, debt-service payments on account of official bilateral flows from DAC member countries are expected to average at least $2.6 billion annually during the period 1974–1979 (see Table 6). This is approximately 20 percent of the projected debt-service payments of these countries in 1976.

MSA countries accounted in 1971–1973 for roughly one-third of debt-service payments to DAC member countries on account of official bilateral flows. During that period, approximately 43 percent of these debt-service payments was on account of official bilateral debt. In 1974, it is estimated

Table 5. Annual debt-service payments, 1974-1980, after hypothetical refinancing of amortization payments on commercial debt a/ as a percentage of annual payments due in the absence of refinancing (Percentages)

(67 non-oil-exporting developing countries)

	1974	1975	1976	1977	1978	1979	1980
Total (67 countries)	71.6	74.4	77.4	110.9	113.7	116.6	117.5
of which:							
countries with per capita GNP in 1972 of:							
$376 and above	69.7	72.2	75.0	111.9	114.7	118.1	119.4
$375 and below	75.5	79.2	82.5	108.9	111.2	113.5	113.8
of which:							
under $200	84.4	85.7	87.2	106.0	107.7	109.7	109.9
MSA countries	84.8	87.4	89.4	105.5	107.0	108.6	108.6
least developed countries	87.5	87.9	88.4	104.4	105.6	107.1	107.1

Source: UNCTAD secretariat, based on information supplied by the World Bank.

a/ Amortization payments on suppliers' credits and private bank loans outstanding at end-1973 were assumed to be refinanced during the following three years by new loans with terms of 9 per cent interest, three years grace period and 15 years maturity.

Table 6. Average annual gross disbursements of official bilateral loans from DAC member countries, 1971-1973, and average annual debt-service payments on such loans; 67 non-oil-exporting developing countries

($ million)

	1971-1973		1974-1979[a]
	Disbursements	Debt service	Debt service
Total (67 countries)	5 524	1 5o7	2 557
of which:			
countries with _per capita_ GNP in 1972 of:			
$376 and above	1 758	7o4	1 313
$375 and below	3 776	8o3	1 245
of which:			
under $2oo	2 454	488	776
MSA countries	2 471	5o3	8o9
least developed countries	746	44	88

Source: UNCTAD secretariat, based on information supplied by the World Bank.

_a/_ Projected on the basis of debt outstanding at end-1973.

that their debt-service payments to DAC member countries was about $715 million, and that a moratorium on such payments in 1974 would have provided these countries with additional financing equivalent to 15.5 percent of the increase in their current-account deficit. It is further estimated that a moratorium on debt-service payments on official bilateral debts owed to DAC member countries would reduce the aggregate debt-service ratio for MSA countries in 1976 from about 13 percent to about 7 percent.

The known distribution among MSA countries of debt-service payments due on bilateral official debt is shown in Table 7, where it may be seen that 26 such countries account for $281 million, or 29 percent, of projected debt-service payments on official loans for the period 1974-1979. These payments represent 15 percent of the total net transfer of resources to these countries in 1973 and 20 percent of the net transfer effected by official bilateral grants and loans in that year. The remaining 71 percent of projected debt-service payments on official loans is due from India and Pakistan. These sums represent 77 percent of the net transfer of resources to those two countries in 1973 and 98 percent of the net transfer generated by official grants and loans to these countries in 1973.

A further question for consideration concerns the way in which the burden of providing relief to MSA countries in this form would be distributed among donor countries. As may be seen from Table 8, the largest creditors of MSA countries on account of bilateral official transactions are the Federal Republic of Germany, Japan, the United Kingdom and the United States, which together accounted for roughly 73 percent of the total outstanding official bilateral debt of MSA countries at the end of 1973 and 68 percent of projected debt-service payments during the period 1974-1979.[5] These countries, to be sure, are also important sources of new bilateral official lending to MSA countries. As may be seen further from Table 8, 15 percent, or $160 million, of projected debt-service payments in 1974-1979 are owed to the socialist countries of Eastern Europe.

For the least developed among the developing countries, annual debt-service payments on account of all official bilateral flows were, on average, only $43 million during the period 1971-1973. The proposal to convert ODA loans to grants for these countries, therefore, implies a very small cost to the donor countries, particularly since not all of these official flows are ODA.

The question arises whether a moratorium on the servicing of official debt would yield an additional net flow of resources to MSA countries and whether such relief would alter the existing distribution of concessional flows. It should be noted in the first instance that both these outcomes cannot occur simultaneously. The possibility that debt relief would alter the distribution of concessional financial flows exists only when relief yields additional funds to one or more debtor countries.

Table 7. Projected annual average debt-service payments (1974-1979) by MSA countries on official bilateral debt outstanding at end-1973

Country	Owed to DAC member countries		Owed to socialist countries of Eastern Europe		Total	
	$ thousand	% of total	$ thousand	% of total	$ thousand	% of total
Afghanistan	11 608	1.43	30 373	18.95	41 981	4.33
Bangladesh	14 330	1.77	13 697	8.54	28 027	2.89
Burundi	224	0.03	...	...	224	0.02
Central African Republic	1 580	0.20	325	0.20	1 905	0.20
El Salvador	2 431	0.30	...	...	2 431	0.25
Ethiopia	8 831	1.09	3 024	1.89	11 855	1.22
Ghana	9 988	1.23	...	...	9 988	1.03
Guyana	7 703	0.95	...	...	7 703	0.79
Haiti	3 567	0.44	...	...	3 567	0.37
Honduras	1 847	0.23	...	...	1 847	0.19
Ivory Coast	24 619	3.04	...	...	24 619	2.54
Kenya	18 947	2.34	76	0.05	19 023	1.96
Lesotho	158	0.02	...	...	158	0.02
Madagascar	7 810	0.97	...	...	7 810	0.81
Mali	3 884	0.48	8 468	5.28	12 352	1.27
Niger	4 829	0.60	...	...	4 829	0.50
Rwanda	106	0.01	...	...	106	0.01
Senegal	9 036	1.12	687	0.43	9 723	1.00
Sierra Leone	3 257	0.40	...	...	3 257	0.34
Somalia	1 591	0.20	6 032	3.76	7 623	0.79
Sri Lanka	24 565	3.04	4 689	2.93	29 254	3.02
Sudan	8 452	1.04	3 606	2.25	12 058	1.24
Uganda	5 885	0.73	5 072	3.16	10 957	1.13
United Republic of Cameroon	12 530	1.55	586	0.37	13 116	1.35
United Republic of Tanzania	10 387	1.28	3 966	2.47	14 353	1.48
Upper Volta	2 610	0.32	...	...	2 610	0.27
Sub-total (26 countries)	200 775	24.81	80 601	50.28	281 376	29.02
India	463 999	57.33	64 819	40.44	528 818	54.54
Pakistan a/	144 526	17.86	14 874	9.28	159 400	16.44
Total	809 300	100.00	160 294	100.00	969 594	100.00

Source: UNCTAD secretariat, based on information supplied by the World Bank.

a/ Assumes that all debt relief is on official bilateral debt.

In principle, debt relief should be provided for by additional financing arrangements in donor countries so as to generate a larger flow to developing countries as a whole. If such an additional flow to MSA countries were not generated, debt relief would nonetheless play an important role in improving the quality of the assistance by releasing a sizeable part of foreign exchange earnings for the financing of necessary imports.

In the final analysis, however, it would appear highly unlikely that the annual average debt-service payments (1974-1979) and gross disbursements (1973) by donor countries

Creditor	Debt outstanding, including undisbursed (end-1973)		Debt-service payments (annual average 1974-1979)		Gross disbursements (1973)			
	$ million	Percent of total	$ million	Percent of total	Loans	Grants $ million	Total	Percent of total
Australia	-	-	12.3	1.1	...	12.5	12.5	0.5
Austria	27.5	0.2	3.0	0.3	2.7	0.5	3.2	0.1
Belgium	47.6	0.3	2.2	0.2	5.1	37.1	42.2	1.8
Canada	957.8	5.8	33.5	3.1	144.0	105.4	249.4	10.7
Denmark	93.9	0.6	2.9	0.3	11.5	17.3	28.8	1.2
Finland	5.6	-	0.2	-	0.8	...	0.8	0.0
France	812.8	5.0	79.8	7.4	128.1	170.7	298.8	12.8
Germany, Federal Republic of	2 452.3	14.9	210.7	19.5	230.3	127.4	357.7	15.4
Italy	227.0	1.4	25.4	2.4	15.4	14.3	29.7	1.3
Japan	1 225.4	7.5	131.0	12.1	137.5	26.0	163.5	7.0
Netherlands	257.1	1.6	11.3	1.1	38.4	24.7	63.1	2.7
New Zealand	-	...	...	...	...	0.1	0.1	...
Norway	-	...	...	...	...	28.1	28.1	1.2
Sweden	226.1	1.4	4.9	0.5	29.9	53.3	83.2	3.6
Switzerland	49.0	0.3	4.9	0.5	12.9	12.4	25.3	1.1
United Kingdom	1 972.0	12.0	113.9	10.6	208.3	48.0	256.3	11.0
United States	6 293.9	38.3	283.8	26.3	328.7	247.0	575.7	24.7
Total DAC	14 648.0	89.2	919.5[a]	85.2	1 293.6	924.8	2 218.4	95.3
Socialist countries of Eastern Europe	1 777.3	10.8	160.3	14.9	109.8	...	109.8	4.7
Total	16 425.3	100.0	1 079.8	100.0	1 403.4	924.8	2 328.2	100.0

Source: UNCTAD secretariat, based on information provided by the World Bank.

a/ Includes debt relief granted to Pakistan, for which the distribution by donor is not yet available.

addition of debt relief as a financial instrument would lessen the influence that donor countries at present exert on the geographical distribution of their aid programmes. Debt relief would have implications for the geographical distribution of concessional flows only if donor countries chose to allow the relief to generate additional flows to a particular recipient country or if debt-service payments due from a particular MSA country to a particular donor country exceeded the amounts of new development assistance planned by the donor country to that recipient. In the first of these two cases the geographical distribution of assistance would still remain entirely under the control of donor countries. In the second case, some loss of control by donor countries over the distribution of concessional funds is clearly implied. It should be noted, however, that this outcome would occur only because the planned concessional disbursements by donor countries to the MSA country in question would have resulted in a negative net transfer to that country. Given the international commitment to assist MSA countries, some redistribution would appear to be in order when such a situation arises.

Notes

1. For further details on definitions and coverage, see UNCTAD, *International Financial Co-operation for Development: Report by the UNCTAD Secretariat. Addendum* (TD/188/Supp.1/Add.1), 20 February 1976, Annex IM.
2. For further details of the indebtedness of developing countries, see ibid.
3. In more than one-third of a large sample of developing countries, the servicing of external debts absorbed 10 percent or more of total export earnings in the 1970-1973 period; see annex table. Footnote added by the editors.
4. For a small number of countries, debt rescheduling did affect the magnitude of debt-service payments in 1974. These agreements had been concluded prior to 1974, however, and the rescheduling did not, therefore, respond directly to the extraordinary situation that emerged in that year.
5. These figures on projected debt-service payments do not reflect recent debt relief accorded India and Pakistan, since information on the distribution of that debt relief among donors is not yet available.

Annex Table 1. Ratio of debt-service payments[a/] to exports of goods and services[b/] in 83 developing countries, 1965 and 1970-1973

(percentages)

Country[c/]	1965	1970	1971	1972	1973	Average 1970-1973
*Egypt	15.3	26.2	19.4	31.5	34.6	27.9
Uruguay	6.9	18.4	22.2	34.0	30.1	26.2
*India	15.0	28.0	25.9	24.5	20.1	24.6
Mexico	24.8	25.2	24.1	23.5	25.2	24.5
*Peru	6.8	13.7	20.0	19.3	32.5	21.4
Afghanistan	7.4	20.0	19.2	26.0	19.9	21.3
*Pakistan	11.0	24.3	19.4	23.4	16.1	20.8
Argentina	20.2	21.0	19.5	20.3	18.3	19.8
Republic of Korea	2.8	23.4	21.7	18.8	13.9	19.5
Turkey	28.5	22.5	19.0	18.8	10.4	17.7
Israel	22.5	18.6	13.4	17.7	20.8	17.6
Tunisia	7.7	19.5	16.9	16.3	13.8	16.6
*Burma	4.6	16.1	14.2	17.5	18.6	16.6
Chile	12.4	18.3	21.0	11.6	11.0	15.5
Brasil	12.4	15.3	15.8	14.3	13.9	14.8
Bolivia	4.8	10.9	12.2	17.9	14.8	14.0
Zambia	2.7	5.1	10.0	10.7	28.0	13.5
Colombia	14.4	11.9	14.8	12.6	13.0	13.1
Nicaragua	4.3	10.6	13.4	10.3	17.8	13.0
Iran	5.4	11.5	11.5	17.1	10.6	12.7
*Sri Lanka	2.0	9.7	10.8	14.2	12.6	11.8
Paraguay	4.2	11.0	13.1	13.2	9.5	11.7
*Sudan	5.5	9.2	12.1	12.3	11.1	11.2
Panama	2.8	7.8	9.3	10.8	16.4	11.1
Morocco	4.8	8.3	11.6	10.7	9.7	10.1
Costa Rica	10.3	9.7	10.1	10.0	10.2	10.0
Ecuador	6.5	9.1	12.2	10.6	7.5	9.9
Algeria	...	7.4	9.7	10.9	11.3	9.8
Greece	4.0	8.4	10.2	9.1	9.7	9.4
*Ethiopia	5.0	11.6	10.6	8.7	6.4	9.3
Malawi	6.4	8.7	8.8	8.9	9.0	8.9
Congo	6.5	7.8	8.0	8.3	10.7	8.7
*Sierra Leone	5.7	9.0	8.5	8.6	8.4	8.6
*United Republic of Tanzania	7.5	7.2	8.4	11.6	6.7	11.5
Syrian Arab Republic	5.5	9.2	8.9	8.1	7.3	8.4
Philippines	5.4	7.5	7.0	9.9	6.3	7.7
Guatemala	5.2	7.7	8.2	10.6	3.8	7.6
Swaziland	4.5	4.7	5.3	9.5	10.5	7.5
Yugoslavia	14.4	9.6	6.5	6.4	6.9	7.4
Indonesia	10.3	6.6	7.6	6.7	7.1	7.0
Liberia	8.4	8.0	7.1	6.7	6.3	7.0

Annex Table 1 (continued)

Country[c/]	1965	1970	1971	1972	1973	Average 1970-1973
Gabon	...	5.2	7.1	7.0	7.3	6.7
*Ivory Coast	4.5	6.0	6.8	7.2	6.3	6.6
*Upper Volta	2.1	5.9	5.9	5.1	8.3	6.3
*Lesotho	2.5	8.5	7.1	5.1	3.2	6.0
Zaire	...	4.0	4.6	7.5	7.0	5.8
*United Republic of Cameroon	...	4.6	4.9	7.7	5.4	5.7
*Uganda	...	4.6	6.2	6.0	5.6	5.6
*Kenya	5.9	5.3	5.8	5.7	5.2	5.5
Dominican Republic	19.2	5.1	6.7	4.1	4.5	5.1
*Senegal	...	2.3	5.1	3.7	8.1	4.8
*El Salvador	3.6	3.7	5.8	3.1	5.3	4.5
*Ghana	19.0	5.0	7.1	3.0	2.3	4.4
*Chad	...	3.2	8.1	1.7	...	4.3
*Guyana	4.1	4.0	2.8	4.9	5.4	4.3
Jamaica	1.9	3.2	3.9	5.2	5.0	4.3
*Madagascar	...	3.6	4.4	3.9	5.0	4.2
Spain	2.1	4.0	5.2	3.5	3.6	4.1
Malta	0.7	2.0	12.5	0.7	0.6	4.0
Jordan	1.2	3.6	3.8	4.7	3.7	4.0
Togo	2.2	3.2	2.9	4.9	4.7	3.9
Venezuela	1.8	2.6	3.3	4.4	4.2	3.6
Trinidad and Tobago	3.7	3.7	3.3	3.0	4.1	3.5
*Benin	3.0	2.9	4.4	3.1	...	3.5
*Burundi	...	1.9	2.2	7.0	3.0	3.5
*Mauritania	-	3.1	3.0	5.5	2.1	3.4
*Niger	1.3	3.9	3.1	2.9	...	3.3
*Honduras	2.4	2.8	3.2	3.4	3.9	3.3
Mauritius	2.3	3.7	5.1	2.1	1.7	3.2
Thailand	3.7	3.6	3.4	2.9	2.6	3.1
Nigeria	3.2	4.0	2.8	2.4	2.1	2.8
*Somalia	1.3	2.1	2.5	3.0	3.6	2.8
*Central African Republic	...	3.2	2.1	1.5	4.0	2.7
Malaysia	1.3	3.0	2.7	2.7	2.3	2.7
Cyprus	1.5	2.5	2.9	2.2	2.0	2.4
Iraq	1.2	2.1	1.9	2.7	3.0	2.4
Botswana	3.7	2.1	1.4	2.0	2.5	2.0
*Rwanda	...	1.2	1.8	2.4	1.3	1.7
Republic of South Viet-Nam	2.9	0.8	0.9	2.2	2.7	1.7
*Mali	8.4	1.8	0.7	1.2	1.6	1.3
Fiji	0.8	0.9	0.7	0.9	0.8	0.8
Singapore	0.1	0.4	0.4	0.9	0.4	0.5
Gambia[d/]	-	-	-	-	-	-

Annex Table 1 (continued)

Source: UNCTAD secretariat, based on data supplied by the World Bank.

Note: An asterisk (*) indicates one of the most seriously affected (MSA) countries.

a/ Debt-service payments on public and publicly-guaranteed debt.

b/ For certain countries for which exports of goods and services were not available, exports of goods only were used.

c/ In descending order of average ratio for 197o-1973.

d/ Debt-service ratio less than o.1 per cent.

15 *Toward a New Framework for International Resource Transfers*

Mahbub ul Haq

The essence of the present demand for a new order lies in a realization by the poor nations that they can negotiate a better deal at the international level through the instrument of collective bargaining. While the new trade unionism of the poor nations has yet to take a concrete and specific form, its objectives are clear: a greater equality of opportunity and participation as equals around the bargaining tables of the world. The demand for a new economic order—similar to the demand for political liberation in the 1940s and 1950s—has to be viewed, therefore, as part of a historical process rather than as a set of specific proposals at the moment. What is important for an orderly dialogue between the rich and the poor nations is to agree that serious negotiations are necessary and acceptable in principle; to narrow down the areas of negotiation to manageable proportions in the first instance; to develop certain negotiating principles as an umbrella for such discussions; and to determine the negotiating forums through which an agreement should be reached in a specified period.

Besides trade, the monetary system, and restructuring of international institutions, an essential element in these negotiations must be the search for a new framework for orderly resource transfers from the rich to the poor nations, which is based on some internationally accepted needs of the poor rather than on the uncertain generosity of the rich. As was the case in the evolution of progressive national orders, provision of equal opportunity to the poor nations should come to be regarded not as a matter of charity but as part of the new deal giving them a significant stake in a stable social order. It is in this spirit that we can explore certain negotiating principles for the evolution of a more enlightened framework for international resource transfers.

Reprinted with permission from Mahbub ul Haq, "Toward a New Framework for International Resource Transfers," *Finance and Development* 12 (Sept. 1975): 6-9, 40, with minor adaptations.

Characteristics of the Present Aid Order

Before considering the new basis for international resource transfers, it is important to sketch out some of the implicit assumptions of the present order and what is wrong with them.

The present resource transfers from the rich to the poor nations are totally voluntary, dependent only on the fluctuating political will of the rich nations. The volume and terms of most assistance are dictated by short-term decisions, with no long-term perspectives or assurances. As such, there is no agreed basis for resource transfers. "Aid" is given for a variety of reasons, including cold war considerations, international leadership, political impact, special relationships with former colonies, domestic and international economic interests, and moral considerations. The relative weight of these factors changes greatly over time with regard to each country. As an illustration, about 25 percent of total resource transfers at present are still governed by "special relationships" with a few former colonies (constituting only 3 percent of the total population of the developing world) rather than by the relative poverty or growth needs of the developing countries.

The only international deal which presently exists on resource transfers is enshrined in the acceptance by the rich nations of a target of 1 percent of gross national product (GNP), with 0.7 percent as official development assistance (ODA) on fairly concessional terms. However, the acceptance of this target by the rich nations was grudgingly slow (with many nations still not officially subscribing to this target or, as in the United States, not having agreed to a date by which this target should be met). The actual performance has been most disappointing: official development assistance from 17 countries of the Development Assistance Committee (DAC) of the Organisation for Economic Co-operation and Development actually declined from 0.52 percent in 1960 to 0.30 percent in 1975 and, according to the current World Bank projections, is expected to decline further to 0.22 percent by 1980, given the present trends. So far, international resource transfers have been regarded primarily as the responsibility of the Western industrialized nations. Centrally planned economies have given little aid bilaterally and have not participated in any major multilateral channels of assistance. The newly liquid countries of the Organization of Petroleum Exporting Countries (OPEC) are recent arrivals on the scene and have already started transferring significant amounts (an estimated 2 percent of their 1974 GNP in disbursements and over 5 percent in commitments) but are not yet systematically integrated into the overall framework of international resource transfers.

Sufficient attention has not been paid in the past to the terms of international assistance or to the concept of *net* transfer of resources. As a result, the developing countries have accumulated by now a total financial debt of over $120 billion, so that annual debt servicing is already taking away about one half of the new assistance they receive. While foreign assistance has played an important role in the development of some countries at certain times, the overall contribution of this kind of resource transfer to the level and character of economic development remains shrouded in controversy. There have been repeated accusations by the developing countries that such assistance has at times been given in such a way as to undermine national resolve, conflict with national planning priorities, transfer irrelevant technologies, education systems, and development concepts, tie the recipient down to the source of assistance at a prohibitive cost, and promote the interests of a privileged minority in the recipient country rather than the vast majority. The critics of aid in the developed countries allege that aid is largely wasted, that it goes to support repressive governments (or experiments in socialism), and that it discourages indigenous efforts to save and invest. These controversies are not an invariable guide to the truth in each case but they generally illustrate how unhappy the recipients are with the present pattern of assistance, how thankless the donors regard their current task to be, and how urgent it is to get a new start.

Search for a New Framework

There must, therefore, be a search for a new framework for international resource transfers as an essential part of the effort to establish a new economic order. It will take time to negotiate such a framework and to put its various elements in place—a logical forum for such negotiations could well be the Joint Bank-Fund Development Committee if the members of the World Bank and the Fund wish to use it for this purpose—but at least some of the principles on which this framework should be based can be spelled out.

An element of automaticity must be built into the resource transfer system. The world community is still in a stage of evolution where the concept of international taxation of the rich nations for the benefit of the poor nations may be regarded as unrealistic. But the concept need not be accepted in its entirety now; it can be introduced gradually over time through a variety of devices: (1) a larger share of liquidity created by the International Monetary Fund (either through SDRs or gold sales) can be made available for development either through international financial institutions or directly to the developing countries; (2) certain sources of international financing can be developed—such as tax on nonrenewable resources, tax on international pollutants, tax on multinational corporation activities, rebates to country of origin of taxes collected on the earnings of trained immigrants from the developing countries, taxes on or royalties from commercial activities arising out of international commons such as ocean beds, outer space, the polar region; (3) if the rich industrialized nations are unwilling to tax themselves, others can collect and distribute these tax proceeds on the basis of what the rich nations consume—for example even a one dollar per barrel "development levy" by the OPEC could create a development pool of over $10 billion a year. The devices can be many: the more difficult aspect is to convince the rich nations that a more automatic system of international resource transfers will be in their own interest in the longer run as it will greatly reduce the present conflicts and endless controversies over the question of aid between the rich and the poor nations.

Aid to Poorest Nations

The focus of international assistance must shift to the poorest countries and, within them, to the poorest segments of the population. These are generally the countries with per capita incomes below $200, mostly in South Asia and Sahelian Africa, containing over one billion of the poorest people in the world. For higher income developing countries, access to international capital markets and expanding trade opportunities, not concessional assistance, is important. It is also essential that such redirected assistance be in the form of grants, without creating a reverse obligation of mounting debt service liability at a low level of poverty. Even the thought of the poorest sector repaying huge debts to the richest sector under the eyes of a benign government would be found abhorrent at the national level, but it is still tolerated at the international level because of the lamentably slow growth of our perceptions as an international community.

It would also be logical to link international assistance to national programs aimed at satisfying minimum human needs. This would give both a focus and direction to international assistance effort and make it a limited period affair until some of the worst manifestations of poverty—malnutrition, illiteracy, and squalid living conditions—are overcome both through the international effort and the expanding ability of national governments to launch a direct attack on poverty. These programs, however, should not be based on the concept of a simple income transfer to the poor—which would create permanent dependence—but on increasing the productivity of the poor and integrating them into the economic system.

Minimum Level of Investment

It is difficult to estimate how much investment it may take to bring the majority of mankind to the level of minimum human needs; much conceptual and empirical work needs to be done. Such work is being undertaken presently in the Dag Hammarskjold Foundation and the World Bank. A very rough estimate, based on various World Bank studies, shows that it may require a total investment of about $125 billion (in 1974 prices) over a 10-year period (food and nutrition $42 billion, education $25 billion, rural and urban water supply $28 billion, urban housing $16 billion, urban transport $8 billion, population and health programs $6 billion). Of course, these estimates will vary considerably depending on the style of development pursued by various countries. However, the merits of articulating such a target for removal of poverty are that it can be easily understood by the public (and, hopefully, by the politicians) in the rich nations; it can be the basis of a shared effort between the national governments and the international community; it provides an allocative formula for concessional assistance; and it establishes a specific time period over which the task should be accomplished.

International assistance, on a more automatic and purely grant basis, should be accepted by the international community as a transitional arrangement, to be terminated as soon as some of the worst manifestations of poverty can be removed. This is necessary both to protect the urge for self-reliance in the developing countries and to underline that the essential element in the new international economic order is not so much the redistribution of past incomes and wealth as the distribution of future growth opportunities. The stress must be on the equality of opportunity, not the equality of income. Each developing country must shape its own pattern of development and its own life style and, for this to be accomplished, international assistance can only be regarded as a temporary supplement to domestic efforts in the poorest countries.

Source and Channels of Assistance

Who should provide this assistance and how should the burdens be shared? Obviously, it should be done by the richest nations as measured by their per capita incomes. The problem for the next few years, however, is going to be that the rich industrialized nations—with an average per capita income of about $4,700 for DAC members—may experience balance of payments difficulties, while most of the liquid OPEC countries (other than Saudi Arabia, Kuwait, Libya, Qatar, and the United Arab Emirates with an average per capita income of about $4,000) are hardly rich enough to provide large subsidy funds since their average per capita income is still less than $500. An obvious solution would be to combine the volume of lending from the OPEC with the availability of subsidy funds from the industrialized countries and from the richest OPEC nations. But such a formula is likely to provide resources at intermediate terms, with about a 50 to 60 percent grant element, rather than the pure grants recommended above. However, this "second-best" solution may be the only course available for the next few years unless some of the automatic mechanisms come into play.

A major effort must also be made to provide a framework within which the richer socialist countries can play a much more substantial role than their present limited contribution. If the framework of international resource transfers is to be restructured, it is a logical corollary that multilateral channels should be used for directing this assistance, in preference to bilateral channels. This will be consistent with greater automaticity of transfers, allocations based on poverty and need (rather than on special relationships), and a more orderly system of burden sharing.

In order to put in a new framework of assistance, it would also be important to wipe the slate clean at least in two directions. First, arrangements must be made to provide a negotiating forum for an orderly settlement of past debts. It is time to revive the proposal of the Pearson Commission that a conference of principal creditors and debtors should be convened to discuss and agree on the principles for a major settlement to ease past burdens, particularly for the poorest countries. Second, since the concessions, leases, and contracts negotiated by the developing countries with the multinational corporations in the past often reflect their unequal bargaining strength, and since there is an environment of constant agitation and uncertainty surrounding foreign private investment at present, a mechanism should be provided to permit an orderly renegotiation of past contracts within a specified period of time under some international supervision. The recent report of the Group of Eminent Persons to the UN Secretary General[1] provides a sensible framework within which a new code of conduct for both the multinationals and the developing countries can be negotiated and arrangements for international monitoring of agreements can be provided.

It is not going to be easy to negotiate all the above principles simultaneously or to implement them immediately. The basic idea in spelling them out is to indicate the sense of direction that must be generated in negotiating a new framework for international resource transfers, rather than to offer a concrete blueprint which can only emerge out of hard, tough bargaining that seeks to balance various conflicting interests. An ideal framework should include most of the elements mentioned in the preceding text; a more practical framework will naturally have to settle for many compromises and second-best solutions, at least in the short run.

Implications for the World Bank

Any new framework that is negotiated will have major implications for the future of the World Bank as the premier international institution at present for the channeling of assistance to the developing countries. The primacy of the role of the World Bank in the future will naturally depend on how well and how quickly it can adjust to changing realities. Before indicating the nature of the changes that the World Bank will have to face and accept, it would be useful to review very briefly the underlying philosophy of this institution since its inception in 1946.

The World Bank started out primarily as a U.S.-sponsored effort for the reconstruction of Europe and Japan, not as an international effort to channel assistance to the developing countries. It is worth noting the opening remarks of John Maynard Keynes at the first meeting of the Bretton Woods Commission on the Bank: "It is likely, in my judgment, that the field of reconstruction from the consequences of war will mainly occupy the proposed Bank in its early days. But as soon as possible, and with increasing emphasis as time goes on, there is a second primary duty laid upon it, namely to develop the resources and productive capacity of the world, with special reference to the less developed countries." As late as 1964, about one third of Bank disbursements were still to the developed countries no longer included in its lending program (the so-called past borrowers). Over the last three decades, it has shown considerable dynamism and brilliant improvisation in the light of changing situations. At first, it became an intermediary (through the instrument of World Bank lending) between the capital markets of the world and the more creditworthy developing countries which could still not raise this capital on their own guarantee. As debt burdens increased in the poorest countries, it established a "soft" window, the International Development Association (IDA) in 1960 to provide long-term concessional resources to this group of countries. Its sectoral priorities also changed with the changing requirements of its recipients.

While it provided mainly equipment and consultants for infrastructure projects in the earlier phase, it has been promoting a direct attack on poverty in the last five years: for instance, about two-thirds of its total lending went to transport, power, and communications in 1964-68 but a similar proportion now goes into rural development, industry, education, water supply, nutrition, and population projects. The Bank has increasingly phased out higher-income developing countries with per capita incomes above $1,000 and focused its attention on the poorest countries with per capita incomes below $200, subject only to the limitations of the total availability of concessional resources. Over 90 percent of IDA resources are now directed to countries with per capita incomes below $200. Thus, the essential vitality of the World Bank has been reflected in its ability to adapt and improvise as the situation demanded.

The need to adapt will be much greater in the future. It is not possible to go over this ground in any great detail here but at least the general direction of change is already clear and can be summarized quite briefly. In order to become a truly international institution and to shed off its image of a Western club, the World Bank must aim at universality of membership, both among its potential contributors and among its recipients. Some of the original rules of the game, which make it difficult for new members to join the club, may therefore have to be changed. For instance, if the World Bank capital base is expanded, the existing members have the first right to pre-empt the additional capital subscriptions so that new members can be inducted or relative quotas changed only with the tacit permission of the existing members. Similarly, the voting rights in the IDA are based on cumulative contributions since 1960 so that if the OPEC, for instance, is willing to contribute even 50 percent to the next replenishment of the IDA, it will obtain only about 10 percent of the total voting rights, which is not likely to encourage its participation unless the formula is revised. The main point is that, while it was inescapable that the World Bank should be conceived primarily as a Western club at the time of the Bretton Woods conference, it must now find ways of becoming truly international and actively negotiate the participation of OPEC and richer socialist countries in its affairs. In the emerging climate, universality of membership becomes one of the most important principles to pursue in its future evolution.

New Formulas for Voting Rights

New formulas must be found for the restructuring of voting rights in the World Bank (including the IDA). While voting rights have been revised over time, they still essentially represent the balance of economic, financial, and political power which prevailed in the 1940s. For instance, the United Kingdom continues to have twice the voting power of the Federal Republic of Germany and nearly three times that of Japan; Belgium and the Netherlands together have more voting strength than OPEC combined; Iran has a lower voting power than India; and Pakistan nearly twice as much as Saudi Arabia, despite the fact that both India and Pakistan are by now aid recipients from Iran and Saudi Arabia. Overall, the developing countries (excluding OPEC) have only 31 percent of the total voting power. It is important, therefore, to carry out a general and thorough-going review of the voting power structure which replaces the historical past with current realities so that the OPEC can be persuaded to play a larger role, the developing countries get an increased assurance that their voices will be heard more attentively on decisions which affect their development, and the established lenders continue to have an important, though necessarily reduced, role in the running of the institution. It is not necessary to start out with preconceived formulas: what is really needed is to set out with a clear recognition of the need for change and to provide appropriate negotiating forums where acceptable formulas can be hammered out.

If international resource transfers tend to become more automatic, the World Bank can emerge as the primary channel for these transfers, provided it can win the confidence of the international community as a whole. More automaticity in World Bank financial resources is needed in any case to free it increasingly from bilateral pressures and to enable it to play a truly multilateral role in the new economic order. Thus, efforts must be made to link at least a part of the future IDA replenishments with SDR creation, or gold sales, or some sources of international taxation. For the World Bank, it would be logical that, instead of seeking the concerned government's permission before floating its bonds, it should have an automatic right to borrow in any capital market where the country has been enjoying an overall balance of payments surplus.

While the World Bank has shown considerable vitality in deepening its activities (by turning its attention to productive programs for the lowest 40 percent of the population), it has not shown the same vitality in extending the range of its services, such as buffer stock financing, export credit financing, and use of its guarantee powers. These services are likely to become even more crucial in the 1970s as trade expansion comes to be recognized as an increasingly important supplement to resource transfers.

"Third Window" for Medium-term Aid

Though the World Bank and the IDA have served admirably as mechanisms for channeling assistance to the developing countries, it is becoming increasingly necessary to evolve a new mechanism for obtaining and directing assistance at terms intermediate between the IBRD and the IDA. The introduction of a "Third Window" [approved in 1975], is, therefore, a pragmatic and inevitable response to the changing circumstances.

At some stage, consideration should also be given to a general review of the Articles of the World Bank which were conceived and drafted in the environment of the 1940s. This is becoming necessary as the basic economic situation of the developing countries is undergoing a fairly rapid change, calling for a greater measure of flexibility in the Bank operations. For instance, the original Articles expected, quite rightly at that time, that the bulk of the Bank assistance would be in projects and in foreign exchange, so that restrictions were built into the rules of the game against program lending and local cost financing. The Bank has improvised pragmatically in its actual operations to get around these restrictions as the need arose: still the long shadow of the Articles is always there and the needed flexibility is sometimes missing. Program lending and local cost financing still have to be justified, on a case-by-case basis, as deviations from a normal trend which is bound to influence the form and character of lending. One can find other instances of such restrictions in the Articles: for example, procurement of goods and services restricted only to Bank members; extremely limited preference margin to developing countries for procurement within their own country; a strict financial rate-of-return criterion.

The Bank practice has moved considerably, though not sufficiently, away from some of the restrictive aspects of the Articles. But the Articles themselves may have to be reviewed, not only to bring them into conformity with the actual practice but also to build into them enough flexibility to accommodate the needs of the 1970s and the fast changing role of the World Bank in the future. It should be recognized at the same time that a general review of the Articles is likely to be a very difficult and treacherous process and can only be undertaken if the necessary political consensus for such a step is available. In the meantime, there is no alternative to pragmatic improvisations.

Notes

1. United Nations, Department of Economic and Social Affairs, *The Impact of Multinational Corporations on Development and on International Relations* (New York: United Nations, 1974).

16 *Restructuring the International Monetary System: The Main Issues*

Group of Twenty-Four

The Ministers of the Group of 24 on International Monetary Affairs held their 12th meeting in Kingston, Jamaica, on January 6, 1976.

Ministers noted with grave concern the continuing deterioration in the international environment for the development of their economies as reflected in highly discouraging trends of aid flows and trade of developing countries. Performance of developed countries in fulfilling obligations under internationally agreed targets has fallen far short of both their capacity to provide assistance and the objective needs of developing countries. They pointed out that the Development Committee, which was charged with the function of finding effective solutions to these problems, has not made progress for want of adequate cooperation and exercise of political will on the part of major developed countries. Ministers also expressed their strong disappointment that the interests and concerns of developing countries have received so little attention in the negotiations on international monetary reform and that decisions affecting all countries continued to be taken in restricted groups of countries. They emphasized that unless there was a fundamental change in the attitude of developed countries, the dialogue on international economic cooperation now under way in many forums is unlikely to produce any constructive results.

Ministers agreed that the various issues before the Interim and Development Committees were closely interrelated. They stressed that a successful conclusion of the forthcoming meetings of the Committees would, as a

---

The text of the "Communiqué of 7 January 1976 of the Intergovernmental Group of Twenty-Four on International Monetary Affairs." The communiqué was issued following a meeting of the Group of 24 in the context of the Kingston meeting of the Interim Committee of the Board of Governors of the International Monetary Fund. The Group of 77 had decided, in 1971, to establish the Group of 24 for the purpose of coordinating the positions of the developing countries in matters related to the international monetary system.

minimum, depend on a set of measures of particular importance to developing countries being adopted by those Committees, and agreed, to that end, to be in close consultation with each other in the coming days.

Ministers noted that, as had been amply shown by studies undertaken by the International Monetary Fund (IMF) and the World Bank, the current account position of non-oil exporting developing countries had deteriorated by approximately $7.5 billion from 1974 to 1975 to reach a deficit of $35 billion. By contrast, that of developed countries had improved by $27 billion over that period to register a surplus of $16 billion in 1975. Ministers pointed out that the inelasticity of demand for imports of developing countries has helped the developed countries by serving as a buffer to deeper recession, and that expansion of the import capacity of developing countries would alleviate significantly the problems of both developed and developing countries.

Ministers, recalling the strong reservations registered at the last meeting of the Interim Committee in connection with the proposed arrangements on gold, expressed strong dissatisfaction with the fact that those proposed arrangements would grossly distort the distribution of international liquidity at the expense of developing countries, and undermine the position of the Special Drawing Right (SDR). They strongly emphasized that the developing countries would not accept or condone any infringement of the Fund's Articles of Agreement regarding purchases by national monetary authorities of gold above the present official price. Ministers were of the view that ways existed for activating the trust fund prior to amendment of the Articles without violating the present Articles.

Ministers urged that, in the future, in the course of disposing of the portion of its gold holdings remaining after the disposal of the first 50 million ounces, the Fund should arrange for the bulk of the benefit to go to the developing countries, with the Fund empowered to distribute to developing countries directly a portion of the profits on the basis of quotas, either in currency or in specie. There was strong support among Ministers in favor of an enabling clause for a gold substitution account in the amended Articles of Agreement.

Ministers agreed that the reconstitution requirements for special drawing rights should be abrogated both entirely and immediately. Ministers agreed that each member of the IMF should undertake to collaborate with the Fund and with other members in order to ensure that the policies of the member with respect to reserve assets is consistent with the objective of making the special drawing right the principal reserve asset in the international monetary system.

Ministers agreed that, in interpreting the obligations and applying the principles under the amended Articles dealing with exchange arrangements, the IMF should pay due regard to the special circumstances of the developing countries and to the importance of currencies for the international financial system. Ministers were opposed to calling upon the Fund, explicitly, to discourage the maintenance of unrealistic par values. They were prepared to see the Fund encourage realistic par values, but the Fund should do so particularly with respect to the par values of major currencies.

Ministers expressed strong support for a substantial enlargement, on a permanent basis, of the access of developing countries to Fund credit. They advocated the immediate action of two credit tranches with the same conditionality as the first credit tranche. Ministers agreed that the conditionality attached to the use of Fund resources in the higher credit tranches was currently excessive and required reduction. Ministers reaffirmed their request for early action to establish a trust fund to provide substantial and additional balance of payments assistance to low-income developing countries.

Ministers noted that the liberalization of the compensatory financing facility agreed to by the Executive Board fell far short of the expectations of the developing countries, and suggested that there should be an early review of the facility to (a) provide for shortfalls to be calculated in real terms and (b) expand the facility and extend the repayment period. Ministers noted that although it had been decided at the final meeting of the Committee of 20 that the link [between the SDR and development financing] should be considered as part of the interim package, it was not included in the package before the Interim Committee. Ministers reaffirmed their strong support for an enabling clause to permit the link to be established.

Ministers expressed grave concern at the maintenance and intensification of restrictions on access to markets for primary commodities, which were causing great damage to the balance of payments positions of the producing countries, and stressed the need to remove such restrictions immediately. Ministers were also agreed that there was an urgent need to stabilize the prices of primary products; the Development Committee should undertake an early review of the IMF buffer stock financing facility.

Ministers were of the view that the relevant provisions of the Rome Communiqué and the trade pledges in the Organisation for Economic Co-operation and Development had as their rationale the discouragement of escalation of trade restrictions in developed countries. They expressed regret that those pledges were not being fully observed by the industrial countries at the same time as the developing countries were being pressed to avoid trade restrictions, even when these were necessary for the maintenance of their development programs.

Regarding access to capital markets by developing countries, Ministers urged the early completion of studies in the Development Committee which would enable prompt and effective measures of an operational character to be taken, particularly regarding obstacles to access to capital markets and the creation of a multilateral guarantee fund designed to secure additional resources for developing countries that do not have access to private capital markets. Ministers were of the view that developing countries with access to private capital markets should not for that reason be denied access to borrowing from development finance institutions.

Ministers stressed the need for international financial agencies to help establish a secondary market for debt instruments issued by developing countries, by investing part of their liquid assets in such paper and by other means. Ministers also emphasized that co-financing could make a substantial contribution to meeting the capital needs of developing countries.

Ministers acknowledged with satisfaction that OPEC countries have increased substantially their financial assistance to other developing countries, noting that it has multiplied fivefold between 1973 and 1974 to a figure approaching $15 billion, divided roughly evenly between bilateral and multilateral aid. On an annual basis, commitments in the first half of 1975 were running well in excess of $21 billion.

Ministers reaffirmed the urgent need for developed countries to reach the 0.7 percent target for official development assistance, and stressed that the Development Committee could and should serve to strengthen the political will required to achieve that target by the end of the decade.

Ministers reiterated their strong support for the lending program proposed by the management of the World Bank. They also expressed strong support for a two-step increase in the capital of the Bank of which the first step, which should be undertaken immediately, would consist of a selective increase of approximately $10 billion, and the second of a general increase at a later stage. They stressed that a firm recognition should be obtained that the general increase would continue to be an urgent necessity and that it should be completed as soon as possible to avoid any restrictions in the Bank's lending program in the near future.

In this connection, Ministers also affirmed that the voting power of the non-oil exporting developing countries should not be reduced from their present level and that the Board representation of those countries should at least be maintained or increased, if necessary, to preserve a balanced geographical representation.

Ministers acknowledged with satisfaction the contributions made by some countries to the Third Window of the World Bank and urged that all countries in a position to do so should contribute to that facility without further delay, so as to allow the original target of $1 billion to be reached. They stressed that such contributions should be additional, and that the Third Window should be administered flexibly with regard to access.

Ministers expressed concern at the diminishing share of upper- and middle-income countries in the IBRD's lending program and considered that present lending to these countries should be increased. The Ministers strongly supported a substantially increased replenishment of International Development Association (IDA) in real terms. Negotiations for the replenishment of IDA should be completed by June 1976, in time to ensure continuity of operations. The Ministers also stressed the need to expand the capital of the regional development banks and of the International Finance Corporation.

Ministers expressed their concern at the apparent lack of political support from the developed nations for the Development Committee, as well as at the lack of concrete measures to be adopted so as to increase the transfer of resources to developing countries. They were of the view that the Committee, its Executive Secretary, and associated international organizations, should proceed promptly to consider concrete solutions to existing problems, so as to achieve the objectives of the Committee. Urgent action was seen to be necessary if the minimum acceptable growth targets are to be attained.

Part 5

Technology

17 *Technological Dependence*

UNCTAD

Technological Dependence and Recent Development Experiences

Although the application of imported science and technology over the last quarter century has brought some progress in accelerating the growth of output, improving material standards of life and spreading modernization, the low-income countries still find themselves unable to meet the basic needs of the majority of their populations. The purpose of this chapter is briefly to consider the extent to which the prevailing approach to industrialization, based on a reliance on the transfer of technology from developed country enterprises, is capable of contributing to a diminution of this problem.

In the 15 years following the Second World War, over 60 countries gained formal independence and the total number since then has grown to nearly 80. These countries entered political independence with a backlog of crushing poverty, massive illiteracy and little accumulated capital or industrialization experience. Emancipation from alien rule was accompanied by a rising political consciousness, which expressed itself in demands for modernization. The best way of accelerating industrialization, it seemed, was to tap the vast fund of production technologies that had already been developed in the advanced countries. The technology was not free but, like the goods that it was used to produce, it was traded and could be bought or leased—mainly from transnational corporations domiciled in the industrialized countries, which had made themselves its proprietors.

The Historical Pattern

Traditionally, the transfer of technology to developing countries, largely in the form of direct foreign investment, has taken place in the extractive

Reprinted, with permission, from UNCTAD, *Transfer of Technology: Technological Dependence, Its Nature, Consequences and Policy Implications. Report by the UNCTAD Secretariat* (TD/190), 31 December 1975, pp. 9-24, with minor adaptations.

sector (petroleum, mining and export agriculture). This can be seen from the accumulated stock of foreign investment, in which the share of this sector was very high in the past and accounted for nearly one-half as late as 1967, compared with about 30 percent in manufacturing.[1] Additions to this stock (by United States firms at least) more recently, however, have been strongly dominated by manufacturing,[2] reflecting in part the results of deliberate policies adopted by the developing countries.

The motivation for foreign investment in the extractive sector has been and is to secure access to critical imports of raw materials for the metropolitan countries and, although the resulting exports have in recent years helped to generate foreign exchange resources needed for the financing of development, the direct effects on modernization, on the dissemination of skills and on the creation of employment have been quite small.

For all but a small minority of developing countries, the main feature of industrialization after the war was, following the example set by continental Europe and the United States in the latter part of the 19th century, an attempt to create internal markets for manufactured goods by the establishment of a system of high tariffs and other types of restrictions on imports. The fledgling industries thus created would produce domestic substitutes for goods that had previously been imported. The desire for greater economic independence was a natural outgrowth of political independence. The aim was to secure control of one's own instruments of production and to end "dependence on 'centres of decision' situated abroad."[3] In the absence of a sufficiently developed entrepreneurial spirit among potential industrialists, protection was felt to be necessary in order to stimulate local initiative, mobilize savings and enhance the establishment of small enterprises that could not become firmly established without the umbrella of tariffs.

Thus, there were two cornerstones to the strategy of industrialization: importation of technology from the industrialized countries, and the substitution of domestic manufactures for imports.

Transnational Firms, Dependence, and the Conditions of Exchange

In reviewing the results of this strategy, it is essential to keep in mind the pervasive influence of the world-wide market for technology and of the respective positions of transnational enterprises and developing countries in that market. The market has the following peculiarities: it is highly imperfect, with great monopoly advantages for the seller because of secrecy and/or the protection of patents and trade marks. The production technology (whether in the form of pure knowledge or embodied in foreign investment or machinery) is transferred under terms that are the outcome of negotiations between buyers and sellers in situations approximating monopoly or oligopoly. The final returns and their distribution depend on the relative power of the bargainers.[4]

The probability of an unfavourable outcome is highest in the case of developing countries because of the existing asymmetry of technical knowledge. Evidence of this is most vividly seen in the negligible participation of developing countries in the ownership of patents, reported in an earlier study by the UN Conference on Trade and Development (UNCTAD) secretariat, which shows that only 6 percent (200,000) of the estimated 3.5 million patents in existence in 1972 were granted by developing countries, and that less than one-sixth of that total was owned by nationals of those countries.[5]

It is true that several developed countries are also heavy net importers of technology and may have few patented inventions to their credit. The seriousness of technological dependence as it applies to the poorer countries, however, is that, because of an absence of experience with modern technology generated by historical factors, there is a lack of skills. This can be of two kinds: (a) a shortage of relatively abstract, high-level skills needed in order to make technological choices—both in firms and in government—to appraise technology and to carry out research on the development of new technologies; and (b) a lack of the more down-to-earth expertise needed in order to use tools and operate mechanical equipment. Table 1 shows the decidedly low endowment of developing compared with developed countries in terms of type (a) skills. Thus, in 1970 there was an average of only about 6 engineers and scientists per 10,000 population for the 8 African countries for which data were available, compared with figures of 22 for Asia and 69 for Latin America. This contrasts with a figure of 112 per 10,000 in developed market economy countries. The poorer performance of developing countries repeats itself for every socio-economic indicator about which it was possible to obtain information. Among developing regions, Africa consistently fares the worst and Latin America generally the best, with Asia in between.

It should not be inferred from the table that the solution to the technology problem is simply to make good the deficiencies shown, e.g., by educating a greater amount of high-level manpower. The existing outflow of scientific personnel from developing countries already demonstrates a probable outcome if such a policy were undertaken in the absence of a parallel increase in the domestic demand for such skills. Moreover, the quantitative deficiencies in science and technology depicted in the table may be less significant than the fact that a great deal of scientific and technological activity in developing countries is unconnected with fundamental needs.[6] There is no quantitative measure of the comparative lack of the second type of more mundane skills and capabilities directly connected with the productive process. These capabilities are not the product of formal

Table 1. Technological dependence: Selected socio-economic indicators
(Averages expressed as medians for 197o or latest year available)

		Developed market economy countries[a]	Developing countries and territories		
			Africa[b]	Asia[c]	Latin America[d]
I.	SCIENCE AND TECHNOLOGY				
(i)	Ratio of total stock of scientists and engineers per 1o,ooo pop.	112	5.8	22.o	69
(ii)	Ratio of technicians per 1o,ooo pop.	142.3	8.3	23.4	72.2
(iii)	Scientists and engineers engaged in R & D per 1o,ooo pop.	1o.4	o.35	1.6	1.15
(iv)	Technicians engaged in R & D per 1o,ooo pop.	8.2	o.4	o.6	1.4
(v)	Expenditure on R & D as percentage of GNP	1.2	o.6	o.3	o.2
II.	HIGH LEVEL MANPOWER				
(vi)	Professionals and technicians as percentage of economically active [illegible]	[illegible]		[illegible]	[illegible]

(vii) Percentage of the economically active population employed in manufacturing sector	25.4	3.5	1o.5	14.1
(viii) Literacy rates (per cent)	96 e/	High f/ 2o Low f/ 15	32	77
(ix) Ratio of primary and secondary enrolment to school age population	92 e/	32	56	78

Sources: (i)-(v): UNESCO, Statistical Yearbook, 1973, table 8.3; and UNITED NATIONS, Statistical Yearbook, 1974, table 199.

(vi) and (vii): ILO, Yearbook of Statistics, 1974, tables 2A and 2B.

(viii) and (ix): Handbook of International Trade and Development Statistics, supplement for 1973, table 6.8.

a/ The size of the sample in this column varies by indicator, ranging from four countries in line (ii) to 25 countries in line (ix).

b/ The size of the sample in this column varies by indicator, ranging from eight countries in lines (i) and (ii) to 46 countries in lines (viii) and (ix).

c/ Excludes China. The size of the sample in this column varies by indicator, ranging from seven countries in line (vi) to 36 countries in lines (viii) and (ix).

d/ The size of the sample in this column varies by indicator, ranging from seven countries in lines (i) and (ii) to 43 countries in line (viii).

e/ Includes Greece and Turkey.

f/ Taking upper limit of estimates where no precise figures were given, e.g., for lo-15 per cent, 15 per cent would be used for high estimate and lo per cent for low estimate.

Note: The classification used in this table is intended for statistical convenience and does not necessarily imply any judgment regarding the stage of development of any particular country.

technical training so much as on-the-job experience which is more difficult to produce. Consequently, their scarcity is the most acute for developing countries.

The most commonly cited advantage for developing countries provided by the transnational corporation is that it offers at one and the same time technology and a package of other crucial inputs such as financial resources, organizing capability, machinery and intermediate goods, and distribution channels for exports. It is frequently overlooked that the transnational corporation also strives to maintain this advantage by consolidating its control over the capacity to generate all of these inputs. In doing so, it deprives the developing country of the capacity to make its own technological and economic decisions. A few statistics will document the dominance that is exercised over one of the above inputs—technology. In the United States, where 70 percent of all (public and private) expenditure on research and development in non-socialist countries occurs, the transnational corporations accounted for an average of 52 percent of total private R&D expenditure in 1966, of which only 6 percent occurred overseas—mostly in Canada, the United Kingdom and Europe.[7] Of the $2,760 million in overseas receipts of royalties and fees for the transfer of technology by United States firms in 1972, it is estimated that between 35 to 90 percent went to transnational corporations and three-quarters of that sum originated from their affiliated firms.[8]

The impact of the transfer of technology is strongly conditioned by the multi-plant (or multi-branch) spread of the transnational corporation and its unified approach to the management of its activities so as to maximize global rather than national profits. Although it may have a clear logic in terms of the efficient operation of the corporations, the location of decision-making centres outside the borders of the developing countries in which these corporations operate tends to foster an international division of labour which accentuates the dominance/dependence relationship between developing and developed countries.

The discussion below of the effects of the technological aspects of recent industrialization strategies of developing countries will concentrate on three main issues: (a) the foreign exchange cost of technology transfer, (b) the appropriateness of technology, and (c) the possibility of technological development.

Foreign Exchange Costs: Some Determining Factors

As has been shown in previous studies issued by the UNCTAD secretariat, the foreign exchange cost of transfer of technology represents a considerable burden on the balance of payments of developing countries[9] and the over-all balance-of-payments impact of individual investment projects has often been on the negative side.[10] Those findings are indirectly supported by other studies which have shown a negative value added calculated at world prices for a number of industries in developing countries[11] and a negative aggregate impact from the activities of transnational corporations on the balance of payments of host countries.[12] At least three types of practices by transnational corporations tend to diminish the balance-of-payments benefits to developing countries. These include the tendency to rely on sources of finance within the host country (though this is sometimes acknowledged to mobilize domestic savings); the imposition of formal and informal restrictions on exports and sources of supply for their affiliates and independent licensees; and the over-pricing or under-pricing of exports by these enterprises.

In no small part, these practices represent the inevitable exercise of market power. But the ease with which supplying firms have been able to extract excessive returns on their technology with these or other practices is due in part to the nature of import substitution policies enacted by governments of developing countries. High tariffs and restrictions shutting out competing imports of consumer goods combined with low tariffs on capital goods have permitted protected industries to price their products well above world market prices.[13] For nationally owned "infant industries," the protection creating a monopoly market may have been necessary as a temporary measure permitting them to attain an efficient scale of production. It has not been justified on an indefinite duration to prolong the existence of excess capacity, or of units too small ever to operate efficiently in domestic markets of limited size.[14] When, as is frequently the case, the protection has applied to the foreign affiliates of dominant, well-established transnational firms it is simply a free gift further inflating potential monopoly profits that are then remitted through the familiar channels of transfer pricing, payments for know-how and trade marks, etc. which appear as costs on the affiliates' income statements.[15] Opportunities for excessive payments for imported technology have also been enhanced by the provision of a host of other investment incentives, such as generous tax holidays, low-cost credits and under-pricing of utilities. It may be said that the competition among developing countries to offer the most generous terms for the attraction of technology is itself a result of technological dependence.

Appropriateness of Production Technologies

A major cause of disappointment with the progress of the Second Development Decade has been the persistence of unemployment and underemployment and the failure of the growth rate of employment to keep up with the growth of population in much of the third world. It has become evident that the rapid expansion of industrial output is not by itself sufficient to solve this problem. In the great amount of literature on the subject, the most frequently prescribed remedy is a greater reliance on efficient technologies using a high ratio of labour to capital. A strong case may exist for choosing more labour-intensive techniques, even in those cases when they are somewhat inferior to others in terms of productive efficiency, if they are preferred by workers and are more suitable to local institutions and traditions.[16] In general, the industries of developing countries have tended to employ techniques which have not led to adequate utilization of domestic resources, including environmental resources. Moreover, there is a pronounced tendency for capital intensity to increase over time—partly owing to shifts in industrial patterns—which is another way of saying that the amount of investment necessary in order to create a job is becoming progressively greater.[17] The technology marketed by transnational firms in import-substituting industries has been of the same labour-saving type used in industries in their own countries. In contrast, the same firms have in recent years been a major source of labour-intensive methods where they have established wholly owned subsidiaries for the export of manufactures, usually to their own countries.[18] But these essentially assembly-type operations continue to represent a small proportion of manufacturing investment in the vast majority of low-income countries where emphasis has been on the exploitation of domestic markets. It can be concluded, therefore, that the powerful combination of technology, capital and organizational skills at the disposal of firms in developed countries has not contributed optimally to the solution of the employment problem and may actually have aggravated it in those instances where it has replaced traditional patterns of production.[19]

The accumulating body of scattered empirical evidence on the existence of labour-using techniques—some in current use and others long discarded by developed country firms—removes the absence of such techniques as a satisfactory explanation for the prevalence of capital-intensive production processes in the transfer of technology to developing countries.[20] Among the other explanations, the most important is that the market prices paid for capital and labour in developing countries do not correctly portray their relative scarcities or, more generally, give the wrong incentives to firms choosing techniques of production. Technologies designed where labour is scarce are transferred unaltered to poor countries where labour is abundant because they already exist and because the heavily protected, monopolistic or oligopolistic markets of these countries obviate the need to develop new ones. Even under competition, market wage rates and interest rates on borrowed capital are an insufficient guide for choosing techniques that are the most desirable from society's point of view. Moreover, government policies such as tax incentives for investment, low tariffs on imported machinery and subsidized credit have had the effect of artificially lowering the price of capital relative to labour in developing countries.

The impact of particular techniques of production is not only conditioned by the intensity with which they use labour, but also by the general social, economic and natural environments in which they are applied. This point applies especially to agriculture, a sector that has only lately begun to attract the kind of attention it deserves in countries with rising food deficits and growing unemployment. Developed country agricultural techniques based on large-scale, highly mechanized methods of cultivation in temperate climates are not adapted to the tropical conditions, low land-to-labour ratios and lack of skills prevailing in developing countries. Development literature abounds with examples of imported farm machinery that falls into disuse the moment the experts have left.[21] Moreover, the socio-economic effects of imported technology depend critically on systems of land tenure, class structure and income distribution. Thus, although the introduction of high-yielding seeds through the green revolution succeeded in achieving spectacular increases in per acre yields in some cases, it mainly benefited rich landlords with access to credit who farmed in areas where irrigation and fertilizers were available.[22] A considerable potential exists for furthering the indigenous adaptation and development of simple technologies directed toward small-scale peasant farming and the creation of rural industry.[23] However, for many Latin American and some Asian countries, land reform would be a necessary precondition.

Appropriateness of Consumption Technologies

Although transnational firms have been the principal source for the transfer of production technology, it has until recently been overlooked that they are also the main avenue for the transmission of "consumption technology."[24] A large proportion of the modern manufactured products consumed in developing countries today are either imported or were formerly imported from developed countries. Through their mastery of the techniques of advertising and product differentiation, and their application of global distribution and marketing strategies, transnational companies have helped to shape the consumption patterns of these countries. At the same time, consumer goods markets in these countries are dominated by urban middle and upper classes who have been the group most favoured by the unequal income distributions that have accompanied the type of import-substituting industrialization that has been pursued. It is these enclaves of affluence that have provided the main target for transnational firms.[25]

The main charge against import substitution is that it has concentrated on the wrong products. The inappropriateness of many of the rich country products introduced and promoted in the domestic markets of poor countries derives from the fact that they embody technological characteristics that are either unnecessary, undesired or too costly to meet the basic needs of nutrition, health, clothing and shelter.[26] Labour-intensive methods of production are sometimes excluded if these modern products of high quality are to be manufactured. The transnationals and their client firms in developing countries are not likely to be keen about or able to undertake the manufacture of goods that cater to the above-mentioned needs, for at least three reasons.[27] First, although the gains to society from their doing so would be high, private profitability is low on account of the limited purchasing power of the income groups that would consume the products. Secondly, the specific production of appropriate goods tailored to the unique environments of individual developing countries would be inconsistent with the principle of efficiency based on standardization and uniform specifications and quality characteristics. Modification of product characteristics is rendered more difficult in the case of highly differentiated goods that are covered by trade marks or brand names identified in consumers' minds, rightly or wrongly, with a certain standard of quality.[28] Finally, such a policy would be inconsistent with the corporate ideology of achieving a "global structure of excellence" based on the Western model.[29] In sum, the efforts needed to respond to the basic wants of the great majority of the third world's population are beyond the field of interest of the transnational corporations.

Self-perpetuating Features of Dependence

The conclusion of the preceding discussion is that the prevailing model of industrialization based on the introduction and application of rich country technologies to reproduce rich country consumption patterns is both too costly and ill-suited for the satisfaction of basic material needs in developing countries. But the technologies and the goods they produce are inseparable from one another. The acquisition of know-how from developed country enterprises, chiefly transnational corporations, demands the use of techniques of production that are biased against labour and towards the manufacture of commodities catering mainly to an affluent tiny minority of the population in the third world. Conversely, to produce these same commodities demands the application of technologies obtainable under the terms and conditions set by the enterprises. Dependence is built into this industrialization process.

Moreover, the technological dependence of developing countries may be self-perpetuating. While thc transfer of technology may facilitate the expansion of industrial output in these countries, it does not necessarily further the ability to produce that output, or, more precisely, the capacity to adapt and modify existing technology and to evolve new technologies.

There are several reasons for this.

First, a large part of the transfer of technology takes place as part of direct foreign investment which in many instances results in majority owned subsidiaries. So long as an industry or product group is under foreign control, the possibility of launching domestic technological initiatives in that industry remains academic. Because of the narrow, fragmented domestic markets for manufactures in many developing countries, a relatively minor capital outlay from the standpoint of a transnational company is sometimes sufficient to result in control or near control of an entire industry. In such industries, a national technology policy, if there ever is to be one, will have to await and be co-ordinated with nationalization.

Secondly, the other two major sources of the technology employed in the industrial sectors of developing countries are (a) licensing agreements concluded with nationally owned firms and covered by patents and/or trade marks (disembodied technology) and (b) imports of machinery or intermediate goods (embodied technology) by nationally owned firms without licensing agreements. In the case of trade marks, the duration of validity has no limit. Consequently, so long as the trade mark is used, it is necessary to use the technology that goes with it. Once the branded product has gained widespread consumer acceptance, there is little incentive for the licensee to abandon it and sustain the expense and risk of promoting his own trade mark. Because of their limited duration, patent licensing agreements offer greater opportunities for developing domestic technological skills—*a fortiori* for the use of imported machinery without licensing. But in both cases the long-term gain to society from the use of a domestic technology is greater than the private gain to the entrepreneur. In the absence of special inducements to the contrary, the entrepreneur is likely to opt for the proven performance of foreign technology.[30]

Thirdly, in the consumer goods sector the superiority of transnational enterprises is based on constant product innovation coupled with highly sophisticated advertising and marketing techniques.[31] As a result, the consuming elite in developing countries is presented with a succession of new or "improved" products, each of which makes the one that preceded it obsolete. In following the kinds of policies described previously, developing countries have in effect committed themselves to the eventual domestic production of each new product and thus to the importation of the technology that corresponds to it. The technology comes both directly as pure know-how and already embodied in imported intermediate goods and machinery. The constant change together with the sophistication of some of the required technology deter its domestic replication. Hence import substitution is extremely incomplete and dependence is prolonged. This contrasts sharply with the experience of nineteenth century developing countries for which the main thrust of technology transfer and technological advance was centred in the production of machinery and intermediate goods rather than new types of consumer goods.[32] The luxury consumption of the rich at that time mainly consisted of goods produced by the artisan class rather than imports, and the manufacture of capital goods, which was initially highly labour-intensive, developed in an organic relationship with domestic consumer goods production for the masses.

Fourthly, since foreign technology has tended to be a substitute for technologies that might have been developed by local scientists and engineers, and since the pre-capitalist sector (i.e. subsistence, agriculture and rural craft industries) as at present organized generates very little demand for these local inputs, science and technological institutions in developing countries have become alienated from productive activities. Whereas in developed countries the inputs of local scientists and engineers are an investment item, in developing countries they are largely an item of consumption. In these circumstances, science and technology cannot contribute to the development of domestic technical capability.

The preceding discussion is not intended to suggest that the import of technology from developed countries is inherently undesirable, or that the solution is some kind of individual or collective autarky. Provided that a particular technology is in fact needed, the only alternative may in fact be to import it from a developed country in many instances. However, it is clear that the gains from the technologically dependent industrialization that has actually taken place have not been equitably distributed either between receivers and suppliers of technology or among different income groups. Individual countries will have to decide on the special objectives of their technological and development policies in terms of their own priorities. For the majority of developing countries, the elimination of mass poverty and unemployment will be high on the list of objectives. This study has shown that it will be difficult to advance toward this goal without the elaboration of a major new strategy emphasizing not only control over the transfer of technology, but also the creation of an authentic, indigenous technical capability.

Notes

1. Based on Organisation for Economic Co-operation and Development (OECD), Development Assistance Directorate, *Stock of Private Direct Investments by DAC Countries in Developing Countries, end 1967* (Paris: OECD, 1972), table 1.
2. Based on statistics tabulated in S. Pizer and F. Cutler, *United States Business Investments in Foreign Countries* (Washington, United States Department of Commerce, 1960); and United States Department of Commerce, *Survey of Current Business* (August 1961 and August 1974).
3. A strategy of export-based development of the manufacturing sector seemed less desirable because of the implied dependence on the markets of the "centre," the trade barriers facing the traditional items most suitable for export to these markets, and the difficulty of meeting the quality requirements for consumer acceptance of more technologically-sophisticated products. For a discussion of the origins of import substitution policies see I. Little, T. Scitovsky, M. Scott, *Industry and Trade in Some Developing Countries: A Comparative Study* (Paris: OECD, 1970 and London: Oxford University Press, 1970).
4. For a full discussion of these issues see C. Vaitsos, *Transfer of Resources and Preservation of Monopoly Rents,* Economic Development Report No. 168, Centre of International Affairs (Harvard: Harvard University Press, 1970).
5. United Nations, *The Role of the Patent System in the Transfer of Technology to Developing Countries* (United Nations publication, sales no. E.75.II.D.6), tables 7 and 12.
6. See Amilcar Herrera, "Social Determinants of Science Policy in Latin America. Explicit Science Policy and Implicit Science Policy," *The Journal of Development Studies* (October 1972).
7. United States Senate, Committee on Finance, *Implications of Multinational Firms for World Trade and Investment for United States Trade and Labor* (Washington, D.C.: United States Government Printing Office, 1973), p. 557.
8. Ibid., p. 600.
9. United Nations, *Major Issues in Transfer of Technology to Developing Countries: A Study by the UNCTAD Secretariat* (United Nations publication, sales no. E.75.II.D.2).
10. See Paul Streeten and S. Lall, *The Flow of Financial Resources: Private Foreign Investment: Main Findings of a Study of Private Foreign Investment in Selected Developing Countries* (TD/B/C.3/111 and Corr. 1), 23 May 1973, summarizing the results of an analysis of 159 firms in six developing countries.
11. See ECAFE, *Intraregional Trade Projections, Effective Protection and Income Distribution Vol. II, Effective Protection* (United Nations Publication, sales no.: E.73.II.F.12), p. 18; Stephen Lewis Jr., *Pakistan Industrialization and Trade*

Policies (Paris: OECD and London: Oxford University Press, 1970), pp. 84-85; and Bela Balassa and associates, *The Structure of Protection in Developing Countries* (Baltimore: Johns Hopkins University Press, 1971).

12. During the period 1966-1970 when the aggregate United States balance of payments (current account plus long-term capital account) as a whole deteriorated, that of transnational corporations improved by $2.3 billion leading to the conclusion expressed in the United States Senate study, op. cit., p. 29, that transnationals "in their transactions with the United States, exert a uniformly large, negative impact on the current accounts of balance of payments of host countries (conversely, of course, they have a favourable impact on the corresponding account of the United States balance of payments)."

13. It is worth noting that, apart from Czarist Russia and the United States, present-day developed countries appear to have had significantly lower tariffs than developing countries at comparable stages of development. See Little, Scitovsky, Scott, op. cit., pp. 162-163.

14. Value added calculations in eight Asian countries have demonstrated in a sizeable number of manufacturing industries that if protection were eliminated the technologies would no longer be viable. See ECAFE, *Intraregional Trade Projections, Effective Protection and Income Distribution*, op. cit., p. 18.

15. Cf. Constantine V. Vaitsos, *Intercountry Income Distribution and Transnational Enterprises* (Oxford: Clarendon Press, 1974), p. 123.

16. See Amartya Sen, "The Concept of Efficiency," in M. Parkin and A. R. Nobay, eds., *Contemporary Issues in Economics* (Manchester: Manchester University Press, 1975).

17. In studying high-technology industry in Colombia, for example, one economist found that whereas it took 45,000 pesos to employ one worker in 1957, by 1966 it took 100,000 pesos of 1957 value. See *Towards Full Employment: A Programme for Colombia Prepared by An Inter-Agency Team Organized by The International Labour Office* (Geneva, 1970), p. 113.

18. See G.K. Helleiner, "Manufactured Exports from Less Developed Countries and Multinational Firms," *Economic Journal,* March 1973.

19. For a convincing theoretical demonstration of how capital-intensive technology transfer may lead to a reduction of both employment and net output see, Pranab K. Bardhan, *Major Issues Arising from the Transfer for Trade, Growth and Distribution in Developing Countries,* mimeographed (UNCTAD, TD/B/C.6/5), 29 September 1975.

20. See D. Morawetz, "Employment Implications of Industrialization in Developing Countries: A Survey," *Economic Journal,* September 1974, for a summary of some of this evidence. See also the studies prepared under the World Employment Programme of the International Labour Office, in particular, A.S. Bhalla, ed., *Technology and Employment in Industry: A Case*

Study Approach (Geneva: ILO, 1975).
21. Even for a relatively more technologically sophisticated country such as India, a recent review of all existing empirical studies of that country's massive tractorization campaign failed to find solid evidence of a clear overall advantage compared with older techniques based on animal power. See Amartyr Sen, "A Study of Tractorization in India" in his *Employment, Technology and Development* (London: Oxford University Press, 1975), appendix D.
22. See Keith Griffin, *The Green Revolution: An Economic Analysis* (Geneva: United Nations Research Institute for Social Development, 1972).
23. For an example of such an experiment in the United Republic of Tanzania, see George MacPherson and Dudley Jackson, "Village Technology for Rural Development—Agricultural Innovation in Tanzania," *International Labour Review,* July 1975, pp. 97-118.
24. See Frances Stewart, "Choice of Techniques in Developing Countries," *The Journal of Development Studies*, October 1972.
25. Thus, Peter Drucker, a business consultant to transnational companies, has pointed out that within the "vast mass of poverty that is India" there is "a sizeable modern economy, comprising ten percent or more of the Indian population or, 50,000,000 people." See his *The Age of Discontinuity* (New York: Harper & Row, 1969), p. 107, cited by R. Barnet and R. Müller, *Global Reach: The Power of the Multinational Corporations* (New York: Simon and Schuster, 1974), p. 169.
26. Thus, the "brightening" agent in detergents is superfluous for making clothes clean; automobiles consume more energy per passenger mile than any other form of transportation; dacron shirts are uncomfortable in hot climates.
27. This does not mean that there have not been superficial modifications in packaging and other characteristics in particular markets. Genuine efforts by Ford, Philips and National Cash Register have been made to develop appropriate products with relatively labour-intensive production technologies, but these appear to be isolated cases.
28. See *Systems, Including Industrial Property Systems, for Improving the National Scientific and Technological Infrastructures of Developing Countries* (TD/B/C.6/AC.2/4), para. 39.
29. As described in Barnet and Müller, op. cit., Chapter 2.
30. There is a great deal of empirical evidence that this has frequently occurred in India. See K. K. Subrahmanian, *Import of Capital and Technology: A Study of Foreign Collaborations in Indian Industry* (New Delhi: People's Publishing House, 1972).
31. In the United States, the principal objective of the research programme of 90 percent of manufacturing corporations is reported to be development of new products and improvements of old ones. See W. E. Gustafson,

"Research and Development, New Products and Productivity Change," *American Economic Review Proceedings,* May 1962.

32. See David Felix, "Technological Dualism in Late Industrializers: On Theory, History and Policy," *Journal of Economic History*, March 1974.

18 Regulating the Transfer of Technology

UNCTAD

Transfer of technology is a process that affects nearly every aspect of economic and social change in a country. The issues that it raises are therefore as broad as the area of its effect. The very breadth of the issues has also influenced the nature and scope of regulatory action. After all, the government of a country acts only according to its own perception of the most important issues. Issues that may be considered important in one country are almost entirely neglected in others, which emphasize a different set of issues. In the government's actions, this perception is tempered by an assessment of its ability to undertake a particular type of regulatory action and to establish the necessary administrative or other machinery for implementation.

Apart from the differences in the aspects covered by national regulatory action, the nature of the action taken also varies greatly from country to country. Some countries have made regulatory action statutory by adopting national laws or general regulations. Others, relying on the force of other legislative enactments, have issued guidelines to regulate the transfer process. There are yet other countries where broad policy declarations have been made to serve as the necessary policy framework.

Moreover, the policies affecting the transfer process are many, and national regulatory action in each country has to a large extent centred upon aspects considered most relevant for achieving the country's given objectives. It will therefore be useful to identify the main areas in which governments have taken one or another type of regulatory action affecting some aspect of the transfer process.

Reprinted, with permission, from UNCTAD, *The Possibility and Feasibility of an International Code of Conduct on Transfer of Technology: A Study by the UNCTAD Secretariat* (TD/B/AC.11/22), 6 June 1974, 11-25, 34-37, with minor adaptations.

Principal Issues in National Regulation of Technology Transactions

The features of the various measures of national regulatory action, whether they have only a general effect on the transfer process or whether they are more specifically related to the transfer process itself, are summarized in Table 1. It should be emphasized right at the beginning that the information contained in the table is incomplete, both in the coverage of the countries as well as in the list of the main features of the regulatory action. Before taking up in some detail the discussion of the six major headings in Table 1 and the 39 sub-headings under which the principal issues in national regulation practices are classified, it would be useful to draw attention to some of their general characteristics.

General Features of the Information on Regulatory Action

In the first place, regulatory action of this type is rather recent in origin. Full details of the degree of its spread over countries and its specific form as well as its content are not easily accessible. In consequence, if a country does not figure in the table against any of the features mentioned this does not mean that that country does not have any regulatory instruments to deal with the problem concerned. It simply means that, at this first phase of gathering information, data on the country in question were not easily available to the secretariat for inclusion in the table.

A mere glance at the table shows that the list encompasses a very large number of countries with different economic and social systems—both developed market economy, and developing countries. The absence against many of the items of any particular socialist country, whether from Eastern Europe or from other parts of the world, needs an explanation. This particular omission does not mean that these countries do not have any instruments for regulating the transfer of technology. In fact it needs to be emphasized that the regulatory instruments in these countries are perhaps much more rigorous, because of the role of central planning, than in any of the countries mentioned in the table. To get a proper perspective of the spread of regulatory practices, therefore, the names of the socialist countries should in general be added for nearly all the items listed in the table.

Secondly, the listing of the features in Table 1 has also to be regarded as an initial effort. A detailed examination of the clauses in the contractual arrangements covering the transfer of patented or non-patented technology and of the implicit practices of foreign investments in dealing with the transfer process began only a few years ago. It has been the general experience of countries that such clauses and practices were kept confidential and were therefore not available for analytical treatment. In many

Table 1: Principal issues in regulatory practices of selected countries concerning imports and use of technology

Principal Issues	Countries
I. Limitations on field of activity and ownership by external enterprises	
1. Exclusion of some areas of the economy from direct foreign investment	Algeria, Argentina, India, Indonesia, Mexico, Sri Lanka, Andean Pact countries, Portugal
2. Nationalization in some areas of the economy	Algeria, Chile, Guinea, Guyana, Iraq, Libyan Arab Republic, Syria, United Republic of Tanzania, Venezuela
3. Promotion of joint venture arrangements	Argentina, India, Indonesia, Mexico, Afghanistan, Yugoslavia, Andean Pact countries, Hungary, Romania
4. Acquisition of control of national enterprises by foreigners	Argentina, India, Mexico, Andean Pact countries, Canada
5. Guarantees given by investor's country in cases of nationalization, expropriation or other measures adopted in receiving country	Australia, Canada, Denmark, Germany (Fed. Rep. of), Japan, Netherlands, Norway, Portugal, Sweden, Switzerland, United States of America
II. Policies on controlling costs	
6. Ceiling on remittance arising from foreign direct investments	Algeria, Argentina, Brazil, India, Paraguay, Andean Pact countries
7. Ceiling on remittance of royalties	Argentina, Brazil, India
8. Limitations regarding payment of royalties between subsidiary and parent company	Brasil, India, Andean Pact countries
9. Technological contributions entitled only to royalties and cannot be registered as capital contributions	Andean Pact countries
1o. Control on payments for unused patents	Andean Pact countries
11. Control on package licensing	Japan, Germany (Fed. Rep. of), Spain, United States of America
12. Control on the payment of royalties during the entire duration of manufacture of a product, or the application of the process involved without any specification of time, or excessively long terms of enforcement	Mexico, Spain
13. Control on price fixing practices	Japan, Spain, United States of America, Argentina Mexico, Andean Pact countries
14. Control on excessive prices of technology	Spain, Argentina, Mexico
15. Control on improper or discriminatory royalties	United States of America
III. Abusive practices either deemed to be illegal or otherwise controlled	
(a) Territorial restrictions	
16 Territorial restrictions on exports	Japan, Spain, Argentina, Brazil, Mexico, Andean Pact countries
(b) Restrictions on purchases, output or sales	
17 On sources of supply of raw materials, spare parts, intermediate products, capital goods and/or competing technologies	Australia, Ireland, Japan, New Zealand, Spain, United Kingdom, United States of America, European Economic Community Argentina, Brazil, India, Mexico, Malawi, Zambia, Andean Pact countries
18. On pattern of production	Japan, Spain Mexico, Andean Pact countries
19. On sales and/or distribution	Japan, Spain, United States of America, Brazil, Mexico, Andean Pact countries

Table 1 (cont'd)

(c) Post-expiration effects	
2o. Limitations on or payment for the use of a patented invention even after the patent has expired	New Zealand, Spain, United Kingdom, United States of America, India, Malawi, Zambia
21. Limitations on or payment for the use of related know-how even after the agreement has expired	Spain
(d) Limitations affecting the dynamic effects of the transfer	
22. Control on the purchase of technology already available in the country	Spain Argentina, India, Mexico
23. Limitations on field of use	United States of America
24. To use staff-designated by the supplier	Mexico, Andean Pact countries
25. Grant-back provisions	Japan, Spain, United States of America Argentina, Brazil, Mexico, Andean Pact countries
26. Limitations imposed on the management of the recipient enterprise	Spain Mexico
27. Limitations on the research or technological development of the recipient enterprise	Spain Mexico
(e) Other practices	
28. Not to contest validity of patents	United States of America
29. Authentic text of contract in foreign language	Spain Argentina

IV. Patent policies	
3o. Patents protected provided they are in the social interest	Peru
31. Patents granted, as a general policy, to ensure that new inventions are worked in the country	Canada India
32. Compulsory licenses, revocation or expropriation of patents are recognized for reasons other than non-working	Austria, Canada, Denmark, France, Finland, Germany (Fed. Rep. of), Ireland Norway, Sweden, United States of America Czechoslovakia, Hungary, Poland, Romania, Soviet Union Algeria, Brazil, Colombia, India, Iraq, Israel, Nigeria, Peru
33. Regulations on employees' inventions	Denmark, Finland, Germany (Fed. Rep. of), Norway, Sweden
34. Recognition of inventors' certificates notwithstanding the grant of patents	Bulgaria, Czechoslovakia, German Democratic Republic, Poland, Romania, Soviet Union, Algeria
V. Promotion of national technological capabilities	
35. Incentives to export-oriented activities	Algeria, Argentina, Brazil, India, Mexico, Philippines, Republic of Vietnam, Sri Lanka, Yugoslavia, Romania
36. Provision regarding training of national personnel in foreign collaboration agreements	Algeria, Argentina, Central African Republic, Egypt, Gabon, Ghana, India, Indonesia, Kenya, Liberia, Libyan Arab Republic, Madagascar, Nigeria, Philippines, Somalia, Uganda
37. Preferential schemes for national supply of goods and/or services from national sources	Argentina, Gabon, India, Andean Pact countries
38. Measures to facilitate absorption and diffusion of foreign technology and development of indigenous technology	Brazil, India, Peru, Republic of Korea
VI. Settlement of disputes	
39. Specific reference in recent regulations to national jurisdiction	Argentina, Mexico, Andean Pact countries

instances, they are still not available even to the national government of the country concerned. The recent concern of the international community, and particularly of the governments of developing countries, with overcoming the obstacles to an improved access to modern technology, and the regulatory machinery established by the governments of these countries as a result of this concern, have made it possible to gather some of the necessary information. Any listing which is based on such partial data—as is the case with Table 1—should be treated as only a start towards a more comprehensive listing. Even then, the spread of the issues—some 59 individual policy items figuring in one or another regulatory instrument—is very wide indeed.

Thirdly, it may be noted that the information on policies and countries shown in Table 1 concerns regulation of clauses in licensing contracts and practices followed by suppliers and receivers of technology. The anti-trust legislation of the developed market economy countries is concerned with practices adversely affecting their domestic commerce. In a strict sense, therefore, these regulatory provisions do not apply if similar practices were followed outside the borders of the countries concerned—that is, in transactions which relate to the supply of technology to foreign recipients and which do not restrain the foreign trade of the exporting country.

A significant part of the regulatory action in the technology-receiving countries, particularly the developing ones, has been concerned with the need to regulate and control problems arising from their imports of technology. In this sense, such action can be taken as an attempt to prohibit or control practices, which are inadmissible under the anti-trust legislation of the technology supplying countries, but which, in the absence of any international regulation, are followed by enterprises of technology-supplying countries in their transactions with the technology-receiving countries.

Specific Issues in National Regulatory Action

The available information on this subject has been classified for analytical convenience under six major headings. They are (a) limitations on field of activity and ownership by external enterprises; (b) policies on controlling costs; (c) abusive practices either deemed to be illegal or otherwise controlled; (d) patent policies; (e) promotion of national technological capabilities; and (f) settlement of disputes. The separate sub-headings under each of these six points are presented here as the main elements in the regulatory mechanisms that have been employed at national levels for governing the relations between suppliers and recipients of technology. It would need considerable space to describe each of these points in detail and to point out the wide variety of practices that have prevailed under each of the headings in the countries mentioned in Table 1. The main purpose of this study is not, however, to undertake such a detailed comparative analysis but only to point briefly to the main lines of national regulatory action.

Limitations on field of activity and ownership by external enterprises. Under this general heading, five areas of regulatory action are described in Table 1. Foreign investors are excluded from specific sectors, which are reserved for public, semi-public or private national enterprises concerned. Such reservation is generally for defence industries, public utilities, means of public communications, insurance, commercial banking and exploitation activities of mineral resources, and in some cases for special sectors which are given priority for national development.

Another relevant aspect in the relationship between suppliers and receivers of technology has been the exercise by some developing countries of rights over their natural resources,[1] through nationalization or the adoption, as in the case of Venezuela, of reversion policies (see the Ley de Reversion de Hidrocarburos of 1971). A group of other countries,[2] having defined their priorities and needs in the field of foreign direct investment, have undertaken to guarantee, through their national laws, that those sectors where foreign investment is accepted are free of measures such as nationalization, expropriation, etc. In this field, bilateral agreements to this effect have been signed.[3]

The table shows that most developed market economy countries have devised investment guarantee schemes for protection of their national private enterprises doing business abroad, which might be adversely affected by some of the measures described above.

Joint-venture arrangements have emerged among the technology-receiving countries as a possible technique for reducing conflicts and securing greater benefits from the transfer. In some of these countries, emphasis has been placed on national majority participation. In the Latin American countries listed in the table and in India, this has to be reflected in the decision-making process of the enterprise. Algeria, Argentina, Sri Lanka and the countries of the Andean Pact have stated their policies towards the continuing and gradual process of transformation of existing foreign-owned enterprises into joint ventures or wholly nationally-owned enterprises.

Closely linked with the features described above, a number of developing countries and Canada have, in the last decade, adopted measures to protect national enterprises, or sectors of the economy adequately served by national enterprises, from acquisition of control by foreign enterprises. Competent national authorities have been established to implement these measures.

Policies on controlling costs. Countries which have established one or another type of screening procedures for foreign technical collaboration agreements use these instruments for controlling various items of foreign-exchange costs of the transfer. Sub-heading II of Table 1 refers to 10 different aspects which have been subject to one or another type of national regulatory action in many developing and some developed market economy countries.

Some of the policies, particularly those limiting the remittances arising from foreign direct investments and payments for royalties and restricting payments over excessively long periods or excessive prices in general, have been adopted by many developing countries. The new regulations on transfer of technology recently adopted in Spain also deal with these aspects.

Some developed market economy countries, in their anti-trust legislation, have been concerned with package licensing and improper royalties. In Spain it is provided that the following will be regarded as unfavourable: "Provisions for the transfer of technology in the form of packages which include unnecessary parts or elements in respect of which there is a proven domestic supply capacity of equivalent quality and reliability, provided that the parts or elements in question are technically separable from the package of services covered by the contract."[4] In the United States, for instance, the improper formulation of or imposition of royalties in licence agreements includes situations where royalties are imposed after the expiration of the patent involved or where they are used to cripple certain competitors or exclude new entrants, or as a device to achieve an unlawful allocation of markets among potential competitors.[5]

Many developing countries consider as abusive practices the inclusion in transfer of technology agreements of package licensing, price fixing and improper or discriminatory royalties.

Abusive practices either deemed to be illegal or otherwise controlled. Some of the abusive practices related to financial limitations have been included under sub-heading II of Table 1. Other practices, listed under sub-heading III, are the following: territorial restrictions; restrictions on purchases, output, or sales; post-expiration effects; limitations affecting the dynamic effects of the transfer; and other practices. These practices and policies for controlling them have been discussed at length in the study "The role of the patent system in the transfer of technology to developing countries" under the heading "Safeguards against abuses of the patent monopoly in licensing agreements."[6] The adverse effects of such abusive practices, limitations or restrictive practices on the trade and development of developing countries have been widely recognized.

The Havana Charter of 1948, which did not enter into force, had already listed in article 46, paragraph 3, practices by or among enterprises which had harmful effects on the expansion of production or trade, or interfered with the achievement of any of the objectives set forth in the Charter. Among others, these included:

(a) fixing prices or terms or conditions to be observed in dealing with others in the purchase, sale or lease of any product;
(b) excluding enterprises from, or allocating or dividing, any territorial market or field of business activity, or allocating customers, or fixing sales quotas or purchase quotas;
(c) discriminating against particular enterprises;
(d) limiting production or fixing production quotas;
(e) preventing by agreement the development or application of technology or invention whether patented or unpatented;
(f) extending the use of rights under patents, trade marks or copyrights granted by any Member, to matters which, according to its laws and regulations, are not within the scope of such grants, or to products or conditions of production, use or sale which are likewise not the subject of such grants.

The International Development Strategy, in paragraph 37, had already set a deadline of 31 December 1972 for considering appropriate remedial measures against restrictive business practices. Following the adoption of the Strategy in the General Assembly two important developments have taken place. In March 1973, a Group of Experts convened by UNCTAD considered and identified some restrictive business practices which adversely affect the trade and development of developing countries. The second development concerns a recommendation of the Council of the Organisation for Economic Co-operation and Development (OECD) adopted on 22 January 1974 recommending the Governments of member countries to be particularly alert to the harmful effects on national and international trade which may result from abusive practices in which their patentees and their licensees may engage. The recommendation listed seven specific practices considered to produce harmful effects.

Patent policies. Under this heading in Table 1, five different aspects of patent policies, marking a significant recent departure from earlier practices, have been singled out for consideration.

The 1970 Peruvian General Law relating to Industry contains the basic regulations on industrial property. At the outset, the Law states: "The State shall guarantee and protect the various constituent elements of industrial property provided that: (a) they contribute to permanent and self-sustaining industrial development; (b) they are in the social interest; and (c) they are not contrary to morality."[7]

The Canadian Patent Act, as revised in 1972, provides in section 67 (3) "that patents for new inventions are granted not only to encourage invention but to secure that new inventions shall so far as possible be worked on a commercial scale in Canada without undue delay." In this connexion the Indian Patents Act of 1970 goes a step further when in section 83 it provides that patents "are not granted merely to enable patentees to enjoy a monopoly for the importation of the patented article," but "that patents are granted to encourage inventions and to secure that the inventions are worked in India on a commercial scale and to the fullest extent that is reasonably practical without undue delay."[8]

As indicated in Table 1, a group of countries including developed market economy countries, socialist countries of Eastern Europe and developing countries have provided for remedies against abuses of the patent monopoly by enacting regulations on compulsory licensing and revocation or expropriation of patents for reasons not exclusively related to the non-working of the invention. In this area particular measures are provided in cases of refusal to grant a licence under reasonable terms or on grounds that a patented invention cannot be worked without also using another invention for which a patent has been granted to another person on the basis of an earlier application; on grounds of failure to satisfy a demand in the market; on grounds that the holder of the patent is not supplying or helping to develop an export market for the patented article manufactured within the country; on the grounds of national defence, public health, national economy, etc.

A number of socialist countries of Eastern Europe and Algeria have, in addition to granting patents, introduced inventors' certificates, by which the exclusive rights in the invention are transferred to the State and the inventor has a right to receive a remuneration when savings are made through the use of the invention.

Taking into account the fact that big corporate units are now responsible for a considerable part of R&D activities, new legislation on patents in a number of countries provides for the regulation of "service inventions," which are products of the activity of employees of such units, and for the settlement of disputes.[9]

Promotion of national technological capabilities. Table 1 attempts, under subheading V, to point to some new trends in policies and legal enactments designed to promote national technological capabilities. These four items included in the table are not intended to constitute comprehensive coverage, particularly since they do not even refer to educational policies specifically directed towards this end. The purpose of this provisional list is rather, to provide illustrative examples of national policies aimed at regulating foreign technical agreements in order to promote national technological capabilities.

Under measures to facilitate the absorption and diffusion of foreign technology and development of indigenous technology, those introduced by the countries listed in the table are described below. In Brazil, the Patent Law provides that all rights to improvements made by the licensee to the product or process licensed shall belong to him.[10] In India it is provided that under technical collaboration agreements Indian scientific, technological and engineering institutions should be associated, to the maximum extent practicable, with the foreign collaboration, so that foreign "know-how" is absorbed into the Indian economy as quickly as possible and further developments can take place within the country. It is also provided that, while approving a case of foreign collaboration, stress should be laid on acquiring indigenous know-how as early as possible, so that it may be possible to discontinue the collaboration after the period of validity of the agreement.[11] Peru obliges all industrial enterprises to deduct 2 percent of their net income to be employed in scientific and technological research for the industry.[12] The Republic of Korea enacted in December 1972 a Law for Encouraging Technology Development designed to contribute "effectively to the sound development of national economy and strengthen the competitive power of Korean products in the world market through our development of our industrial technology and the proper transplanting of imported technology into the Korean environment situation, and also to improve Korea's industrial technology through the proper dissemination of advanced technology." With these objectives in mind, the law sets up a Reserve Fund for Technology Development constituted by the funds that may be collected from persons importing foreign technology and to be used to cover expenditures for technology development.

Settlement of disputes. National regulations have also concerned themselves with the settlement of disputes. Of particular relevance in this connexion are the provisions laid down in a number of Latin American countries, which have stressed the principle that disputes arising from foreign technical collaboration agreements are to be settled under the national jurisdiction of the technology-receiving country. In the Mexican law on the transfer of technology it is provided, moreover, that actions, contracts and agreements covered by the law and to be implemented in the national territory shall be governed by Mexican law.

Some Other Practices Among Suppliers Requiring Regulation

So far the discussion has concentrated on highlighting the issues that are relevant in transactions between the suppliers and the recipients of technology. It has not concerned itself with cartel practices or activities in the sale of goods and services which have, or could be expected to have, harmful effects on the expansion of production or trade, and in general on an orderly exchange of technology. Some of these issues were considered by the Ad Hoc Group of Experts on Restrictive Business Practices established under Conference resolution 73 (III) of 19 May 1972. In its report the Group agreed that all horizontal cartel activities involving restrictions limiting territory, quantity, price and customers should be considered likely to have significant adverse effects on developing countries. According to the Group, the following cartel activities should be classified as category A and should not be retained or imposed:[13]

a. Import cartels.
b. Rebate cartels and other price fixing arrangements.
c. National export cartels.
d. International cartels, which allocate markets or control exports or imports.

The Group also agreed that the following types of cartel activities might also be avoided:[14]

a. Private and semi-official agreements on certain standards in developed countries.
b. Specialization cartels, insofar as they do not lead to a dominant position.
c. Cartels for the exchange of technical information.
d. Rationalization cartels, insofar as they do not lead to a dominant position.
e. Small-scale industry and small-scale marketing cartels.

Possible Legal Forms of the Regulation of the Transnational Transfer of Technology

It is evident that facilitation and regulation of the transfer of technology across national boundaries can be pursued through any number of legal techniques. Each of these techniques has its advantages and disadvantages in the context of the need to bring about a more equitable balance of economic advantage between the supplier and the purchaser of technology, taking into account the particular economic needs of developing States. It would appear that an important consideration in a basic decision on the feasibility and possibility of a code of conduct would be the advantages provided by one type of technique of international lawmaking as compared to others.

International Regulation of Transfer of Technology in the Framework of National Law

At present the formulation of substantive rules for the transfer of technology is generally left to national legal systems. Thus, the international legal consequences (i.e. when another national legal system has to deal with the consequences) of the transfer are left to the discretion of that other legal system. If the law of State A, which is at present a purchaser of technology (and a developing country), invalidates certain types of contractual clauses, bars certain restrictive business practices, or refuses recognition to certain foreign enterprises, the courts or administrative agencies of State B (supplier) have no obligation to recognize or enforce State A's laws or the application thereof by the courts of State A. Similarly, State B's laws on facilitation, protection and regulation of its enterprises engaged in the export of technology do not extend beyond its borders and enforcement of its laws in State A depends on A's own public policy.

In the absence of an appropriate international agreement, the only recourse to a refusal by the national authorities of one State to enforce the domestic law of another State or to give effect to what the latter believes is international public policy is to raise the matter from a commercial question to a higher level issue to be settled by the States concerned.

National legislation on transfer of technology has certain advantages and certain natural limitations. Since national legislation has as its unlimited field of operation only the national economy, it can take into account all the pecularities of the national economy, of national politics, and of all the pressure groups both internal and foreign, such as foreign-based corporations operating in the country. Nonetheless a State is subject to all sorts of economic and business pressures either to refrain from enacting effective legislation in the field, to enact weak legislation or to brave the pressure, enact legislation and have the transnational enterprises move their operations to countries which do not have similar legislation. States which wish to control certain practices by their nationals who are suppliers of technology find their efforts confined within their borders and place their enterprises in an economically vulnerable position with respect to supplier States which will not enact appropriate domestic legislation. It should be noted here that while national laws are confined within national boundaries, transnational companies operate across such boundaries and engage, inter alia, in those very commercial transactions which are the subject of this inquiry—transfer of technology.

Moreover, much of national regulatory action is not integrated. It is fragmented into a number of instruments dealing separately with various aspects of the transfer process, e.g. foreign investment, patents and trade marks, foreign exchange transfer, etc. The widespread divergencies in national legislation are creating a basis for conflicts in interpretation, thus underlining the need for establishing international standards. An alternative approach to exclusively national action might be regional action by recipient countries, very much on the lines of the action taken by the Andean Pact countries. Regional action of this type has, however, placed the burden of regulation on technology-receiving countries only. But not being able to co-ordinate policies of technology suppliers along similar lines it could lead to conflicts of interpretation. An international regulation would obviously be more effective for orderly exchange of technology across national frontiers. Furthermore, if international regulation is to perform the function of harmonizing national laws, it must itself have the status of international law, i.e. be accepted as a treaty.

Limited or Regional Multilateral Action for Controlling the Importation of Technology

The rules on transfer of technology of the Andean Pact represent a multilateral approach at tackling the issues which, from the point of view of the country of the purchaser of technology, are crucial to fair and equitable conditions of transfer of technology. In following this approach to international action in the transfer of technology a general convention could be formulated applicable to States which are not importers of technology and more particularly the developing countries. Its existence would undoubtedly eliminate many of the economic pressures felt by countries which are importers of technology. This type of multilateral instrument would serve as a basis for the incorporation of its rules into the national legislation of developing countries. On the other hand, this type of convention would not legislate on the rights and duties of supplier States; the brunt of the regulation of the transfer of technology would thus be borne by the importers of technology. The lines between supplier States and recipient States would be drawn even more sharply than now.

An International Code of Conduct on Transfer of Technology

An alternative to a convention entered into only by States which are purchasers of technology would be a multilateral code of conduct regulating the relationship between supplier and purchaser of technology that would take into account the particular needs of developing countries. Such a code might set minimum standards based on a fair and equitable balance of the various economic interests involved and might make such standards specifically enforceable through national legislation. A variety of existing multilateral instruments in related fields, as was described above, can provide guidance in choosing a framework for a code of conduct on transfer of technology. Furthermore, given the disadvantaged position of the developing countries, such a code could also take fully into account the special needs of these countries in the new international rules of conduct in the trade of technology.

Any code on the transfer of technology must reflect the need for a set of basic principles governing the economic relations of States in the context of the transfer of technology, as well as the need for specific legal rules governing the commercial relationships between suppliers and purchasers of technology in the context of specific transactions between individuals or enterprises of the various countries. The standards thus established in an international code would act as the ground rules for enterprises of both technology-supplying and technology-receiving countries.

The first part of such a code might consist of certain general economic principles to which the States would adhere. These might include principles on the encouragement of transfer of technology under fair and equitable conditions and on the encouragement of the development of local technology in States which are recipients of technology. More specifically, the code might aim at:

a. Striking an equitable balance between the economic interests of suppliers and receivers of technology, by eliminating unfair and discriminatory practices in the commercial relationships under which the transfer of technology takes place, by eliminating certain restrictive business practices, restricting the ability of commercial enterprises to undertake certain concerted activities, and by assuring the supplier of technology fair and equitable financial treatment.
b. Taking into account the special requirements of developing countries with a view to ensuring that the terms and conditions of the transfer of technology are consistent with the development objectives of the developing countries.
c. Developing effective and generally acceptable methods for the settlement of disputes.

The second part of the code might include rules to govern the specific commercial relationships between suppliers and receivers of technology. In line with a formula used in many multilateral conventions, the States which become parties to the code would be bound to enact the specific provisions of the code in their national law.

The settlement of disputes requires thorough study. It might possibly be entrusted exclusively to the national courts of the country of the purchaser of the technology on the theory that it is the country with the greatest interest in settling the dispute. Resort to international arbitration procedures or other forms of settlement of disputes might be envisaged, subject to the provisions of national law. In this connexion appropriate conventional machinery might be set up and patterned, to the extent desirable, after well-known and established courts or institutions or arbitration such as the Permanent Court of Arbitration, the International Centre for Settlement of Investment Disputes, the Gdynia Maritime Arbitration Court, etc.[15]

Notes

1. In the case of Cuba and the United Republic of Tanzania the process covered also larger sectors of the economy.
2. Including Afghanistan, Algeria, Indonesia, Niger, Philippines, Portugal and Sri Lanka.
3. See Belgium and Luxembourg-Tunisia Investment Agreement, 1964, ratified in 1966; Investment Guarantee Agreement between the Government of the United States of America and the Government of the United States of Brazil, 1965; Germany (Fed. Rep. of)-India Investment Guarantee Agreement, 1964; Sweden-Malagasy Republic Commercial Agreement, 1966.
4. See Ministry of Industry, Order of December 1973 (Madrid, 1973).
5. See Mark R. Joelson, "International Technology Transfers and the United States Antitrust laws," *The Journal of International Law and Economics,* June 1973, pp. 85-112.
6. See UNCTAD, *The Role of the Patent System in the Transfer of Technology to Developing Countries* (TD/B/AC.11/19), 23 April 1974, Chapter III.
7. World Intellectual Property Organization (WIPO), *Industrial Property,* April 1973, p. 112. This provision is a long way from the philosophy embodied in the French Patent Law of 1791 as expressed in its Preamble: "Every novel idea whose realisation or development can become useful to society belongs primarily to him who conceived it, and it would be a violation of the rights of man in their essence if an industrial invention were not regarded as the property of its creator." (See UNCTAD, *The Role of the Patent System in the Transfer of Technology to Developing Countries* (TD/B/AC.11/19), 23 April 1974, para. 296.)
8. Ibid, para. 316, p. 103.
9. See, *inter alia,* patent laws in Brazil, Colombia, Israel, Nigeria, and Peru. Special regulations in the Federal Republic of Germany, Denmark, Finland, Norway and Sweden contain provisions concerning the rights and obligations of employee's inventions.
10. Brazilian Patent Law, article 29 (3).
11. Indian Guidelines: Policies and Procedures concerning foreign collaboration agreements (January 1969).
12. Ley General de Industrias, Decreto Ley No. 18.350 of 27 July 1970, article 15.
13. For details, see UNCTAD, *Restrictive Business Practices in Relation to the Trade and Development of Developing Countries: Report by the Ad Hoc Group of Experts* (New York: United Nations publication, sales no. E.74.II.D.11), paras. 26 and 27.
14. This is what the Group defined as category B practices, where the adverse effects were less clear and might be offset by corresponding

advantages and therefore more complete economic analysis was required.
15. Mandatory or model rules for the settlement of disputes would eventually have to be drafted to suit specific needs. For a detailed discussion of a code of conduct for the transfer of technology, see the following contribution by Dieter Ernst.

19 A Code of Conduct for the Transfer of Technology: Establishing New Rules or Codifying the Status Quo?

Dieter Ernst

Introduction

The subject of an international code of conduct for the transfer of technology has been on the international agenda for some time. Since the middle of the 1960s, specific proposals have been presented by various social scientists, and the initiatives taken by international, regional, and privately sponsored organizations have multiplied.[1] The International Chamber of Commerce, for instance, in its "Guidelines for International Investment" (published in November 1972), included a chapter dealing specifically with "technology (including inventions and know-how skills)" and related policies, to be pursued by technology-receiving and technology-exporting countries.[2] Thus, the international business community demonstrated its interest in having a code be included among the respectable political issues of the transfer of technology-bargaining package. Among independent groups, a special Working Group of the Pugwash Conferences on Science and World Affairs adopted in April 1974 a draft code which later served as a basis for the United Nations (UN) Conference on Trade and Development's (UNCTAD's) activities in this field.[3] Finally, in May 1975, an Intergovernmental Group of Experts submitted two separate draft outlines for the preparation of an international code of conduct for the transfer of technology to UNCTAD's Committee on Transfer of Technology: one submitted by Brazil on behalf of the Group of 77, the other one by Japan on behalf of the Group B countries.[4]

In general, there seems to be an amazingly broad consensus with regard to

---

The views expressed here do not necessarily reflect those of the Vereinigung Deutscher Wissenschaftler, with whom the author is currently affiliated.

the necessity of a code. Representatives of Group B countries have repeatedly stated that they would strongly support a code as one of the key instruments to facilitate the international transfer of technology. The Group of 77 countries, both in their "Proposal for the Revision of the International Development Strategy" and in their Manila Ministerial Meeting of January-February 1976 (which was called in preparation of UNCTAD IV), assigned "urgent priority . . . to the formulation and adoption and implementation of a legally binding code" and declared their intention to have it adopted "prior to the end of 1977."[5] Finally, UNCTAD's Trade and Development Board, in drafting the provisional agenda for its Fourth Conference, included "decisions on a code of conduct for the transfer of technology and, in the light of those decisions, a decision on the modalities for its establishment" among UNCTAD's major initiatives at UNCTAD IV.[6] Although the Nairobi Conference did not produce concrete results with regard to the code, the resolutions adopted there clearly showed that a code will remain among the top priorities of further negotiations concerning transfer of technology.

So far, the code seems to be one of the very few "success stories" among the attempts to regulate and/or restructure international relations. During the process of preparing such a code within UNCTAD, much very helpful material has been generated, *inter alia,* regarding the international patent system and restrictive business practices related to the international commercialization of technologies, including some of their effects on the developing countries' growing technological dependence.

Furthermore, the very fact that the Group of 77 has adopted a common position on this highly complicated and controversial issue confirms this positive evaluation. But a closer look is necessary. It is not at all clear whether a code will, as one UNCTAD background information paper put it, establish "new rules of the game." Rather, it might well serve to codify rules governing the status quo of the international commercialization of technologies. From the viewpoint of a company's global risk-minimization policy, this might rightfully be termed a positive effect. By the same token, however, such a code would not be a very helpful instrument for establishing the New International Economic Order (NIEO).

Main Shortcomings of the Present System

Why is a code needed; that is, what would be its function with regard to the international flow of technologies? To answer this question, let us briefly outline some of the major structural deformations of the existing system of international technology transfer. We can skip details here, because most of these issues have been widely covered elsewhere.[7]

Inputs into, and outputs of, worldwide research, development, and engineering (R,D & E) activities are to a very high degree unequally distributed. Not only are the forces of technological progress highly concentrated within some private and state institutions of the most highly developed countries, but this high degree of concentration is increasing significantly. This state of affairs has had considerable consequences for the kind of technology transfer with which the developing countries are confronted. Both the conditions of transfer into and the nature of the technologies received by developing countries display some basic structural deficiencies that are decisive impediments for the further development of these countries. In many cases, the technologies received have been considerably overpriced, and the local technology receivers' right to make appropriate use of the imported technologies has been restricted to a very high extent. But the most important point is that there exists a strong tendency to transfer inappropriate technologies into the developing countries.

The *inappropriateness* of the technology transferred can be roughly described under three main headings. First, both the factor intensity and the plant-size requirements of the technology transferred do not correspond to the socially optimal factor endowment or plant size in the Third World. For instance, the production technologies imported are either relatively capital-intensive and depend on economies of scale or, as is the case, for example, with assembly lines producing for the world market, the labor-force requirements relate to low-wage labor, i.e., to unskilled, easily replaceable labor. Thus, the technologies transferred tend to obstruct the most urgent need of developing countries, that is, to establish new, permanent and productive jobs for their exploding populations—the job-destructing capacity of imported technologies. The same argument applies to other factors of production that are of key importance for the development process such as, e.g., local raw materials or specific local skills.

Second, in many cases the imported technologies have led to the production of goods that are entirely inessential for the fulfillment of basic needs and for an enlarged social reproduction of the receiver country. To give some examples, we note luxury consumption goods for the national elites; certain means of production for some enclave-type production activities for the world market that are only very marginally related to local social reproduction (the case of Free Export Zones being only the most extreme expression of this phenomenon); and, especially, the production of a growing variety of arms and other military-related goods.

Third, the massive influx of modern technologies into developing countries has not resulted in a significant strengthening of the receiver countries' technological capacity. Instead, the very fact that nearly no transfer of non-marginal R,D & E activities has occurred to the Third World may have been a major factor behind the further accentuation of the

Third World's technological dependence.[8] Technological dependence is understood to encompass three aspects: (1) the need to import technology, (2) the need to import the capacity to utilize and apply the imported technology, and, finally, (3) the incapacity for the autonomous adaptation, reproduction, and improvement of the technologies received. Most of the technologies imported by developing countries are of an end-product type, i.e., they are more or less ready-made for local use. Whatever knowledge is needed—especially with regard to system- or company-specific technologies and their integration into local processes of production—must be bought in the form of imported foreign consultant services.[9]

But the most basic shortcoming of the present system of transfer of technology into developing countries is the nearly complete absence of a complementary transfer of R,D & E activities that are integrated into local production requirements. Except for some process and product control, some engineering involved in scaling down production techniques to a market of more limited size, and for most modest adjustments to local consumer tastes, nearly no engineering, development or research has actually been transferred to developing countries by the main agents of the transfer of technology, the transnational enterprises (TNEs).

Objectives of a Code

Obviously, the present system of the international transfer of technology needs some kind of control and regulation, to say the least. According to the UNCTAD secretariat, a code would be an important element of an integrated approach toward restructuring the international system of technology generation and transfer. Clearly, the worldwide proliferation of technologies is characterized by some major structural deformations, especially with regard to the conditions of transfer into, and the nature of technologies received by, developing countries. Given the inherent weaknesses of most of the existing national and regional systems of legislation, an "internationalized" framework for the regulation of technology transactions is required. Together with the reform of the international patent system, a code would then serve to adapt and change the current arrangements concerning the transfer of technology, i.e., its "legal and juridical environment." Thus, it would help to prepare the ground for the second component of this overall strategy, which would consist of policies aimed at "strengthening the technological capacity of developing countries and thereby reducing their technological dependence."[10]

Within this framework, a code would have a specific, albeit somewhat limited, objective, i.e., to smooth out existing transfer conditions for the worldwide flow of technologies and to establish rules for a less unequal distribution of costs and benefits of technology generation and transfer, taking into consideration particularly the needs of developing countries. Pursuant to these main objectives, a code would have to deal with the following main problem areas:[11]

a. To develop the instruments for the control and regulation of the costs of access to technology, particularly those arising from transfer pricing and transfer accounting.
b. To register and eliminate the countless restrictions associated with the worldwide commercialization of technologies.
c. To enlarge the possibilities of receiver countries to unpackage technology imports with regard to the choice of various elements of technology, evaluation of costs, organizational forms, and institutional channels for the transfer.
d. To establish a set of guarantees to recipients and suppliers of technology, taking into account the extreme unequal distribution of bargaining power specific to the international transfer of technology.
e. To establish minimum international standards with regard to the implementation of national laws and policies on transfer of technology.
f. To include provisions that would reduce the negative effects of technology imports for the development of local technological capacities in developing countries.

Possible Shortcomings of a Code

Given the structure of the present international economic order with its concomitant distribution of power and knowledge, and taking into account the experience of the Seventh Special Session of the United Nations, any code that will be adopted in the near future is likely to have the following main shortcomings:

a. It will tend to be of a much too general nature to become an effective instrument for the regulation of the international transfer of technology.
b. The main agents of the international generation and distribution of technologies, the TNEs, may well be least affected by a code; thus, the real issues of transfer of technology would be left untouched.
c. It seems highly improbable that the Group B countries' resistance against the adoption of an international legally binding code could be overcome, even if one would assume optimal bargaining conditions for the Group of 77 (which actually do not exist).
d. Equally unlikely are the chances to find "effective and generally acceptable methods and institutions" for the settlement of disputes.[12]

Any code that does not overcome the aforementioned limitations could develop into a decisive hindrance for the establishment of the NIEO. First, such a code would be an important set-back behind some of the existing national and regional sets of regulations like those, for example, of Mexico or the Andean Pact countries. Thus, the possibilities for other countries to legitimize the establishment of further national and regional institutions for controlling and selecting technology imports might even be diminished. Second, and most important, this could mean that the attention dedicated to the formulation of such a code could impede other more important activities with regard to the restructuring of the international system of technology generation and exchange.

Let us now discuss in more detail some of the aforementioned potential main shortcomings of a code. Despite many dissimilarities, the existing draft codes have one characteristic in common: they all contain some general criteria with regard to the prevention of restrictive business practices and they suggest relatively vague principles concerning the "special requirements of developing countries," principles that have already been included in countless UN resolutions and "which up to now have not had a major repercussion in actual business conduct given the power relations and relative knowledge (or ignorance) among participants in the foreign investment process."[13] Even those parts that specifically deal with the commercial relations of suppliers and receivers of technologies are devoid of any sufficient differentiation. Thus, for instance, no distinction is made between the different types of receiving countries and institutions, and the branch-specific characteristics of the trade in technology remain untouched. Finally, there is no differentiation with regard to different supplying institutions and the types of firms involved.

Consequently, the net with which the countless open and hidden restrictions should be seized (which today characterize the trade in technology) remains extremely wide-meshed. Thus, there will be many possibilities legally to circumvent these regulations, possibilities that will stimulate the imagination of the planning staffs of TNEs. Most importantly, however, a code that is a watered-down smallest common denominator may very well obstruct the possibilities of further development of existing, progressive national and regional legislations.

Among the various supplying institutions of technology, those that dominate the process of worldwide creation and diffusion of technologies, TNEs, will be least affected by a code.[14] This statement may at first seem rather startling. Chapter IV of the Group of 77's revised draft outline of a code enumerates, for example, altogether 40 types of "restrictive business practices in transfer of technology transactions" which the governments of the respective receiver countries "shall prohibit or otherwise control."[15]

This provision could seem to mean that a code would have far-reaching possibilities of intervention, at least if it would be adopted as proposed by the Group of 77 countries.

But this interpretation is probably misleading. No code, even the most shrewdly worked out one, can effectively deal with the following three main problems of the worldwide commercialization of technologies:

a. Intra-firm transfer pricing.
b. The countless restrictions that characterize any transfer of technology.
c. The problem of how to affect decisively the economic, legal, and political environment of the decisions of TNEs with regard to selecting products, techniques and the location of activities.

Within the framework of a code, the control of intrafirm transfer pricing appears to be unfeasible. To refer to "fair" or "market-conform" prices presupposes the solution of the problem. After all, the real problem is that a growing part of a parent enterprise's expenditures on R&D, production, packaging, communications, and marketing of a product has to be financed through cost-saving expansion into new geographic areas. Here, the worldwide commercialization of technologies is going to have a growing importance. According to an inquiry of the U.S. Senate, already in 1966 U.S.-based TNEs received nearly 40 percent of their overall R&D expenditures from the sale of goods and technologies in foreign markets, a huge part of these sales being related to interaffiliate trade.[16] Various research projects have shown that interaffiliate trade is usually characterized by an over-invoicing of imported inputs of at least 50 percent and an under-invoicing of exported products of somewhere around 40 percent.[17] Consequently, there exists considerable room for the realization of oligopolistic rents and global tax minimization or tax avoidance. Strategies for the optimal management of the global financial system within TNEs (developed only very recently) have further enlarged these possibilities.

It is obviously not possible to codify the measures and mechanisms of transfer pricing that have been made possible to a large extent by the very processes of the worldwide commercialization of technologies. Constantine Vaitsos has lucidly stated the problem:

> What is a "just" price that a host country should pay for the training and R and D expenses of Swiss pharmacologists, Japanese auto engineers, and US electronics specialists whose costs are charged by the respectively based parent firms when they sell to or buy products from their foreign subsidiaries? Or what is a "fair" price that a host country should pay to cover part of the expenses assumed by foreign firms lobbying in front of their home

governments for the application of economic sanctions in case of nationalization of their assets abroad?[18]

It may be doubted whether a code may be able to deal efficiently with the countless restrictions usually accompanying the transfer of technology. For the main actors of the global commercialization of technologies, TNEs, restrictions are a decisive key to effective control. Effective control, defined to mean the ability to influence the future course of operations of the recipient firms, is one of the basic conditions for the worldwide "sourcing," production, and marketing strategies of TNEs.[19] If direct control through ownership should be impossible or insufficient, i.e., if technologies have to be sold through license- or management-contracts, TNEs will attempt to obstruct not only the access to technologies through the existing international patent system but also to control the selection of sources of supply of materials and components, market outlets, production standards, etc. The variety of such restrictions is nearly unlimited. At least twenty-two separate types of restrictive terms have been identified by an UNCTAD study based on a sample of 2,640 contracts in eleven developing countries.[20] According to UNCTAD, some of the broad categories of restrictions and limiting conditions have been found to be as follows:

a. Restrictions on exports.
b. Restrictions on sources of supply of capital goods, material inputs, and competing technologies.
c. Excessively long periods for payments of royalties.
d. Demand of guarantees against changes in taxes, tariffs, and exchange rates affecting profits, royalties, and remittances.
e. Limitations on competing sources of supply by restricting competing imports, preventing competition for local resources, and obtaining local patents to eliminate competition.
f. Constraints obstructing possibilities to enlarge local innovative capacities related to the necessities of local social reproduction through the use of expatriate personnel in technologically decisive activities; grant-back provisions and post-termination clauses stipulating that all technical and organizational information collected during the agreement period shall be returned; and discouragement of the development of local technical and R&D capabilities.

To appreciate the importance of these restrictions, it might be convenient to look at the degree of denationalization of patents registered in the Third World. True, the distribution of patent ownership is but one indicator—albeit an essential one—of the TNEs' worldwide control over R,D & E activities and, thus, of their ability to impose restrictions. But we may very well use it as a rough indicator of the overall dimension of the problem.

A patent protects the knowledge embodied in the respective products, process of production, and trade marks against appropriation by others and enables the patent owner to reap monopoly rents, at least within a certain time limit. Only the patent holder can decide the use of patented knowledge in a country in which a patent is registered.

In 1972, 3,500,000 patents were registered worldwide. Of these, some 200,000 patents, that is 6 percent, accrued to developing countries. The overwhelming majority of the patents registered in developing countries—that is, 84 percent—were controlled by foreigners. The United States, the Federal Republic of Germany, Switzerland, the United Kingdom, and France alone controlled 80 percent, the socialist countries not more than 1.8 percent.[21] In Tanzania, for instance, 0.9 percent of the registered patents were owned by Tanzanians, while 46.9 percent had owners in the United Kingdom, 15.4 percent in the United States, and 6.1 percent in Switzerland (1972).[22] And in Chile, to take just one other example, the domestic ownership of patents decreased from nearly 35 percent in 1937 to hardly over 5 percent in 1967.[23]

Obviously, a few developed market economies are more and more monopolizing the patents in the Third World. Owing especially to the pioneering studies of the UNCTAD Secretariat, evidence has been made available that the list of owner countries reflects to a considerable degree a small group of TNEs. Thus, in Colombia (in 1970), less than 10 percent of all firms that had received patents in the pharmaceutical industry owned nearly two-thirds of this industry's patents. Similar percentages have been found to prevail during the same period in the production of synthetic fibers and for the chemical industry in general.

The degree of monopolization of the developing countries' patents by a few TNEs becomes even more prominent if one looks at the distribution of the receipts from the technology trade with the Third World. In the second half of the 1960s, over 80 percent of the developing countries' overall expenses on commercial technology imports went to the United States. Of these, roughly 90 percent went to its TNEs, and seven firms alone received over 60 percent of the industrial group's income (in 1966).[24] Most of the patents registered in developing countries remain unused.[25] Thus, only a very small part of these patents will lead to the establishment of local assembly activities, let alone integrated production. In the majority of cases, patents serve to continue, with other means, the protection of traditional export markets. In the Third World as elsewhere, patents are used to restrict local production and to grant protection against oligopolistic competition.

Any attempt to control and finally eliminate restrictions should differentiate between two types: explicit restrictions—expressed as part of an agreement for the sale of technology—and implicit restrictions—those that are an integral part of intrafirm transfers between the parent company and its affiliates and that for anyone who is not a member of the firm's top management can hardly be detected, since no obligations exist to publish such data. While today implicit restrictions predominate, a code will only aim at explicit ones.

Only a few years ago, explicit restrictions were used relatively liberally as parts of written contracts. Even when a TNE directly owned a subsidiary, explicit restrictions were imposed in the majority of cases.[26] Although this might seem unnecessary, such clauses can be useful for a TNE if ownership changes (e.g., through nationalization) occur, or if the local government demands, for instance, a certain share of exports from the subsidiary's production. In the meantime, the sophistication of TNEs in this field—their capabilities to hide restrictions used by them—has increased considerably. Especially the initiatives taken by the Andean Pact countries, Mexico, and India since the end of the 1960s to identify and obtain a reduction of contractual export restrictions (which, at least during the initial period, did produce some spectacular success) have to be given some credit for these new developments. Moreover, in most industrial branches there exists today a tendency to transfer, whenever possible, technologies only to wholly owned affiliates. Thus, explicit restrictions are increasingly replaced by implicit ones. Even in countries that, like India, do not allow the foreign investor to hold more than 40 percent of the shares of a joint venture, no effective obstacles exist to the application of implicit restrictions. First, if the government is eager to attract a particular technology (for whatever reasons) considered important, the foreign partner may be permitted to hold a majority of shares or even to establish a wholly owned local affiliate.[27] Second, the fact that the Indian government, with regard to technical cooperation agreements between local firms and foreign partners, allows only restrictions of a relatively mild type should not be interpreted as if this would mean a significant limitation for a TNE's capacity to impose implicit restrictions. As Peter Neersø showed:

> . . . in many cases the Indian company fears that the foreign collaborator will not be prepared to conclude an agreement which does not include tight restrictions; if these are forbidden by the Government, the Indian company enters into a 'gentleman's agreement' with the foreign company on such restrictions. Of course, the foreign collaborator cannot sue the Indian company if it breaks the agreement. But most often the Indian company depends on the foreign collaborator for specialised inputs and technical services, including the transfer of new technologies, and therefore does not dare to offend the collaborator.[28]

Analogous tendencies have been found to exist, for example, in the Andean Pact countries and Kenya.[29]

Any code, even the most radical one, could at best help to soften the use of contractual restrictions. The far more important implicit restrictions could only be effectively dealt with if agreement could be reached to make their publication mandatory—a somewhat hopeless venture under given political realities.

To complete the picture, two types of restrictions have to be added that none of the existing draft codes have the means to deal with and that nevertheless are decisive for the existing international system of transfer of technology. One type comprises restrictions limiting the access to technologies that are regarded by the governments of both developed-market and centrally planned economics as being critical for their national-defense capacity (the militarily conditioned technologies) and/or as crucial for their capacity to make further and continuous advances in *avant garde* technologies. These technologies are "unfree goods" in a very extreme sense: they could not even be bought if the potential buyer would be willing to pay the maximum price. The ever-increasing arms trade with the Third World and the proliferation of the means to produce them locally do not contradict this statement. On the contrary, all research available on this topic points to the fact that the basic technologies relevant to military production, such as key electronic devices, jet propulsion, high quality alloys, or steel varieties are not allowed to be exported. Given the fact that expenditures of this kind of technology represent, for instance, over 50 percent of the overall R&D expenditures of the United States (which points to their key importance for developments in global science and technology), this type of restriction on the transfer of technology into developing countries warrants further research.[30] It is obvious that, so far, a code has no instruments available to deal with this kind of restriction.

The second type comprises restrictions that are embodied in transferred technologies themselves and that prevent the technology-receiver from reproducing or even further developing these technologies by means of "reverse engineering."[31] Four categories of these *technology-embodied restrictions* can be distinguished:

a. Adaptation to TNEs' global industrial standards restricting adaptation of possibilities to local conditions.[32]
b. Planned diversification and obsolescence of all products transferred, including subsystems, intermediates, and spare parts.
c. Maintenance and repair techniques that make an overhaul of the imported machinery impossible, or at least extremely costly without using the company's maintenance and repair manual.

d. Planned technological indivisibility as a result of the transfer of technologies within a package.

This last point is of increasing importance. Packages consist of main components (e.g., to take the example of the Green Revolution, miracle grains) and of complementary inputs (for instance, fertilizers, insecticides, pesticides, irrigation systems, pumps, etc.). Without these inputs, the package cannot function. A package consists of a combination of mutually dependent innovations and improvements that are, for all practical purposes, indivisible or could be divided only at a very high cost. The use of package deals in the export of technologies tends to enlarge the possibilities of the technology supplier to realize built-in and planned technological indivisibility. Thus, sellers of a package are in a very favorable position to make themselves irreplaceable for a long time.

Basic Conditions for an Effective Code

Even if a code would have the means to deal with some of the major deficiencies related to the conditions of the transfer of technology, the question of whether a code would be able to codify and effectively sanction any deviations from its established guidelines still remains. To accomplish this, it would have to fulfill two basic conditions: (a) it would have to be a multilateral legally binding code and (b) mechanisms for the settlement of disputes would have to be institutionalized in such a way that they would be able to enforce the guidelines even in cases of basic conflicts of interest.

Whereas the Group of 77 countries have repeatedly declared that for them a code means nothing but "an international legally binding instrument as the only form capable of effectively regulating commercial transfers,"[33] the Group B countries have made it clear that in this respect they would not accept any compromise. The formulations chosen in the Group B countries' draft code are unequivocal:

> Such a Code should be an international instrument of a non-binding character. It is the responsibility of governments to promote all appropriate means of facilitating the transfer of technology. An international Code should permit each government to so act, leaving it full and complete freedom of decision, including the right to legislate on the subject of technology transfer, within the framework of international law. The provisions of a Code should be of a general and voluntary nature. . . . Specific rules would immediately result in their frequently being inappropriate or

> counter-productive. On the other hand, general guidelines can be useful, provided that they are not mandatory.

This position is even more bluntly stated in the final sentence of the paragraph from which this quote has been taken: "The failure of parties to a mutually agreed contract to observe one or more of such guidelines should not in itself invalidate such contract."[34] Thus, it would be highly unrealistic to expect the adoption of a multilateral legally binding code.[35]

In addition, the question of the settlement of disputes remains highly controversial. Four minimum requirements with regard to the establishment of an effective machinery for the settlement of disputes have been identified by the Pugwash draft code (this code had been unanimously adopted by participants from developed market economy, socialist, and developing countries):

> (a) the technology transfer agreements between technology suppliers and recipients from different countries should be subject, with regard to their scope, enforcement and interpretation, to the laws of the technology-receiving country; (b) in the event of a dispute between a supplier of technology and a receiver of technology, legal jurisdiction for settlement of the dispute shall reside in the courts of the technology-receiving country; (c) if the laws applicable to the technology transfer agreements do not exclude recourse to arbitration in this field and the parties concerned agree in their contracts to submit their possible disputes to arbitration, such disputes will be settled according to the procedures set out in the contract; (d) in order to permit the solution of technical disputes at an early stage and thus minimize the need for legal arbitration or judicial settlement of disputes, parties may insert in their arbitration procedures provisions whereby disputes of a technical nature would be submitted as soon as possible after they arise to impartial technical experts appointed in a way acceptable to all parties concerned.[36]

In the meantime, the competing positions on this issue have considerably stiffened. Whereas the Group of 77 countries declare that with regard to "the settlement of disputes pertaining to transfer of technology arrangements" only "the technology-receiving country shall exercise legal jurisdiction" and that "any dispute among the States with regard to the interpretation of the present Code shall be settled through consultation and through such conciliation and arbitration procedures as may be established by the States concerned,"[37] the Group B countries' draft states dryly "that the parties to a contract [shall] be free to have recourse to international arbitration or other appropriate methods of dispute settlement where they so agree."[38]

Conclusions

Let us now restate the problem in a somewhat broader context. To establish new rules for the international transfer of technology, a code would not only have to control and regulate transfer conditions related to the trade in technologies, such as, for instance, transfer pricing and restrictions. It would also have to have the means to decisively influence the decision criteria of TNEs with regard to the selection of the exported products and technologies and with regard to the transfer modalities chosen.

Even if we would suppose that a code would have the instruments necessary to implement the control of transfer conditions and that it would be an international legally binding code, one could hardly assume that such a code would suffice to induce significant changes in the economic, legal, and political "environment conditions" for the worldwide sourcing and transfer decision of TNEs with regard to technologies. If this should be obtained, a code would have to have the capacity to influence at least some determinants of the present international division of labor. For instance, it would have to be able to modify, on a worldwide scale, relative factor costs at alternative locations with regard to a redistribution of flows of technology, defined as optimal. Obviously, this is far beyond any international form of regulating international economic relations.

A code needs the corrective of workable, efficient, and effective national and regional instruments for the control and regulation of technology transactions, especially on the part of the receiver countries. Only then would it be possible to implement some of the very challenging formulations of the existing draft codes, namely that a code, besides regulating transfer conditions, should aim at increasing "the contributions of technology to the identification and solution of . . . the special problems of developing countries" and at strengthening "the national technological and scientific capabilities of . . . developing countries, for selecting imported technologies, assimilating them into their national economies and adapting them creatively to domestic conditions, as well as for ensuring the increasing participation of these countries in world production and exchange of technology."[39]

In principle, a code will play only a supplementary role. In practice, however, it could be of some use, at least during a middle-range period, because of the presently lacking regulative capacities of individual receiver countries and regional groupings. A pragmatic instrument to bridge existing control and regulative bottlenecks on the national and regional levels, concentrating especially on transfer conditions—such an instrument could be of some positive value for the realization of the NIEO, if it were accompanied by the parallel establishment and improvement of national and regional laws and policies with regard to both the generation and the transfer of technology.

Establishing a code and related activities are but a part of the developing countries' activities aimed at a general restructuring of the international system of technology generation and distribution. The definition of a new role for science and technology in the development of the Third World is one essential precondition for establishing the NIEO. Further bargaining during and after UNCTAD IV related to the technology transfer to and from the Third World (that is, including the reverse transfers of technology[40]) could produce a minimum of positive results if it would succeed in transforming two essential questions into political issues.

First, under what conditions could developing countries succeed in overcoming technological dependence on the national, regional, and international levels? Technological dependence is defined to mean a country's structural inability to produce the capital goods needed for its own social reproduction and to initiate local R,D & E activities sufficiently interrelated with productive activities. The proliferation of nearly all varieties of technology into the Third World has, in fact, not decreased but rather increased the technological dependence of these countries. The question is: what is to be understood under strategies of national and collective technological self-reliance and what consequences will such strategies have for the restructuring of the international economic order?

Second, under what conditions will it be possible to induce those institutions that control the worldwide distribution both of inputs into and outputs of R, D & E activities, the TNEs, to transfer technologies *appropriate* to the development needs of the Third World, including the transfer of capacities for autonomous technological innovation? Until now, politically relevant discussions concentrated on a much more restricted problem, that is, how to facilitate the transfer of capabilities for local adaptation of existing technologies?[41] Obviously, for the sake of establishing indigenous innovative capacities in developing countries, this is but one aspect of the problem. Thus, attempts to reformulate the concept of "appropriate technology" and to make it politically operational with regard to the above-mentioned question, should deserve high priority.

A considerable amount of impressive scientific work has now been done on the internationalization of capital, worldwide commercialization of technologies, technological dependence, and criteria for "appropriate technologies." Nevertheless, what is really needed is to transform these findings into a catalogue of policy issues that in turn will have to be translated into strategies, policies, and tactics. Thus, the choice of relevant policy issues will not only depend on an analysis of the nature, scope, and consequences of technological dependence and the role of the present system of transfer of technology but also on an explicit determination of strategic priorities, the paths of tactical procedures, and the time horizons involved.

It is in this context that any discussion of a code of conduct on the transfer of technology has to be located. The program of action to strengthen the technological capacity of developing countries, outlined by the UNCTAD secretariat for UNCTAD IV, might turn out to be a first step in this direction.

Notes

1. The list of participants in this game is impressive; see UNCTAD, *The Possibility and Feasibility of an International Code of Conduct in the Field of Transfer of Technology* (TD/B/AC.11/22), 6 June 1974, paras. 87-99.
2. International Chamber of Commerce (Paris: ICC, 1972).
3. Pugwash Conferences on Science and World Affairs, "Draft Code of Conduct on Transfer of Technology," contained in UNCTAD, *The Possibility and Feasibility of an International Code of Conduct in the Field of Transfer of Technology*.
4. UNCTAD, *Report of the Intergovernmental Group of Experts on a Code of Conduct on Transfer of Technology* (TD/B/C.6/1), 26 May 1975, Annexes I-III. Group B encompasses the developed market economies, Group of 77 the developing countries, and Group D the socialist countries of Eastern Europe.
5. Vienna Institute for Development, *Preliminary Proposal by the Group of 77 for the Revision of the International Development Strategy for the Second United Nations Development Decade, 4 June 1975* (Vienna: Vienna Institute for Development, 1975).
6. UNCTAD, *Technological Dependence: Its Nature, Consequences and Policy Implications* (TD/190), 31 December 1975, p. 1.
7. See for instance, Charles Cooper, "Special Issue on Science and Technology in Development," *The Journal of Development Studies*, 9/1 (October 1972).
8. National Academy of Sciences, *U.S. International Firms and R, D & E in Developing Countries* (Washington, D.C.: National Academy of Sciences, 1973), Chapter 5.
9. The sale of consulting services into developing countries has become one of the fastest growing markets. Estimates put it at around $4 billion a year. For a differentiation between general technology (information common to an industry or trade), system-specific technology (information concerning the manufacture of a certain item or product), and firm-specific technology (information that is specific to a particular firm's experience and activities)

see E. Mansfield, "International Technology Transfer: Forms, Resource Requirements, and Policies," *The American Economic Review* 65 (May 1975): 372ff.

10. UNCTAD, *Technological Dependence,* p. 3.

11. Other objectives have been included, too, but their character is more or less accessory.

12. UNCTAD, *The Possibility and Feasibility*, para. 125(c).

13. Constantine Vaitsos, *'North-South' Economic Relations: The Case of Foreign Investments and Productive Knowledge*, mimeographed. Secretariat of the Andean Common Market (Lima: Secretariat of the Andean Common Market, January 1974).

14. With regard to the dominance of TNEs in the international transfer of technology, see, for instance, OECD, *Science, Growth and Society: A New Perspective. The 'Brooks Report'* (Paris: OECD, March 1971).

15. UNCTAD, *Report of the Intergovernmental Group,* Annex III, pp. 7-10.

16. U.S. Senate, *Implications of Multinational Firms for World Trade and Investment and for U.S. Trade and Labor* (Washington, D.C.: Gov. Printing Office, 1973).

17. See, for instance, Constantine Vaitsos, *Intercountry Income Distribution and Transnational Enterprises* (Oxford: Clarendon Press, 1974); Raymond Vernon, *Sovereignty at Bay—The Multinational Spread of U.S. Enterprises* (New York: Basic Books, 1971), pp. 137ff.

18. Constantine Vaitsos, *'North-South' Economic Relations*, p. 22.

19. National Academy of Sciences, *U.S. International Firms and R, D & E in Developing Countries*, Chapter 2.

20. UNCTAD, *The Role of the Patent System in the Transfer of Technology to Developing Countries* (TD/B/AC.11/19), 23 April 1974, tables 1, 3 and accompanying text.

21. Ibid., table 12, p. 92 and table 9, p. 86.

22. H. E. Grundmann, "What Kind of Patent Law does Tanzania Need?" (Dar es Salaam: University College, 1968), mimeographed.

23. Constantine Vaitsos, "Patents Revised: Their Function in Developing Countries," *Journal of Development Studies* 9 (October 1972).

24. U.S. Department of Commerce, *Policy Aspects of Foreign Investment by U.S. Multinational Corporations* (Washington, D.C.: Gov. Printing Office, 1972).

25. See UNCTAD, *The Role of the Patent System,* para. 280ff.

26. This has been shown, for instance, by Vaitsos in his investigation of 451 technical agreements in the Andean Pact countries. In 409 of these agreements, there were export clauses, and in three-fourths of them there was a total prohibition of exports: Constantine Vaitsos "Patents Revised," pp. 20ff.

27. Peter Neersø, "Some Aspects of India's Policies on the Import of

Technology," *Development and Change* 6 (January 1975): 41, 42.
28. Ibid.
29. See, for instance, J. Carlsen, *Some Reflections on Government Policies Towards Private Foreign Investment: The Cases of Colombia, India and Kenya* (Copenhagen: Institute for Development Research, 1974).
30. This is simply a statement of the status quo. It does not imply that this would be in any sense an optimal situation for overall scientific and technological progress; see Milton Leitenberg, "The Dynamics of Military Technology Today," *International Social Science Journal* 25 (March 1973).
31. Reverse engineering has been extensively used in Japan up till the middle of the 1960s. Thus, especially proponents of a "Japanese model" for the developing countries' policies regarding technology imports should take into account these technology-embodied restrictions. There are indications that China has been able to circumvent some quite fanciful techniques of reverse engineering; see, for instance, Jon Sigurdson, "Technology and Employment in China," *World Development* 2 (March 1974).
32. "Local affiliates are generally required to adhere to global standards, but in some cases affiliates are permitted to modify material output standards and specifications so long as they comply with performance and worldwide interchangeability criteria," National Academy of Sciences, *U.S. International Firms*, p. 39.
33. See UNCTAD, *Report of the Intergovernmental Group,* para. 9, stating that "such a code of conduct must, as had been so often expressed formally by the Group of 77, take the form of a legally binding instrument."
34. Ibid., Annex II, p. 2.
35. In any case, there are signs that at least some developing countries may be inclined to accept compromises even on this subject.
36. Pugwash Draft Code, in UNCTAD, *The Possibility and Feasibility*, p. 11.
37. UNCTAD, *Report of the Intergovernmental Group,* Annex I, p. 14.
38. Ibid., Annex II, p. 2.
39. Ibid., Annex I, para. 1.1.
40. See, for instance, UNCTAD, *The Reverse Transfer of Technology: Its Dimensions, Economic Effects and Policy Implications* (TD/B/C.6/7).
41. See, e.g., National Academy of Sciences, *U.S. International Firms*, p. 1, stating that TNEs were supposed to assist developing countries in "(1) implanting indigenous capability to adopt technology to their particular needs, (2) training research and engineering personnel (that has not been drained off by means of international brain drain, D.E.) to perform a wider range of adaptive engineering, and (3) enabling enterprises in LDCs to acquire, control and use more industrial technology."

Part 6

Industrialization and Transnational Enterprises

20 *Industrial Growth in Developing Countries*

UNIDO

Historically, the industrial sector has been the most dynamic force contributing to structural change in the economic and social system. The agricultural sector, which is heavily dependent on natural conditions, has traditionally been less strong in stimulating economic growth. According to national accounts and income statistics by origin and to agricultural production indices, the maximum growth rates of the primary sector have been about 2 or 3 percent per annum in nearly all countries. Often these rates have not matched the annual rates of growth in population.

By contrast, the industrial sector has generally attained rates of growth in excess of the rates of population increase. On the supply side, technical progress is typical and rapid for this sector, resulting in considerable increases in labour productivity. On the demand side, the market for industrial products has expanded at a rate exceeding *per capita* growth of income owing to the high income elasticity of demand for such products. National income statistics by industrial origin or time series data on industrial production indicate that the secondary sector in many countries has attained annual rates of growth of more than 10 percent.

The tendency of industry to grow rapidly indirectly affects the economy as a whole in a number of ways. Considerable spread effects result from the adoption of new technologies and production methods. The new demand for various industrial inputs links the industrial sector with other economic activities, and the income generated may contribute to changes in the pattern and level of demand for a variety of products.

The tertiary sector, which encompasses a wide range of diverse economic activities, such as transportation, communications, electricity, commerce, finance and public administration, is closely linked with the industrial

---

Reprinted, with permission, from United Nations Industrial Development Organization (UNIDO), *Industrial Development Survey: Special Issue for the Second General Conference of UNIDO* (New York: United Nations, 1974), pp. 9-19.

TABLE 1. AVERAGE ANNUAL GROWTH RATES OF WORLD MANUFACTURING OUTPUT, BY DEVELOPING REGION AND ECONOMIC GROUPING, 1955-1973
(Percentage)

	Developing countries						
Year	Total	Africa[a]	Asia	Latin America	Developed market economies	Centrally planned economies	World
1955-1960	7.2	8.3	8.5	6.2	4.0	10.7	6.0
1960-1965	6.6	10.6	6.9	5.9	6.4	8.5	6.9
1965-1970	6.2	4.5	5.1	7.2	5.3	8.8	6.4
1971	8.2	19.1	6.7	7.8	1.3	8.4	4.4
1972	8.8	7.8	8.8	8.9	7.2	7.8	7.3
1973	11.2[b]	...	15.4[b]	...	9.8	8.2	10.3[b]

Sources: Based on *The Growth of World Industry, 1969 Edition,* vol. I (United Nations publication, Sales No. 71.XVII.6); *The Growth of World Industry, 1971 Edition,* vol. I (United Nations publication, Sales No. 73.XVII.6) (for 1955 and 1965 data); and *Monthly Bulletin of Statistics,* February 1974.

[a]Manufacturing output for Africa is taken from national income data and is not strictly comparable with the data for the other developing regions and economic groupings. Furthermore, coverage of this region by country is not always sufficiently complete for the United Nations Statistical Office to provide separate regional estimates for some production and employment data. While statistical coverage for all developing countries is usually sufficient to provide reliable figures for this economic grouping as a whole, it does not follow that the precise figures for Africa can be derived by subtracting data for Asia and Latin America from the totals for the developing countries.

[b]Preliminary estimates for the first six months of 1973 compared with the first six months of 1972.

sector. Value added in the tertiary sector occurs in the distribution of necessary inputs and products, the provision of financial resources, the flow of information and the supply of public utilities and services. The real growth rate of the tertiary sector is normally between the rates of the primary and secondary sectors in the developing countries. Past experience suggests that, as development continues, the tertiary sector tends to become more prominent in terms of its contribution to Gross Domestic Product (GDP) and to employment, as has been the case in many of the developed countries.

Recent Trends in the Growth of Manufacturing Output

The growth rates for manufacturing, shown in Table 1, reveal that the pace of industrial development in many of the developing countries quickened in the early 1970s. Manufacturing output of all developing countries increased by 8.2 percent in 1971, 8.8 percent in 1972 and 11.2 percent in the first six months of 1973. These rates exceeded those for preceding periods, as evidenced in Table 1. They suggest that the developing countries have made a good start towards achieving the target of a minimum average growth of 8 percent per annum set in the International

Development Strategy for the Second United Nations Development Decade.

In the developed market economies, growth rates of 7.2 percent in 1972 and of 9.8 percent in 1973 indicate a recovery from 1971 when the rate was 1.3 percent. In the past, growth rates for the output of manufacturing in the centrally planned economies have not fluctuated as they have in the developed market economies and, to a lesser extent, in the developing countries. In 1973, the growth rate for the centrally planned economies was calculated to be 8.2 percent. Although only preliminary estimates of industrial growth are available for the developing countries for the first half of 1973, it appears that the rate of increase in manufacturing output of this economic grouping well exceeded the rates recorded by the developed market and the centrally planned economies.

With regard to the individual developing regions, the growth rates of manufacturing output for Latin America increased steadily over the period 1955-1972, approximating the target rate set for the Second Development Decade in 1971 and 1972 with rates of 7.8 percent and 8.9 percent, respectively. In Africa, growth rates were somewhat erratic (see Table 1, footnote a), but in this region the 7.8 percent increase in 1972 was also close to the over-all target. Growth rates for Asia in 1971 and 1972 were equally encouraging (6.7 percent and 8.8 percent, respectively). The high preliminary estimate for Asia for the first half of 1973 (15.4 percent) is reflected in the estimated growth rate for all developing countries in the first six months of 1973 compared with the first six months of 1972.[1]

It is too early to assess, on the basis of the data for the first quarter, the possibility of reaching the targets set for the manufacturing sector for the Second Development Decade. In 1972, the developing countries accounted for 6.9 percent of total manufacturing output, and this proportion represents only a slight change from 1955 when it was 6.2 percent.[2] This fact is discouraging when a comparison is made of the growth rates for the three economic groupings shown in Table 1; the smallness of the share of the developing countries in the total world manufacturing output suggests that it will take these countries a long time to achieve a more equitable share of world industrial activity even if they reach the target growth rates set for the Second Development Decade.

Table 2 gives the distribution of manufacturing output among the developing regions and for selected countries over the period 1960-1972. Latin America produced the largest share of the output of the developing countries, followed by Asia. In 1972, the share of Latin America in the manufacturing output of the developing countries was 54.6 percent, and that of Asia was 37.3 percent; the share of Africa was far less, or 8.1 percent. This pattern persisted throughout the First United Nations Development Decade, as shown in Table 2. In 1960, the individual countries shown in the table

TABLE 2. DISTRIBUTION OF MANUFACTURING OUTPUT, BY DEVELOPING REGION AND SELECTED COUNTRIES, 1960, 1970, 1971 AND 1972

(Percentage)

Region and country	*1960*	*1970*	*1971*	*1972[a]*
Developing regions, total	100.0	100.0	100.0	100.0
Latin America	53.9	54.7	54.5	54.6
Asia	39.4	37.9	37.3	37.3
Africa	6.7	7.4	8.2	8.1
Individual countries				
India	15.7	15.2	16.2	15.8
Brazil	14.0	14.7	15.2	...
Argentina	12.9	12.0	12.5	12.3
Mexico	8.8	10.7	11.3	11.3
Indonesia	4.4	2.9	3.2	...
Chile	3.5	2.8	2.9	2.8
Iran	2.8	2.5	2.2	2.4
Colombia	2.8	2.8	3.1	...
Venezuela	2.8	3.3	3.5	3.3
Pakistan	2.6	3.0	3.5	3.3
Philippines	2.4	2.1	2.3	2.2
Egypt	1.8	2.5	2.5	...
Cuba	1.5	0.8	0.8	...
Peru	1.4	1.6	1.6	...
Republic of Korea	1.4	3.5	4.1	4.5
Thailand	0.9	1.0	1.1	...
Morocco	0.9	0.9	0.9	...
Burma	0.8	0.7	0.7	...
Total	81.4	83.0	87.6	...

Sources: Based on *The Growth of World Industry, 1969 Edition,* vol. I (United Nations publication, Sales No. 71.XVII.6); *Monthly Bulletin of Statistics,* May 1974 and July 1974; and other data supplied by the United Nations Statistical Office.

[a]Country figures are based on preliminary estimates.

accounted for 81.4 percent of the manufactured output of all developing countries. By 1971, this figure had risen to 87.6 percent. By way of comparison, the same countries accounted for 70 percent of the total population of all developing countries in both years.[3]

One conclusion that may be drawn from the pattern of concentration of industrial output evidenced in Table 2 is that the averages for the developing regions obscure great variations in the level of industrial development of individual countries. It is thus apparent that the growth targets for manufacturing output established in the International Development Strategy may not be applicable to all developing countries. The attainability of the target growth rate for the Second Development Decade depends heavily on the achievements of large countries such as Argentina, Brazil, India and Mexico. Since the target is simply an average and it conceals the different performances of individual countries, review and appraisal of industrial development in the Second Development Decade may be most meaningful at the country level, especially if their purpose is to pin-point problem areas and to establish the basis for international policy decisions.

Industrial Growth in Selected Developing Countries

Industrial growth in a country depends largely on the size of the population, the natural resource endowment and the industrial development strategy and policies the Government has adopted. To determine the progress made in industrial development at the country level, a sample of 29 developing countries has been selected for study. The countries included were at different stages of development in 1960. Various ways are used to define stages of industrial development. The method adopted here is to classify a country according to the share of the manufacturing sector in GDP: thus, a country is *industrialized* when the share of the manufacturing sector in GDP is more than 30 percent, it is *semi-industrialized* when this share is between 20 and 30 percent; it is *industrializing* when this share is between 10 and 20 percent; and it is *non-industrial* when this share is less than 10 percent.

According to Table 3, in 1970, 7 of the 29 developing countries[4] (Argentina, Brazil, Chile, Iran, Mexico, the Republic of Korea and Venezuela) had reached the semi-industrialized stage of development compared with 4 countries (Argentina, Chile, Iran and Venezuela) in 1960. In 1970, 17 countries were classified as industrializing countries and 5 as non-industrial countries, compared with 18 industrializing countries and 7 non-industrial countries in 1960. At present, most of the developing countries characterized as semi-industrialized also have populations of over 20 million. It is noteworthy that the two exceptions, Chile and Venezuela, are both economies in which natural resource endowment plays a particularly important role.

Some small countries appear to have overcome successfully other obstacles to industrial development, at least in the initial phases. However, when countries are grouped according to size of population, a distinction appears in the growth rates of manufacturing output between more and less populated countries. In the period 1960-1970, 7 of the 14 developing countries in Table 3 with a population of over 20 million achieved growth rates of more than 8 percent per annum, the target set for the Second Development Decade, whereas only 5 of the 15 countries with a population of less than 20 million had annual growth rates for manufacturing output of more than 8 percent.

TABLE 3. GROWTH RATES OF MANUFACTURING OUTPUT AND SHARE OF MANUFACTURING OUTPUT IN GDP FOR 29 SELECTED DEVELOPING COUNTRIES, 1960-1970

(Percentage)

Country[a]	Average annual rate of growth of manufacturing output 1960-1970	Share of manufacturing output in GDP 1960	1970
Population over 20 million			
India	4.9	13	13[b]
Pakistan	8.1[c]	9	13
Indonesia	2.9	8	9
Brazil	6.4	18	20[b]
Nigeria	11.8[d]	4	7[b]
Mexico	9.5	19	23
Philippines	4.9	16	16
Thailand	11.1	13	16
Republic of Korea	17.2	14	22
Iran	13.1	25	28[c]
Burma	1.0[e]	10[f]	9[g]
Ethiopia	11.8[h]	6[i]	10
Argentina	5.7	29	28[c]
Colombia	5.7	18	19
Population less than 20 million			
Morocco	4.0	13	14
United Republic of Tanzania	10.9[j]	6[k]	9
Sri Lanka	7.4[l]	8[m]	9
Kenya	7.5[j]	10[k]	11
Venezuela	6.7	21[n]	21
Chile	5.5	23	28
Guatemala	8.2	13	15[c]
Bolivia	7.3	13	14
Haiti	−0.1	10	10
Zambia	12.5[p]	6[k]	11
Dominican Republic	4.9	17	19
El Salvador	8.8	15	19
Honduras	7.6	11	12
Jamaica	5.9	12	11
Panama	10.6	12	15[n]

Sources: Based on *Monthly Bulletin of Statistics,* May 1974; and *Yearbook of National Accounts Statistics, 1972,* vol. III (United Nations publication, Sales No. 74.XVII.3).

[a]Countries arranged according to decreasing population.

[b]1969. [g]1967. [l]1963-1970.
[c]1960-1969. [h]1961-1970. [m]1963.
[d]1960-1966. [i]1961. [n]1968.
[e]1962-1967. [j]1964-1970. [o]1965.
[f]1962. [k]1964. [p]1965-1970.

Structural Change in the Manufacturing Sector

Growth patterns in the manufacturing sector may differ widely among the various heterogeneous branches, leading to changes in the industrial structure of this sector. Logically, the share of an industry that attains a higher rate of growth than the average for this sector increases and that of an industry with a growth rate lower than the average decreases. In this section, past trends in the growth of various manufacturing industries are examined in relation to changes in the industrial structure.

If the growth rates of output and employment in the manufacturing sector are analysed at the ISIC two-digit level for the developing regions of Asia and Latin America and for the economic groups,[5] several noteworthy trends emerge (see Table 4). First, the growth rate of output in the period 1960-1972 was higher in heavy industry than in light industry for Asia and Latin America and for each of three economic groupings. Increases in the share of heavy industry were specially evident for the developing countries and the centrally planned economies. Heavy industry grew more rapidly in Asia (at a rate of 9.5 percent) than in Latin America (at a rate of 8.6 percent), while the converse was true of light industry (4.6 percent in Asia compared with 5 percent in Latin America). Comparable data for Africa are not available. Among the major groups of manufacturing industry, chemicals and petroleum products and metal products and machinery registered relatively high rates of growth, while the textile industry lagged behind in Asia and Latin America and in all economic groupings.

In the developing countries, the metal products and machinery industry attained the highest average growth rate, or 10.1 percent per annum, followed by the chemicals and petroleum products industry (8 percent), the non-metallic mineral products industry (7.9 percent), and the basic metals industry (7.4 percent). It should be noted that the wearing apparel and wood products industries, which are highly labour-intensive, grew much more rapidly than they did in the developed market economics.

Secondly, employment in the manufacturing sector increased at annual rates of 3.4 percent in the developing countries as a whole, and at a rate of 3.2 percent in Asia and 2.7 percent in Latin America. These growth rates were much higher than those achieved in the developed market economies. As was the case for output, heavy industry evidenced higher growth rates for employment in manufacturing than light industry in Asia and Latin America and in the economic groupings.

In the developing countries, the highest rate of increase in employment in the period 1960-1970 was recorded in the metal products and machinery industry (5.6 percent), followed by basic metals (5.1 percent) and wearing apparel (4.9 percent). The textile industry registered the lowest rate of employment growth, or only 11 percent annually. In Latin America, a

TABLE 4. AVERAGE ANNUAL GROWTH RATES OF OUTPUT AND EMPLOYMENT BY MAJOR GROUPS OF MANUFACTURING INDUSTRY

(Percentage)

Industry	ISIC	Developing countries		Asia		Latin America		Developed market economies		Centrally planned economies	
		Output[a]	Employment[b]	Output[a]	Employment[b]	Output[a]	Employment[b]	Output[a]	Employment[b]	Output[a]	Employment[b]
Total manufacturing	3	6.7	3.4	6.5	3.2	6.7	2.7	5.5	1.5	8.5	3.3
Light manufacturing	31-33, 342, 355 and 356, 39	5.0	2.8	4.6	2.5	5.0	2.5	4.3	1.1	4.6	2.3
Heavy manufacturing	341, 351-354, 36-38	8.8	4.8	9.5	5.1	8.6	3.1	6.1	1.9	10.5	4.0
Food, beverages and tobacco	31	4.7	2.8	4.3	1.9	4.6	3.4	3.9	0.9	6.1	2.6
Textiles	321	4.6	1.1	4.5	0.4	4.7	0.8	3.8	−0.9	5.1	1.3
Wearing apparel, leather and foot-wear articles	322-324	5.1	4.9	5.2	5.1	4.9	2.7	2.4	1.7	6.4	3.1
Wood products, furniture	33	6.2	4.4	7.3	4.2	5.0	2.5	4.8	0.9	6.5	1.5
Paper, printing and publishing	34	7.3	3.5	8.3	3.4	6.6	2.9	4.7	1.5	7.3	2.8
Chemicals, petroleum, coal and rubber products	35	8.0	4.6	8.3	5.0	7.8	2.7	8.7	2.0	11.4	4.5
Non-metallic mineral products	36	7.9	3.8	8.7	3.8	7.4	2.2	4.7	0.8	8.5	2.9
Basic metals	37	7.4	5.1	8.7	6.1	7.5	3.6	4.6	0.5	7.3	2.3
Metal products and machinery	38	10.1	5.6	11.0	6.1	9.8	3.4	5.8	2.4	11.5	4.4

Source: Based on *The Growth of World Industry, 1971 Edition*, vol. 1 (United Nations publication, Sales No. 73.XVII.6); and *Monthly Bulletin of Statistics*, August 1973.

Note: The period of observations is as follows:

(1) For output the period 1960-1972 is applicable for all economic groupings.

(2) For employment the periods are 1960-1970 for the developing countries and 1960-1971 for the developed market and centrally planned economies.

[a] Based on production index numbers. [b] Based on employment index numbers.

relatively high rate was recorded by basic metals (3.6 percent), metal products and machinery (3.4 percent) and the food industry (3.4 percent), whereas in Asia, along with some branches of heavy industry, wearing apparel (5.1 percent) and wood products (4.2 percent) had high growth rates.

Structural Change in Selected Industrial Sectors

Some interesting conclusions may be drawn also by examining structural change in three main sectors of industry—consumer non-durables, intermediate goods and capital goods—at the individual country level. Table 5 indicates average annual growth rates of manufacturing output for the three sectors over the period 1960-1971 (in some cases the period was 1960-1970) for 20 African, 13 Asian and 13 Latin American countries. The output of intermediate goods and capital goods (including consumer durables) increased at a higher rate than that of consumer non-durables in all three regions. In Africa, the average (arithmetic) means of growth rates of the three sectors were 8.6 percent for capital goods, 8.1 percent for intermediate goods and 6.1 percent for consumer non-durables. In Asia the respective average means were 9.4 percent, 9.2 percent and 7.1 percent, and in Latin America they were 8.9 percent, 9.5 percent and 6.8 percent.

The non-uniform growth among these sectors resulted in a change in the industrial structure in favour of capital and intermediate goods. This fact is shown in Table 6 where the distribution of value added among the three sectors in 1960 and 1971 (in some cases in 1970) is indicated for selected developing countries and areas. It is evident that the shares of intermediate goods and of capital goods increased in almost all of the developing countries and areas included.

Table 6 indicates another important fact concerning industrial structure. There are obviously wide variations among the countries and areas considered in the share in value added of each sector. These variations are caused not only by differences in the stage of industrialization, but also by differences in the size of the countries involved and in their natural resource endowments. Thus, size and natural resource endowment appear to be influential factors affecting the industrial structure of an economy.

In Latin America, for example, such countries as Argentina, Brazil, Chile, Mexico and Peru, which are important in terms of size (measured by population and GDP) or resource endowment, also have a relatively large share of value added in capital and intermediate goods. By contrast, in small countries such as Costa Rica and Paraguay, the share of value added in consumer goods is considerably larger. One probable reason is that many economic activities classified as capital goods industries require large markets owing to economies of scale, and it is relatively easy for a large

TABLE 5. AVERAGE ANNUAL GROWTH RATES OF MANUFACTURING OUTPUT BY SECTOR IN SELECTED DEVELOPING COUNTRIES, 1960-1971 *(Percentage)*

Region and country or area	*Mainly consumer non-durables*[a]	*Mainly inter-mediate goods*[b]	*Mainly capital goods (including consumer durables)*[c]
Africa			
Algeria[d]	1.5	0.2	8.2
Angola	6.8	11.6	9.1
Egypt[d]	7.4	11.5	16.3
Ghana	6.3	10.7	7.6
Ivory Coast	6.6	7.0	7.6
Kenya	7.1	7.2	7.5
Libyan Arab Republic[d]	8.0	6.3	14.9
Malawi	6.0	9.8	7.7
Mauritius	6.6	7.9	7.0
Morocco[d]	6.6	8.2	7.0
Mozambique	4.7	8.4	6.4
Namibia	4.8	7.4	7.9
Nigeria	8.9	11.4	7.2
Senegal	2.6	4.0	7.8
Sudan[d]	6.0	9.0	14.4
Tunisia[d]	6.5	6.0	8.9
Uganda	4.9	10.6	7.2
United Republic of Tanzania	6.5	7.1	10.5
Zaire	5.6	6.8	2.0
Zambia	8.3	10.3	7.2
Average (arithmetic) mean	6.1	8.1	8.6
Asia			
Burma	5.4	8.0	8.1
Hong Kong	8.2	10.7	9.6
India	5.6	8.6	8.7
Indonesia	2.4	4.3	9.1
The Khmer Republic	6.8	9.7	9.0
Malaysia, West[d]	4.9	5.2	7.7
Pakistan	9.4	8.0	9.0
Philippines	5.6	6.8	7.7
Republic of Korea	16.8	20.4	17.0
Republic of Viet-Nam	4.5	8.9	8.2
Singapore	7.1	6.0	9.0
Sri Lanka	8.3	10.2	11.2
Thailand	7.5	13.1	7.8
Average (arithmetic) mean	7.1	9.2	9.4

TABLE 5 (cont'd)

Region and country or area	Mainly consumer non-durables[a]	Mainly inter-mediate goods[b]	Mainly capital goods (including consumer durables)[c]
Latin America			
Argentina	4.8	8.0	7.0
Bolivia	10.8	14.2	4.4
Brazil	4.5	9.2	9.4
Chile	4.2	4.9	6.4
Colombia	7.3	7.7	7.7
Costa Rica	6.4	9.2	11.0
Ecuador	9.3	12.0	12.7
Honduras[d]	10.3	17.7	14.5
Mexico	7.9	10.7	9.9
Paraguay	6.5	8.1	7.1
Peru	6.8	10.4	9.0
Uruguay	3.5	2.7	3.7
Venezuela	6.4	9.3	12.8
Average (arithmetic) mean	6.8	9.5	8.9

Source: Based on data supplied by the United Nations Statistical Office.

[a]ISIC 31, 32, 33, 342, 385 and 390.
[b]ISIC 341, 35 and 36.
[c]ISIC 37 and 381-384.
[d]1960-1970.

TABLE 6. DISTRIBUTION OF MANUFACTURING VALUE ADDED BY SECTOR IN SELECTED DEVELOPING COUNTRIES, 1960 AND 1971

(Percentage)

Region and country or area	1960			1971		
	Mainly consumer non-durables[a]	Mainly inter-mediate goods[b]	Mainly capital goods (including consumer durables)[c]	Mainly consumer non-durables[a]	Mainly inter-mediate goods[b]	Mainly capital goods (including consumer durables)[c]
Africa						
Algeria[d]	51.6	36.5	11.9	48.8	30.1	21.1
Angola	79.4	16.5	4.1	71.3	24.1	4.6
Egypt[d]	70.0	17.6	12.4	56.7	20.9	22.4
Ghana	87.4	5.2	7.4	84.0	7.8	8.2
Ivory Coast	53.0	17.0	30.0	51.0	17.0	32.0
Kenya	58.0	16.5	25.5	57.3	16.6	26.1
Libyan Arab Republic[d]	81.3	15.8	2.9	81.1	13.5	5.4

TABLE 6 (cont'd)	*1960*			*1971*		
Region and country or area	*Mainly consumer non-durables*[a]	*Mainly inter-mediate goods*[b]	*Mainly capital goods (including consumer durables)*[c]	*Mainly consumer non-durables*[a]	*Mainly inter-mediate goods*[b]	*Mainly capital goods (including consumer durables)*[c]
Africa (continued)						
Malawi	83.9	8.9	7.2	79.5	12.5	8.0
Mauritius	79.8	10.4	9.8	78.2	11.7	10.1
Morocco[d]	66.8	17.2	16.0	64.6	19.3	16.1
Mozambique	79.3	13.8	6.9	73.6	18.7	7.7
Namibia	78.9	4.4	16.7	73.2	5.4	21.4
Nigeria	75.1	14.5	10.4	73.3	18.1	8.6
Senegal	80.4	9.3	10.3	73.7	9.9	16.4
Sudan[d]	71.8	20.2	8.0	62.0	23.2	14.8
Tunisia[d]	78.5	13.6	7.9	77.5	12.8	9.7
Uganda	81.8	8.8	9.4	74.8	14.4	10.8
United Republic of Tanzania	96.5	1.3	2.2	95.4	1.4	3.2
Zaire	34.3	8.2	57.5	41.3	11.2	47.5
Zambia	57.1	20.0	22.9	55.9	24.0	20.1
Asia						
Burma	80.4	15.8	3.8	75.8	19.5	4.7
Hong Kong	77.5	11.3	11.2	73.8	13.9	12.3
India	60.7	17.4	21.9	53.0	20.8	26.2
Indonesia	59.9	37.8	2.3	54.0	41.7	4.3
The Khmer Republic	76.9	12.3	10.8	71.9	15.5	12.6
Malaysia, West[d]	38.9	49.9	11.2	37.0	49.1	13.9
Pakistan	68.5	23.9	7.6	70.9	21.5	7.6
Philippines	64.3	26.0	9.7	60.8	27.9	11.3
Republic of Korea	71.6	17.0	11.4	66.8	22.3	10.9
Republic of Viet-Nam	84.3	13.7	2.0	77.6	19.7	2.7
Singapore	46.7	38.5	14.8	47.2	34.7	18.1
Sri Lanka	77.9	17.2	4.9	74.1	19.8	6.1
Thailand	79.5	13.2	7.3	72.2	20.9	6.9
Latin America						
Argentina	46.3	21.1	32.6	39.8	25.1	35.1
Bolivia	70.4	20.3	9.3	68.0	27.3	4.7
Brazil	46.8	23.6	29.6	35.0	28.6	36.4
Chile	48.5	21.1	30.4	44.4	20.7	34.9
Colombia	62.4	24.3	13.3	61.4	24.9	13.7
Costa Rica	85.1	9.7	5.2	80.1	12.1	7.8
Ecuador	74.0	22.9	3.1	63.4	27.6	4.0
Honduras[d]	81.7	13.9	4.4	71.2	23.2	5.6
Mexico	57.8	24.5	17.7	51.7	28.9	19.4
Paraguay	81.7	10.7	7.6	79.7	12.4	7.9
Peru	62.7	14.9	22.4	56.0	19.0	25.0
Uruguay	57.5	24.6	17.9	58.5	23.0	18.5
Venezuela	46.3	37.0	16.7	36.4	38.9	24.7

Source: Based on data supplied by the United Nations Statistical Office.

[a]ISIC 31, 32, 33, 342, 385 and 390.
[b]ISIC 341, 35 and 36.
[c]ISIC 37 and 381-384.
[d]1970 instead of 1971.

country to establish these markets domestically through policies of import substitution. Tendencies similar to those described above may be observed for the African and Asian countries listed in Table 6.

Notes

1. The industrial growth discussed here precedes certain recent world events that might alter patterns to such an extent that it would be seriously misleading to gauge future prospects on the basis of past performance.
2. Based on United Nations, *The Growth of World Industry, 1970 Edition,* vol. I (New York: United Nations, 1972) and *Monthly Bulletin of Statistics,* August 1973.
3. Calculated from United Nations, *Statistical Yearbook, 1972* (New York: United Nations, 1973), and *Monthly Bulletin of Statistics*, February 1971 and September 1973.
4. The selection of countries is not fully representative; because of the unavailability of data, a number of developing countries with relatively large manufacturing sectors are not included.
5. The data presented in Table 4 cover only organized manufacturing and generally exclude such activities as cottage industries and home workers, which are specially important in terms of employment in developing countries. The coverage is thus incomplete, and the structural changes described concern only the organized sector.

21 *The Lomé Convention and Industrial Cooperation: A New Relationship Between the European Community and the ACP States?*

Steven J. Warnecke

Among the issues raised by the Third World's call for a New International Economic Order (NIEO) have been demands for a more acceptable global distribution of industry and ownership of industrial assets. As a result of their weak bargaining position, lack of confidence in the private sectors of the industrialized states, discontent with existing trade and aid policies, and distrust of the present General Agreement on Tariffs and Trade (GATT) framework, the solutions proposed by the developing countries have combined moral and legal arguments with demands for more involvement by the governments of industrialized countries in bringing about the establishment of industries in the developing world. To a certain extent, this approach rests not only on combining industrial policies in the Third World with better access to Northern markets, but also on the premise that there must be a parallel contraction of competing sectors in the Organisation for Economic Co-operation and Development (OECD) member states. This would allow a "shift of industries" to occur from the Northern to the Southern hemisphere in sectors in which the developing countries purportedly have a comparative advantage. The fulfillment of these demands raises basic questions about the relationship of government and the private sector in the industrialized nations, the role domestic and international markets are to play in resource allocation, and the value of intergovernmental agreements in influencing this process.

At present, world attention has been focused on these issues by actions taken by the United Nations (UN) and its agencies. In May 1974, the UN General Assembly approved two resolutions that call for the establishment of a NIEO.[1] In February 1975, the Dakar Declaration—adopted by a large number of developing countries—comprehensively reviewed the developing states' positions on international economic issues, particularly in regard to commodities.[2] It elaborated an integrated program for commodities (including price stabilization), more processing at the source, and measures to prevent synthetic and substitute products from undermining the export earnings of the Third World states. Next, the UN Industrial Development Organization (UNIDO) Lima Declaration of March 1975 called for a comprehensive effort by the industrialized countries to develop industries in developing countries.[3] This document is an all-inclusive catalogue of demands that reflect the developing states' aspirations to emulate the industrial structures of the OECD countries. It also proposed that UNIDO's mandate be expanded to include the establishment of an Industrial Development Fund (IDF), and it called upon the General Assembly to convert UNIDO into a specialized agency of the UN. The demands regarding industrialization were synthesized into section four of the resolution adopted at the Seventh Special Session of the General Assembly, held in September 1975.[4]

The increased assertiveness of the developing world has led to what is termed a "North-South" confrontation, and further pressure for translating words into deeds has been added by the successes of the Organization of Petroleum Exporting Countries (OPEC). Because of their greater vulnerability, the European Community (EC) and Japan among the OECD states were the first to be more conciliatory toward the Third World. The United States, which initially offered great resistance, belatedly has begun to strike a conciliatory note. Secretary of State Henry A. Kissinger, in his speech on global consensus and economic development (which was read to the UN General Assembly on 1 September 1975), suggested several ways of responding to these issues. They included the expansion of the resources of the World Bank's International Finance Corporation, the creation of an International Investment Trust, the establishment of an International Center for the Exchange of Technological Information, and an International Industrialization Institute.[5] In part, this change in the American position was motivated by a desire to counteract the drift toward trade blocs by placing the discussion of world development problems back in a global forum.[6]

While the UN may be the best forum within which the developing nations collectively can exert a general pressure on the industrialized states, it is open to question whether it is the most suitable institution through which to implement many of the industrial goals contained in the Lima Declaration and the resolution adopted by the Seventh Special Session. As a result of the developing countries' rhetoric, as well as their voting patterns, the UN has become too politicized; even if the UN could be one of the international fora for dealing with some of these issues, the realization of many of these proposals is, by and large, far off in the future. In addition, much of the North-South dialogue, which owes its origin to the pressure of developing countries within the UN, is now taking place parallel to the UN in the context of the Conference on International Economic Co-operation (CIEC). And, finally, the negotiations concerning the transfer of real resources and the granting of practical concessions are taking place in the International Monetary Fund (IMF), the General Agreement on Tariffs and Trade, with the European Community, and between specific banks and corporations and individual developing nations.

The Lomé Convention

Many of the proposals on industrialization in the Lima Declaration and the Kissinger speech are contained in the Lomé Convention which was concluded on 28 February 1975 between the EC and 46 developing states located in Africa, the Caribbean, and the Pacific (ACP states).[7] This agreement, which is the successor to the Yaoundé and Arusha Conventions,[8] bears the imprint of the structural changes in the EC and the developing world. As a result of the United Kingdom becoming a full member of the Community in January 1973, the Yaoundé associates (nineteen with Mauritius) decided to join Commonwealth Africa in negotiating a pan-African successor to the existing agreements. In May 1973, African trade ministers met in Abidjan to draft a mandate for themselves to negotiate as a group. The fact that the Anglophone and Francophone states could agree to negotiate collectively was a major development. It reflected the continued loosening of bilateral ties between them and their former metropolitan countries as well as their efforts to multilateralize their relations with European states.[9] Much to the surprise of the Europeans, the ACP states were able to reconcile internal differences throughout the course of the negotiations and to deal effectively with their European interlocutors.

The Lomé agreement includes provisions for moving beyond traditional trade and aid policies to include more active forms of industrial, technical, and financial cooperation (Titles III and IV) and a commodity price-support system (Title II). In regard to trade, the Convention provides for 46 one-way free trade areas between the individual ACP states and the EC. In other words, the developing states that are signatories to the agreement do not have to grant the reverse preferences that were a major point of contention under the Yaoundé and Arusha accords. This includes duty- and quota-free access for ACP products to Community markets and nondiscriminatory most-favored-nation treatment of European exports to the ACP countries. Three-hundred ninety million dollars is to be provided through the European Investment Bank and three billion dollars worth of aid through the European Development Fund. Finally, Title III provides for the establishment of a Committee on Industrial Co-operation and a Centre for Industrial Development; and Title VI provides for the establishment of three major institutions for joint administration of the Convention: the Council of Ministers, the Committee of Ambassadors, and the Consultative Assembly.

The EC Commission has hailed this agreement as a new model for the relationship between the advanced industrialized states and the Third World. This view is contained in one of the points of the Convention's preamble in which the signatories have resolved "to establish a new model for relations between developed and developing States, compatible with the aspirations of the international community towards a more just and more balanced economic order."[10] While the official ACP response has also been favorable, the Convention has not been at a loss for European critics who do not share the optimistic interpretation of the Commission. Among the criticisms that have been leveled are (a) the real benefits to be derived from the sections that govern trade in manufactured products are quite restricted as a result of severe rules of origin; (b) preferences granted to ACP agricultural products are not as liberal as they appear to be, because they are hemmed in by relevant provisions of the EC's common agricultural policy; (c) the STABEX scheme for supporting the prices of a selected group of raw materials is quite limited in scope; (d) the levels of funding for the European Investment Bank and the European Development Fund are inadequate; and finally, (e) Title III on industrial cooperation is dismissed as being programmatic at best.[11]

In the context of pressures for a NIEO, the negotiation of the Lomé agreement, as well as the implementation of its provisions on industrial and technical cooperation, provide a practical basis for studying the current evolution of these functional issues. What makes Lomé of particular interest is that some of the poorest developing countries in the world are among the signatories.[12] While Africa is the least developed continent in the Third World, the countries associated with the EC are among the least developed and least industrialized in Africa; sixteen are on the UN's list of the twenty-five least developed countries.

Consequently, does the conclusion of this intergovernmental agreement between two regional secretariats constitute a new departure in the relationship between advanced and developing states—particularly in regard to influencing the international distribution of production? Does it provide a framework through which private enterprises can be induced to invest in the ACP economies? And, most important of all, what expectations has it awakened in the developing world and what model value does it have for implementing the various UN resolutions on establishing a NIEO?

Industrial Cooperation and the Lomé Convention

Since the Lomé Convention has been overshadowed by the many UN resolutions, the impression has arisen that the agreement, and particularly

Title III on industrial cooperation, is derived from the declarations of the Sixth Special Session concerning a NIEO. Although this session did have an impact on the ACP states, the Convention, and particularly its articles on industrial cooperation, are primarily a direct outgrowth of a series of prior agreements between the EC and several African countries that preceded actions taken at the UN.

At first, the relationship of the six states that founded the Community to Africa was defined unilaterally by Title IV of the Treaty of Rome. This section associated the overseas territories of four of them to the EC in a free trade area. The first Yaoundé Convention of 20 July 1963 changed this into a negotiated association with eighteen now independent African states.[13] This was followed by the Arusha Convention of 1969 and the second Yaoundé Convention of 1969. These agreements did not have the impact on trade and investment desired by the African signatories. In spite of guaranteed access to the EC in a specific range of products, the associated African states failed to increase their penetration of European markets. As it quickly became obvious, discriminatory trade concessions are only theoretical preferences; in order to have any value for inducing trade and investment, a variety of other conditions must be present. Since the Yaoundé and Arusha states were more or less devoid of modern industry and its supporting infrastructure, their prospects for attracting or generating the investments required to produce the goods which could have benefited from the preferences listed in the Yaoundé and Arusha Conventions were extremely reduced.

Consequently, in the course of the transition from one agreement to the next, at the insistence of the African states, the subject of active industrial cooperation between the EC and the African associates took on greater importance.[14] If Title IV of the Rome Treaty had been limited to protecting colonial markets and implementing trade and aid policies, the first Yaoundé Convention shifted the emphasis to policies "to facilitate the economic diversification and industrialization of the Associated countries" and the statutes of the European Development Fund were expanded to include a provision for aid for trade promotion. These objectives were reaffirmed in the second Yaoundé agreement. Shortly before this agreement was to terminate, the last meeting of the Yaoundé Association Council held in Luxembourg on 10 October 1972 approved a five-point program for the general guidance of Community action to support the industrialization efforts of the African associates.[15] The main points were the establishment of an EC investment guarantee system and the promotion of links between European industrialists and the Yaoundé states. During the Lomé negotiations, these goals reappeared in a somewhat expanded form on 24 March 1974 when the ACP representatives submitted four questions to EC officials. These covered the possibilities for (a) free and unimpeded access to European knowledge in the area of industrial development, (b) the mobilization of the EC's scientific and technical infrastructure for development, (c) the adjustment in EC production patterns to enable a new and more rational international division of labor, and (d) arrangements to reconcile the interests of private industry and investors in Western Europe with the ACP member states' policies of increased control over their own industrial sectors.[16]

In July 1974, quite to the surprise of the EC negotiators, the ACP representatives—encouraged by the Sixth Special Session—provided their own answers to these questions in what has come to be called the Kingston Memorandum on Industrial Cooperation.[17] This memorandum (and Title III of Lomé which is almost entirely based on the memorandum) contains most of the broad issues and general solutions raised later in 1974 in the UN Charter on Economic Rights and Duties of States and in the UNIDO Lima Declaration. The Kingston Memorandum—in emphasizing active EC policies for establishing industrial and commercial links between European firms and those of the ACP countries, the accelerated transfer of technology, and EC policies to permit a better international division of labor by encouraging the reduction of selected industrial sectors in the EC—indicated that the ACP states no longer wished to rely on general and theoretical concessions from the industrialized states. Such general preferences would have to be supplemented by ongoing intergovernmental bargaining on a wide range of issues to insure that the theoretical value of an agreement would be translated into reality. Thus, the Kingston Memorandum called for the establishment of specific targets and objectives to be obtained in the promotion of particular industries for the duration of the Convention. Among the broad areas in which such targets could be established were processing of raw materials for export, import substitution industries, and heavy industries involving multinational arrangements on both sides. The memorandum also called for EC assistance in expanding international subcontracting and licensing arrangements.[18] Finally, it proposed the establishment of a Committee on Industrial Co-operation and an Information Centre on Industrial Development.

While the EC negotiators did not accept the inclusion of specific targets in Title III, the final version did include most of the positions and goals of the ACP states.[19] This is reflected in the first section of the industrial cooperation section, article 26. In this article, the Community agreed to promote the diversification of industry in the ACP states as well as the marketing of their industrial products in foreign markets; to establish new industrial and trade links between the industries of the Nine and those of the ACP nations; to encourage Community firms to participate in the industrial development plans of the 46; and to facilitate the transfer of technology. In addition, the EC agreed to contribute to the establishment and extension in the ACP states of raw materials processing industries[20] and industries manufacturing finished and semifinished products, and to provide funds through the European Investment Bank and the European Development Fund for industrial infrastructure projects, manpower training, technology and research, industrial information, trade cooperation, and promotion. Finally, agreement was reached on establishing a Committee on Industrial Cooperation (Article 35)[21] and a Centre for Industrial Development (Article 36).[22] The structure, size, and responsibilities of these two institutions were deliberately left vague and attention is now being focused on how they will be related to the ambitious programmatic goals of Title III as well as to the titles on trade and technical and financial cooperation.

In spite of the institutional weaknesses of Title III, the Lomé Convention is the first important agreement between developed and developing states that not only accepts in principle many of the goals of the NIEO but also combines them with some economic and political mechanisms of varying efficacy for translating them into specific policies. In fact, the EC official responsible for negotiating the title on industrial cooperation has compared Lomé with the UNIDO Lima Declaration: "though the theme is the same, the nature and objectives of the two documents are quite different. The Lomé Convention is a contract, the Declaration of Lima ranks as a resolution."[23] Such a political interpretation does afford the ACP representatives a potentially significant basis upon which they can forcefully negotiate with the EC in implementing the various provisions of the agreement.

At a minimum, Lomé does put more emphasis on intergovernmental bargaining on a wide range of industrial issues; but both the reasons for the expectations from governmental involvement differ appreciably between the European and the ACP states. The key role that this approach plays for the ACP governments is to be expected because their domestic private sectors are weak, and in many cases nonexistent, or because the ruling parties are socialist. As a result of their tutelary relationship to their own economies and their inexperience in dealing with the European private sector directly, they hope that the Commission and the governments of the EC member states will and can play a more active role in influencing the decisions of the private sector.

Thus, in the context of increased pressures from the developing world, can the Lomé institutions and the regional secretariats that negotiated the agreement play meaningful roles in stabilizing political and economic relations among the countries these secretariats represent? In turn, can this framework have an impact on implementing Title III on industrial cooperation? And, finally, what will be the response of the private sector, because ultimately it is the key to any long-range success. Most of the problems that must be faced were raised during the negotiations.

General Political and Economic Problems Confronting the Implementation of Title III

The Commission of the European Community

From the outset, the EC representatives were positively inclined toward the aspirations of their ACP counterparts. In addition, the negotiations on Title III seemed to occur in a relatively favorable climate. The ACP demands for a more acceptable international division of labor were reinforced by UN declarations in 1974 and by the simultaneous discussion in the member states of the EC about which industries should be allowed to decline in Western Europe and gravitate toward the Third World.[24]

In spite of these developments, there are difficulties inherent in the implementation of Title III as a result of the Commission's weak relationship to the member states' governments and their private sectors. On the most general political level, there has been an extremely important policy difference between the Commission and the EC governments on the goals to be obtained through the Lomé negotiations. The EC commissioner responsible for development policy, Claude Cheysson, had consistently staked out positions in favor of the developing countries that frequently went beyond what many of the EC member states are currently prepared to accept. In fact, for many of them, the EC, by accepting too much of the rhetoric of the Third World in the context of an agreement that involves specific political and economic commitments, may have placed itself and the Nine in a very exposed position.[25] Many observers have wondered subsequent to the conclusion of the negotiations whether the Commission has in fact contributed to an awakening of expectations in the ACP states that neither the EC nor its members can fulfill. Moreover, both explicitly and implicitly, the ACP demands require the EC and the governments of the Nine to exert more pressure on their private sectors as well as to intervene in the operation of international markets to the benefit of the developing states. However, on both of these accounts, the Commission is poorly situated to exercise effective influence over either the member state governments or their private sectors. The Nine, in turn, as a result of the existing distribution of power between governments and their private sectors, also have limits placed upon the influence they can exert over banks and businesses.[26] These points are obvious in regard to the problems of technology transfer. It is clear that the EC cannot offer the ACP states know-how and techniques which do not belong to it, but rather are the sole property of the private sector. What the Commission might do is to provide information and assistance in selecting relevant technologies, to facilitate contacts, and (within the limits of certain financial arrangements) to help in the acquisition of these technologies. However, the role the Commission can play in this as well as other areas, in part, depends on the extent to which the governments of the Nine are prepared to accord it a larger role in development policy, particularly if this is at the political and financial expense of the member states.

Furthermore, the policies advocated by the ACP negotiators would, as they themselves have recognized, have serious repercussions on the EC's own industries. According to the Kingston Memorandum, this would mean that the EC would have to actively encourage the reduction of certain activities in Western Europe, to program in advance the transfer of specific productive capacities to the ACP states, and to implement special measures to deal with the problems of structural adjustment in the EC. Title III, however, does not contain references to any of these points. As the EC representatives indicated, the evolution and adaptation of industries in Europe is mainly in the hands of the private sector, and advanced programming of structural change is very difficult to undertake in the mixed market economies of the Nine. In any case, although the Commission has tried to define a role for itself in "industrial policy," public policies toward industry are the responsibility of the member states. Consequently, they do not lend themselves to negotiation at the Community level.[27]

The Private Sector

Since the participation of the private sector is central to the goals of the Convention, the Commission, in the course of the Lomé negotiations, obtained advisory opinions on the Kingston Memorandum from the Union of Industries of the European Community (UNICE)[28] and the "Club of Seven,"[29] a group of private associations of firms with business interests in Africa. While both organizations expressed support for the general industrialization goals of the ACP states, they were concerned about two problems. First, since Lomé includes provisions for increased government efforts to influence private sector activities, both UNICE and the Club of Seven expressed concern that the Convention might open the way for political considerations to intrude upon business decisions. Such a development, in turn, might lead to an unwarranted distortion in the operation of market forces. This question, in particular, has come up in regard to the developing world's demand that the Europeans permit a "shift of industries" to take place. The Federation of Belgian Industries, among others, was worried that a demand of this kind opens the door to decisions by government decree to determine industrial location, and, in common with UNICE and the Club of Seven, this position reflects the conflict between business decision-making in a market system and the domestic and international dirigisme of most of the ACP states. However, such a perspective does not necessarily represent a resistance to industrialization in the Third World, but rather a concern about the role markets are to play in determining this development. Thus, the Federation of Belgian Industries has noted that there is a continuous redistribution; and a practical and constructive policy for European governments would be to speed up this process insofar as it works through market forces.[30]

But in this regard, the two organizations and the Commission shared the concern that the text of the Convention did not contain sufficiently specific provisions about investment guarantees.[31] Although the EC negotiators had continuously emphasized the importance of some form of guarantee that would ensure suitable reception and working conditions for Community businesses, some of the ACP countries viewed a detailed article concerning investment as an interference with their sovereign right to determine their own development policies. Their position was a reflection of the contradictory and often self-defeating positions many of the ACP states have taken in their efforts to attract investors and corporations. On the one hand, they have insisted that the Community influence its private sector to expand activities in the developing world. On the other hand, they have insisted on maintaining an exclusive right to nationalize industries and to unilaterally control capital flows. This is as much the remnant of an anticolonialist reaction and nationalistic self-assertion as it is one way in which the ACP states have attempted to demonstrate that they are negotiating as equals with the Europeans. In addition, these contradictory goals cover the fear that the Europeans would continue to impose a pattern of industrial development on the ACP countries that is tailored to European needs and, therefore, unacceptable to the 46 developing world signatories of the Convention.

In attempting to allay these fears, the Commission took the position that in industrial matters, more than in other fields, the Western Europeans should help the ACP states to fulfill their own developmental choices and should not attempt to persuade them to accept outside patterns. The extent to which the ACP states were prepared to agree to some form of investment guarantee is contained in article 38.[32] This article is a watered-down version of the original Commission proposal and only provides that the ACP countries shall take the necessary measures to promote effective cooperation with businesses that respect the development plans and priorities of the host countries.

While UNICE and the Club of Seven indicated their readiness to respect the laws of the host ACP states, their doubts about the investment environment was not removed by what ultimately became article 38. In a position paper, UNICE stated that the encouragement of West European investments in the ACP states would require (a) clear and well defined legislation so that investors and managers know their rights and obligations,

(b) the free movement of capital, (c) prompt, just and equitable compensation in the case of nationalization and in accordance with the principles of international law, and (d) the settlement of disputes by courts that are acceptable to both parties.[33]

However, the Club of Seven memorandum did contain some interesting suggestions which, in part, were similar to the views the ACP negotiators had tried to have embodied in the final version of the Convention. In regard to free access to European markets for industrial products, the memorandum accepted the ACP position that more was necessary than just lowering tariff barriers and removing quotas. On the one hand, in the past, in too many cases when ACP firms have been able to export to the EC, the benefits of tariff concessions have been lost to European importers who have acted as intermediaries between EC industries and developing world producers.[34] On the other hand, since the importers have many producers from among whom to choose, Third World firms have found themselves exposed to the risk and uncertainty of finding buyers for their products.

Consequently, the Club of Seven suggested that successful exploitation of these theoretical preferences as well as the establishment of a stable context for ACP industrialization programs is only possible if *structures d'accueil* are established.[35] This implies something more than a simple buyer/seller relationship. In other words, the club has proposed that ACP firms become directly and more closely integrated with corresponding EC firms which can provide them with continued access to marketing networks, new technologies, training programs, and financial resources. At first, such a relationship would assist ACP firms in learning how to produce for, and sell in, EC markets and this, in turn, might be a step to selling in the markets of other industrialized countries. Inevitably this would mean more emphasis on EC industries establishing affiliates in ACP states as well as expanding subcontracting.

The ACP States

In common with other developing countries, the ACP states emphasized the link between their own industrial development and the policies in the advanced states toward their own industries. While there is a general connection between the policies of the public and private sectors in Western Europe and the development plans of the ACP states, this connection has been defined in terms that insufficiently take into account the economic and political context in which industries and investors operate. Thus, understandably—given the ACP states' planned approach to their own economies—their approach to influencing the location of industry between the EC and themselves is economically static and geographically limited rather than dynamic and global in scope. First, it depends upon European industry confining the scope of its activities to the ACP countries, although European industrialists have a global approach to markets. Second, it depends upon political decisions to allocate resources between the EC and the developing world, rather than relying on markets. Third, by formulating the dynamics of industrial location in terms of a North-South dichotomy, problems affecting Lomé as a result of the nature of international competition are camouflaged. In general, as the example of textiles has illustrated (but other sectors could be used), it is not always possible to predict which developing countries will successfully expand productive capacity and exports if competing suppliers in Europe cannot meet domestic demand or are phased out. In addition, competition for access to West European markets does not only take place among developing countries; in many types of textiles, for instance, they also compete with suppliers from other advanced industrialized states. Furthermore, it is not possible to foresee whether "declining" industries in the EC can rejuvenate themselves technologically, thus, to some extent, stemming or reversing the shift in comparative advantage to the developing world. The introduction of synthetic fibers in the European natural fiber textile industry and the technological modernization of some branches of the shoe industry are cases in point.[36]

Moreover, much of the discussion conducted under the heading of the "shift of industries" is mechanical since it completely neglects how the changing environment for business in Western Europe is affecting the freedom of governmental and managerial decision-making. These changes include greater pressures by workers for participation in managerial decision, increased government responsibility for high levels of growth and employment, and national regional and industrial policies to influence the development and distribution of specific industrial sectors. The motivation for and the goals of these policies often have little to do with the dictates of the market place as seen from the perspective of managerial efficiency. Such developments in the EC will inevitably have an effect on the formulation of policies based upon Title III of Lomé.

What Are the Possibilities for Implementing Title III?

It would be very difficult to add anything new to the theoretical literature on development or to propose policies that have not been tried in one form or another. The basic problems are well known and have been described at great length. On the one hand, they involve developing countries which often have not consolidated politically or economically.[37] On the other hand, the efforts of the developing countries face impediments created by the developed states.

Although the Lomé Convention does introduce some novel schemes and goals, its importance for the industrialization of the ACP states can only be understood if it is placed in a broader context. This involves the potential implications of ongoing intergovernmental negotiations for interregional economic cooperation. It may be simplistic to say that as a result of the privileged economic and political relationships the Convention has established between the Community and the ACP states, its major significance may be that it has provided the 46 states with a general framework through which they can compel attention and can exert pressure.[38] Several reasons suggest this conclusion. First, while industrialization of the Third World (to the extent that it is possible) ultimately depends on economic efficiency, realistic use of resources and managerial skills, the political context within which this occurs should not be underemphasized. Regional secretariats can play a potentially vital role in stabilizing interregional political and economic relations and, at the moment, the future of the Convention appears to be under a relatively favorable star. In November 1975, the president of Tanzania, speaking for the ACP states, told the EC Commission that he had always been suspicious of the Community's "neo-colonialist approach"—even under the Yaoundé Convention. However, for whatever value it may have, he now felt that the EC was genuinely trying to help the Third World with its plans to industrialize.[39] The reverse side of this coin is the active interest that Community industrial associations have taken in Title III (to be discussed in the next section).

Second, to a large extent many of the problems that have arisen in efforts at industrial cooperation are a result of the apparent or real political relationships between the EC and the ACP states. Thus, the image of an industrial economy which many ACP states have is designed to give them complete independence from and equality with the developed countries. In good measure this is part of a continuing reaction against a colonial past marked by economic exploitation. While the political and psychological causes of this reaction are understandable, the goal of emulating the developed countries in many industries is often unrealistic and self-defeating. The existing distribution of industry and historically determined technological leads and market patterns still favor the OECD states. Consequently, it is vital for the leaders of the ACP countries to transform feelings of dependence into ones of self-confidence that they can successfully negotiate and cooperate with the more advanced and stronger economies of Western Europe.

This not only entails an evolution in political perceptions but a more differentiated view of the range of industrial links that can be established between the industrialized states and the developing nations. Thus, a new international division of labor cannot be seen exclusively in terms of emulating or duplicating the industries of the OECD states or of redeploying certain industries from the Northern to the Southern hemisphere, but it also must be seen in terms of firm integration into the West European industrial structure through subcontracting, through supplying products that do not compete with those produced in the EC, and through obtaining some share of EC markets in products produced by the industries of the Nine and the ACP states.

Third, as the operation of the European Community Generalized System of Preferences (GSP) scheme has illustrated, general policies are empty concessions to those states that are too weak to compete in an international economic system dominated by the main industrial states.[40] As was mentioned, many of the African signatories of the Lomé Convention are among the poorest developing states in the Third World. They are not only in competition with industries in advanced states, but also with similar ones in other developing states. Moreover, among the various Third World states, some have a more favored place in the EC's external relations than others. These include the developing states on the Mediterranean littoral and, more recently, for obvious reasons, the OPEC members.

Consequently, behind the facade of Third World unity (which has been used to extract general trade and aid concessions from developed countries), a fierce competition among the developing states takes place for privileged relations with individual or groups of industrialized states. The EC, for its part, has contributed to this competition by concluding contradictory trade, aid, and industrial cooperation agreements with many developing states.[41] Thus, the value of the discriminatory trade framework established by the Lomé Convention must be judged in the context of the evolution of the EC's commercial policies in the last ten years. The theoretical value of the trade preferences granted to the ACP states under Title I of the Convention have been eroded by the EC's GSP for developing countries and by the continued reduction of tariffs in successive GATT negotiations. Moreover, the membership of the United Kingdom, Denmark, and Ireland in the EC and the conclusion of free trade agreements with the remaining European Free Trade Association (EFTA) states have established a bloc of industrialized states whose trade relations with each other in manufactures are more privileged than the concessions granted to the ACP states.

In this context, the institutions and principles of Lomé may permit the ACP states the opportunity to exert more pressure to champion their own interests. But this involves a basic question concerning the current revolution of the international economic system established after 1945. Such agreements not only undermine efforts to maintain a liberal multilateral basis for international trade, but divide developing nations from each other. However, are special arrangements with industrialized states necessary to insure the economic development of poor nations? Perhaps, at the outset, continuity and stability are more important than insuring full adherence to multilateral rules. In this regard, Japan plays a central role in Southeast Asia, the United States in Latin America, and the EC in Africa. These developments, in part, are the inevitable outgrowth of geographic proximity, which, in turn, has had an impact on political relations and trade and aid patterns. In a world in which many states have comparative advantages in similar industries, political ties and their economic implications can be decisive in influencing which states gain access to new markets and receive investments and which do not.

In all of these respects, Lomé establishes special ties between the ACP and the EC states. For the various governments involved it provides institutional foci such as the Council of Ministers, the Committee of Ambassadors, the Consultative Assembly, the Committee on Industrial Co-operation, and the Centre for Industrial Development. Since the Convention was signed in February 1975, the ACP states have been trying to exploit the leverage the agreement potentially gives them with the EC Commission, the governments of the Nine, and the banks and businesses of Western Europe. In the first instance, this requires maintaining cohesion and a sense of collective interests among themselves, because there is always the danger that the unity they achieved during the negotiations will fall apart as they compete with each other during the implementation of the Convention's various titles. The central political cleavage that may emerge could be between the Anglophone and Francophone states in Africa, a division that predates the Convention. In addition, the Caribbean and Pacific signatories may find themselves pushed to the sidelines. At present, however, the 46 countries have a common interest in protecting the advantages negotiated in the Convention—not only against other developing countries that are the recipients of privileged treatment under the EC's GSP Scheme, but also against further erosion of their tariff advantages in the context of the current GATT round.

On 6 June 1975, the ACP foreign ministers adopted the Georgetown Declaration.[42] Among the goals they have set for themselves are the establishment of a permanent ACP Secretariat in Brussels to perpetuate the cooperative organization set up for the negotiations of the Convention; the collective realization of the agreement's goals; closer economic and trade relations among themselves; and the promotion of effective regional and interregional cooperation. These developments have encouraged more cooperation among the ACP embassies in Brussels. Whereas previously many of these states had to deal on an individual basis with the Commission and the nine member governments of the EC, they are now organizing to act in a concerted fashion on a wide range of EC policies that are of concern to them.

The Committee on Industrial Co-operation and the Centre for Industrial Development

Structure and Organization

Although the Convention was signed in February 1975 and the ACP states have attached great importance to Title III, for many reasons the delineation of the organization, responsibilities, and size of the Committee and the Centre has been slow. By and large, in spite of their efforts to have both the symbols and substance of equality during the implementation stage of the Convention, the ACP states are the demandeurs. Consequently, they have been dependent on the formulation of detailed responses to their suggestions by the Europeans. This task has not been an easy one for the EC Commission because of the difficulties of relating the ambitious goals of Title III to the institutions described in articles 35 and 36, the problem of establishing meaningful contacts with the EC's private sector, and the obstacles that stand in the way of coordinating Title III with the other sections of the agreement.

Industrial cooperation as defined in Title III is dependent on the availability of instruments for granting technical and financial assistance. Not only has a provision for funding been omitted from Title III, but, to a large extent, the necessary instruments are located in different parts of the Convention. Thus, trade promotion—which is to be funded by the European Development Fund (article 13)—is contained under Title I on trade cooperation. More importantly, Title IV on financial and technical cooperation is to be administered by the European Investment Bank and the European Development Fund. Therefore, as the Commission itself has admitted, Title III is not really on the same basis as the other parts of the Convention. It is in many cases a repetition of provisions that figure elsewhere in the agreement, a device that was required because of the ACP states' pressure to have a separate and distinct section on industrial cooperation.[43]

In whatever way the problems of coordination within the Convention will be handled, Title III's main purpose is to interest the EC's private sector in the Lomé states. In their advisory opinions to the Commission, both UNICE and its affiliates stated the obvious point that the Centre for Industrial Development will require the logistical support of employer federations to be effective. But they also emphasized that industrial cooperation depends not only on the active participation of peak organizations, but even more so on the response of individual enterprises. On the one hand, this is simply a practical observation. On the other hand, it is an indication of concern in industrial circles that the Convention may be one more example, this time at a European level, of government bureaucrats contributing to the shift of power between the public and private sectors. Consequently, UNICE has stated that industrial cooperation is the responsibility of individual enterprises, and the institutions established under Title III can neither supersede nor replace the private sector, but must rely upon it.[44]

In order to insure that this position is translated into organizational terms, UNICE and its affiliates have insisted that the persons chosen to staff the Centre be selected according to extensive industrial and financial experience in the EC and ACP states and not according to political or national considerations. Moreover, in a letter to the Commission and the Council of Ministers, UNICE stated that the "organizations representing Community industrialists should have the right to nominate their representatives on the Committee on Industrial Development's bodies." The letter stressed that there should be compulsory provisions that "the agreement of enterprise representatives must be sought on all important questions. This would apply particularly to the drafting of the annual work programme of the Centre and also to any decision which necessitates the direct or indirect participation of enterprises."[45] A more extreme position concerning the organization of the Centre has been advanced by the Arbeitsgemeinschaft Entwicklungsländer, an organization coordinated by the Bundesverband der Deutschen Industrie. In a memorandum to its members, the association suggested that the Centre should not be established as a government institution and be independent from the EC Commission.[46]

By April 1976, after a year of negotiations with the ACP states and discussions with the private sector, the Commission completed its proposal for the institutions specified in Title III.[47] According to the Title, the Committee on Industrial Co-operation is to be responsible to the Committee of Ambassadors and to supervise the Centre for Industrial Co-operation and the application of Title III. Thus, it will be essentially an intergovernmental, political body, composed of fifteen ACP and eleven EC representatives, but with a single spokesperson.

The Centre for Industrial Development is to be strictly operational and will be run jointly by the Community and the ACP members. The Commission has proposed that the director of the Centre be nominated by the Committee on Industrial Co-operation. However, the European Investment Bank, and several of the employer organizations, are of the opinion that the director should be chosen from the private sector. This suggestion has been unacceptable to the Commission, the EC member state governments, and the ACP nations.

In order to associate the Community's business and financial sectors (both public and private) with the Centre's activities, the Commission has proposed the establishment of a "Council of Economic Operators" to assist the director of the Centre. Even though the Commission and the member states share the view that the Council should be composed of people with business and financial experience and with close ties to the private sector, they have not been able to reach agreement on its exact composition. One delicate question has been to decide who should present candidates to the Committee on Industrial Co-operation for inclusion on the Council of Economic Operators. The European Investment Bank and the Commission have suggested that they themselves consult with business circles in the member states of the EC, and then the Commission would draw up a list of candidates which it would present to the Committee on Industrial Co-operation for approval. This procedure has proved to be unacceptable to the nine member states. They wish to present their own lists after having consulted with relevant business circles. However, the names proposed by the national governments would then be examined by the Community with the aid of the Commission and the European Investment Bank. The Commission fears, however, that this procedure runs the risk of politicizing a body that should essentially remain professional.

As a result of the polycentric political structure of the EC and the structure of the Lomé Convention, similar conflicts have arisen in drafting the financial and budget arrangements for the Title III institutions. The nine EC member states, by having agreed that the Centre for Industrial Development will be financed from the resources of the European Development Fund, have diluted the Centre's administrative autonomy. In addition, as originally conceived by the Commission, the director of the centre would draw up an annual budget which would be submitted to the Committee for Industrial Co-operation for approval. If approved, the director would then present the budget to the Commission which would consult with the European Development Fund (EDF) Committee according to standard procedures for allocating EDF aid. Some member states, however, would like the EDF Committee (on which the nine member state governments are represented) to review the Centre's budget proposal before the Committee for Industrial Co-operation has an opportunity to discuss it. In this way, the member governments could exert control over the draft budget before it is adopted by the Committee for Industrial Co-operation.

Substantive Responsibilities

At least two of the roles that the Centre for Industrial Development will play are derived from its responsibilities for providing information and promoting industrial cooperation. One will be that of an intermediary facilitating contacts between the ACP and EC public and private sectors.

The other will be that of transmitting information on financial, technical, and commercial matters. While this intergovernmental framework can set the context for intensifying economic contacts between the EC and the ACP states, what ultimately counts is the success that the ACP states have in attracting the EC's private sector and in securing its cooperation. This means industrial firms, financiers, brokers, suppliers of services—all of those who are able to carry out industrial projects, insure the regular transfer of technological know-how, supply the requisite technical and administrative frameworks, and guarantee the orderly marketing of products.

Consequently, as both the Commission and UNICE have emphasized, the prospects for industrial cooperation depend not only upon concessions from the Europeans, but on the readiness of the ACP states to create the practical and psychological preconditions for cooperation with the EC private sector, particularly in regard to attracting investments.[48] In this regard, the Centre can become an extremely important institution for creating an understanding of the obstacles and disincentives faced by a potential investor and for assisting the ACP states in devising policies to eliminate these hurdles. The Arbeitsgemeinschaft Entwicklungsländer has suggested that the Centre could advise the ACP states on legislation concerning investments.[49] And UNICE has proposed that the Centre—in collaboration with the EDF—could assist the ACP states in formulating development projects, expressing them as tenders, assessing them, drafting contracts, and supervising their implementation.

Finally, the Arbeitsgemeinschaft Entwicklungsländer has underscored both the possibility and necessity of the Centre aiding the ACP states to establish more efficient administrative foci in order to improve chances for more effectively attracting investments. The Belgian Federation of Industries has referred to such administrative units as *cellule d'accueil des operateurs.* These would be central bureaus for facilitating and expediting contacts between foreign investors and the various branches of the host country government as well as for promoting information and for conducting research studies. This suggestion is based on a similar unit established in the Belgian Ministry of Foreign Affairs in the early 1960s.[50]

Does Title III Have a Model Value for the New International Economic Order?

Only future developments can tell whether the Lomé Convention in general and Title III in particular can play a role in expanding industrial links and investment flows. But the continuous interregional negotiations that will occur in the Lomé framework can create a favorable political climate within which the specific economic goals of the agreement can be approached. However, the viability and meaningfulness of these interregional contacts, both on the public and private levels, depend on several factors. First, whatever possibilities for aiding the ACP states are inherent in the Convention depend upon the political stability of the ACP states. If a reasonable degree of political stability can be attained (and this is their responsibility), the next important question is whether more realistic models for development can be transmitted to the 46 Third World signatories. This includes a more differentiated perspective on the dynamics and standards of the West European political, industrial, and financial systems. UNICE and its affiliates have repeatedly emphasized the necessity of applying standards of managerial and economic efficiency to ACP industrial plans. But the severity with which European industry has advanced these views may produce a counter-reaction among the ACP states because of their fears that such standards are wedges both for undermining their sense of independence and autonomy as well as for justifying the existing distribution of industry. However, it will force them to confront the problems they face in becoming involved in a dynamic world economy. One dimension involves understanding that attracting investment means dealing with bankers and industrialists. These persons are accustomed to clarity and rapidity of decision-making, and they are interested in performance and efficiency—goals that are not at all incompatible with the industrial development plans of the ACP states. In fact, as I. William Zartman has noted, Europeans are finding increased receptivity to these standards as the generation of Third World leaders who guided their nations to independence is being replaced by a new generation interested in performance, a generation that is more pragmatic in its approach to domestic economic problems.[51]

Whether or not Title III has a model value for realizing some of the goals of the NIEO raises two fundamental questions. For those who believe that the realization of such an order depends upon maintaining Third World unity in the face of the industrialized nations, the Lomé Convention is divisive. For those who support a multilateral liberal international economic system, Lomé is an important derogation. If the Convention and Title III do have model value, this probably means accepting that a complex mixture of special relations between groups of developing states and industrialized states is necessary, even though this entails the danger of a drift toward blocs. In spite of these broad structural questions about the future of the international economic system, Title III institutions can potentially assist those developing states that are capable of sustaining industrial development plans by integrating their economies more closely into those of the EC member states, but also with their Third World neighbors.

Notes

1. United Nations General Assembly resolution 3201 (S-VI) *Declaration on the Establishment of a New International Economic Order* and General Assembly resolution 3202 (S-VI) *Programme of Action on the Establishment of a New International Economic Order,* adopted 1 May 1974. See also United Nations, General Assembly resolution 3281 (XXIX) *Charter of Economic Rights and Duties of States,* adopted 21 November 1974.
2. *The Dakar Declaration Adopted at the Conference of Developing Countries on Raw Materials, Dakar, 3-8 February 1975* (United Nations document E/AC.62/6), 15 April 1975.
3. UNIDO, *Report of the Second General Conference of the United Nations Industrial Development Organization* (A/10112), 13 June 1975. For an example of European industry's reaction to the preparations of the Lima Conference, see Union des Industries de la Communauté Européene (UNICE), *Report on the General UNIDO Conference at Lima,* mimeographed (Brussels: UNICE, 17 February 1975). For the Commission of the European Community's (CEC) report on the results of the conference, see *Deuxième conference générale de l'organisation des Nations-Unies pour le développement industriel (ONUDI). Rapport de mission de la délégation de la Commission des Communautés Européenes*, mimeographed (Brussels: CEC, 17 May 1975).
4. For the text of this resolution, see Chapter 2.
5. Henry A. Kissinger, "Global Consensus and Economic Development" (Washington, D.C.: Department of State, Bureau of Public Affairs, Press Release, 1 September 1975).
6. Ernest H. Preeg, *Economic Blocs and U.S. Foreign Policy* (Washington, D.C.: National Planning Association, 1974).
7. The 46 ACP countries consist of former dependencies of Belgium, France, and the United Kingdom in Africa, the Caribbean, and the Pacific, plus a few other African states, emphasizing the essentially African nature of the link. Specifically, they consist of the following:
   a. The nineteen countries already associated with the Community under the Yaoundé Convention: Benin, Burundi, Central African Republic, Chad, Congo, Gabon, Ivory Coast, Madagascar, Mali, Mauritania, Mauritius, Niger, Rwanda, Senegal, Somalia, United Republic of Cameroon, Upper Volta, Togo, and Zaire.
   b. Twenty-one Commonwealth countries—twelve in Africa (Botswana, Gambia, Ghana, Lesotho, Malawi, Nigeria, Sierra Leone, Swaziland, Uganda, United Republic of Tanzania, Zambia), six in the Caribbean (Bahamas, Barbados, Grenada, Guyana, Jamaica, and Trinidad and Tobago), and three in the Pacific (Fiji, Tonga, and Western Samoa).
   c. Six other African states (Equatorial Guinea, Ethiopia, Guinea, Guinea-Bissau, Liberia, and Sudan).

d. In addition, Cape Verde, Comoros, Papua New Guinea, and Sao Tomé and Principe have applied for membership. The EC is also receptive to potential applications from Mozambique and Angola.

8. The members of the Arusha Convention were Kenya, United Republic of Tanzania, and Uganda.

9. I. William Zartman, "Europe and Africa: Decolonization or Dependency," *Foreign Affairs* 54 (January 1976): 325-343.

10. See the preamble to the Convention. The entire agreement and supporting documents are published in "Lomé Dossier," a special issue of *The Courier: European Community/Africa, Caribbean, Pacific,* no. 31 (March 1975). This is a publication of the EC Commission.

11. For critical views of the Convention see "The Lomé Convention," mimeographed (London: Overseas Development Institution, Briefing Paper, October, 1975); David Wall, "The European Community's Lomé Convention: Stabex and the Third World's Aspirations," mimeographed (London: Trade Policy Research Centre, Guest Paper No. 4, 1976); and Peter Tulloch's brief commentary "The New Lomé Convention: There is Much Praise for It 'But Let Us Not Get Too Carried Away'," *Commonwealth*, April/May 1975, pp. 12-13.

12. Countries defined as least developed under article 48 of the Lomé Convention are Benin, Botswana, Burundi, Central African Republic, Chad, Ethiopia, Gambia, Guinea, Guinea-Bissau, Lesotho, Malawi, Mali, Mauritania, Niger, Rwanda, Somalia, Sudan, Swaziland, Togo, Tonga, Uganda, United Republic of Tanzania, Upper Volta, and Western Samoa.

13. For a study of the Yaoundé negotiations, see I. William Zartman, *The Weak Confront the Strong: The Politics of Trade Negotiations between Africa and the European Economic Community* (Princeton: Princeton University Press, 1971).

14. André Huybrechts, "EEC Support for Industrialization in Associated Countries," *Association News,* no. 25 (May/June 1974) pp. 42-48; Dieter Frisch, "Industrial Cooperation with Associated Countries," *Association News,* no. 26 (July/August 1974), pp. 47-50; and "Industrialization of the A.A.S.M.," *Association News,* no. 21 (September/October 1973), pp. 15-40. Also, see the series of studies prepared by the EC Commission's Directorate General for Development and Cooperation: *Preselection of Export Industries Suitable for Establishment in the AASM* (Brussels: Commission of the European Communities, Directorate-General for Development and Cooperation, 1971), summary and five annexes; *Industrialization Potential in the Associated African States and Madagascar* (Brussels: Commission of the European Communities, Directorate-General for Development and Cooperation, 1966), 16 volumes and summary; and *The Establishment of the Textile Exporting Industries in the AASM* (Brussels: Commission of the European Communities, Directorate-General for Development and Cooperation, 1975).

15. For the five point plan, see *Association News,* no. 21 (September/October

1973), p. 27.
16. "ACP Memorandum to the EC Commission," mimeographed, Communication to the Commission of the European Community, 27 March 1974.
17. ACP Group for Negotiations with the EEC, *Memorandum Presented by the ACP Ministers to the EEC on the Subject of Industrial Cooperation* (ACP/AG.89/74 (Amb) Rev. 1.), 23 July 1974.
18. Sergio Zambetti, "Developing Countries and International Subcontracting," *Association News,* no. 24 (March/April 1974), pp. 33-38.
19. For the complete text of Title III, see "Lomé Dossier."
20. For the EC Commission's proposals on industrialization and processing at the source see *Development and Raw Materials. Bulletin of the European Communities,* Supplement 6, 1975.
21. Article 35 reads as follows:

1. A Committee on Industrial Co-operation shall be established. It shall be supervised by the Committee of Ambassadors.
2. The Committee on Industrial Co-operation shall
   a. see to the implementation of this Title;
   b. examine the problems in the field of industrial co-operation submitted to it by the ACP States and/or by the Community, and suggest appropriate solutions;
   c. guide, supervise and control the activities of the Centre for Industrial Development referred to in Article 36 and report to the Committee of Ambassadors and, through it, to the Council of Ministers;
   d. submit from time to time reports and recommendations which it considers appropriate to the Committee of Ambassadors;
   e. perform such other functions as may be assigned to it by the Committee of Ambassadors.
3. The composition of the Committee on Industrial Co-operation and the details for its operation shall be determined by the Council of Ministers.

22. Article 36 reads as follows:

1. A Centre for Industrial Development shall be set up. It shall have the following functions:
   a. To gather and disseminate in the Community and the ACP States all relevant information on the conditions of and opportunities for industrial co-operation;
   b. to have, at the request of the Community and the ACP States, studies carried out on the possibilities and potential for industrial development of the ACP States, bearing in mind the necessity for adaptation of technology to their needs and requirements, and to ensure their follow-up;
   c. to organize and facilitate contacts and meetings of all kinds between Community and ACP States' industrial policy-makers, promoters, and firms and financial institutions;
   d. to provide specific industrial information and support services;

e. help to identify, on the basis of needs indicated by ACP States, the opportunities for industrial training and applied research in the Community and in the ACP States, and to provide relevant information and recommendations.

The Centre's Statutes and rules of operation shall be adopted by the Council of Ministers on a proposal from the Committee of Ambassadors upon the entry into force of this Convention.

23. Dieter Frisch, "Lima (Peru): Towards a New International Economic Order," *The Courier,* no. 33 (September/October 1975), p. 28.

24. For a discussion of the relocation of production to developing countries see Frank Walter, "A Sound Case for Relocation," *Intereconomics,* no. 12 (December 1975), pp. 366-368. For a French view see "La nouvelle politique industrielle de la France: un entretien avec Hugues de l'Estoile, Directeur General de l'Industrie," *Révue Française de Gestion,* May 1975, pp. 11-16. An interpretation of the policy directions outlined in this interview are contained in "Je redeploie, tu redeploies," *Economie,* no. 11 (April 1975), pp. 18-19. Similar views in regard to the Federal Republic of Germany are discussed in "Gut hat's, wer schon draussen ist," *Wirtschaftswoche,* no. 3 (10 January 1975), pp. 62-63.

25. For an examination of the problems of formulating and coordinating the external policies of a multistate customs union see Robert McGeehan and Steven Warnecke, "Europe's Foreign Policies: Economics, Politics or Both?," *Orbis* 17 (Winter 1974): 1251-1279.

26. This relationship is discussed in Steven J. Warnecke's introduction to *Industrial Policies in Western Europe,* eds. Steven J. Warnecke and Ezra N. Suleiman (New York: Praeger, 1975), pp. 1-19.

27. For an analysis of the EC's efforts at industrial policy see Steven J. Warnecke, "Industrial Policy and the European Community," in *Industrial Policies,* eds. Warnecke and Suleiman, pp. 155-191.

28. "Brief Observations by UNICE on the ACP Memorandum," mimeographed (Brussels: UNICE, 29 October 1974). In addition to UNICE, information was obtained directly from the following national federations which are members of UNICE: Fédération des entreprises de belgique, Industriraadet Danmark, Conseil national du patronat français, Bundesverband der Deutschen Industrie, Confederation of Irish Industries, Confederazione Generale dell' Industria Italiana, Fédération des industriels luxembourgeois, Confederation of British Industries, and Raad van Nederlandse Werkgeversverbonden.

29. Club of Seven, "La cooperation industrielle CEE-ACP: vue du secteur privé. Synthese des notes recues au sujet de la réunion du 26 Novembre 1974," mimeographed (n.p.: Club of Seven, 1974). The "Club of Seven" is composed of the following national organizations: Afrika Institut (Netherlands), Afrika Verein (Federal Republic of Germany), Association Interna-

tionale pour le développement économique et l'aide technique (France), Centre d'études et de documentation pour les investissements outre-mer (Belgium), East Africa and Mauritius Association (United Kingdom), Instituto Italo-Africano (Italy), and West Africa Committee (United Kingdom).

30. Fédération des entreprises de belgique, "Belgian Private Enterprise and Industrial Development in the Third World" (n.d., n.p.), pp. 13-14.

31. See the documents cited in footnotes 28 and 29. For the Commission's views see "Industrial Cooperation," mimeographed (Brussels: Directorate-General for Development and Cooperation, June 1975).

32. Article 38 reads as follows:

> 1. Each ACP State shall endeavor to give as clear an indication as possible of its priority areas for industrial co-operation and the form it would like such co-operation to take. It will also take such steps as are necessary to promote effective co-operation within the framework of this Title with the Community and the Member States or with firms or nationals of Member States who comply with the development programmes and priorities of the host ACP State.
>
> 2. The Community and its Member States, for their part, shall endeavor to set up measures to attract the participation of their firms and nationals in the industrial development efforts of the ACP States concerned, and shall encourage such firms and nationals to adhere to the aspirations and development objectives of those ACP States.

33. UNICE, "Brief Observations," p. 2.

34. For an analysis of how European importers have all too often derived the advantages from the EC's generalized preference system at the expense of the developing countries, see Richard N. Cooper, "The EEC Preferences: A Critical Evaluation," *Intereconomics*, no. 4 (1972), pp. 122-124.

35. Letter to the author from the Fédération des entreprises de belgique, 26 March 1976.

36. For a discussion of technological upgrading in "declining" industries in Western Europe, see Hans-Werner Staratzke, "The Textile Industry: An Unsuitable Development Primer," pp. 369-371, and Philipp Urban, "Not Much Chance for Developing Countries in the Shoe Industry," pp. 371-372, both in *Intereconomics,* no. 12 (December 1975). Although both articles do describe the positive impact of the introduction of new technologies in the European textile and shoe sectors, the authors are, respectively, officials of the West German textile and shoe associations. Moreover, the Commission, as a result of its structure, is pursuing contradictory policies in regard to industrial cooperation with the developing world. On the one hand, the Directorate-General for Development and Cooperation has identified the shoe industry as one which should be expanded in the Third World and contracted in the EC. On the other hand, the Directorate-General for Industrial Policy has made proposals for further upgrading the EC's shoe

sector. See "Geld für neue Schuhe," *Die Zeit,* no. 52 (26 December 1975), p. 16.

37. For a survey of these problems see Ian Little et al., *Industry and Trade in some Developing Countries: A Comparative Study* (London: Oxford University Press, 1970).

38. Charles P. Kindleberger develops this point in *Foreign Trade and the National Economy* (New Haven: Yale University Press, 1962), pp. 8-25.

39. "ACPs: Success Story," *The Economist*, 27 December 1975.

40. Peter Tulloch, *The Politics of Preferences* (London: Croom Helm, 1975). See also Chapter 12 above.

41. "Cheysson Stresses Importance of Maghreb Pacts. Sums up ACP State of Play," *European Report,* no. 292 (14 January 1976), external relations section, p. 2.

42. "ACP Council of Ministers Meets in Georgetown," *The Courier,* no. 33 (September/October 1975), p. 14.

43. See "Industrial Cooperation," pp. 2-3, document cited in footnote 31.

44. "The Centre for Industrial Development," mimeographed (Brussels: UNICE, 20 February 1976).

45. Cited in *European Report,* no. 311, (17 March 1976), business brief section, p. 6.

46. Arbeitsgemeinschaft Entwicklungsländer, "Überlegungen der Wirtschaft zur Errichtung des Zentrums für industrielle Entwicklung," mimeographed (Cologne: Arbeitsgemeinschaft Entwicklungsländer, 1 January 1976).

47. The discussion of the structure of Title III institutions is based on articles in the 17, 20, and 27 March 1976 issues of *European Report.*

48. Arbeitsgemeinschaft Entwicklungsländer, "Überlegungen der Wirtschaft"; Commission of the European Community, "Industrial Cooperation"; and UNICE, "Brief Observations."

49. Arbeitsgemeinschaft Entwicklungsländer, "Überlegungen der Wirtschaft."

50. Letter to the author from the Fédération des entreprises de belgique, 26 March 1976.

51. Zartman, "Europe and Africa," pp. 338-39.

22 *Controlling Transnational Enterprises: A Review and Some Further Thoughts*

Karl P. Sauvant

Transnational enterprises (TNEs) occupy a central position in all major areas of the New International Economic Order (NIEO): trade, financial resources for development, technology, industrialization, and agriculture. It is, therefore, important for the restructuring of the international economic system to find mechanisms through which TNEs are appropriately integrated into the new order. These mechanisms have to ensure that TNEs, in the pursuit of their activities in the interest of the corporate good, also serve the public good to the largest extent possible. The essence of this mechanism is, therefore, control—control of the activities of the TNEs in the interest of the public good.

In this chapter, I shall review approaches pursued by the most important institutions interested in such control: host governments—their strategies at the national, regional, and international levels—and labor unions. In distinction to these approaches which almost exclusively rely on external frameworks for constraining and directing TNE activities, the final section examines the possibility of establishing Host Country Councils at the seat of TNE headquarters. Through these councils, host countries would gain immediate influence on the decision-making of the main enterprises operating in their territories. First, however, a few introductory observations are necessary on why the question of controlling TNEs has become an important issue and for what specific purposes control should be exercised.

This chapter incorporates most of the observations made in the introduction to Part III of *Controlling Multinational Enterprises: Problems, Strategies, Counterstrategies,* ed. Karl P. Sauvant and Farid G. Lavipour (Boulder, Colo.: Westview Press, 1976). The views expressed here do not necessarily reflect those of the United Nations Centre on Transnational Corporations with whom the author is currently affiliated.

The Need for Control

TNEs have come to play a crucial role in the international economic system. In the international delivery of goods to market economies, the aggregate production by foreign affiliates has already become more important than aggregate exports; in the case of some major countries (e.g., the United Kingdom and the United States), the value of foreign production is actually several times higher than that of exports. A substantial part of world trade itself consists of intracompany transactions, i.e., is channeled through the transnational network of TNEs. This is particularly the case in natural resources industries (industries of vital importance to most developing countries) where, as a rule, a very limited number of enterprises manage most transactions and usually keep them within their transnational corporate system—from prospecting to distribution. Obviously, this situation provides TNEs with great opportunities to influence, through income allocation mechanisms, the distribution of benefits associated with trade.

The internationalization of production has been accompanied, quite naturally, by an internationalization of service industries. For example, the financing of international trade, as well as the promotion of its goods, is controlled by transnational institutions in the respective industries. These institutions allocate, on an international level, private financial resources, as well as consumption patterns and the social values and behavioral models reflected by them.

Similarly, since in market economies large enterprises—most of them transnational in nature—account for most R&D expenditures, TNEs contribute in an important way to the international allocation of scientific and technological capacities and associated benefits. As available data indicate, TNEs almost exclusively allocate these values to their home countries. Host countries benefit from them to the extent (and under the conditions) to which technology is made available to them through transfer of technology processes.

Finally, in the area of industry and agriculture, the internationalization of production has brought a growing share of the domestic sector of host countries' economies under the influence of TNEs. In this situation, headquarters' centralized transnational allocation of production according to its type (e.g., high-technology vs. low-technology; mining vs. fabrication) determines the production stage at a which foreign affiliates are integrated into the intra-firm division of labor. In developing countries in particular, where foreign capital is often of considerable importance, the aggregation of these decisions by all TNEs operating in a given economy may constitute a crucial parameter for determining the development path of the country in question.[1]

I do not intend here to document in detail the dimensions of international business in the areas just outlined. For such a documentation and discussion the reader is referred to the expanding literature and research on TNEs.[2] But I should like to draw attention to one particularly important characteristic of international business: its concentration.[3]

At the end of the 1960s, over 10,000 enterprises had an estimated 70,000 foreign affiliates, representing a book value of approximately $165 billion. However, about half of this book value is accounted for by only about 150 enterprises. Most of them are headquartered in only five countries—the U.S., followed by the United Kingdom, the Federal Republic of Germany, France, and Switzerland—who together originate about four-fifths of total international direct investment. Virtually all TNEs are owned and controlled almost exclusively by home-country nationals. Furthermore, the distribution of book value and foreign affiliates across developing countries closely reflects historical interests. As a result, one home country alone supplies at least 75 percent of the stock of foreign direct investment in about half of the developing countries and over 50 percent in about four-fifths of them. The magnitude of international business is, thus, further amplified by the characteristics of its ownership, control, and geographical distribution.

Given the importance and characteristics of TNEs, their activities have profound—both short- and long-term—economic, social, and political effects on host countries, home countries, and the international system. Again, the reader is referred to the extensive literature and research on TNEs for a documentation of this impact. The short-term effects mostly involve the division of the immediate benefits associated with the activities of these enterprises. The long-term effects involve the stage at which host economies are integrated into the international division of labor, changes in the social fabric of host societies and their value systems, and the position of host countries in the international system. As to the international division of labor, the patterns described in the previous paragraph reflect, of course, the uneven global distribution of the major factors and conditions of production. The availability of capital, skills, governmental support for R&D, large and sophisticated markets, and various external economies, in conjunction with a safe and predictable investment climate, largely explains why more advanced, valuable, and sophisticated aspects of the production process are clustered in a few countries. But the structure of the international economic system not only *reflects* the uneven distribution of the major factors and conditions of production, it also *reproduces* it—in part, at least, because of the operations of TNEs. An enterprise, like any institution based on the principle of profitability, cannot afford to act *counter* to a particular distribution of factors and conditions; it has to work with it.[4] This holds true of operating within, as well as across, national borders. However, while in the former case any undesirable consequences, especially regional imbalances, can be rectified by the national government, no equivalent remedial institution or mechanism exists at the international level. In the absence of any corrective intervention, then, TNEs will tend to perpetuate existing inequalities.[5]

The transnational allocative power of TNEs, on the basis of its magnitude and its effect, has made these enterprises important international political actors in a very traditional sense: they determine who gets what, when, and how. At the same time, this power has created a number of concerns. Many host countries—frequently competing with each other—are in a weak bargaining position vis-à-vis enterprises (especially in manufacturing) able to choose among a multitude of investment sites or investment-expansion possibilities. This is particularly true for developing countries who are often regarded as representing a poor investment risk. As a result, the power of host countries to influence the allocative decisions of TNEs—decisions that are important for the development of their economies—is limited.

Closely related to the problem of influencing allocative decisions of TNEs is the question of the purpose these allocations are meant to serve once they have been made. While host countries perceive them as serving primarily their national economic and (aggregate) welfare objectives, TNEs perceive them, quite naturally, as serving primarily their global corporate objectives. Although these objectives may, and to a considerable extent do, overlap, the degree and nature of this overlap and the benefits associated with it (where these benefits are not merely accidental) are a function of the bargaining power of both sides as well as of their capacity to implement and supervise agreements concluded between them.[6]

It is not surprising, then, that efforts are increasingly being made to develop and use mechanisms that permit the supervision of allocative decisions of TNEs and that are capable of preventing or correcting undesirable effects resulting from them. More concretely, the objectives of these efforts at controlling TNEs are threefold. The first is to ensure that host countries (and especially developing ones) obtain an equitable share of the benefits associated with the activities of TNEs. The second is to influence, if not to channel, the activities of TNEs into desired directions. The third, finally, is to restore the accountability of these enterprises. The last objective is a very fundamental one. It is based on the recognition that the internationalization of production has increased the "option space" of TNEs.[7] Consequently, their autonomy concerning public policies has increased and, conversely, their accountability to the institutions of public policy has decreased. This is especially the case for host countries, but increasingly also for home countries.[8] Controlling TNEs, therefore, also aims at restoring the accountability of these enterprises.[9]

Although attempts to control TNEs can be pursued at various levels, the best solution is one in which the domain of the means of control is as wide as the domain of TNEs, i.e., global. If such an approach is not feasible, a second-best solution is groupings of a limited number of countries—either on a regional basis (e.g., the European Community (EC) or the Andean Common Market) or on a producers' basis (e.g., the Organization of Petroleum Exporting Countries (OPEC)). A third-best solution would be actions by individual host countries. Apart from host countries, another major political counterweight is the labor union movement, operating essentially at the same three levels. In principle, the smaller the domain governed by a control institution, the wider the choices for TNEs and the greater their bargaining power. Moreover, in the absence of a global approach, host governments attempting to regulate TNEs, either individually or in collaboration with others, have to be careful in striking an acceptable balance between what they have to offer to international business and the severity of their restrictions. Too unfavorable a balance may just lead to a decrease in investment inflows; in the case of capital-exporting countries, retaliatory measures may result.

National Approaches

Policies to control foreign investment are difficult to formulate and to implement.[10] This is particularly true of policies directed at long-term effects of TNEs. To arrest a further ossification of current inequalities in the structures of the international economic system and, especially, to eventually rectify them, requires a long-term perspective and a determined policy. Such long-term objectives are best served by a development plan that indicates what sector and industry is to be developed, and where and what inputs by TNEs are desirable or necessary. A long-term perspective is of crucial importance, since, without it, decisions concerning the relevance of particular foreign direct investment projects tend to be made on an ad hoc basis, aimed at best at increasing immediate benefits. The implementation of such a development plan, in turn, requires determination on the part of national decision makers to refuse authorization of projects that threaten to siphon off scarce resources into nonpriority industries and that may launch or keep the country on an undesirable development path.

A precondition for a clear policy is the establishment of a central institution in the host country solely responsible for foreign direct investment matters. (Otherwise, several institutions, each with different interests, may work at cross-purposes or compete with each other.) The increasing stress on the establishment of (frequently interministerial) investment boards, or similar bodies, in countries in which foreign direct investment plays an important role appears to indicate that this necessity is being recognized. Often, these bodies receive the applications for investment projects and are responsible for their screening, authorization (including eligibility for incentives), administration, and supervision.[11]

Although most countries do not possess detailed long-term economic plans, many of them have exercised at least a minimum of strategic selectivity by specifying key sectors which, in their opinion, are vital to the economy and its development and, therefore, should remain closed or restricted to foreign capital. Most countries, for example, protect their financial institutions (especially banks and insurance companies) and their communication industries. The former are crucial instruments for the implementation of governmental economic policy, and the latter are important agents for influencing host countries' sociocultural systems and especially the allegiances of their citizens. Restrictions in the transportation sector, including shipping, probably originate in military considerations, while the increasing limitations on real estate and property acquisitions are probably based largely on emotional grounds. Finally, very important in this key sector approach is the protection of natural resources. While some of the developed market economies that are traditional raw material suppliers—such as Sweden and Norway—have long accorded a special status to their natural resource industries, developing countries, for whom these resources are often of central importance, are only now beginning to move in the same direction. A number of countries, moreover, have restricted foreign direct investment in selective manufacturing industries, especially when these are defense-related. Developing countries are also increasingly embarking on a policy directed toward the indigenization of their wholesale and retail trade.

It should be noted, however, that in all these cases the policy regarding TNE activities is selective-restrictive rather than selective-channelling. In other words, foreign direct investment is kept out of certain sectors as opposed to being deliberately channelled—with proper safeguards and continuous supervision—into particular industries or projects that are given priority by host governments within the framework of a comprehensive plan. Only a few governments, among them those in socialist countries, appear to be using the selective-channelling approach to any appreciable extent. While other governments are moving in this direction by actively courting foreign partners for specific projects or industries (or by designating "eligible industries"), these activities are often carried through on an ad hoc basis and not necessarily within the framework of a larger plan and a longer perspective.

Of course, a number of policies between those that are selective-restrictive and those that are selective-channelling can be pursued to influence TNE behavior in an attempt to increase the benefits for host countries.[12] Entry criteria can be formulated to assess the desirability of any particular project,[13] and incentives may be offered in the hope of attracting desirable investment.[14] Regulatory provisions are being made by many host countries regarding export and R&D performance, local employment and training requirements, ownership and managerial control, takeovers,[15] financial transactions (e.g., repatriation of capital, profits, and fees), transfer of technology, terms of licensing agreements, domestic borrowing, etc. The government itself can employ certain policies (notably those relating to procurement of goods and services, grant and loan programs, and taxation) in a selective manner—that is, in such a way as to favor, if appropriate, domestic enterprises over foreign ones.[16]

The ambiguities of the criteria to be applied in most of these approaches provide governments, in principle, with a considerable latitude within which they can regulate the amount, type, and direction of foreign direct investment. A combination of well-defined entry selection criteria (based on the requirements of a long-term economic plan), a sophisticated central screening machinery (determining the desirability of each major project), and continuous review of the performance of foreign affiliates (according to well-defined standards) potentially constitutes a powerful set of instruments in the hands of host-country governments resolved to channel TNE activities in appropriate directions and to increase their share of the benefits associated with them.

In general, however, and with the notable exception of the socialist countries, such an integrated approach has rarely been adopted and, more important, implemented and enforced. Developed countries, as a rule, have been reluctant to adopt any specific laws and regulations dealing with foreign direct investment. On the contrary, the liberalization of international capital movements and current invisible operations, coupled with nondiscriminatory treatment of domestic and foreign enterprises, has been their dominant approach to foreign direct investment.[17] As far as regulatory measures are taken, this is usually done in the context of the administration of exchange control laws or through a key sector approach.

In the case of developing countries, the pattern is mixed (see table 1). According to a United Nations (UN) study:

> One general pattern, which prevails in most African and certain Asian countries as well as the CACM [Central African Common Market], is characterized by relatively few regulations and restrictions and a greater number of incentives. Formal investment legislation applies without discrimination as to the nationality of the investor. While there are indigenization policies as regards management and the labour force, these are often not mandatory. Screening is required in connexion with the award of incentives, but is seldom a prerequisite for the approval of foreign investment as such. Few foreign ownership ceilings are in effect and relatively few sectors are

Table 1. Patterns of foreign direct investment regulation in selected developing countries

Parameter	Pattern 1 (mostly Asia - excluding India - Africa, CACM)	Pattern 2 (mostly Middle East, North Africa)	Pattern 3 (mostly South America)
Administration	Case-by-case screening largely restricted to award of <u>incentives</u> (nondiscriminatory)	Case-by-case screening at establishment (degree of discrimination varies)	Separate administration for foreign investment. Screening at establishment
Investment screening criteria	Emphasis on functional contributions of investment. Little indication of extensive cost/benefit analysis. Screening largely for award of incentives	Emphasis on functional contributions and conditions of investment. Little indication of extensive cost/benefit analysis	Criteria formulated for cost/benefit analysis, often extensive. Includes social cost criteria in some cases
Ownership	Few requirements. Few sectors closed to foreign investment	Joint ventures prevalent	Strict regulations on ownership and investment (except Brazil). A large number of closed sectors
Finance	Few repatriation limitations	Few repatriation limitations	Repatriation ceilings in most areas (except Mexico). Screening of foreign loans. Special control of payments to parent company
Employment and training	Announced indigenization policies but little headway in practice	Local quotas for work force. Few local quotas for management	Specific across-the-board indigenization requirements
Technology transfer	No controls	No controls	Screening and registration of all technology imported
Investment incentives	Long-term tax incentives for establishment	Establishment incentives limited to five years - in most cases non-renewable	Incentives tied to specific contributions, but incentives may be curtailed for foreign-owned firms
International dispute settlement	Adherence to international dispute regulations. Regional investment regulation: UDEAC, OCAM, EAC, OAMP	Same as pattern 1. Regional investment regulation: Arab Economic Union	Local adjudication and regional harmonization of investment regulation: ANCOM, CACM

Source: Taken from United Nations, Secretariat, <u>National Legislation</u>, pp. 21-22.

> closed to foreign investment. Most countries in this group accept international dispute settlement procedures. Often they have bilateral agreements with capital exporting countries that provide further protection against discrimination and prescribe procedures for compensation in the case of nationalization.[18]

The Arab countries (see table 1, pattern 2) largely exhibit a similar approach, although they have introduced a number of more regulatory provisions. For instance, local participation quotas are frequently mandatory (especially with respect to the petroleum industry), incentives are less generous, and capital and profit repatriation ceilings, as well as employment and training requirements, are specified. A number of countries—like Egypt and the Syrian Arab Republic—permit foreign direct investment only in a limited number of eligible industries.

Finally, the least permissive approach among developing countries is pursued by South American states (see table 1, pattern 3). Most of these countries submit foreign direct investment projects (including their technology contribution) to screening, are less generous with incentives, have strict regulations for financial transactions, strongly encourage local managerial control, and insist on exclusive local jurisdiction in the case of investment disputes.

Thus, while a wide array of instruments is available to direct and regulate the activities of TNEs, host countries have rarely exhausted them. In the case of the developing countries, the key reason is often the lack of administrative capabilities. Virtually all of the measures reviewed above require a relatively sophisticated apparatus capable of formulating, implementing, and overseeing an intricate array of criteria, rules and provisions—all this vis-à-vis organizations with access to worldwide resources and talent. It is exactly this capability which the developing countries, in particular, do not possess. Except in the case of projects that have attracted special government attention, developing countries are usually incapable of dealing effectively with TNEs with respect both to the short-term as well as the long-term consequences of their activities.

A united approach, on the other hand, whether based on territorial contiguity or product identity, appears to be more effective in dealing with a number of problems inherent in most individual attempts to regulate foreign direct investment: most importantly, it reduces or eliminates costly incentive competition; it pools resources available for dealing with TNEs; and, as a consequence, it increases the bargaining power of each individual party to the common agreement.

Regional and Producers' Groupings

Regional Groupings

Coordinated policy is of special relevance in a common market where the absence of national administrative limitations on the flow of goods and factors eliminates one important locational determinant and thereby punishes more restrictive member countries.[19] France learned this when, during a relatively restrictive period of French policy vis-à-vis foreign direct investment, TNEs tended to establish themselves elsewhere in the EC. It is, therefore, hardly surprising that France was (and is) one of those members of the EC most interested in a common (regional) approach to non-Western European TNEs.

The EC has dealt with questions related to TNEs for some time. The Community's main objective has been "to stimulate European firms to greater efficiency and competitiveness, and to encourage a[n] EEC-wide perspective in their ownership, financing, research, production, and distribution."[20] This has been done partly to promote economic integration and partly to encourage the development of strong Western European industries, competitive on a global level. To this purpose, several harmonizing measures have been taken,[21] including, in 1972-73, a limitation of national incentives offered to any enterprise—whether foreign or domestic.[22]

Finally, in November 1973, a comprehensive communication was submitted to the Council of Ministers of the EC, recommending various measures aimed at controlling TNEs operating inside the EC. This attempt to actively limit "the growing hold of multinational undertakings on the economic, social and even political life of the countries in which they operate" is based on the belief that "it will be impossible to find solutions and allay anxieties in this area unless suitable counterweights are introduced at Community and international level[s] so as to re-establish the conditions for a balance between the parties concerned." It is the first endeavour by a group of developed market economies to establish, at the supranational level, a "suitable legal framework" aimed at guarding the member countries against harmful effects by counterbalancing the power of large enterprises, irrespective of whether they are foreign- or community-controlled.[23]

Specifically, the commission recommended action in seven areas: (1) protection of the general public, with special attention to taxes, TNE-related capital movements and investment incentives; (2) protection of workers (particularly noteworthy is the fact that "the Commission considers the setting up of a trade union counterweight as essential for a balanced solution" to the problems of TNEs[24]); (3) possible restrictions of competition and the abuse of dominant market positions; (4) rules governing acquisitions; (5) harmonization of policies regarding TNEs among Organisation for Economic Co-operation and Development (OECD) countries; (6) conditions of establishment of TNEs in developing countries; and, finally, (7) information about TNE activities.[25]

The implementation of this program, as the Commission document observes, will take several years. So far, hardly any progress has been made. However, it represents an important first step, since it contributes to the identification by an official body of some of the problems connected with TNEs, recognizes that the most effective control strategies have to be pursued on at least the regional level,[26] and, finally, outlines a concrete action program.

While the EC is still considering what steps to take next, another regional group, the Andean Common Market (ANCOM), is already implementing a comprehensive Foreign Investment Code.[27] Decision 24 of the Junta del Acuerdo de Cartagena, as amended, epitomizes Latin America's continued dissatisfaction with foreign direct investment. In its comprehensiveness, detail, and relevance it "may represent the most concrete resolution of the foreign investment problem possible in Latin America today, and perhaps even the truest consensus of the entire Third World."[28] Indeed, the Code deserves special attention, since it combines concern with many of the immediate consequences of TNE activities with an attempt to integrate foreign direct investment into a comprehensive, long-term, developmental-emancipatory framework designed to build a strong and independent regional economy.[29]

As far as ANCOM's economic framework is concerned, its core is a Sectoral Program for Industrial Development. Under this scheme, the production of commodities for which economies of scale are important is assigned to specific countries. Trade is liberalized in such a way as to favor, for a period of years, the assigned country. Similarly, no foreign direct investment will be authorized for a considerable period of time by other members in the nonassigned industries.[30] With this emphasis on development planning, a strong element of selectivity and channelling of foreign resources is introduced which encourages specialization, reduces inefficient duplication, and avoids competing incentives for foreign direct investment. At the same time, the possibilities of economies of scale may be a special attraction to foreign investors.

To ensure that foreign direct investment has, in fact, a developmental-emancipatory effect, and that the immediate benefits accruing to the host economy are as favorable as possible, complete control over the activities of foreign affiliates was thought to be necessary. Decision 24, the Andean

Foreign Investment Code, was adopted with these objectives in mind. Its basic assumption is that (1) foreign capital and technology have to be acquired selectively; (2) that these inputs only become fully effective if they are eventually domestically controlled; and (3) that considerable information is required, on the one hand, to make proper choices regarding what, when, and under what conditions foreign direct investment is to be admitted and, on the other, to avoid irregularities by existing foreign affiliates. A number of provisions of the Code are designated to implement these objectives.

Under the Code, certain sectors, in principle, are excluded from foreign direct investment: public utilities, financial institutions, media, advertising, and transportation. Each member, however, is free to determine additional industries. In extractive industries, TNEs can operate under a system of concessions. In the remaining sectors, foreign investors have to submit applications for each new investment (and reinvestment), containing detailed information on various aspects of the project. No approval is given in areas where the members of ANCOM are adequately serviced by existing enterprises. Authorization is granted if the project "meets the development priorities of the receiving country" (Article 2). Acquisitions are not allowed, except in cases of bankruptcy. To avoid draining the national capital market, no domestic long-term credits are permitted to foreign affiliates. In addition, interest rates paid for foreign credits, as well as the remittance of earnings, require authorization. Similarly, any contract regarding the import of technology or the use of patents and trademarks has to be submitted for approval and is reviewed for its "effective contribution" (Article 18). The protection and development of regional technology is encouraged.[31] Restrictive business practices, particularly as embodied in technology transfer agreements, are prohibited.

In order to maximize benefits and diffuse foreign inputs throughout the economy, all new investment projects must contain a plan to "fade out" gradually to a maximum foreign ownership of 49 percent during a period not exceeding 15 years in the more advanced countries of Chile, Columbia, Peru and Venezuela, and 20 years in the case of Bolivia and Ecuador. Similarly, existing foreign affiliates have to commit themselves to divestment if they desire to take advantage of the subregional duty-free trade.

Finally, the individual national agencies that administer and register foreign direct investment also supervise the foreign investors' compliance to the obligations undertaken. They are charged with establishing an information-and-control system regarding the major activities of foreign affiliates, including transfer pricing and restrictive business practices. The national agencies are aided in their task by the Junta and the Secretariat of the Acuerdo de Cartagena which are empowered to supervise the implementation of and compliance with the Code. The Secretariat is also requested to centralize and disseminate information on questions related to foreign direct investment and the transfer of technology.

The Code is in force to varying degrees in all ANCOM member countries. Of course, it still has to pass the test of time. But it has already been acknowledged that ANCOM has increased the negotiating strength of all countries involved[32]—an objective expressly stated in the preamble of the code. Moreover, the comprehensiveness and the detail with which the various problems have been dealt with may well help and inspire other countries, or groups of countries, to move in a similar direction. Harvey W. Wallender III, vice president of the Council of the Americas, felt that such a demonstration effect is probably the most important consequence of ANCOM.[33] Over 20 countries have already accredited observers to the group.[34] In fact, developed market economies may well be able to learn from the Latin American experience—the EC has established a special committee to study ANCOM and it might, in due course, take a close look at Decision 24.

Apart from EC and ANCOM, a number of other regional groupings promote, as one of their objectives, the harmonization of foreign direct investment legislations and regulations. Among them are, for instance, the African and Malagasy Common Organization, the Arab Economic Union, the Association of South-East Asian Nations, the Caribbean Community, the Central African Customs and Economic Union, the Central American Common Market, and the East African Community. In most of these groupings, however, hardly any progress has been made to achieve the objective of harmonization. Furthermore, no grouping exists for the sole purpose of controlling TNEs or aspects of their activities.

Regional groupings may represent an effective overall approach to controlling the activities of TNEs. Indeed, they may be the only possible approach in response to manufacturing TNEs. The effectiveness of such groupings probably depends most on the the extent to which markets can be made available or withheld; important markets—like the EC or, increasingly, the centrally planned economies—probably can afford greater restrictions than a grouping such as ANCOM. Although the experience with regional groupings so far has only been as part of a more comprehensive regional integration effort, it is not inconceivable that common regional policies will be formulated and implemented in the future specifically for the purpose of controlling TNEs.

Producers' Groupings

As far as raw materials are concerned, an alternative approach to controlling TNEs, and especially to increasing the host countries' share in the benefits associated with their activities, is the organization of suppliers.

Clearly, producers' groupings have broader functions than controlling TNEs: generally speaking, they are instruments to increase the benefits that can be reaped from raw materials exported by the members of a grouping. However, since TNEs have traditionally been the exploiters of many of these raw materials, since even after a series of recent nationalizations they often play (as observed below) the role of a "tax collector" for exporters, and since many producers' associations have their genesis in the assertiveness of host countries vis-à-vis TNEs, producers' associations are also important instruments for controlling TNEs. As such, they represent an attempt to increase the bargaining power of exporters by pursuing a common policy vis-à-vis the enterprises that exploit the raw materials in question. At the same time, this approach decreases the possibilities for enterprises to defect into alternative geographic locations or to play off exporter countries against each other. It is from this perspective that producers' groupings are discussed in this section.[35]

The prototype of a producers' association is, of course, OPEC. The experience of the oil exporting countries exemplifies how the major issues surrounding foreign direct investment in general, and natural resource ventures in particular, progressively became the subject of negotiations and actions. Successively, and with each step drawing closer to the heart of the relationship between the foreign investor and the host country, attention focused on issues involving (1) the division of total net revenues from the operations of transnational enterprises in the host country; (2) control of the factors affecting revenue (notably prices and output); (3) control over the foreign affiliates themselves; and (4) the role of foreign affiliates in long-term domestic development.[36] Since this pattern might well be repeated by other product groups, it is appropriate briefly to trace OPEC's development.

OPEC, like most commodity agreements, began as an attempt to deal with price fluctuations or, more precisely, to restore prices that had unilaterally been cut by the major transnational oil companies.[37] Although price restoration was the key issue of OPEC's first conference in 1960, this demand was quietly dropped when formal negotiations began a few years later. Attention focused entirely on obtaining more favorable provisions regarding the treatment of marketing and royalty expenses. The royalty question took two years to settle. Four years later, in 1968, certain amendments were made which raised the oil exporting countries' revenues by less than $25 million.[38] The whole decade of the 1960s, in other words, was spent on negotiating minor improvements in the division of revenues.

OPEC did not deal with prices again until late in 1970. Suffice it to say that due to a combination of factors—most important among them the willingness of major members of OPEC to take concrete and concerted actions in the event that negotiations should fail[39]—the price question was settled, beginning with the February 1971 agreement in Tehran, in a manner highly favorable to the oil exporting countries.[40] Since then, oil prices have increased further and were nearly five times as high in 1974 as in 1970. As a result of these changes, the oil exporting countries' revenues in 1974 rose by more than $80 billion over the 1970 level.

Aware of their bargaining strength, the oil exporting countries also took steps to gain control over the amount of crude produced by the oil companies, either by setting minimum production rates with fines in the case of noncompliance (e.g., Venezuela) or by assuming majority ownership of production facilities. The change in ownership patterns is particularly striking. While in 1970 hardly any crude oil production facilities in OPEC countries had been domestically controlled, foreign majority-ownership was the exception rather than the rule by the end of 1974 (see table 2).[41] In the words of one observer, the transnational oil enterprises had become the "tax collecting agency" of the exporting countries.[42]

Finally, a number of oil exporting countries also used a sizeable share of their revenues and their bargaining power to advance large-scale industrialization programs, which included convincing oil enterprises to locate more advanced processing stages on their territory.

Although the bargaining power of OPEC is probably unique,[43] even a cautious observer like Stephen D. Krasner noted, however, that "the basic market prerequisites for oligopoly behavior are present for many other raw materials. . . ."[44] Of course, the existence of these prerequisites alone does not necessarily mean that alliances will, in fact, be formed. But there are a number of reasons for expecting that new (or renewed) efforts will be forthcoming. For one, host countries have become increasingly aware that the exploitation of their natural resources through TNEs is frequently conducted in a manner not fully responsive to their needs—both in terms of distribution of immediate benefits as well as in terms of the developmental effect on the host economy. Second, OPEC's success had added considerably to the foreign exchange expenditures of non-oil-producing developing countries, resulting in a current account balance of payments deficit for them of $28 billion in 1974 and $35 billion in 1975 (as compared to $9 billion in 1973). As a result, non-oil-producing developing countries have to make every effort to increase their export earnings in order to cover their increased foreign exchange needs; and one (if not the only) way is to collude in order to increase the price of their (mainly raw material) exports. In this context, OPEC's success, and the absence of strong retaliatory responses on the part of TNEs and consuming countries, should have, and has had, a seductive demonstration effect on other raw material exporters. In addition, it is not inconceivable that the oil exporting countries will actively support the creation of other producers' associations,[45] for instance, in the context of the nonaligned movement.

Finally, and this may well be the most important factor, the developing countries have become much more assertive and organized. Their assertiveness expressed itself, for instance, during the Sixth (1974) and Seventh (1975) Special Sessions of the UN General Assembly, in the adoption of the Charter of Economic Rights and Duties of States by the regular Twenty-ninth UN General Assembly (1974), and in the various international economic conferences that have taken place since 1974. Their organization occurred mainly through the Group of 77 and, since the beginning of the 1970s, in the framework of the nonaligned movement.[46] In the context of the nonaligned movement, developing countries also expressly supported and encouraged the formation of producers' association[47]—an approach that also found its way into such documents as the resolutions adopted at the Sixth Special Session and the Charter of Economic Rights and Duties of States. The Non-Aligned Countries further decided, at the Fifth Conference of Ministers for Foreign Affairs of Non-Aligned Countries, to establish a Council of Associations of Developing Countries Producers-Exporters of Raw Materials and to create a Special Fund for the Financing of Buffer Stocks of Raw Materials and Primary Products Exported by the Developing Countries.[48] Table 3 shows which producers' associations have been proposed for initial membership in the council; it also indicates for these associations their individual country membership. It should be noted that multiple membership (including of important OPEC countries) is quite frequent—a situation that facilitates coordination among producers' associations and thus facilitates the functioning of the Council. If these institutions should become effective coordinating bodies, the various producers' associations could become important instruments for exercising control over transnational raw material enterprises and for achieving improvements in the economic situation of developing countries.

In fact, the years 1974 and 1975 saw a number of efforts aimed at activating and strengthening producers' associations. For instance, exporters of bauxite, copper, iron ore, bananas, coffee, mercury, natural rubber, and phosphate, made (or renewed) attempts—blessed with mixed success—at improving their bargaining positions. The exporters of the first three of these commodities were particularly active.[49] Among them, the major bauxite exporting countries (which had agreed, in March 1974, to establish the International Bauxite Association) were especially successful in substantially increasing their share in the benefits associated with transnational mining on their territory. Less successful were the copper exporters (organized in CIPEC) whose efforts to prevent a price decline of their commodity through the introduction of a quota system on exports failed in the face of the depressed economic situation in major consumer countries;

Table 2. Ownership patterns in the petroleum industry in OPEC countries, 1970 and mid-1974 (percentage)

Country and company	Share in country's crude oil production		Equity							
			Major international							
			British Petroleum		Compagnie française des pétrôles		Exxon		Gulf	
	1970	1972	1970	1974	1970	1974	1970	1974	1970	1974
ALGERIA										
Sonatrach	22.4	76.9	-	-	-	-	-	-	-	-
Total Algérie)	77.2	13.6	-	-	-	49.00	-	-	-	-
Elf Algérie)		9.1	-	-	-	-	-	-	-	-
Getty	0.4	0.4	-	-	-	-	-	-	-	-
ECUADOR										
Texaco/Gulf	-	96.2	-	-	-	-	-	-	50.00	50.00 a/
Anglo Ecuadorian	-	2.5	-	-	-	-	-	-	-	-
CEPE	-	1.3	-	-	-	-	-	-	-	-
Cautivo	-	-	-	-	-	-	-	-	-	-
Adobe	-	-	-	-	-	-	-	-	-	-
INDONESIA										
Caltex	82.8	77.0	-	-	-	-	-	-	-	-
Pertamina	11.4	16.0	-	-	-	-	-	-	-	-
Stanvac	5.6	6.9	-	-	-	-	50.00	50.00	-	-
Pusdiklap	0.1	0.1	-	-	-	-	-	-	-	-
Calasiatic	-	-	-	-	-	-	-	-	-	-
IRAN										
Iranian Oil Participants b/	91.4	90.4	40.00	-	6.00	-	7.00	-	7.00	-
LAPCO	3.7	3.3	-	-	-	-	-	-	-	-
IPAC	2.4	2.7	-	-	-	-	-	-	-	-
IMINOCO	1.3	1.6	-	-	-	-	-	-	-	-
SIRIP	0.8	1.7	-	-	-	-	-	-	-	-
NIOC	0.3	0.3	-	-	-	-	-	-	-	-
IRAQ c/										
IPC	75.7	50.4	23.75	-	23.75	-	11.88	-	-	-
BPC	22.6	44.6	23.75	23.75	23.75	23.75	11.88	-	-	-
MPC	1.7	1.6	23.75	-	23.75	-	11.88	-	-	-
INOC	-	3.4	-	-	-	-	-	-	-	-
KUWAIT										
KOC	91.5	91.3	50.00	20.00	-	-	-	-	50.00	20.00
AOC	5.8	6.2	-	-	-	-	-	-	-	-
Aminoil	2.7	2.4	-	-	-	-	-	-	-	-
LIBYA										
Oasis	28.5	35.6	-	-	-	-	-	-	-	-
Occidental	20.0	18.9	-	-	-	-	-	-	-	-
Esso Standard	17.2	11.7	-	-	-	-	100.00	49.00	-	-
Arabian Gulf Explo. Co.	12.5	9.5	50.00	d/	-	-	-	-	-	-
Amoseas	9.7	10.4	-	-	-	-	-	-	-	-
Mobil/Gelsenb.	7.6	7.3	-	-	-	-	-	-	-	-
Esso Sirte	3.7	4.1	-	-	-	-	50.00	24.50	-	-
Aquitaine _et al._	0.6	0.7	-	-	-	-	-	-	-	-
Amoco	0.2	0.4	-	-	-	-	-	-	-	-
AGIP	-	0.8	-	-	-	-	-	-	-	-
NOC	-	0.6	-	-	-	-	-	-	-	-
NIGERIA										
Shell/BP	72.9	66.5	50.00	22.50	-	-	-	-	-	-
Gulf	21.4	17.9	-	-	-	-	-	-	100.00	45.00
Mobil	5.0	9.1	-	-	-	-	-	-	-	-
AGIP/Phillips	0.4	2.9	-	-	-	-	-	-	-	-
SAFRAP	-	3.0	-	-	-	-	-	-	-	-
Texaco Chevron	0.1	0.6	-	-	-	-	-	-	-	-
QATAR										
QPC	52.5	50.4	23.75	9.50	23.75	9.50	11.88	4.75	-	-
Shell	47.5	49.8	-	-	-	-	-	-	-	-
SAUDI ARABIA										
Aramco	93.4	95.3	-	-	-	-	30.00	12.00	-	-
AOC	4.5	3.4	-	-	-	-	-	-	-	-
Getty	2.1	1.3	-	-	-	-	-	-	-	-

participation

oil companies

Mobil		Shell		Standard California		Texaco		Other foreign companies		National companies	
1970	1974	1970	1974	1970	1974	1970	1974	1970	1974	1970	1974
-	-	-	-	-	-	-	-	-	-	100.00	100.00
-	-	-	-	-	-	-	-	100.00	-	-	51.00
-	-	-	-	-	-	-	-	100.00	49.00	-	51.00
-	-	-	-	-	-	-	-	-	49.00	-	51.00
-	-	-	-	-	-	50.00	50.00 [a/]	-	-	-	a/
-	-	-	-	-	-	-	-	100.00	100.00	-	-
-	-	-	-	-	-	-	-	-	-	-	100.00
-	-	-	-	-	-	-	-	-	-	-	100.00
-	-	-	-	-	-	-	-	-	100.00	-	-
-	-	-	-	50.00	50.00	50.00	50.00	-	-	-	-
-	-	-	-	-	-	-	-	-	-	100.00	100.00
50.00	50.00	-	-	-	-	-	-	-	-	-	-
-	-	-	-	-	-	-	-	-	-	100.00	100.00
-	-	-	-	100.00	50.00	-	50.00	-	-	-	-
7.00	-	14.00	-	7.00	-	7.00	-	5.00	-	-	100.00
-	-	-	-	-	-	-	-	50.00	50.00	50.00	50.00
-	-	-	-	-	-	-	-	50.00	50.00	50.00	50.00
-	-	-	-	-	-	-	-	50.00	50.00	50.00	50.00
-	-	-	-	-	-	-	-	50.00	50.00	50.00	50.00
-	-	-	-	-	-	-	-	-	-	100.00	100.00
11.88	-	23.75	-		-	-	-	5.00	-	-	100.00
11.88	-	23.75	9.50	-	-	-	-	5.00	-	-	43.01
11.88	-	23.75	-	-	-	-	-	5.00	-	-	100.00
-	-	-	-	-	-	-	-	-	-	100.00	100.00
-	-	-	-	-	-	-	-	-	-	-	60.00
-	-	-	-	-	-	-	-	80.00	40.00	20.00	60.00
-	-	-	-	-	-	-	-	100.00	100.00	-	-
-	-	16.67	-	-	-	-	-	83.33	40.80	-	59.20
-	-	-	-	-	-	-	-	100.00	49.00	-	51.00
-	-	-	-	-	-	-	-	-	-	-	51.00
-	-	-	-	50.00	-	50.00	-	50.00	d/	-	100.00 [d/]
-	-	-	-	50.00	d/	50.00	d/	-	-	-	100.00 [d/]
65.00	31.85	-	-	-	-	-	-	35.00	17.15	-	51.00
-	-	-	-	-	-	-	-	50.00	12.00	-	63.30
-	-	-	-	-	-	-	-	100.00	100.00	-	-
-	-	-	-	-	-	-	-	100.00	100.00	-	-
-	-	-	-	-	-	-	-	100.00	50.00	-	50.00
-	-	-	-	-	-	-	-	-	-	100.00	100.00
-	-	50.00	22.50	-	-	-	-	-	-	-	55.00
-	-	-	-	-	-	-	-	-	-	-	55.00
100.00	45.00	-	-	-	-	-	-	-	-	-	55.00
-	-	-	-	-	-	-	-	100.00	45.00	-	55.00
-	-	-	-	-	-	-	-	100.00	45.00	-	55.00
-	-	-	-	50.00	22.50	50.00	22.50	-	-	-	55.00
11.88	4.75	23.75	9.50	-	-	-	-	5.00	2.00	-	60.00
-	-	100.00	40.00	-	-	-	-	-	-	-	60.00
10.00	4.00	-	-	30.00	12.00	30.00	12.00	-	-	-	60.00
-	-	-	-	-	-	-	-	80.00	40.00	90.00	10.00
-	-	-	-	-	-	-	-	100.00	100.00	-	-

Table 2 (continued)

Country and company	Share in country's crude oil production		Equity: Major international							
			British Petroleum		Compagnie française des pétrôles		Exxon		Gulf	
	1970	1972	1970	1974	1970	1974	1970	1974	1970	1974
UNITED ARAB EMIRATES										
ADPC	61.2[e]	58.1[e]	23.75	9.50	23.75	9.50	11.88	4.75	-	-
ADMA	38.8[e]	41.9[e]	66.67	14.67	33.33	13.33	-	-	-	-
ADOCO	..	..	-	-	-	-	-	-	-	-
DPC	..	..	-	-	25.00	-	-	-	-	-
VENEZUELA[f]										
Creole	42.6	43.1	-	-	-	-	95.40	95.40	-	-
Shell	26.1	24.9	-	-	-	-	-	-	-	-
Meneg	11.5	12.2	-	-	-	-	-	-	100.00	100.00
Ven. Sun	6.4	5.8	-	-	-	-	-	-	-	-
Mobile	3.1	3.0	-	-	-	-	-	-	-	-
Texaco	2.0	1.6	-	-	-	-	-	-	-	-
Texas	1.6	1.4	-	-	-	-	-	-	-	-
Chevron	1.5	1.2	-	-	-	-	-	-	-	-
CVP	1.2	1.9	-	-	-	-	-	-	-	-
Sinclair	1.2	1.0	-	-	-	-	-	-	-	-
Others	3.9	3.9								

Source: Taken from United Nations, Secretary-General, Permanent Sovereignty over Natural Resources, (A/9716 and Corr.1), 20 September 1974, pp. 17-18.

Note: The table depicts the equity holdings of eight of the largest international oil companies in selected companies with production rights in individual OPEC countries.

The following abbreviations have been used for companies:

Ecuador
CEPE - Corporación Estatal Petrolera Ecuadoriana

Iran
LAPCO - Lavan Petroleum Company
IPAC - Iran Pan-American Oil Co.
IMINOCO - Iranian Marine International Oil Company
SIRIP - Société irano-italienne des pétroles
NIOC - National Iranian Oil Company

Iraq
IPC - Iraq Petroleum Company
BPC - Basrah Petroleum Company
MPC - Mosul Petroleum Company
INOC - Iraq National Oil Company

Kuwait
KOC - Kuwait Oil Company
AOC - Arabian Oil Company
Aminoil - American Independent Oil Company

Libya
Oasis - Oasis Oil Company of Libya, Inc.
Amoseas - American Overseas Petroleum, Ltd.
Amoco - Amoco International Oil Company
NOC - National Oil Company

Nigeria
SAFRAP - Elf-Nigeria

Qatar
QPC - Qatar Petroleum Company

CIPEC succeeded, however, in persuading Indonesia to join as a member and Australia and Papua New Guinea to join as associates. Finally, major iron ore exporters, after a number of preparatory meetings, agreed in 1975 to form the Association of Iron Ore Exporting Countries. However, as table 4 demonstrates, members of all three producers' associations made progress in establishing local control over mining facilities. In the case of the copper exporters, this development largely dates back to the late 1960s and the early

participation

oil companies

Mobil		Shell		Standard California		Texaco		Other foreign companies		National companies	
1970	1974	1970	1974	1970	1974	1970	1974	1970	1974	1970	1974
11.88	4.75	23.75	9.50	-	-	-	-	5.00	2.00	-	60.00
-	-	-	-	-	-	-	-	-	12.00	-	60.00
-	-	-	-	-	-	-	-	100.00	40.00	-	60.00
-	-	-	-	-	-	10.00	10.00	65.00	90.00	-	-
-	-	-	-	-	-	-	-	4.60	4.60	-	-
-	-	100.00	100.00	-	-	-	-	-	-	-	-
-	-	-	-	-	-	-	-	-	-	-	-
-	-	-	-	-	-	-	-	100.00	100.00	-	-
100.00	100.00	-	-	-	-	-	-	-	-	-	-
-	-	-	-	-	-	100.00	100.00	-	-	-	-
-	-	-	-	-	-	100.00	100.00	-	-	-	-
-	-	-	-	100.00	100.00	-	-	-	-	-	-
-	-	-	-	-	-	-	-	-	-	100.00	100.00
-	-	-	-	-	-	-	-	100.00	100.00	-	-

Saudi Arabia

Aramco	- Arabian American Oil Company
AOC	- Arabian Oil Company

United Arab Emirates

ADPC	- Abu Dhabi Petroleum Company
ADMA	- Abu Dhabi Marine Areas
ADOCO	- Abu Dhabi Oil Company
DPC	- Dubai Petroleum Company

Venezuela

CVP	- Corporación Venezolana del Petroleo

a/ Negotiations are in process aimed at the acquisition by the Government of Ecuador of 25 percent of Texaco/Gulf's operations; the first down-payment for compensation has already been made.

b/ Legally, the Iranian Oil Participants have been owned by Iran since the Nationalization Act of 1951, but in practice the management role of the national oil corporation was somewhat limited.

c/ After nationalization, the company became the Iraq Company for Oil Operations (ICOO).

d/ The nationalization is being contested by the companies involved.

e/ For Abu Dhabi only.

f/ Legislation has been drawn up aimed at establishing participation in the oil industry.

[Author's note: Since the middle of 1974--when this table was prepared--further changes toward national ownership occurred. Venezuela, for instance, nationalized all foreign oil producing affiliates on 1 January 1976. In addition, Gabon became a full member of OPEC in 1975.]

1970s, but in the case of bauxite and iron ore, initiatives were taken mostly beginning with 1974.

Clearly, none of the three products just mentioned approach the economic significance of oil. In addition, copper and aluminum can be substituted for each other with relative ease. They are, in fact, close competitors, with the latter having lost some of its advantage due to its comparatively high energy content.[50] In this situation, producers' associations may find it

Table 3. Membership in the producers' associations constituting the Council of Producers' Associations, 1976[a]

Producers' association[b]	Africa	Asia
African Groundnuts Council	Gambia, Mali, Niger, Nigeria***, Senegal, Zaire***	
Asian and Pacific Coconut Community (1969)		Fiji, India*****, Indonesia******, Malaysia*, Philippines, Sri Lanka**, Thailand**, Western Samoa
Asian Pepper Community (1970)		India*****, Indonesia******, Malaysia**
Association of Natural Rubber Producing Countries (1970)		Indonesia******, Malaysia**, Rep. of South Vietnam, Singapore Sri Lanka**, Thailand**
Cocoa Producers Alliance (1962)	Ghana**, Ivory Coast**, Nigeria***, Togo*, United Rep. of Cameroon**	
Inter-African Coffee Organization (1960)	Benin, Burundi, Central African Rep.*, Congo*, Ethiopia, Gabon**, Ivory Coast**, Liberia*, Madagascar*, Nigeria***, Rwanda, Sierra Leone**, Togo*, Uganda*, United Rep. of Cameroon**, United Rep. of Tanzania**, Zaire***	
Intergovernmental Council of Copper Exporting Countries (1967)	Zaire***, Zambia	Indonesia******, (Papua New Guinea)
International Association of Iron Ore Exporting Countries c/ (1975)	Mauritania, Sierra Leone**	India*****
International Bauxite Association (1974)	Ghana**, Guinea, Sierra Leone**	(India)*****, Indonesia******
International Committee for Tea	Kenya, Malawi, Mozambique, Uganda*, United Rep. of Tanzania**	Bangladesh*, India*****, Indonesia******, Sri Lanka**
Jute International d/		Bangladesh*, India*****, Nepal, Thailand**
Latin American and Caribbean Group of Sugar Exporting Countries		
Organization of African Wood Producing and Exporting Countries (1975)d/	Central African Rep.* Congo*, Gabon**, Ghana**, Equatorial Guinea, Ivory Coast**, Liberia*, Madagascar*, United Rep. of Tanzania**, United Rep. of Cameroon**, Zaire***	
Organization of Petroleum Exporting Countries (1960)	Gabon**, Nigeria***	Indonesia******
Union of Banana Exporting Countries (1974)		

a/ Countries in parenthesis have associate or observer status. Countries with double membership (regardless of whether a full member or observer) are starred once; those with triple membership, twice, etc.

Middle East	Western hemisphere	Other
Oman, Sudan		
	Brazil*	
	Chile*, Peru**	(Australia)**
Algeria*, Tunisia	Chile*, Peru**, Venezuela**	Australia**, Sweden
	Dominican Rep.*, Guyana*, Haiti Jamaica*, Surinam, (Trinidad and Tobago)*	Australia**, (Greece), Yugoslavia
	Argentina, Barbados, Brazil*, Colombia*, Costa Rica*, Cuba, Dominican Rep.*, Ecuador*, El Salvador, Guatemala*, Guyana*, Honduras*, Jamaica*, Mexico, Nicaragua*, Panama*, Paraguay, Peru**, Trinidad and Tobago*, Venezuela**	
Algeria*, Iran, Iraq, Kuwait, Libya, Qatar, Saudi Arabia, United Arab Emirates	Ecuador*, Venezuela**	
	Colombia*, Costa Rica*, Guatemala*, Honduras*, Nicaragua*, Panama*	

b/ In parenthesis: year of formation.
c/ Final membership is not determined.
d/ Not yet functioning.

Table 4. Nationalization or takeover in the bauxite, copper and iron-ore industries, 1974

Country	Year	Name of affiliate	Parent enterprise affected
A. Bauxite (in IBA[a/] countries, end-1974)			
Ghana	1972	British Aluminium Co.	British Aluminium Co. b/
Guinea	1961	Société des bauxites du Midi (Los islands)	Alcan Aluminium
	1972	FRIA	Olin-Mathieson British Aluminium Co. b/ Schweizerische Aluminium AG Vereinigte Aluminium Werke AG Pechiney Ugine
Guyana	1970	Demarara Bauxite Co.	Alcan Aluminium
	1974	Reynolds Guyana Mines, Ltd.	Reynolds Metal Co.
Jamaica	1974	Kaiser Bauxite Co.	Kaiser Aluminum and Chemical Corp.
	1974	Revere Jamaica Alumina, Ltd.	Revere Copper and Brass, Inc.
Surinam	1974	N.V. Grasshopper Aluminum Co.	Reynolds Metal Co.
B. Copper (in CIPEC[g/] countries, mid-1974)			
Chile	1967	El Teniente[h/]	Kennecott[h/]
	1969	Chuquicamata) El Salvador)	Anaconda
	1971	Chuquicamata) El Salvador) Exotica)	Anaconda
	1971	Rio Blanco	Cerro
	1971	El Teniente	Kennecott
	1972	Cia. Disputada de Los Condes	Le Nickel
Peru	1974	Cerro de Pasco	Cerro
Zaire	1966	Société Générale des Minirais	Union Minière du Haute Katanga
Zambia	1970	Roan Selection Trust[o/]	American Metal Climax
	1970	Zambian Anglo-American	Anglo-American Corporation of South Africa
C. Iron-ore (end-1974)			
Chile	1971	Bethlehem Chile Iron Mines	Bethlehem Steel Corporation
Gabon	1974	Société des mines de fer de Mekambo (SOMIFER)	Bethlehem Steel Corporation ... ...
Mauritania	1974	Société des mines de fer de Mauritania (MIFERMA)	USINOR and others Bureau de recherches géologiques et minières British Steel Corporation FUNISIDER Thyssen
Morocco	1967	RIF Iron Ore Mine	...
Venezuela	1974	Iron Mines Company of Venezuela	Bethlehem Steel Corporation
	1974	Orinoco Mining Company	United States Steel Corporation

Source: United Nations, Secretary-General, Permanent Sovereignty over Natural Resources, (E/C.7/53), 31 January 1975 and United Nations, Secretary-General, Permanent Sovereignty over Natural Resources, (A/9716 and Corr.1), 20 September 1974.

Investor country affected	Compensation (millions of dollars)	Year settled	Parent equity Before nationalization (percentage)	Parent equity After nationalization (percentage)	Government equity Before nationalization (percentage)	Government equity After nationalization (percentage)
United Kingdom, United States	...	1973	100	45	-	55
Canada	c/	1967	100	-	-	100
	d/	1972			-	49
United States			48.5	24.73		
United Kingdom			10.0	5.10		
Switzerland			10.0	5.10		
Germany, Federal Republic of			5.0	2.55		
France			26.5	13.52		
Canada	53.5	1971	100.0	-	-	100
United States	14.5	1974	100.0	-	-	100
United States	15.0	1974	100.0	49.0	-	51
United States	e/	1974	-	e/	-	e/
United States	3.5[f]	1974	50.0	-	50.0	100
United States	80	1967	100	49	-	51
United States	175[i]	1969	100	49	-	51
		1969	100	49	-	51
United States	253[i]	1974	49	-	51	100
		1974	49	-	51	100
	j/	j/	75	-	25	100
United States	42[k]	1974	70	-	30	100
United States	l/	l/	49	-	51	100
France	13	1972	86	42	-	44
United States	75-79[m]	1974	100	-	-	100
Belgium	500[n]	1969	82	-	18	100
United States	118	1970	100	49	-	51
South Africa[p]	175	1970	100	49	-	51
United States	22.3[q]	1971	100	-	-	100
	-	1974			-	60
United States			50	20.0		
France			34	13.6		
Other European countries			16	6.4		
	-	Un-settled		-	5	100
France			32			
France			24			
United Kingdom			19			
Italy			15			
Germany, Federal Republic of			5			
Spain	-	...	100	-	-	100
United States	17.7	1974	100	-	-	100
United States	83.7	1974	100	-	-	100

NOTES--TABLE 4

a/ International Bauxite Association.

b/ Owned 52 per cent by Tube Investments Ltd. (United Kingdom) and 48 per cent by Reynolds Metals Company (United States).

c/ Bauxites du Midi's mining assets on the Los islands and its undeveloped concessions in the Boké region were transferred, in 1962/63, to Cie. des Bauxites de Guinée, a company 49 per cent owned by the government of Guinea. ALCAN later received a 14 per cent participation in the company's new Boké project. The Los islands deposits have been exhausted in the meantime.

d/ $2.2 million of FRIA's equity was transferred to a new company, FRIGUIA, in which the government of Guinea held a 49 per cent interest and to which the government provided additional bauxite concession areas (valued about $1 million by the companies involved). The rest of FRIA's equity ($34.8 million), as well as the subordinated open account indebtedness (advances approximately $10 million) was converted into debt of the new corporation.

e/ The government has agreed to purchase all land owned by Revere at written-down book value. It will be paid for in 10 equal annual instalments at 7 per cent. The government may also establish a 51 per cent interest in a new mining company and has the option to participate in major expansions of Revere's alumina plant.

f/ The project involved was an exploration joint venture; it was terminated by joint agreement.

g/ Intergovernmental Council of Copper-exporting Countries.

h/ The 1967 sale of 51 per cent equity in El Teniente was negotiated on the initiative of Kennecott.

i/ The government of Chile paid $11-12 million towards the compensation sum agreed upon in 1969 before discountinuing payments in 1971. The settlement reached in 1974 encompassed all claims of Anaconda, that is, including the balance of the 1969 transaction. Total receipts of Anaconda from Chile therefore will total $264-265 million.

j/ Anaconda received, in 1972, $11.9 million insurance payments for its Exotica assets from the Overseas Private Investment Corporation (OPIC) and thereby transferred its claim against the government of Chile to that body.

k/ Cerro had insured, with OPIC, a $14 million debt investment in Compañia Minera Andina, the company that operated the Río Blanco mine. Cerro's equity interest in the mine was not insured. After nationalization, Cerro reached agreement (early 1974) with the government of Chile concerning compensation; OPIC guaranteed payment of a portion of the deferred payment attributable to the insured investment.

l/ Kennecott had insured, with OPIC, its debt investment of $80 million in El Teniente, but not its 49 per cent equity interest. Upon nationalization, Kennecott received from OPIC, in 1972, a lump-sum cash payment of $66.9 million for the outstanding $74.9 million of the OPIC-insured loan. After the death of President Allende, the company commenced negotiations with the government of Chile about a compensation settlement.

m/ Cerro received a cash payment of $67 million covering partial compensation for Cerro de Pasco; an additional $8-12 million is expected out of a lump-sum settlement of $76 million concluded between the governments of Peru and the United States and covering the compensation of various assets nationalized by Peru.

n/ The total payment of $500 million, which Union Minière will eventually receive, is the largest single compensation payment ever negotiated.

o/ At the time of nationalization, approximately 80 per cent of the Roan Selection Trust (RST) in Zambia was owned by American enterprises, with American Metal Climax (AMAX) holding a plurality interest of 42.3 per cent and thus controlling and operating the facilities. After nationalization, RST International became a wholly owned subsidiary of AMAX and continued to remain, with 20.4 per cent the principal partner of the government of Zambia's majority-owned Roan Consolidated Mines Ltd. The Anglo-American Corporation holds another 12.25 per cent minority share in Roan Consolidated Mines Ltd.

p/ United Kingdom and other European investors hold a 40 per cent share in the company.

q/ Bethlehem's Chilean mine was purchased by the government of Chile. OPIC, with whom Bethlehem had insured its equity investment of the Chilean branch, agreed to guarantee payment of a portion of the purchase price attributable to the insured investment.

necessary to enter into intergroup alliances or to develop parallel strategies to forestall interproduct substitution. The Council of Producers' Associations may have to play an important role in this area. In any case, the objectives of the strategies pursued by each group have to be highly differentiated and have to reflect, as closely as possible, the ability of a respective group to withhold important supplies effectively. Obviously, an attempt by the major tea exporters to imitate OPEC's strategy could only end in disaster. Rather, most product groups have to select an incremental and cautious, but nonetheless firm, approach—if necessary, in cooperation with related groups—and they have to remain below the threshold at which enterprises or consumers would defect to substitutes or change consumption patterns. The developments in these industries unmistakably indicate, however, that host countries are increasingly assuming control in their relations with transnational raw material enterprises.

International Approaches

Although the prospects for some producers' associations appear to hold promise, it should not be overlooked that such an approach would only improve the situation of the relatively few major raw material suppliers—and even that perhaps at the expense of other developing countries. Regional groupings, on the other hand, are difficult to establish, particularly where neighboring and conflicting national jealousies or resentments have to be overcome. In addition, it should be kept in mind that an optimal control strategy should have the same domain as TNEs, i.e., it should be global. What, then, is the situation regarding international attempts at dealing with TNEs?

International instruments[51] dealing with TNEs or aspects of their transnational activities are summarized in Appendix A.[52] It is obvious from this appendix (on the basis of which the following discussion is conducted) that these instruments vary widely in terms of such defining characteristics as legal form, purpose, coverage, status, and enforcement. Most importantly, no international instrument is in force that sets out, in a comprehensive manner, agreed rules governing the whole range of issues associated with the transnational activities of TNEs. In other words, all instruments are either issue-specific or represent the point of view of only one group.

The instruments that are relatively comprehensive have been elaborated by nongovernmental groups or organizations and normally represent—with the notable exceptions of the Stikker Report, the Report of the Group of Eminent Persons, and the Pugwash transfer of technology draft code—only one point of view. Particularly well known here are the 1972 International Chamber of Commerce (ICC) Guidelines for International Investment (and its forerunners), as well as such instruments as the Pacific Basin Charter, the

Japanese Guidelines for Investment Activities in Developing Countries, and codes developed by various individual enterprises. The purpose of these instruments—which are mostly formulated in the form of recommendations and rely on voluntary enforcement—is usually to create a stable environment conducive to the activities on transnational enterprises.[53]

Governmental efforts at dealing with TNEs are highly fragmented and, as far as they exist, deal with specific issue-areas. Furthermore, most of them have a promotional character, i.e., are aimed at facilitating the transnational activities of TNEs and at creating a predictable external environment. Virtually all instruments developed under the auspices of the OECD fall into this category. They deal with such matters as the liberalization of capital movements and current invisible operations, the protection of foreign property, and the avoidance of double taxation. A number of non-OECD official instruments have an essentially similar character. They include the pertinent paragraphs of the Lomé Convention, the Paris Convention for the Protection of Industrial Property, and most of the early resolutions adopted within the UN system (e.g., those pertaining to foreign private investment, as well as those pertaining to permanent sovereignty over natural resources—which include references to appropriate compensation and recourse to international law), as well as most of the projects carried out or discussed within its framework (e.g., the Multinational Investment Guarantee Scheme, the establishment of the International Centre for Settlement of Investment Disputes (ICSID)). Moreover, virtually all pertinent bilateral instruments, be they in the form of treaties of commerce, friendship and navigation, the form of bilateral treaties specifically dealing with foreign direct investment, or in the form of double taxation treaties, have as their major purpose the promotion and protection of the activities of TNEs. All major capital exporting countries have concluded a large number of the first two types of treaties, which are frequently also the precondition for obtaining home-country foreign direct investment insurance which, in turn, is often an important factor entering the locational decision making of TNEs. As far as these governmental instruments have the status of treaties, they are, at least in principle, enforceable through court action or sanctions under international law. Virtually none of them, however, provide for a monitoring mechanism.

It is only in recent years that regulation and control elements are being discussed and introduced into international instruments dealing with TNEs and that efforts are being undertaken to make their activities more transparent.[54] This was largely a result of the growing dissatisfaction among developing countries with the role of private foreign direct investment in the development process, the revelations resulting from hearings initiated in 1973 in the U.S. Senate, and the discussions conducted at the UN. Together, these developments made TNEs the object of widespread discussion and led to increasing demands for actions aimed at their control. The current code discussions in the OECD, the Organization of American States (OAS), the ILO, UNCTAD (regarding seaborne trade, transfer of technology (see Chapter 19 of this volume), and restrictive business practices), the UN Group of Experts on Tax Treaties between Developed and Developing Countries, the UN Group of Experts on International Standards of Accounting and Reporting, the nonaligned movement, the UN Commission on Transnational Corporations, and the recent resolutions of the UN General Assembly—all have to be seen in this context. Deserving special attention are the efforts of the OECD, the nonaligned movement and particularly the UN Secretariat, since they are aimed at comprehensive interregional instruments dealing with the whole range of issues related to TNEs.

The OECD

The OECD initiative originated in part from a U.S. suggestion to liberalize the policies of capital-exporting countries toward the investments of TNEs. In the course of this process, the United States further sought to improve the pertinent existing OECD instruments (especially the Code of Liberalisation of Capital Movements and the Code of Liberalisation of Current Invisible Operations) by a strong declaration binding governments to accord national treatment to foreign affiliates. Other governments, however, were reluctant to assume further responsibilities without a *quid pro quo* which, in their view, should consist of relatively elaborate guidelines setting out the responsibilities of TNEs. This turn of events was quite unexpected for the U.S. But it was irreversible, since the proposal had been put on the table (and embraced especially by the Nordic countries) and since parallel developments in the UN made it advisable for the developed countries to clarify their position and agree upon a common platform. The result was, thus, an agreement to work toward an investment package consisting of a code of conduct for TNEs, a declaration on national treatment, and a declaration on official incentives and disincentives for investment.[55]

Consequently, in January 1975, the OECD established a Committee on International Investment and Multinational Enterprises. It was charged to prepare (a) action proposals on the formulation of a code of conduct containing uniform standards applicable to TNEs; (b) procedures for dealing with complaints that might emerge in the context of such a code; (c) arrangements for the exchange of improved information and for improved and harmonized statistics; (d) consultations to achieve better cooperation, notably on official investment incentives or disincentives; and (e) consultations on the national treatment of enterprises under foreign control.[56]

After several drafts and intensive consultations with labor unions and especially the business community, an investment package was adopted by an OECD ministerial meeting in Paris in June 1976. This package consists of four interrelated instruments: "Guidelines for Multinational Enterprises," "Inter-governmental Consultation Procedures on the Guidelines for Multinational Enterprises," "National Treatment," and "International Investment Incentives and Disincentives."

In the final months of negotiation, one of the key discussion points involved the question of whether and in which form the Committee on International Investment and Multinational Enterprises—which had been selected as the vehicle for intergovernmental consultations—should monitor the observance of the Guidelines. Virtually all governments agreed that the OECD should not pass judgment on the actions of individual governments or firms. At the same time, a number of governments felt that governmental and corporate behavior should be discussed somewhere and somehow in order to introduce an element of accountability; otherwise, they feared, the whole interrelated package would not have served any purpose. The Swedish government, in particular, desired that the Committee should have the right to cite specific abuses by specific TNEs and to bring the enterprises involved before the Committee. The United States, on the other hand, argued that since the Guidelines are voluntary, no company should be obliged to appear before the Committee. A compromise was finally reached which provided that the Committee (comprised of all member governments), after a unanimous decision, could extend invitations to enterprises to express their views. Enterprises, however, are still free to accept or decline such invitations. A double veto possibility, in other words, protects TNEs from having to explain their activities before this intergovernmental body.

The disagreements on the various components of the package were such that until the end of the deliberations it was not certain whether the package as a whole would be adopted by all governments. Canada, in particular, regarded the trade-off between guidelines and the national treatment obligation with strong reservations; similar feelings were shared by Australia, Japan, and New Zealand.

The Guidelines are addressed to enterprises (and their affiliates) established in different countries and regardless of whether their ownership is private, state, or mixed. (In fact, where appropriate, they also apply to domestic enterprises.) The Guidelines note that transnational enterprises "now play an important part in the economies of Member countries and in international economic relations" and that they "can bring substantial benefits to home and host countries." But they also recognize that transnational enterprises "may lead to abuse of concentrations of economic power and to conflicts with national policy objectives." Moreover, "the complexity of these multinational enterprises and the difficulties of clearly perceiving their diverse structures, operations and policies sometimes give rise to concern" (paragraph 1). In this situation, the code of conduct has as its purpose "to encourage the positive contributions which multinational enterprises can make to economic and social progress and to minimise and resolve the difficulties to which their various operations may give rise"; in addition, the Guidelines are designed "to contribute to improving the foreign investment climate" (paragraph 2). To obtain these objectives, the OECD "set out . . . recommendations jointly addressed by Member countries to multinational enterprises operating in their territories"; it laid down "standards for the activities of these enterprises in the different Member countries" (paragraph 6).

However, the observance of the code "is voluntary and not legally enforceable" (paragraph 6). General consensus supported this approach, although the OECD's Trade Union Advisory Committee strongly urged mandatory guidelines. If disputes between enterprises and OECD countries should arise, the Guidelines encourage the use of "appropriate international dispute settlement mechanisms" (paragraph 10). The Committee on International Investment and Multinational Enterprises is furthermore empowered (by the Consultation Procedures) to deal with any matters that may arise with the Guidelines. This provision may provide the Committee with certain rudimentary supervisory powers through which, to a certain extent, the observance of the Guidelines could be monitored, although no plans appear to exist to give the Committee the necessary administrative capacity to do more than cursory reviews or to simply file complaints. Furthermore, beyond this limited authority, the Committee has no sanctions at its disposal.

These provisions do not preclude that OECD countries can regulate individually the activities of the TNEs operating in their territories. Such regulations, however, are not only "subject to international law and the international agreements" (paragraph 7) to which a country has subscribed, but member countries should also take into account the principle of national treatment and fulfill their responsibilities to treat enterprises equitably. Thus, "Member countries should . . . accord to enterprises operating in their territories and owned or controlled directly or indirectly by nationals of another Member country . . . treatment . . . consistent with international law and no less favourable than that accorded in like situations to domestic enterprises" (Declaration II.1). The instrument on National Treatment provides that exceptions have to be communicated and explained to the Committee on International Investment and Multinational Enterprises. And each OECD country can request consultations (in the framework of the Committee) regarding any matter related to national treatment. The instrument on Incentives and Disincentives, furthermore, specifies that any measures giving official incentives or disincentives to international direct investment should take into account the interests of other OECD countries. In cases of perceived adverse effects, the countries affected may request consultations within the framework of the Committee. These consultation provisions are novel in that they make certain aspects of foreign direct investment policies subject to international review.

As to substantive coverage, the code addresses itself to a wide range of issues. In its general policies section, it encourages TNEs, *inter alia,* to take fully into account the general policy objectives and the aims and priorities of the countries in which they operate; not to restrain the commercial activities and competitive advantage of their foreign affiliates; and to refrain from rendering or soliciting bribes.

With respect to disclosure of information—an area that was debated intensely because of the question whether or not information should be disclosed on a country-by-country basis—enterprises are requested to publish regularly additional information in order to increase the transparency of their activities. Thus, information should be published for the enterprise as a whole (a) on sales and important new capital investments in major lines of business; (b) on sources and uses of funds; (c) on R&D expenditures; and (d) on intragroup pricing and accounting policies. Furthermore, information by geographical area is expected (a) on the operations and principal activities of the parent enterprise and its main affiliates (whereby the latter should be identified, including the percentage of parent ownership in them); (b) on corporate operating results and sales; (c) on important new capital investments; and (d) on the average number of employees. The definition of "geographical area" is left to each individual enterprise—a liberty that severely limits the comparability of the data generated.

In the area of competition, TNEs are held not to abuse a dominant position of market power by, for example, anticompetitive acquisitions or the anticompetitive abuse of industrial property rights; not to engage in a variety of restrictive business practices; and to cooperate, including through the provision of information, with national authorities regarding competition questions or investigations. Regarding financing, the Guidelines merely state that enterprises should take into account the balance of payments and credit policies of the countries in which they operate. And concerning taxation, enterprises are encouraged to refrain from non-arm's length transfer pricing and to provide all information that is necessary to correctly assess corporate taxes.

The code gives considerable attention to employment and industrial relations. Among the list of desiderata mentioned here one finds the acceptance of the right of employees to be represented by labor unions as legitimate organizations responsible for industrial bargaining. Furthermore, provisions are made concerning information necessary for employee representatives for collective agreements, including where possible, information on the performance of the foreign affiliate and the enterprise system as a whole; nondiscriminatory training; advanced information about close-downs; nontransferal out of the host country of operating units (or parts thereof) in bargaining situations; and collective international bargaining with employer representatives authorized to make decisions. Finally, in a section on science and technology, enterprises are recommended to contribute to the development of national scientific and technological capacities and to rapidly diffuse technologies at reasonable terms and conditions.

The OECD code is important because countries that are also the major home countries of TNEs have agreed, for the first time, to elaborate certain guiding principles for the behavior of "their" TNEs. As such, the OECD Guidelines represent the response of the developed market economies—the headquarters countries of virtually all TNEs—to growing pressures from many quarters to clarify the conditions under which TNEs should conduct their activities.

The code has, of course, a number of limitations. First of all, many of its provisions are very general. Furthermore, qualifications are attached to many of them, qualifications, moreover, whose exact definitions are usually left to the enterprises affected. More important, however, is the voluntary character of the Guidelines. It is entirely left to TNEs whether or not they choose to obey them. And no authority can interpret to what extent they are doing so or detailize the degree to which they should do so. On the other hand, since the governments of the major headquarter countries stand behind the code, it has a considerable amount of moral suasion which may, in fact, persuade TNEs to volunteer information and to attempt observance. Corporate responsiveness also will depend on the degree to which the Committee on International Investment and Multinational Enterprises will (can) utilize the rudiments of its mandate to monitor the code. In addition, it is conceivable that elements of the code may find their way into national laws and regulations and thereby acquire legally binding power.

Another major limitation of the Guidelines is that while they reflect, to a certain extent, the interests of host countries, they do not reflect the interests of developing host countries. This is, of course, a result of their formulation within the OECD framework and in reference, primarily, to OECD members. Nevertheless, the question of the geographical applicability of the code is ambiguous. The recommendations in the section dealing with disclosure of information, for instance, will probably be interpreted as applying to the world as a whole. In fact, all other sections appear to imply that the desiderata contained in them extend beyond the OECD. This vagueness conjectures at least the expectation that TNEs based in OECD countries will follow the same standards of behavior regardless of where they operate. Review of their behavior, however, appears to be strictly limited to their activities in OECD countries. As such, the Guidelines—and the entire investment package—also represent a bargaining position of the developed countries for their negotiation with the developing countries of a truly international code. The position of the developing countries for these negotiations is beginning to emerge from their deliberations in the framework of the nonaligned movement.

The Non-Aligned Countries

The first time that the Non-Aligned Countries dealt with the question of controlling foreign direct investment was at the Third Conference of Heads of State or Government of Non-Aligned Countries, held in Lusaka in September 1970. At this summit—which brought the enunuciation of the principle of self-reliance and a turn of the Non-Aligned Countries to an increased consideration of economic matters—the attending countries pledged themselves "to adopt as far as practicable a common approach to problems and possibilities of investment of private capital in developing countries"; this pledge was followed up, during the Third Conference of Ministers of Foreign Affairs of Non-Aligned Countries in Georgetown, 1972, with a decision to establish a Committee of Experts of the Non-Aligned Countries on Private Foreign Investment "to draw up a draft set of criteria, techniques and procedures which would make private foreign investment subserve national development objectives and which would govern the adoption of a common approach to private investment."[58] The Committee met in Santiago in August 1973 and submitted its conclusions to the Fourth Conference of Heads of State or Government of the Non-Aligned Countries, held in Algiers in September 1973. Specifically, the summit endorsed a number of considerations in regard to guidelines for foreign private investment,[59] agreed that "for purposes of regulating and controlling the operations and activities of multinational corporations" common rules in respect of these enterprises should be adopted and, finally, approved the establishment of a nonaligned information center on transnational corporations.[60] Pursuant to the decision of the Algiers summit, a second meeting of the Committee of Experts on Private Foreign Investment took place in Lima in July 1975 and elaborated a "Draft Statute for the Treatment of Foreign Investment, Transnational Corporations and the Transfer of Technology."[61]

Like the OECD guidelines—however, without the corresponding instruments specifying the responsibilities of governments—the Statute is addressed to enterprises only, or, more specifically, to "any contribution made from abroad to the capital of an enterprise or corporation in a Non-Aligned Country" (Definitions, paragraph a). It appears, therefore, to be irrelevant whether the foreign investor is a private, mixed, or state-owned entity. In clear contradistinction to the OECD instrument, however, the Statute differentiates between several types of enterprises: national corporations (80 percent of the capital held by nationals), joint ventures (51-80 percent held by nationals), and foreign corporations (less than 51 percent held by nationals). A number of rules apply to foreign corporations only. Most importantly, and following the example of ANCOM, the Statute contains a fade-out clause:

> The foreign corporations operating in the territory of a Non-Aligned Country shall progressively transfer a part of their shares or partnerships to national investors, within a reasonable period of time, on which the Non-Aligned Countries should consult so as to arrive at a common stand, in order to allow the foreign investor to recoup his investment plus a reasonable profit margin (Article 11).

In other words, foreign affiliates in which the parent enterprises hold more than 80 percent of the capital have to be gradually transformed into joint ventures or national corporations.

The purpose of the Statute is to regulate, supervise, and control the activities of TNEs as well as the transfer of technology. To obtain these objectives, the instrument outlines minimum treatment standards (except for transactions among Non-Aligned Countries) for foreign direct investment and transfer of technology which should be implemented through national legal provisions. For this purpose, every Non-Aligned Country is encouraged to establish a national agency responsible for the whole range of issues pertaining to the subject matter of the Statute. In addition, subregional and regional agreements on the basis of the Statute are envisaged. Close cooperation is also urged for the implementation of a special set of rules of conduct for TNEs. As part of this cooperation, Non-Aligned Countries are requested to provide pertinent information to the Information Center of the Non-Aligned Countries on Transnational Corporations and to coordinate their positions in the UN Commission on Transnational Corporations. The improvement of the investment climate is not a concern of the instrument, except in so far as a set of minimum standards in and by themselves diminish the uncertainties for TNEs contained in an otherwise undefined external environment.

The Statute accepts the Calvo doctrine as the guiding principle for the settlement of conflicts between host countries and foreign enterprises. In other words, in case of dispute, TNEs have to "submit to the exclusive jurisdiction of the Law and courts of the State in which they operate" (Article 13d); they also have to "refrain from involving other States, in particular the home State, in disputes that might arise between the transnational corporation and the host State" (Article 13e). This approach differs, of course, markedly from the references to international law and obligations contained in the OECD instrument and the arbitration and consultation procedures envisaged by it.

Although the implementation of the Statute is mainly a national responsibility, provisions are made for international review. Specifically, the Committee of Experts of the Non-Aligned Countries on Private Foreign Investment—which drafted the instrument—suggested that it "will evaluate regularly, on the basis of information provided by each State, the implementation of the present Statute" (Article 24) and that an item on this subject matter should be included in every summit conference (and other major meeting) of the nonaligned with a view to determining what progress has been made and what improvements are necessary. These mechanisms are considerably weaker and less supranational than those envisaged in the OECD instrument.

In its substantive coverage, the Non-Aligned Countries focus on four key areas: conditions for foreign investment, conversion of foreign corporations into joint ventures or national corporations (already discussed earlier), transnational corporations, and transfer of technology. The first area begins with a delineation of strategic economic sectors in which foreign direct investment may be restricted. Key sectors specified include national resources, public utilities, financial services, and a number of other services (e.g., advertising) as well as basic industries (e.g., iron and steel). Other articles provide for the authorization and registration of any investment project and situations in which such authorization should be conditional (e.g., acquisitions); a common ceiling on the repatriation of profits; the treatment of reinvestments as new investments, subject to authorization; conditions for credit operations; harmonization of tax incentives; and environmental safeguards.

The chapter dealing with TNEs contains a set of rules of conduct for their activities in Non-Aligned Countries.[62] They request the observance of such principles as noninterference into domestic and international affairs, permanent sovereignty over natural resources and economic activities, and the Calvo doctrine. Others address themselves to sociopolitical questions and prescribe that transnational enterprises should respect the sociocultural identity of host societies, should not serve as political instruments of other states, and should provide all information requested by host governments. Economic matters receive attention in rules requesting compliance with national development plans, rules asking for a contribution to the host economy and its technological capacity, and rules prohibiting restrictive business practices. All of these rules are very general, brief, and not operationalized.

Finally, in the area of transfer of technology, Non-Aligned Countries are held to request for approval and scrutiny all contracts involving technology imports, patents, and trademarks and to deny authorization for any of them containing restrictive business practices. No royalties should be paid, and no tax deductions allowed, for intangible technology supplied from within the parent system.

The Statute was submitted to the Fifth Conference of Ministers for Foreign Affairs of Non-Aligned Countries (Lima, August 1975). The foreign ministers were asked to approve it for adoption by their respective countries. However, they did not follow this recommendation and only decided to submit the Statute "to the consideration of their Governments so that they may possibly be inspired by it in the framework of their national policies in this field."[63] By taking this action—i.e., by leaving the Statute's implementation entirely to the discretion of each country and by eliminating any (even if only rudimentary) possibilities for internationally monitoring its progress—the Statute has lost virtually all its potential to become the basis of immediate, coordinated Third World action. The ministers did, however, resolve to locate the Information Center of the Non-Aligned Countries on Transnational Corporations in Havana and they decided that a group of experts should meet as soon as possible to revise a draft statute of the center which had been prepared by Cuba. This center may develop into a Third World focal point of work on TNEs and it may provide new impetus for a renewal of cooperation efforts among developing countries aimed at controlling TNEs. Furthermore, as discussed above, several decisions concerning the strengthening of producers' associations were taken.

The efforts of the Non-Aligned Countries represent the first attempt of the Third World to agree on a common approach toward TNEs. They also demonstrate the difficulties involved in such an attempt. Broad support existed among Non-Aligned Countries for the idea of controlling TNEs. This support was also reflected in other situations, most notably in the resolutions adopted at the Sixth Special Session of the UN General Assembly, the Charter of Economic Rights and Duties of State, the resolutions leading to the establishment of the UN Commission and Centre on Transnational Corporations, and various recent documents of the Group of 77.[64] The result was a draft whose emphasis was clearly on national implementation; cooperation at the sub-regional, regional, and international levels was visualized as having only flanking character. Even the suggested role for the committee of experts to monitor the implementation of the agreement was minimal. Nevertheless, in spite of this broad support, in spite of its emphasis on national action, in spite of the strong leadership provided by such countries as Chile (under President Allende), Cuba, Guyana, and Peru, and in spite of the amount of time spent on the matter, not enough common ground could be found among the Non-Aligned Countries for them to agree on a general set of rules concerning the treatment of transnational enterprises—rules that would take into account the interests and experiences of the relatively more developed as well as those of the relatively less developed countries in the nonaligned movement.

Although the efforts of the Non-Aligned Countries to agree on coordinated or parallel actions have not been successful so far, the Statute still represents the basis of a consensus of the Third World in matters relating to foreign direct investment. Obviously, however, further discussions are required. This is reflected in the program of work of the UN Commission on Transnational Corporations (adopted in March 1976 during the second session of the Commission) which recognized the need for regional consultations among developing countries for the purpose of arriving at a common position in preparation for the elaboration of a UN code of conduct dealing with TNEs. But the experience of the nonaligned efforts also indicates that developing countries are very reluctant to accept any international responsibilities—even vis-à-vis other developing countries—that are perceived as infringing on their sovereignty.

The United Nations

The UN's activities concerning TNEs began in July 1972 with the unanimous adoption by the UN Economic and Social Council of a resolution requesting the UN Secretary-General to appoint a Group of Eminent Persons to study the role and impact of TNEs and to submit recommendations for appropriate international action.[65] The evolution of this effort has been described and analyzed elsewhere and, therefore, needs not be summarized here.[66] Suffice it to say that the main stations of the UN effort involved the preparation of a Secretariat study on *Multinational Corporations in World Development;* hearings by the Group of Eminent Persons; the final report of the group; and the establishment of the UN Commission on Transnational Corporations and the UN Centre on Transnational Corporations.[67] At the same time, the UN's involvement in this area received further—even if at times controversial—impetus from strong formulations concerning the regulation and supervision of TNEs contained in the resolutions adopted at the Sixth Special Session and in the Charter of Economic Rights and Duties of States.

During the first two sessions of the Commission, a program of work for the Commission and the Centre was agreed upon. It reflects the intention of these institutions to "serve the interests of all States concerned with the full range of issues relating to transnational corporations, and in particular the subject of the regulation and supervision of their activities."[68] It was decided to assign priority to the establishment of a comprehensive information system; research on political, economic, legal and social effects of TNEs; technical assistance to requesting governments in the area of TNEs; and work leading to a definition of TNEs. Highest priority, however, was assigned to the formulation of a code of conduct.[69]

No agreement has yet been reached on the defining characteristics of the code. Thus, for instance, it still has to be decided to whom the code should be addressed (to TNEs only—including state-owned?—or also to host and home governments?); what its precise purpose should be (beyond the general objective of regulation and control); what legal form it should take (especially whether or not it should be voluntary); what subject matters should be covered and at what level of generality (conceivably, several substantive areas may emerge in which the convergence of interests of all states could allow detailed and specific provisions); what mechanisms (if any) should be created to ensure implementation of and adherence to the code; what procedures for dispute settlement should be followed; and what sanctions for noncompliance can be applied. The code has to synthesize the positions of developed and developing countries and it has to take into account the views of the socialist states. As has become apparent during the preceding discussion, disagreement exists regarding most of its main defining characteristics.

The key question is: what is the *quid pro quo*? This raises immediately the further question of the addressees of the code. In the case of the OECD, the bargain involved agreement on national treatment and incentives and disincentives in exchange for guidelines. The resulting package was addressed to governments and enterprises. In the case of the Non-Aligned Countries, a *quid pro quo* was not necessary, but rather agreement on a common denominator vis-à-vis TNEs—and even that did not (yet) prove feasible. On the international level, the preferred agreement for developed countries is probably one in which they receive (1) an acknowledgement of the positive contributions of TNEs and (2) assurances regarding (a) nondiscrimination of foreign affiliates, (b) noninterference in the management of these affiliates (including convertibility of earnings and capital), and, most importantly, (c) recourse to international law in the case of dispute settlement (including for prompt, adequate, and effective compensation in the case of nationalization). In the eyes of the main capital exporting countries, such an acknowledgement and especially such assurances—which together would guarantee a stable and safe investment climate—may well warrant the disclosure of certain information, rules of conduct for "their" TNEs, and even some monitoring of these rules through an international body. For the developing countries, the preferred agreement is probably one in which (1) rules of conduct are prescribed exclusively for TNEs—especially rules through which developing countries would receive special treatment, e.g., in the location of R&D—and with adherence to these rules ensured (possibly) by home countries and/or an international body, (2) a number of their principles—e.g., the Calvo doctrine—gain international acceptance, and (3) they receive maximum information about the activities of TNEs. On the other hand, the developing countries are hardly interested in accepting officially any guidelines for their treatment of foreign affiliates or any responsibilities that may limit their freedom of action in any way. Thus, the developing countries cannot be expected to give any of the assurances sought by the main capital exporters, although they may be willing to acknowledge the positive contributions of TNEs—balanced by a proper on-the-other-hand clause.

The basic *quid pro quo,* therefore, involves issues in which there have traditionally been disagreements between developed and developing countries. It is unlikely that the UN Commission on Transnational Corporations can resolve them. While this does not make a code impossible, it has to affect its character, making it probably a very general nonbinding instrument. In fact, the UN code may even be less specific in its disclosure requirements and in its behavioral rules than the OECD Guidelines. Such specificity, and especially the monitoring elements of the OECD instruments, may just require too many concessions on the part of the Third World to be, in the final analysis, really desirable for them. Therefore, the formulations contained in Annex IV of the Conclusions and Recommendations adopted at the second session of the Commission on Transnational Corporations—formulations that represent particularly the view of the Latin American states but that are also contained in the Statute of the Non-Aligned Countries[70]—may be indicative of the type of rules to be included in a UN code. Such general formulations have also the advantage of allowing the continuation of differences in opinions among their supporters (including sympathizing developed countries), differences that would inevitably surface—and may not be resolvable—if specific rules were to be discussed. In this situation, the question of the legal character of the code (voluntary vs. mandatory) loses in importance, since it would prove to be difficult to enforce such rules in the first place. The same consideration also applies to the issues of enforcement, dispute settlement, and sanctions. At best, an institution like the UN Centre on Transnational Corporations may be asked to periodically report about developments bearing on the code.

These and other questions are considered (since the beginning of 1977) by an intergovernmental working group of the whole of the Commission on Transnational Corporations which meets between the sessions of the commission and which is charged to prepare, for the Commission's third session (spring 1977), an annotated outline of the code.[71] The Commission expects that the code will be finalized, after further work by the working group, at its fourth session in 1978.

Apart from arriving at a code, the efforts of the UN are also directed at exploring the feasibility and desirability of intergovernmental agreements on specific subjects. For instance, a Group of Experts on International Standards of Accounting and Reporting has been established (see Appendix A). It is conceivable that the work of this group will eventually lead to an international agreement on accounting and reporting standards. Intergovernmental agreements may also be sought and reached for such issues as corrupt practices of TNEs;[72] the extraterritorial application of laws and regulations; the harmonization of investment incentives; taxation and income allocation; restrictive business practices; and transfer of technology.[73] Ultimately, in fact, a General Agreement on International Investment may become feasible,[74] an instrument that could build on the code of conduct and on specialized intergovernmental arrangements, and that would regulate, in a comprehensive manner, the whole range of issues related to TNEs.[75]

Any international effort aimed at regulating and controlling TNEs, whether issue-specific or general in nature, and particularly any approach involving enforcement mechanisms, is difficult and time-consuming to develop. But even if only a general and voluntary code of conduct should be the result of the present efforts, a first step in the direction of creating an international set of rules aimed at regulating and controlling TNEs has been taken. At a minimum, such a code would be a concrete expression of the expectations that host countries (and particularly developing ones) have regarding TNEs—in fact, the more detailed a code, the more it would force host countries to examine and to state what exactly should be the rights and responsibilities of TNEs. As such, a code would be valuable for TNEs since it decreases the unpredictability inherent in a vaguely defined environment. On the other hand, of course, the code would constitute a reference point for the evaluation of TNE behavior, especially if elements of it were incorporated in national or regional instruments that are legally binding. National legislation, after all, will remain the core of any efforts to control TNEs; an international code can only have supplementary character. Moreover, the process of formulating and adopting such a set of rules could be a learning experience for all parties involved, in that it contributes to the clarification of some of the major issues surrounding TNEs which require regulation and especially regulation at the international level. A code of conduct may thus help to prepare the way for specific intergovernmental arrangements or even a General Agreement on International Investment. Although the negotiation of such arrangements and of such an agreement may also be very time-consuming, and special efforts would be required to guarantee their strict application, supervision, and enforcement, it is ultimately the only way to ensure that TNEs do not take advantage of overlapping or underlapping national jurisdictions (or escape them altogether), that they can be directed in a way desired by the countries involved, and that their accountability is restored.

There exists, however, one broad area in which action by the international community is needed and where tangible results can be obtained relatively fast. One of the major comparative advantages that TNEs enjoy in a decentralized world of often competing states is their centralized structure and strategy. This situation provides them with a very substantial information advantage vis-à-vis individual states,[76] and it allows them to use, if necessary, their entire intellectual and financial resources in any place they operate, be it for the assessment of investment projects or situations, the evaluation of local laws, or the negotiation of contracts. A well-organized and well-orchestrated global effort[77] to collect and to analyze information related to TNEs, to research the effects of their activities, and to disseminate the results to interested parties, in conjunction with (if so desired) technical assistance in dealing with TNEs, would therefore be a significant step in the direction of counter-balancing TNEs and achieving at least the type of control that is vested in equal levels of information and expertise.

The UN is now equipped to undertake such an effort. In fact, as outlined above, the Commission's and especially the Centre's main functions—apart from assisting in the formulation of a code of conduct—are information analysis and dissemination, research, and technical cooperation. The Centre has, therefore, the capability to provide governments, especially those of developing countries, with a reliable body of knowledge on which they can draw when making decisions regarding the treatment of foreign direct investment, and it could assist them in the preparation of these decisions. Since these assistance activities are conceived as being closely integrated into the information analysis and research functions of the Centre, a continuous and mutually supporting feedback is ensured.

If these capabilities are utilized, a very important step toward monitoring and, eventually, controlling TNEs would have been taken. The significance of the UN initiative would then be fourfold: (1) it would indicate that the international community has not only recognized but also accepted the need to deal with TNEs at a level equal to their own; (2) it would have established international institutions charged with developing and implementing a comprehensive program designed to make TNEs and their effects more transparent and, ultimately, more beneficial for host countries; (3) it would represent an immediate effort aimed at improving the situation and bargaining power of host countries, and especially of developing ones; and (4) it would tend to restore the accountability of TNEs.

Labor Unions

Many of the problems connected with the transnational character of TNEs are also faced by labor unions. In contradistinction to governments, however, unions do not have legislative power to direct TNE behavior. They are entirely dependent on their bargaining strength. And their bargaining strength is increasingly eroding as a growing number of enterprises and industries are outgrowing the organizational reach of any particular labor union. Three reasons, in particular, are responsible for the diminishing vulnerability of TNEs vis-à-vis labor unions.

For one, labor's capacity to exercise effective pressure has decreased, as less and less production of any TNE is subject to the pressure of any particular national union. Consequently, strikes—the labor unions' ultimate recourse—tend to become less costly for enterprises than for unions. For instance, an affiliate in country *A* may account, for instance, for only 5 percent of a TNE's total production; a shut-down of this affiliate may be sustained practically indefinitely by the enterprise because the losses incurred may be minimal from the system's perspective. Secondly, thanks to centralized control and the resulting flexibility, the loss from strikes in one country can be minimized by switching production temporarily to an affiliate in a second country, *B*;[78] or, more drastically, headquarters may even divert, or threaten to divert, future investments away from countries with an assertive labor movement. Frequently, workers in *B* may not even know why they have been asked, for example, to work overtime: as a rule they do not have sufficient information facilities of a horizontal, transnational kind to be informed on events elsewhere in the enterprise system. On the other hand, however, the financial, organizational, and personnel capacities of the enterprise as a whole can readily be deployed, in a concentrated fashion, wherever its interests need to be defended or advanced. Finally, by expanding into host countries with weak or docile labor unions, TNEs not only minimize chances for strike disruptions but also decrease the likelihood of international union collaboration.[79]

Beginning with the late 1960s, labor unions became increasingly aware of and concerned about these developments, and since then they have been in the forefront of advocating public control of TNEs, both at the national and international levels. Some of the more formal union proposals are mentioned in Appendix A, among them especially those sponsored by the World Federation of Trade Unions and the International Confederation of Free Trade Unions. Noteworthy also is the fact that the International Labor Organization (ILO) is undertaking research aimed at investigating the usefulness and feasibility of various approaches to international guidelines relating to TNE activities which lie within ILO's competence. In addition, unions have also ventured into control efforts of their own. To counter the trends outlined above, and possibly even to improve labor's position, it has increasingly become clear that the basic framework of international labor union collaboration has to be strengthened.

International collaboration has a direct bearing on the most crucial issue faced by labor unions—their diminishing capacity to exercise effective pressure. To reverse this trend, unions have to be able to cover, by their actions, a significant share of a TNE's production. As a rule, this requires regional or even international coordination or cooperation. A precondition for concerted action[80] is the negotiation of common termination dates of collective bargaining agreements—otherwise, legal or tactical problems may seriously impede a joint approach.[81] Common bargaining periods also improve the possibilities for solidarity measures such as sympathy strikes or material support for workers on strike in a second-country affiliate.

In fact, a minimum of solidarity is necessary merely to avoid a further deterioration of labor's situation. Most importantly, workers in affiliates in one country have to refrain from actions that would weaken the position of their colleagues in another affiliate in a second country. Specifically, headquarter efforts to (temporarily) compensate strike-losses from one affiliate by increasing production in a second-country affiliate have to be halted. The effective implementation of this approach rests, of course, on a certain minimum of communication between the individual affiliates of the system.

Finally, regarding the third reason for diminished TNE vulnerability, the effects resulting from the expansion of TNEs into countries with a weak or docile labor movement can possibly only be countered by internationalizing disputes between local employees and foreign affiliates. In other words, the more powerful corresponding union in a headquarter country may have to offer its support, whether by providing information, by assisting in bargaining, or by taking appropriate actions.

In all cases, union effectiveness improves as transnational union collaboration goes beyond information and consultation and reaches at least coordination or possibly even crystallizes itself into some permanent structures. Some of the international trade secretariats[82] are already focal points for concerted actions; similar functions can be fulfilled by world councils.[83] These and other mechanisms have to be strengthened, at least at a regional level, if labor unions desire to develop capacities comparable to those of TNEs.

Obviously, the formulation and implementation of union counter-strategies is faced with formidable obstacles, ranging from language difficulties to bureaucratic egotisms of national or even local organizations to questions of political orientation and objectives of actions.[84] To overcome these obstacles will require great efforts and much time. But it is encouraging for the movement toward transnational labor union cooperation that at least one important Western European institution has expressly recognized its necessity: "the Commission [of the EC] considers the setting up of a trade union counterweight as essential for a balanced solution" of efforts aimed at controlling TNEs.[85]

Host Country Councils

The objective of this essay has been to review approaches aimed at controlling TNEs for the purpose of restoring their accountability; influencing, if not channelling, their activities in desired directions; and increasing the share of host countries in the benefits associated with these activities. Since the autonomy of *internal* decision making in the enterprise system as a whole was tacitly assumed, the discussion focussed on possible *external* frameworks that would constrain and direct TNE activities. The establishment of a sophisticated and comprehensive framework *and* its implementation and enforcement would be sufficient to ensure the desired control over TNE activities. Unfortunately however, hardly any framework of this kind—national, regional, or international—has been established. Nor have existing legislation and regulations always been implemented and enforced. While the picture presented above may have appeared optimistic, it cannot be overlooked that virtually all attempts at controlling TNEs, at least until the present, are very fragmentary and therefore very limited in their effectiveness.

Most efforts at controlling TNEs have been made at the national level. As a rule, however, most of the frameworks established (except, in particular, those in socialist countries) are neither sophisticated nor comprehensive; and where national legislation and regulations exist, they are frequently neither fully implemented nor enforced. In fact, developing countries and even many developed countries do not, as a rule, have the administrative capacities to supervise adequately the activities of TNEs operating in their territories.

As far as groupings of countries are concerned, it was observed that while two regional groupings (ANCOM and the EC) are making efforts at controlling TNEs—albeit in the special context of a regional integration attempt—the progress of these efforts is still very limited, and, as far as decisions have been made, these have still to pass the test of time. In most other regional groupings, foreign direct investment harmonization schemes are largely inoperative. No regional grouping exists for the sole purpose of controlling TNEs or aspects of their activities. Some groupings of raw material producers, on the other hand, have been successful in establishing control over those TNEs exploiting their resources; they have thus succeeded in harnessing these enterprises for an improvement of their national situations. However, while the success of these groupings has strengthened the bargaining position of, particularly, the developing host countries, it has resolved neither the problem of control for other raw material producers nor the problem of control of TNEs in industries other than natural resource industries.

At the international level, no enforceable instrument that deals with the whole range of issues related to TNEs exists. International instruments are highly fragmentary in their coverage of issues and their main purposes is frequently not the control of TNE activities but rather their promotion.

Labor unions, finally, while making their own efforts to redress their bargaining power vis-à-vis TNEs, recognize fully that, ultimately, the control of TNEs is a task of governments. For that reason, they have consistently advocated the adoption of binding instruments at the national and international levels.

There is no doubt that efforts at improving control mechanisms regarding TNEs should continue at all levels and in all spheres. Progress has already been made, and several of the current discussions may eventually lead to new control mechanisms. But, clearly, the achievement of significant improvements—especially for developing countries—of the present situation is a very difficult, painstaking, and long-term process.

Consideration should therefore be given to other approaches through which some measure of accountability could be introduced into the activities of TNEs, through which decision-making of TNEs regarding matters of importance to their host countries can be influenced immediately, and through which some of the negative effects of the externalization of decision-making associated with central control over global TNE systems can be alleviated. Such an approach would be the establishment, at the seats of TNE headquarters, of Host Country Councils. These councils would have as their objective participation in the *internal* decision-making processes of TNEs, thus supplementing policies aimed at setting up *external* control mechanisms. The councils would consist of representatives from host country governments in which the respective TNEs have achieved a certain degree of importance—for instance, in terms of control of key industries, investment expenditures, employment, share in exports, and the like. In determining such importance, the nature of an enterprise's operation—e.g., whether affiliates are majority- or minority-owned—could also be taken into account.

The rights of these councils could range from receiving information and hearing explanations to being consulted or even having a codetermining voice. The specific degree of involvement in decision making could depend, for instance, on the issues at hand. Candidate issues are all those pertaining to long-range planning, i.e., the major allocative decisions of who gets what, when, and how. Candidate issues are also those pertaining to enterprise measures with immediate consequences for host countries—e.g., plant closures. Host country involvement may eventually also be expected in the determination of enterprise policy concerning areas such as transfer pricing and income distribution, restrictive business practices, and capital movements. In this way, host countries would be in a position to monitor the allocative decisions of TNEs—which, after all, affect their economies—or may even be able to influence them directly, a possibility that no external framework can offer.

Even a minimal obligation on the part of TNEs—such as keeping host countries informed about their policies—would make enterprise activities more transparent and predictable. Moreover, by offering host countries a chance to present their views and open a dialogue, possible later conflicts may be avoided. Whether such presentations are taken into account by headquarters or not, host countries would at least know what they have to expect and can plan accordingly.

Clearly, a Host Country Council alone does not suffice to ensure the beneficial operation of TNEs—it can only be supplementary to a long-term development plan and its determined implementation—but it would constitute an important flanking measure contributing to the reduction of uncertainties introduced into national planning by the frequently unknown long-term intentions of TNEs. Host countries with limited capabilities to monitor the activities of TNEs or those desiring some influence over downstream facilities, in particular, should benefit from such a scheme.

The establishment of Host Country Councils could proceed gradually, with progressive enterprises and strong host countries pioneering the way. For instance, TNE headquarters could invite representatives of countries in which they have important operations to participate in periodic sessions of mutual consultation. Or, host countries with a strong bargaining position might make the establishment of a Host Country Council a condition of the entry contract; such a contract could also stipulate the rights of the council and link, for instance, the scrupulous respecting of these rights to the treatment of the affiliate(s) in the host country. Home country governments—realizing that they could be drawn into conflicts between their TNEs and host countries—could also encourage the establishment of Host Country Councils as a means of preventing such conflicts or at least reducing their frequency.

Regarding those TNEs that refuse to collaborate, a second-best solution would be periodic meetings of all host countries concerned with, and especially interested in, a particular enterprise to "compare notes." From such meetings one might be able to infer the long-term strategy of an enterprise. At the same time, immediate problems could be discussed and appropriate action, if necessary, coordinated.

The acceptance of the idea of Host Country Councils would be an acknowledgement on the part of both enterprises and governments that TNEs are not only private organizations dedicated to attaining profits, but are, in fact, institutions with profound consequences for the public good of the countries in which they operate. On the part of TNEs, such acknowledgement would also signify that enterprises realize and accept the responsibilities associated with their activities and their consequences. Given the importance of TNEs for all aspects of the NIEO, it is difficult to conceive that the central area of economic development could continue to remain subject to increasing and non-representative foreign-determination, particularly at a time when transparence, democratic control, accountability, and national self-determination are key values in many parts of the world.

Appendix A. Selected International Instruments Dealing with Transnational Enterprises and Aspects of Their Activities*

Instrument	Organization	Coverage	Purpose
Non-governmental instruments			
The Role of Private Enterprise in Investment and Promotion of Exports in Developing Countries (Stikker Report)	Under the auspices of UNCTAD	The recommendations deal, inter alia, with ownership, training, transfer of technology, exports, reinvestments (TNEs); tariff policy, protectionism, tax treatment, investment guarantees, stimulation of investment (home countries); condition for joint ventures, administrative treatment of TNEs, taxation, tariffs, exports (host countries)	To increase the effectiveness of TNE activities for the development process. Mainly promotional
Group of Eminent Persons: The Impact of Multinational Corporations on Development and on International Relations	Under the auspices of the United Nations	International relations; ownership and control; financial flows and balance of payments; technology; employment and labor; consumer protection; competition and market structure; transfer pricing; taxation; information disclosure and evaluation	Transparency, accountability, distribution of benefits, control
Draft Code of Conduct on Transfer of Technology	Pugwash Conferences on Science and World Affairs	Relations between suppliers and recipients of technology; relations among suppliers of technology; guarantees; action by governments; laws and jurisdiction for settlement of disputes; role of international organizations; measures according special treatment to developing countries; and implementation and revision	To ensure that every country can participate on an equal footing in the international transfer of technology
International Accounting Standards	International Co-ordination Committee for the Accountacy Profession	Disclosure of accounting policies; inventories in the context of the historical cost system; consolidated financial statements; depreciation; information to be disclosed in financial statements; inflation accounting; translation of foreign accounts; source and application of funds; presentation of the income statement, research and development; and others	Harmonization of accounting standards
Guidelines for International Investment	International Chamber of Commerce	Investment policies; ownership and management; finance; fiscal policies; the legal framework; labor policies; technology; commercial policies	Establishment of a stable and favorable framework for TNE activities

*Included are instruments that have obtained some measure of endorsement by private or official groups. Not included are, therefore, proposals advanced by individuals (for references to some of these proposals

Enforcement	Status	Comments
Voluntary	Recommendations	Prepared in 1967 on request of UNCTAD by Dirk V. Stikker. The report covers a number of issues connected with foreign direct investment and contains, in its concluding chapter, a set of recommendations which (apart from some general ones) are addressed to TNEs, home governments, host governments, and international organizations
Voluntary	Report and recommendations	Adopted a number of principles and recommendations, including some leading to the establishment of the UN Commission on Transnational Corporations and the UN Centre on Transnational Corporations
Recommendations. Suggested to be the object of a multilaterally binding instrument		Elaborated in 1974 by a Working Group on Code of Conduct on Transfer of Technology. The Code has been transmitted to governments and international organizations (including UNCTAD) for consideration
Disciplinary action against members	Recommendations. Pronouncements on the first two items have been approved; on the next three items issued but not yet approved. The other items are under consideration	The International Accounting Standards Committee, which drafts the accounting standards, was established in 1973
Voluntary	Recommendations	Issued 1972. Each of the headings is elaborated in greater detail

see the text). Regional instruments are also not included since they are usually part of a more comprehensive integration effort (see the text for a discussion).

APPENDIX A (continued)

Instrument	Organization	Coverage	Purpose
International Code of Fair Treatment for Foreign Investments	International Chamber of Commerce	Conditions to be created and maintained by governments for the most advantageous flow of capital and skills	Facilitation of foreign direct investment
Precepts for Successful Business Operations Procedures in Canada and the United States	U.S. Chamber of Commerce and Canadian Chamber of Commerce	A brief list of desirable objectives concerning the business policies of foreign affiliates in Canada	Ensure successful investment
Guidelines for Investment Activities in Developing Countries	Japan Federation of Economic Organizations, The Japan Chamber of Commerce and Industry, Japan Committee for Economic Development, the Japan Federation of Employers' Associations, Japan Foreign Trade Council	Basic posture; promotion of business based on mutual trust; employment and promotion; selection of personnel for overseas assignment; education and training; fostering related industries; promotion of reinvestment; cooperation with host country's industry; cooperation and harmonization with host country	Establishment of a stable and favorable framework for TNE activities
The Pacific Basin Charter on International Investments	Pacific Basin Economic Council	Responsibilities of international investors; policies regarding ownership, management employment, taxation, financing, transfers; life and property; commercial affairs; international trade; legislation; technology	Promotion of TNE activities
Codes of business practices	Individual enterprises such as Turner and Newall, Caterpillar Tractor Co., Union Carbide, Motorola, Ciba Geigy	These codes cover, with various degree of emphasis, general principles; interests of employees, customers, suppliers, shareholders, society; political contributions and involvement; economic and social contributions; ownership; investment policy; reinvestment; employment; technology; transfer pricing; parent-affiliate relations; foreign exchange and other financial practices; resolutions of investment disputes; public policies conducive to the improvement of the contributions of TNEs to the host country	To improve general understanding of TNEs

Enforcement	Status	Comments
Voluntary	Drawn up in the form of a multilateral treaty, but never acted upon	Approved 1949. Elaborated concurrently with the negotiations concerning the ITO and thought as a presentation of the business point of view on the treatment of foreign direct investment
Voluntary	Recommendations	These guidelines followed the Guidelines issued (in 1966) by the Canadian Ministry of Trade and Commerce (see footnote 16), largely reflecting the objectives contained in them. Added was a clause requesting the containment of extra-territorial applications of laws and regulations by governments
Voluntary	Recommendations	Elaborated on the suggestions of the MITI and issued 1973
Voluntary	Recommendations	Adopted 1972
Voluntary	Adopted by individual enterprises	A task force of the Chamber of Commerce of the United States developed in 1974-75 a working document on "Elements of Global Business Conduct for Possible Inclusion in Individual Company Statements." These "Elements" were distributed for the use of individual enterprises. At the beginning of 1976, about 30-50 US enterprises were in the process of formulating individual statements on their international and domestic business philosophy

APPENDIX A (continued)

Instrument	Organization	Coverage	Purpose
Bilateral governmental instruments			
Treaties of Commerce, Friendship and Navigation	Bilateral treaties	Inflow of capital; non-discrimination; management of affiliates; convertibility of earnings and capital; prompt and adequate compensation in the event of nationalization	Promotion and protection of TNE
Investment protection agreements	Bilateral treaties	Nationalization; convertibility; guarantees; financial transfers; entry permissions for foreign personnel; procedural matters in case of conflict, etc.	Promotion and protection of TNE activities
Agreements on the Avoidance of Double Taxation and Prevention of Fiscal Evasion	Bilateral treaties	(See United Nations Guidelines for Tax Treaties between Developed and Developing Countries)	Harmonization of taxation practices

Enforcement	Status	Comments
Court actions and sanctions under international law	Treaties	Major capital exporting countries--especially the US but also the UK, Japan and the Federal Republic of Germany--have concluded such treaties with developing countries. The treaties also cover subject matters not related to TNEs
Court actions and sanctions under international law	Treaties	The US has concluded such treaties specifically dealing with the protection of investment with over 80 developing countries; the Federal Republic of Germany with about 40; and Switzerland with about 15. A few of these treaties have also been concluded by the UK, Sweden, the Netherlands, Belgium and Luxembourg. France has a network of similar agreements. Treaties of this kind also exist between developing countries. Frequently, home country investment guarantees and insurance are only provided for projects in countries having signed such an agreement
National courts	Treaties	Over 500 such double taxation agreements are in force

APPENDIX A (continued)

Instrument	Organization	Coverage	Purpose
<u>Multilateral governmental instruments</u>			
Charter of the International Trade Organization		Foreign direct investment; restrictive business practices	Regulation
Statute for the Treatment of Foreign Investment, Transnational Corporations and the Transfer of Technology	Non-Aligned Movement	Conditions for foreign investment (including key sectors, authorization and registration, acquisition, financial transactions, credit policy, environment); conversion of foreign enterprises into joint ventures or national corporations; set of rules for TNEs; cooperation among non-aligned countries; collaboration with non-aligned information center; transfer of technology; implementation of ths statute (including adoption of internal legal provisions); institutional mechanisms (including foreign investment agencies, review by Committee of Experts of the Non-Aligned Countries on Private Foreign Investment, review at future non-aligned meetings)	Control of TNEs
Code of conduct for TNEs	OAS	Settlement of disputes; TNEs as policy instruments; role of TNEs in national development and international relations; information; economic and technological contribution of TNEs; restrictive practices; socio-cultural impact	Control of TNEs
ACP-EEC Convention of Lomé	European Community and 46 African, Caribbean and Pacific States	Measures to promote industrialization and the participation of TNEs therein; provisions relating to establishment and services (including non-discrimination of nationals and enterprises) and to current payments and capital movements	Facilitation and promotion of industrial cooperation

Enforcement	Status	Comments
Court actions or sanctions under international law	Never ratified	First major international attempt to deal with some foreign direct investment questions
The Statute was submitted by the Fifth Conference of Ministers for Foreign Affairs of Non-Aligned Countries (1975) to the consideration of member governments as possible reference point for national legislation		The draft Statute had been adopted in 1975 by the second meeting of the Committee of Experts of the Non-Aligned Countries on Private Foreign Investment, but has not been endorsed by the conference of foreign ministers (for background and developments, see text). An Information Center of the Non-Aligned Countries on Transnational Corporation was established
	Under discussion	In 1975 the Permanent Council of the OAS approved a resolution which led to the establishment of a Subcommittee on Transnational Enterprises and a Working Group that met several times and considered principles to be included in a code of conduct. On the basis of the report of the Working Group and in the light of the results of the second session of the UN Commission on TNCs, the Subcommittee prepared a report for the 1976 General Assembly of the OAS
Arbitration	Treaty	Signed on 28 February 1975 in Lomé and superceding the Second Yaoundé Convention and the Arusha Convention. The Convention regulates the economic relationship between the ACP states and the EC

APPENDIX A (continued)

Instruments	Organization	Coverage	Purpose
Convention of Paris for the Protection of Industrial Property	Union for the Protection of Industrial Property	Protection of patents, utility models, industrial designs, trademarks, service marks, trade names, indications of source or apellations of origin, unfair competition	Protection of property
Draft convention on the Protection of Foreign Property	OECD	Treatment and protection of foreign property	Encouragement of foreign direct investment
Draft Double Taxation Convention on Income and Capital	OECD	Fiscal incentives in capital-exporting countries for private investment in developing countries	Harmonization of taxation practices
Code of Liberal-isation of Capital Movements and Code of Liberal-isation of Current Invisible Operations	OECD	Abolition of restrictions on the movement of direct and portfolio investments as well as concomitant invisible transaction. Covered are direct investment, portfolio investment, real estate, commercial credits, personal capital movements, and income and other payments arising from such flows (e.g., dividends, interests, patents, trade marks, etc.). (Short-term capital movements with a duration of less than one year--other than commercial credits--are not included)	Facilitation of TNE activities
Guidelines for Multinational Enterprises; Inter-governmental Consultation Procedures on the Guidelines for Multinational Enterprises; National Treatment; International Investment Incentives and Disincentives	OECD	General policies, disclosure of information, competition, financing, taxation, employment and industrial relations, science and technology; intergovernmental consultation procedures on the implementation of the guidelines, procedures for an exchange of views on the guidelines and their implementation; measures related to national treatment and review of such measures; incentive or disincentive measures their review	Prescription of conditions for TNE operations and improvement of foreign investment climate

Enforcement	Status	Comments
National courts	Treaty	A special European Patent Convention has been drafted and awaits ratification
	Draft	Finalized in 1963
	Draft	Drawn up in 1963. Double taxation treaties signed since 1963 frequently followed the structure and a number of substantive provisions of the OECD draft
Sanctions under international law	Treaty	Both adopted 1961 and amended several times since then
Voluntary	Declaration	Adopted June 1976 by an OECD ministerial meeting. For details see text

APPENDIX A (continued)

Instrument	Organization	Coverage	Purpose
United Nations system			
Convention on a Code of Conduct for Liner Conferences	UNCTAD	Relations among member lines; relations with shippers; freight rates; provisions and machinery for settlement of disputes	To regulate the world shipping industry and the relations between shippers and liners
Code of conduct on transfer of technology	UNCTAD	Objectives and principles; scope of application of code; ownership and control; relations among suppliers; restrictive practices related to the acquisition of technology for production; practices relating to distribution; pricing and costs of technology; development of national technological and scientific capabilities; special preferences for developing countries; legal nature and forms of code; machinery for the implementation of the code; applicable law and settlement of disputes	Regulation; improvement of access; development of technological capacity of recipients
Multilaterally acceptable principles on restrictive business practices	UNCTAD	Restrictive business practices that may affect trade and development of developing countries, especially those pertaining to international cartels, national external trade cartels, domestic restrictive practices, and acquisition or abuse of market power; exchange of information (collection and exchange of information, possible extensions of information collection, establishment of possible consultative procedure)	To ensure the objective control of restrictive business practices affecting trade and development of developing countries
International principles and guidelines concerning TNEs and social policy	ILO	Social aspects within the competence of ILO and especially as covered by the international labor standards	To ensure the observation of international labor standards

Enforcement	Status	Comments
Suspension or expulsion of members	Treaty. Open for signature	Prepared 1973 and 1974 by the United Nations Conference of Plenipotentiaries on a Code of Conduct for Liner Conferences under the auspices of UNCTAD
	Under discussion	Following the recommendations of UNCTAD's Intergovernmental Group on the Transfer of Technology, an Intergovernmental Group of Experts on a Code of Conduct on Transfer of Technology was convened in 1975 (consisting of experts from 43 countries). The Group's mandate is to draw up a draft code of conduct. During the first session of the Group (May 1975), the experts from the Group of 77 submitted a draft outline which served as basis of the deliberation of the Group; a draft outline was also submitted by the experts of the developed countries
	Under discussion	The principles are considered to be an important element in an overall package of measures being considered by an <u>ad hoc</u> Group of Experts meeting under the auspices of UNCTAD. The preparation of a model law (or model laws) is also being considered
	Under discussion	A study examining the usefulness and feasibility of international principles and guidelines, their elements and implications, has been prepared for the Governing Body of the ILO

APPENDIX A (continued)

Instrument	Organization	Coverage	Purpose
Multilateral Investment Guarantee Scheme	IBRD	Guarantees for foreign direct investment	Protection and encouragement of TNE activities
Convention on the Settlement of Investment Disputes between States and Nationals of other States	International Centre for Settlement of Investment Disputes (ICSID) (under the auspices of the IBRD)	Provision of arbitration facilities for the settlement of investment disputes involving a government on one side and a foreign private investor on the other	Encouragement of TNE activities
Guidelines for Tax Treaties between Developed and Developing Countries	United Nations	Taxation of business profits, sea and air transport, profits, dividends, interests, royalties, income from personal services, exchange of information for the prevention of international tax evasion and avoidance	Harmonization of tax practices
Early United Nations resolutions	United Nations system	Permanent sovereignty over natural resources (including compensation and reference to international law); promotion of foreign private investment; financing of development	Primarily promotion of TNE activities
Recent United Nations resolutions (including the resolutions adopted at the Sixth Special Session and the Charter of Economic Rights and Duties of States)	United Nations system	Restrictive business practices; transfer of technology; patents; taxes (including allocation of income); trade law; social policy; corruption; the whole range of issues related to TNEs	Primarily control of TNEs
International standards of corporate reporting	United Nations	Review of existing practices of TNE reporting; country reporting requirements; identification of reporting gaps and of items on which TNEs and their affiliates should report	Increase of transparency of TNEs and improvement of comparative information
Code of conduct dealing with TNEs	United Nations	All issues related to TNE activities	Regulation and supervision of TNE activities

Enforcement	Status	Comments
	Draft "Articles of Agreement of the International Insurance Agency" have been prepared by the IBRD in 1966-68 and are under consideration by governments	Elaborated at the request of the Development Assistance Group of the OECD in 1961
Court action or sanctions under international law	Treaty	Came into force in 1966. As of 1973, 68 states have signed the convention (excluding most Latin American countries). Until 1974, one case had come to arbitration; in 1974, four cases were submitted
Voluntary	Recommendations. Model for bilateral tax treaties	The Guidelines constitute the consolidation of the first five meetings of the UN Group of Experts on Tax Treaties between Developed and Developing Countries. Additional work is under way concerning, inter alia, international income allocation (including transfer pricing, prevention of tax evation (excluding tax havens)) and general relief provisions (including incentives and disincentives)
Public opinion	Resolutions	Mainly during the 1950s and 1960s
Public opinion	Resolutions	Mainly during the 1970s. The resolutions adopted at the Sixth Special Session and the Charter of Economic Rights and Duties called specifically for the control of TNEs
	Under discussion	The first meeting of the United Nations Group of Experts on International Standards of Corporate Reporting took place in September 1976. The Group carried out its work in the framework of the UN Centre on Transnational Corporations
	Under discussion	The code is being elaborated by the United Nations Commission on Transnational Corporations. See text for further details

APPENDIX A (continued)

Instrument	Organization	Coverage	Purpose
Labor union instruments			
Charter of Trade Union Demands for the Legislative Control of Multinational Companies	International Confederation of Free Trade Unions	Public accountability; social obligations; control of foreign direct investment and take-overs; restrictive business practices and oligopolistic pricing; taxation; transfer of technology and the role of TNEs in development; short-term capital movements; main data required on TNEs; social obligations of TNEs	Strong control of TNEs at the national and international levels
Charter of Trade Union Rights and the Economic and Social Demands of the Workers in Capitalist Countries at the Present Time	World Federation of Trade Unions	Exchange of information; joint program; creation of a coordinating committee; achievement of: governmental control over TNEs, control of capital movements, respecting of various trade union rights, elaboration of new ILO norms relating to TNEs, acceptance of countries' rights to nationalization	Coordinated international action against TNEs
Action Programme	Council of Nordic Trade Unions	Rules of establishment; rules of competition; taxation; labor laws	To create the basis for common action concerning TNEs

Enforcement	Status	Comments
Voluntary	Recommendations and guidelines for action. Desired is a general multilateral treaty under UN auspices with a new UN agency supervising its application	Adopted by the XI ICFTU World Congress, Mexico, 1975. The Charter is intended to serve as a guideline for ICFTU actions at the national and international levels. It reflects the conviction of the ICFTU that national legislation frequently has to be supplemented (and sometimes even preceded) by strong international agreements
Voluntary	Recommendations and guidelines for action	Adopted 1973 by the Eighth World Trade Union Congress. Chapter V of the Charter deals with TNEs
Voluntary	Recommendations and guidelines for action	Adopted in 1975. The program constitutes the basis for common actions by the Nordic trade union movement at the national and international levels. At present the program is limited to four areas of concern

Notes

1. See, for instance, the following quote from Philips' N.V. *1972 Annual Report,* p. 12: "In our policy [i.e., that of the management of Philips] with regard to the allocation of factories we are taking account of the fact that in highly industrialized countries, where the general level of education is high and the supply of less skilled labor is relatively limited, a gradual shift is taking place from simple to sophisticated forms of production. As a consequence simple, labor-intensive production plants are increasingly being located in countries where the supply of labor for this category of work presents fewer problems. Since this is a slow process, and since advanced production plants will continue to be expanded in highly industrialized countries, this structural development is reflected only very gradually in the geographic distribution of our labor force."
2. For the most recent and comprehensive review of the literature and research concerning TNEs (including an extensive bibliography and an annotated list of research projects in progress at the beginning of 1976), see United Nations, Secretariat, *Research on Transnational Corporations* (E/C.10/12 and Add.1), 28 January 1976. This document also contains a listing of relevant bibliographies.
3. For the following see Bernard Mennis and Karl P. Sauvant, *Emerging Forms of Transnational Community: Transnational Business Enterprises and Regional Integration* (Lexington, Mass.: D.C. Heath, 1976); and United Nations, Department of Economic and Social Affairs, *Multinational Corporations in World Development* (New York: United Nations, 1973).
4. To quote the International Chamber of Commerce: "It must be understood that industrial enterprises are not established or operated primarily for the purpose of transferring techniques and skills from one country to another," but rather that "they and their affiliates manufacture and market on a worldwide basis the products in which they specialize. They seek to do this as efficiently and profitably as possible. . . ." See International Chamber of Commerce (ICC), *The International Corporation and the Transfer of Technology* (Paris: ICC, 1972), p. 5.
5. This tendency is encouraged by a deliberate incentive policy of many home countries designed to attract advanced production processes—notably those involving raw materials—into their borders. It is also reinforced by the organizational structure of enterprises. As Stephen H. Hymer pointed out, TNEs have different levels of operation for their various activities, the locations of which tend to parallel the distribution of the factors and conditions of production. See Stephen H. Hymer, "The Multinational Corporations and the Law of Uneven Development," in *Economics and the World Order: From the 1970s to the 1990s,* ed. Jagdish N. Bhagwati (London: Macmillan, 1972).

6. Since home countries are favored by the international distribution of the factors and conditions of production, and since performance in TNEs is, as a rule, equated with performance of the parent enterprise, home countries benefit automatically from the activities of "their" TNEs. However, to the extent that corporate performance is equated with the performance of the corporate system as a whole, home countries tend to lose these benefits. The latter approach appears to be becoming more important; witness, for instance, the move out of Canada of several TNEs when Canada imposed a tax measure unfavorable to TNEs based in that country.

7. Franklin R. Root, "Independence and Adaptation: Response Strategies of U.S. Based Multinational Corporations to a Restrictive Public Policy World," in *Controlling Multinational Enterprises: Problems, Strategies, Counter-strategies*, eds. Karl P. Sauvant and Farid G. Lavipour (Boulder, Colo.: Westview Press, 1976), pp. 101-110.

8. See ibid., for some data pertaining to the U.S.

9. For a brief discussion and some material on some of the constraints under which control efforts have to be formulated, see Sauvant and Lavipour, *Controlling Multinational Enterprises,* part II.

10. This section is largely based on United Nations, Secretariat, *National Legislation and Regulations Relating to Transnational Corporations* (E/C.10/8 and Add.1), 28 January 1976; a relevant chapter in Canada, Government of Canada, *Foreign Direct Investment in Canada* (Ottawa: Government of Canada, 1972) (reprinted in Sauvant and Lavipour, *Controlling Multinational Enterprises*); and United States, Department of Commerce, *Foreign Direct Investment in the United States,* vol. 2, *Appendices* (Washington: US Department of Commerce, 1975).

For further information, see the references cited earlier in this footnote, as well as Instituto para la Integración de América Latina and Banco Interamericano de Desarrollo, *Regimen de las inversiones extranjeros en los paises de la ALALC* (Buenos Aires: Instituto para la Integración de América Latina and Banco Interamericano de Desarrollo, 1974); Instituto para la Integración de América Latina and Banco Interamericano de Desarrollo, *Cuadro comparativo de legislaciones sobre inversión extranjero en paises de la ALALC* (Bueno Aires: Instituto para la Integración de América Latina and Banco Interamericano de Desarrollo, 1975); International Centre for Settlement of Investment Disputes, *Investment Laws of the World: The Developing Countries* (Dobbs Ferry, New York: Oceana Publications, various years); National Association of Credit Management, *Digest of Commercial Laws of the World* (Dobbs Ferry, New York: Oceana Publications, various years); and Organization of American States, Department of Legal Affairs, "Estudio comparativo de las Legislaciones Latinoamericanas Sobre Regulación y Control de la Inversión Privada Extranjera" (OEA/Ser. G; CP/INF.680/75), 29 April 1975.

11. The functions of administration and supervision are, however, fre-

quently exercised by individual government departments.

12. Only a few countries, particularly major capital exporters (like the United States, the Federal Republic of Germany, and the Netherlands) with a vested interest in maintaining laissez-faire, are relatively free from restrictions other than of key sectors.

13. Usually, however, these criteria are very vague and refer, for instance, to contributions to the economy, to development or national welfare, or to the use of local resources. See also footnote 15.

14. Most common among incentives—including those granted by socialist countries—are various tax privileges (especially tax holidays). Frequently, incentives and their terms are negotiated on a case-by-case basis—a method that is usually beneficial for foreign investors. For profiles of national incentives to private foreign direct investors in sixty countries, see National Industrial Conference Board, *Obstacles and Incentives to Private Foreign Investment*, vol. II, *Incentives, Assurances and Guarantees* (New York: National Industrial Conference Board, 1969). A reference service of the Business International Corporation, *Investing, Licensing and Trading Conditions Abroad,* provides periodic information on all aspects relevant to foreign direct investment in more than fifty countries.

15. The recently enacted Canadian Foreign Investment Review Act deals mainly with acquisitions. The take-over of any large Canadian business by any noncitizen has to be reviewed and authorized by a screening agency. The government will henceforth authorize only those acquisitions that it believes will significantly benefit Canada. Five criteria are taken into consideration: (1) effects on the level and nature of economic activity and employment; (2) degree and significance of Canadian participation; (3) effects on productivity, industrial efficiency, technological development, and product innovation and variety; (4) effects on competition; and (5) compatibility with national economic and industrial policies (see *Canada Gazette,* part II (27 March 1974), p. 108).

Obviously, these criteria are subject to broad interpretation and often difficult to implement. For instance, would it be likely that an acquisition judged beneficial in terms of the first four criteria is incompatible with (a not-yet-formulated) national industrial policy? Or, what is the trade-off between employment and efficiency?

The Australian experience may serve as an indicator of what can be expected from the new Canadian law. In 1972, Australia passed a Takeover Act, establishing a screening committee which bases its judgment on a broad notion of "national interests," defined in terms of the nature and size of the business to be taken over. Between 5 December 1972 and 31 May 1973, only 6 percent of the take-over proposals from foreign companies were rejected. If proposals that were withdrawn after the government had been notified are taken into consideration, the percentage increases to 13 percent of the offers made (*Financial Times*, 14 June 1973).

16. See United Nations, Secretariat, *National Legislation*, for further details on the prevalence of the measures mentioned in this paragraph.

Before passing the Foreign Investment Review Act, Canada experimented with "Some Guiding Principles of Good Corporate Behaviour for Subsidiaries in Canada of Foreign Companies," issued in 1966 by the Ministry of Trade and Commerce. The guidelines contained a list of 12 desirable objectives concerning the business policy of foreign affiliates. Although the guidelines were voluntary, surveys were conducted by the government to assess the performance of foreign affiliates in relation to the objectives of the guideline. The guidelines were eventually incorporated into the Foreign Investment Review Act.

17. See Appendix A to this chapter.

18. United Nations, Secretariat, *National Legislation*, p. 15.

19. Control efforts in regional groupings are primarily carried out in the framework (and as a part) of a more comprehensive regional integration attempt. For this reason, they are not considered together with international approaches which are specifically designed to deal with TNEs or aspects of their activities.

20. Jean Boddewyn, *Western European Policies Toward U.S. Investors* (New York: New York University, 1974), p. 60. The same source contains a useful summary of the EC's policies regarding TNEs. It should be noted that most EC efforts related to direct investments have to be seen in the larger framework of enhancing Western European economic integration. The same applies to the integration effort of the Andean Common Market states discussed below.

21. Several steps have been taken to harmonize company and tax laws. In June 1970, the EC Commission proposed the harmonization of municipal merger procedures as a first step toward regulating mergers across Community frontiers. In the same month, the Commission submitted a proposal for a European Company Statute. A European Company would have the same status as a national company in every Community country and it would come into existence by registration with the Court of the European Communities. Certain minimum capital requirements, however, make this form of venture relevant only for major concerns. The proposal is still before the EC Council. Furthermore, the European Investment Bank has been encouraged to make loans to Community enterprises interested in cross-border merging as a means of strengthening Western European industries, in particular in such key sectors as aeronautics and electronics. The 1970 memorandum on industrial policy indicates that, for this purpose, discriminatory measures might be admissible (see, European Community, Commission (CEC), *Industrial Policy in the Community* (Brussels: CEC, 1970)). Finally, in 1973, a Business Cooperation Center was established to

assist Community firms in finding partners in other Community countries, be it for cooperation or for merger (the idea of an EC corporate "marriage bureau" had been developed by Christopher Layton, who implemented it on becoming *fonctionnaire* in the EC Commission; see Christopher Layton, *Cross Frontier Mergers in Europe* (Bath: Bath University Press, 1971)).

22. Boddewyn, *Western European Policies,* pp. 51-52. The Commission hopes to further reduce the limit of 20 percent of capital costs it had imposed for 1972-73.

23. The quotes are from European Community, Commission, *Multinational Undertakings and Community Regulations. Commission Communication to the Council* (COM (73), 1930), pp. 2, 3, 5. *Business International,* 16 November 1973, p. 361, observed that this move concerning TNEs "reflects the growing internationalization of efforts to balance their power."

24. European Community, Commission, *Multinational Undertakings,* p. 9. In this context, the Council is encouraged to adopt directives that would protect workers against collective dismissals and regulate the treatment of workers affected by mergers and take-overs. Furthermore, the Commission urged the adoption of the European Company statute which also foresees the participation of employee representatives in the supervisory boards of companies.

25. The Commission suggested the publication of an annual report on major national and international enterprises covering, *inter alia,* investment flows, origin and composition of capital, employment, profits and taxes, research and development expenditures, and income from licenses.

26. In fact, the document even notes that "it is quite obvious that the activities of the Community will be fully effective only to the extent that identically inspired rules are imposed at world level with a view to ensuring a homogenous framework for the operations of multinational undertakings whatever their origin and their geographic field of activity" (EC, *Multinational Undertakings*, p. 3). It is in this context that point 5 of the action program, the harmonization of policies among OECD countries, has to be seen.

27. In May 1969, Bolivia, Chile, Colombia, Ecuador, and Peru signed the Agreement of Cartagena, establishing the Andean Common Market. Venezuela joined the group in 1973. The highest organ of ANCOM is the Junta with its permanent Secretariat located in Lima. ANCOM is a subgroup of the Latin American Free Trade Association, and its main purpose is the advancement of economic integration among its members. Since it was recognized that foreign direct investment would have a considerable influence on the integration process, a special Investment Code was formalized in Decision 24 of the Junta (July 1971). Its full title is "Common Treatment of Foreign Capital, Trademarks, Patents, Licensing Agreements and Royalties in the Andean Common Market." An English

translation is reprinted in the *Journal of Common Market Studies* 10 (June 1972): 339-359.
28. Dale B. Furnish, "The Andean Common Market's Common Regime for Foreign Investments," *Vanderbilt Journal of Transnational Law* 5 (Spring 1972): 314.
29. For this purpose, Decision No. 46 of the Junta also facilitates and regulates the formation of subregional enterprises; at least 60 percent of the capital of these enterprises has to be contributed by national investors from at least two ANCOM states.
30. Thus, the selective program does not establish permanent monopoly rights but rather offers head-start privileges. The first program approved (August 1972) covers about 200 metal-working products.
31. The Code specifically provides for a subregional system for the promotion, development, production, and adaptation of technology.
32. Council of the Americas (CoA), *The Andean Pact: Definition, Origin, and Analysis* (New York: CoA, 1974), part III, p. 81.
33. Ibid., part I, p. 2.
34. Ibid., part II, p. 7.
35. For a general discussion of producers' associations, see especially the literature quoted in footnote 43.
36. See Raymond F. Mikesell, "Conflict in Foreign Investor-Host Country Relations: A Preliminary Analysis," in *Foreign Investment in the Petroleum and Mineral Industries,* ed. Raymond F. Mikesell (Baltimore: The Johns Hopkins Press, 1971).
37. OPEC was founded by Iraq, Iran, Kuwait, Saudi Arabia, and Venezuela. Qatar joined in 1961, Indonesia and Libya in 1962, Abu Dhabi in 1967, Algeria in 1969, Nigeria in 1971, Ecuador in 1973, and Gabon in 1975.
38. Abbas Alnasrawi, "Collective Bargaining Power in OPEC," *Journal of World Trade Law* 7 (1973): 194.
39. The breakthrough was probably greatly helped by Libya's unilateral and successful attempt to increase crude prices, and thereby its oil revenues. In 1970, a mild energy shortage in Western Europe and Japan coincided with the continued closure of the Suez Canal, the disruption of the Saudi Arabia-Sidon pipeline, and a general shortage of long-haul tankers. Oil from Libya, a country which already supplied about a quarter of Western Europe's requirements, was in great demand. Libya, however, decided to cut back its output in an attempt to convince the oil companies to agree to higher prices. The cut-backs were first imposed on the weakest of the oil companies operating in Libya, Occidental Oil, but were later extended to other companies. At the same time, Algeria announced a rise in oil prices. Within a few months (in September 1971), Occidental Oil, which was particularly vulnerable because it had no other source of crude outside the United States, agreed to a price increase and other companies soon followed suit. These

developments set the stage for the successful collective bargaining at the Caracas Conference (December 1970) and the Tehran negotiations (February 1971).

40. The Tehran agreement was solidifed in Geneva in January 1972, when, in the wake of the devaluation of the dollar, further price adjustments were made and prices were linked to an index of nine major currencies. These negotiations proved to be an important test case for OPEC's ability to act jointly vis-à-vis the major international oil enterprises.

41. Actually, the nationalization of foreign affiliates is not a measure that is taken very frequently. A study prepared by the United Nations (United Nations, Secretary-General, *Permanent Sovereignty over Natural Resources* (A/9716 and Corr.1), 20 September 1974) reported over 875 cases (all in developing countries) of nationalization or take-over of foreign affiliates of parent enterprises of any nationality for the period 1960 to mid-1974. (Furthermore, in about 10 percent of the cases, the affiliates were later reverted to the foreign investor.) Of these 875 cases, one-quarter involved affiliates of TNEs headquartered in the US; over one-third involved natural resource assets (including agriculture) and somewhat less than one-third banking and insurance facilities (since the percentages have been calculated on the basis of number of cases, the high percentage for this latter category reflects the presence of a large number of branches in any of the nationalizing countries). Moreover, over two-thirds of the total number of cases is accounted for by only 10 countries, all of them countries that, for sociopolitical reasons, embarked on large-scale indigenization programs (e.g., Algeria, Chile, Egypt, Sudan, Uganda, United Republic of Tanzania). These figures have to be seen against the total number of foreign affiliates, which is over 23,000 for the US and estimated to be about 70,000 for major market economies. (Approximately one-third of the book value which is represented by these affiliates is located in developing countries.) In the overwhelming number of bargaining situations, therefore, TNEs—and especially those in manufacturing—need not fear the ultimate loss of their assets. Conversely, the reluctance of most host governments to have recourse to nationalization represents an effective limitation on their control policies vis-à-vis foreign investors.

42. The board chairperson of British Petroleum, quoted in M.A. Adelman, "Is the Oil Shortage Real? Oil Companies as OPEC Tax-collectors," *Foreign Policy* 9 (1972): 69-107.

43. For a discussion of determinants of the bargaining power of producers' associations and conditions of their success see, for instance, C. Fred Bergsten, "The Threat from the Third World," *Foreign Policy* 11 (Summer 1973): 102-124, and "The Threat is Real," *Foreign Policy* 14 (Spring 1974): 84-90; Stephen D. Krasner, "Oil is the Exception," *Foreign Policy* 14 (Spring 1974): 68-84 (excerpts from these articles are reprinted in Sauvant

and Lavipour, *Controlling Multinational Enterprises*; this volume also contains, in the introduction to its part III, a brief discussion of this subject matter). See also, Zuhayr Mikdashi, "Collusion Could Work," *Foreign Policy* 14 (Spring 1974): 57-68; Bension Varon and Kenji Takeuchi, "Developing Countries and Non-Fuel Minerals," *Foreign Affairs* 52 (1974): 497-510; and Alton D. Law, *International Commodity Agreements* (Lexington: D.C. Heath, 1974).

44. Krasner, "Oil is the Exception," p. 74.

45. Venezuela—an important member of OPEC—financially supported, for instance, Central American coffee producers in their efforts to obtain higher prices.

46. For an analysis of the development of the nonaligned movement into a pressure group for the reorganization of the international economic system, see Odette Jankowitsch and Karl P. Sauvant, "The Evolution of the Non-Aligned Movement into a Pressure Group for the Establishment of the New International Economic Order" (Paper presented at the Seventeenth Annual Convention of the International Studies Association, Toronto, February 1976).

47. The "Economic Declaration" adopted in September 1973 by the Fourth Conference of Heads of State or Government of Non-Aligned Countries (United Nations, *Action Programme for Economic Co-operation* (doc. A/9330) 22 November 1973, pp. 67-68) recommended, for instance, "the establishment of effective solidarity bodies for the defence of the interests of raw material producing countries such as OPEC and CIPEC, which are capable of undertaking wide-ranging activities in order to recover natural resources and ensure increasingly substantial export earnings and income in real terms, and to use these resources for development purposes and to raise the living standard of their peoples." The text continues: "The results obtained in the hydrocarbons sector, which was previously exploited for the sole benefit of the transnational oil companies, demonstrate the power and effectiveness of organized and concerted action by producing and exporting countries."

48. The establishment of both institutions had first been recommended at the February 1975 "Conference of Developing Countries on Raw Materials" (Dakar Conference). Following this conference, several expert group meetings took place during which the Fund to Finance Buffer Stocks as well as the Council of Producers' Associations were discussed (in preparation for the Fifth Conference of Ministers for Foreign Affairs of Non-Aligned Countries). The group of experts dealing with the Council also suggested the initial membership of the Council. For further details, see Jankowitsch and Sauvant, "Evolution of the Non-Aligned Movement."

49. For a review of recent developments in these three industries, see United Nations, Secretary-General, *Permanent Sovereignty over Natural Resour-*

ces (A/9716 and Corr. 1 and E/C.7/53), 20 September 1974 and 31 January 1975. See also Kenneth W. Clarfield, Stuart Jackson, Jeff Keeffe, Michaela Ann Noble, and A. Patrick Ryan, *Eight Mineral Cartels: The New Challenge to Industrialized Nations* (New York: McGraw-Hill, 1975).

50. At the same time, however, all three materials have gained a competitive advantage vis-à-vis petroleum-based plastics.

51. Regional measures relating to TNEs—like those taken by ANCOM or the EC—are not included here, since, as pointed out earlier, they are usually not taken in their own right but tend rather to be carried out in the context of a more comprehensive integration effort.

It should also be noted that a number of international agreements of a more general nature are relevant to TNEs and their activities in that they constitute the framework within which TNEs operate. Among these, particularly important are the General Agreement on Tariffs and Trade (GATT), the Articles of Agreement of the International Monetary Fund (IMF), a large number of conventions relating to labor questions and concluded under the auspices of the International Labour Organisation (ILO), and the "Final Act" of the Conference on Security and Co-operation in Europe.

52. For a more detailed discussion of most of these instruments, see United Nations, Secretariat, *International Codes and Regional Agreements Relating to Transnational Corporations: A Comparative Survey of Selected International Instruments* (E/C.10/9 and Add.1), 30 January 1976. See Annex II of the same source for a listing of additional relevant instruments.

53. The character of the international accounting standards prepared by the International Accounting Standards Committee, however, is different.

54. Earlier attempts—apart from the never ratified Charter of the International Trade Organization (ITO)—were largely pursued in relation to specific political objectives, e.g., the United States Trading with the Enemy Act.

55. This part of the package was added in an attempt to deal within the framework of the general foreign direct investment discussion (as opposed to trade measures) with regional incentives that attract foreign direct investment and result in subsidized exports to third countries. Michelin's decision to service the U.S. market from a plant in Canada was instrumental in putting this issue on the agenda.

56. Organisation for Economic Co-operation and Development (OECD), *Activities of OECD in 1974* (Paris: OECD, 1975).

57. The consultation procedures are to be reviewed within a period of three years. These documents are contained in OECD, *International Investment and Multinational Enterprises* (Paris: OECD, 1976). The following quotes are taken from this source.

58. See, respectively, Third Conference of Heads of State or Government of

Non-aligned Countries, "Declaration on Non-Alignment and Economic Progress," in *Neither East nor West: The Basic Documents of Non-Alignment,* ed. Henry M. Christman (New York: Sheed and Ward, 1973), p. 191, and Third Conference of Ministers of Foreign Affairs of Non-Aligned Countries, *An Action Programme for Economic Co-operation among Non-Aligned Countries*, mimeographed (NAC/FM/CONF.1/18 Add.1), para. 36. The Committee (which was open to all developing countries) was specifically instructed to take into account, *inter alia,* "the introduction of common investment policies" and "mechanisms for collating and exchanging information among the Non-Aligned Countries on the operations of trans-national and multi-national corporations."

59. These considerations did not cover the whole range of issues associated with transnational enterprises but rather were limited to questions relating to host country authorization (including for reinvestments) and control of foreign direct investment; various economic effects; the strict limitation of acquisitions; remittances of profits; and key sectors.

60. See Fourth Conference of Heads of State or Government of Non-Aligned Countries, *Action Programme for Economic Co-operation* (UN document A/9330) 22 November 1973, p. 98.

The center is expected to promote the exchange of experience and information among Non-Aligned Countries, to be responsible for training personnel and to conduct research (ibid., pp. 98-99).

61. See Conference of Ministers for Foreign Affairs of Non-Aligned Countries, Lima, 25-29 August 1975, "Draft Statute for the Treatment of Foreign Investment, Transnational Corporations and the Transfer of Technology," NAC/FM/CONF. 5/5, 20 August 1975. The following quotes are taken from this source.

62. These rules are virtually identical with the "Guidelines of Behavior that could be Observed by Transnational Enterprises," presented on 13 January 1975 by the Latin American Group in an aide-memoire to the Third Preparatory Session of the Working Group on Transnational Enterprises of the OAS. The same set of rules was submitted two months later to the first session of the UN Commission on Transnational Corporations. They were also appended to the conclusions and recommendations of the second session of the UN commission. Thus, these rules have their origin in the concerns of (the relatively highly developed) Latin American countries. Since the experiences of other developing countries are different, differences in approach may be unavoidable. This situation may also be one of the explanatory factors for the ultimate refusal of the Non-Aligned Countries as a group to make the Statute the basis for common actions.

63. Fifth Conference of Ministers for Foreign Affairs of Non-Aligned Countries, *Plan of Action for Strengthening Co-operation, Solidarity and the Action Capacity of Non-Aligned and other Developing Countries and for Achieving th*

Establishment of the New International Economic Order (UN document A/10217) 5 September 1975, para. 164.

64. See, for instance, the *Declaration and Plan of Action on Industrial Development and Co-operation,* adopted in Algiers, February 1975, by the Second Ministerial Meeting of the Group of 77 (relating to UNIDO) and contained in United Nations document E/AC.62/4, 15 April 1975. The provisions contained in this document regarding transnational enterprises were repeated, almost verbatim, in the *Lima Declaration and Plan of Action on Industrial Development and Co-operation,* adopted by the Second General Conference of UNIDO (UN document A/10112), 13 June 1975; and the *Manila Declaration and Programme of Action,* adopted in Manila in February 1976 by the Third Ministerial Meeting of the Group of 77 (relating to UNCTAD) (United Nations document TD/195), 12 February 1976.

65. Resolution 1721 (LIII).

66. See, for instance, N. T. Wang, "The International Community and Transnational Corporations" (with an annex containing the preliminary work program of the UN Commission on Transnational Corporations as agreed upon during its first session in March 1975), in *Controlling Multinational Enterprises,* eds. Sauvant and Lavipour; Michell B. Carroll, *UN Proposals for the Regulation of Transnational Corporations* (New York: The Presidents Association, 1975); Paul A. Tharp, Jr., "Transnational Enterprises and International Regulation: A Survey of Various Approaches in International Organizations," *International Organization* 30 (Winter 1976): 47-73; Werner Feld, "U.N. Supervision over Multinational Corporations: Realistic Expectation or Exercise in Futility?" mimeographed (New Orleans: University of New Orleans, Department of Political Science, n.d.); Wolfgang Gruhler, *Die Kontroverse um die multinationalen Unternehmen: Kritik der Vorwürfe und Forderungen* (Köln: Deutscher Instituts-Verlag, 1974); and Rainer Hellmann, *Die Kontrolle multinationaler Unternehmen* (Baden-Baden: Nomos-Verlagsgesellschaft, 1974).

67. See United Nations, Department of Economic and Social Affairs, *Multinational Corporations in World Development,* (New York: United Nations, 1973); *Summary of Statements Made at Public Hearings Conducted by the Group of Eminent Persons Studying the Impact of Multinational Corporations on Development and International Relations* (New York: United Nations, 1974); *The Impact of Multinational Corporations on Development and on International Relations* (New York: United Nations, 1974); and Economic and Social Council (ECOSOC) resolutions 1908 (LVII) and 1913 (LVII).

The Commission is composed of high-level experts from 48 states (12 African states, 11 Asian, 10 Latin American, 10 Western European and other states, and 5 socialist states of Eastern Europe). The Commission meets annually. It reports to the UN Economic and Social Council and assists that body in questions concerning TNEs by examining and discussing all issues relevant to this subject matter. The Centre on Transnational Corporations, which became functional in November 1975, is a part of the UN Secretariat and conducts its activities under the guidance of the Commission. When it was set up, it had a professional staff of 12 persons.

68. United Nations, Commission on Transnational Corporations, second session, 1-12 March 1976, *Report on the Second Session* (New York: United Nations, 1976), chapter I, "Conclusions and Recommendations of the Commisssion," para. 4.

During its first session (March 1975), the Commission established the priorities for its work and formulated a preliminary work program. During the second session (March 1976), these priorities were confirmed and a detailed program of work was agreed upon. This program was submitted to the Economic and Social Council for its consideration and approval at its sixty-first session (summer 1976).

69. For further details concerning the work of the Commission and especially of the Centre in these priority areas, see the work program of the Commission. See also United Nations, Secretariat, *Information on Transnational Corporations* (A/C.10/11 and Add.1), 23 January 1976; *Research;* and *Proposed Programme of Technical Co-operation on Matters Related to Transnational Corporations* (E/C.10/13), 28 January 1976.

70. As indicated earlier (footnote 62), these rules have already been discussed in the framework of the OAS, and most of them proved to be basically acceptable to the United States; see Organization of American States, Permanent Council, General Committee, Subcommittee to Study Resolution CP/RES.154, "Behavior of Transnational Enterprises," *Report of the Rapporteur of the Working Group of the Subcommittee of the General Committee to Study Resolution CP/RES.154* 'Behavior of Transnational Enterprises Operating in the Region and Need for a Code of Conduct to be Observed by such Enterprises" (OEA/Ser.G, CP/GP/656/76/Corr.1), 26 February 1976. See also Annexes I-III of the same document.

71. In establishing this working group, the Commission largely followed the recommendations of the Centre contained in United Nations, Secretariat, *Possible Methods of Work Related to the Drafting of a Code of Conduct* (E/C.10/10), 19 January 1976. Several documents had been prepared by the Centre for the second session of the Commission in order to assist it in its work on the code of conduct; see, United Nations, Secretariat, *National Legislation* and *International Codes*. The preparation of additional documents was requested at the second session of the Commission; the first of these documents was United Nations, Secretary General, *Transnational Corporations: Issues Involved in the Formulation of a Code of Conduct* (E/C.10/17), 19 July 1976.

The working group, as well as the Commission, can draw on the knowledge of a small group of persons with practical experience in labor unions, academia, and business and consumer groups.

72. In resolution 3514 (XXX), the General Assembly requested the Commission to include the question of corrupt practices of TNEs in its program of work. In addition, the United States submitted a proposal (at the Commission's second session) for an international agreement on this subject (see United Nations, Commission on Transnational Corporations, *Report on the Second Session,* annex VI). See also United Nations, Secretary-General, *Transnational Corporations: Measures against Corrupt Practices of Transnational and other Corporations, Their Intermediaries and Others Involved. Report by the Secretary-General* (E/5838), 11 June 1976.

73. For UN activities regarding the last three issue areas, see Appendix A.

74. The idea of such an agreement was first advanced by Paul M. Goldberg and Charles P. Kindleberger, "Toward a GATT for Investment: A Proposal for Supervision of the International Corporation," *Law and Policy in International Business* 2 (Summer 1970): 295-323.

75. For some additional literature dealing with international control of TNEs see, for instance, George W. Ball, "Cosmocorp: The Importance of Being Stateless," *Columbia Journal of World Business* 2 (November-December 1967): 25-30 and "Making World Corporations into World Citizens," *War/Peace Report* 8 (October 1968): 8-10; A. A. Fatouros, "An International Code to Protect Private Investment: Proposals and Perspectives," *University of Toronto Law Journal* 14 (1961): 77-102 and "Problèms et méthodes d'une réglementation des entreprises multinationales," *Journal du Droit International* 101 (July-August-September 1974): 495-521; Public Affairs Council, *Codes of Conduct* (Washington, D.C.: Public Affairs Council, 1975); Eugene Rostow, Joseph S. Nye, Jr., and George W. Ball, "The Need for International Agreements," in *Global Companies: The Political Economy of World Business,* ed. George W. Ball (Englewood Cliffs: Prentice-Hall, 1975); Don Wallace, Jr., *The Regulation of Multinational Corporations* (New York: Praeger, 1976); Don Wallace, Jr., assisted by Helga Ruof-Koch, eds., *International Control of Foreign Investment: The Düsseldorf Conference on Multinational Corporations* (New York: Praeger, 1974); and N.T. Wang, "The Design of an International Code of Conduct for Transnational Corporations," *Journal of International Law and Economics,* forthcoming. For references to some research projects being conducted in 1976 regarding codes of conduct and problems related to the regulation and control of TNEs, see United Nations, Secretariat, *Research,* p. 48.

76. By way of example the Swiss pharmaceutical company Hoffmann LaRoche sold drugs to the British National Health Service at prices considerably higher than those it charged in Italy for the same product. For years this practice remained undiscovered, simply because nobody compared prices transnationally.

77. In this effort, the Commission and the Centre could be supported by

joint liaison and support units on TNEs set up in each of the United Nations regional commissions pursuant to Economic and Social Council resolution 1961 (LIX).

78. Malcolm Warner and Louis Turner (see "Trade Unions and the Multinational Firms," *Journal of Industrial Relations* 14 (June 1972): 147) quote a report on strikes involving Ford in the United Kingdom: "Ford is known to have one of the best early-warning systems in the motor industry and has on occasion pin-pointed troubles in supplier firms before production has actually stopped. In some cases, it has beaten strikes by 'pulling' tools and dies in time to start alternative production before employees in the original firm have stopped work."

79. On the other hand, TNEs could be agents for the introduction of more advanced labor practices into host countries.

80. In parallel bargaining, demands need not necessarily be the same. Coordination could be based on an agreement that no national union will sign a settlement until agreement has been reached in each country.

81. A legal problem is that sympathy strikes are often illegal; from a tactical point of view, it might be easier to gain worker support in simultaneous bargaining periods.

82. Particularly active were (or are) the International Transport Workers' Federation, the European Committee of Metal Workers, and the International Chemical Workers' Federation.

83. World councils have been established for enterprises like General Electric, Westinghouse, International Harvester, John Deere, Massey-Fergusson, and all major automobile firms.

84. For a review of obstacles see, in particular, David H. Blake, "Multi-National Companies, International Unions and International Collective Bargaining: A Case Study of the Political, Social and Economic Implications of the 1967 U.A.W.-Chrysler Agreement," in *Transnational Industrial Relations: The Impact of Multinational Corporations and Economic Regionalism on Industrial Relations*, ed. H. Günter (London: Macmillan, 1972), "The Multinationalization of Industrial Relations," *Journal of International Business Studies* 3 (1972): 17-32, and "Trade Unions and the Challenge of the Multinational Corporation," *The Annals* 403 (September 1972): 34-45; Rolf Jungnickel and K. Matthies, *Multinationale Unternehmen und Gewerkschaften* (Hamburg: Verlag Weltarchiv, 1973); Duane Kujawa, ed., *American Labor and the Multinational Corporation* (New York: Praeger, 1973); Ernst Piehl, *Multinationale Konzerne und internationalale Gewerkschaftsbewegung* (Frankfurt: Europäische Verlagsanstalt, 1974); and Kurt P. Tudyka, *Multinationale Konzerne und Gewerkschaftsstrategie* (Hamburg: Hoffmann and Campe, 1974). For further reference, see United Nations, Secretariat, *Research,* pp. 39-40.

85. European Community, Commission, *Multinational Undertakings,* p. 9.

Part 7

Self-reliance

23 *Economic Co-operation Among Developing Countries*

UNCTAD

Towards a Global System of Economic Co-operation Among Developing Countries

During the last few years a number of factors and circumstances have given a new thrust to the concept of economic co-operation among developing countries. Foremost among them was the realization that the International Development Strategy was falling far behind the expectations placed on it in 1970. Deep and prolonged recession and severe inflationary pressures in developed market-economy countries, the increase in oil prices, fluctuations in other commodity prices and the consequent financial and balance-of-payments problems, brought about dramatic changes in the world economy. All this gave rise to a greater awareness of the potentialities of collective self-reliance. The developing countries had before them the challenge of acquiring increased strength through unity of action.

The failure of the traditional economic order to solve the problems of poverty and economic backwardness has imparted a sense of urgency to the need for the developing countries to reduce their dependence on the industrialized centres and to secure their interdependent and balanced development. This sense of urgency is also fostered by the growing realization that in the absence of conscious and deliberate efforts to that effect, the opportunities and prospects for co-operative action which exist at present might not necessarily be a permanent feature in the relationships among developing countries. While solidarity among them has been emphasized in several occasions, there is nevertheless a danger that, without effective mechanisms to harmonize a diversity of interests, such solidarity could be negatively affected by the different circumstances and degrees of development in which the countries of the third world find themselves.

Reprinted, with permission, from UNCTAD, *Economic Co-operation among Developing Countries: Report by the UNCTAD Secretariat* (TD/192), 22 December 1975, pp. 1-23.

The International Development Strategy adopted for the Second United Nations Development Decade viewed co-operation among developing countries mainly as "efforts to negotiate and put into effect commitments for instituting schemes for regional and sub-regional integration or measures of trade expansion. . . ."[1] Since then, however, several resolutions and decisions adopted within and outside the United Nations framework have widened the context of co-operation beyond the boundaries set by trade and integration agreements among neighbouring countries. In particular, the Fourth Conference of Heads of State or Government of Non-Aligned Countries held at Algiers in September 1973 approved an Action Programme for Economic Co-operation among Non-Aligned and other Developing Countries which had been adopted at the Conference of Non-Aligned Foreign Ministers held at Georgetown in September 1972. Then, in 1974, the Declaration on the Establishment of a New International Economic Order adopted by the General Assembly of the United Nations underlined the importance of promoting new types of co-operation among the developing countries. Although it has been recognized that the strengthening of the existing economic integration schemes, which in fact embrace about one half of the total number of developing countries, should constitute an essential element of a comprehensive effort towards collective self-reliance, new approaches and ideas are emerging which emphasize the need for co-operation among all the developing countries. This is particularly so in relation to such actions as those leading to the creation of producers' associations which would strengthen the measures being adopted for the creation of a new and equitable international economic order.

The Programme of Action on the Establishment of a New International Economic Order adopted at the sixth special session of the General Assembly envisages, inter alia, measures to be taken by developing countries "to promote collective self-reliance among them and to strengthen mutually beneficial international economic co-operation with a view to bringing about the accelerated development of developing countries."[2] In addition, the resolution on development and international economic co-operation adopted at the seventh special session urged "developed countries and the United Nations systems. . . . to provide, as and when requested, support and assistance to developing countries in strengthening and enlarging their mutual co-operation at sub-regional, regional and inter-regional levels."[3] The development of collective self-reliance is thus an integral aspect of the new international economic order and one supported by all sections of the international community. Within the new global strategy of economic development and the principles governing international economic co-operation, it has been given a new and more profound emphasis.

The resolutions and recommendations referred to above have given special importance to collective action for the establishment of mechanisms to secure equitable and remunerative prices and stabilize markets for basic export commodities; to the concession of preferential treatment in trade relations among developing countries; to the promotion of payments arrangements; to joint action in the fields of industry, science, technology, transport and shipping; and to co-operation in the use of financial resources available for development.

At present, a number of initiatives are beginning to give concrete shape to the new trend towards collective self-reliance. Significant among them are a number of bilateral ventures among developing countries, particularly in the productive sectors; the bilateral and multilateral financial support given by oil exporting States to other developing countries; and the organization of producers' associations and marketing schemes aimed at securing fair and stable prices for certain commodities and increasing the producers' share in their transportation, marketing and distribution. Also, trade relations among developing countries are being facilitated by new preferential arrangements and payments agreements at the sub-regional level.

These new steps towards economic co-operation among developing countries, as well as those leading to the re-structuring and strengthening of existing integration schemes, represent concrete actions which implement the principles of collective self-reliance and interdependence. It should be pointed out, however, that some of the new ventures in co-operation, because of their ad hoc, short-term or discontinuous nature, could fall short of the expectations placed on them if they do not develop a self-generating momentum. Moreover, what has been achieved so far could not by itself lead to the emergence of a consistent set of measures designed to secure the greatest possible advantage from economic interdependence among the developing countries. Also, some caution should be exercised to ensure that special ties based on geography, history or culture, which often give rise to fruitful co-operation among particular groups of countries, do not lead to undue discrimination against other developing countries. Finally, it is becoming increasingly evident that the vigorous pursuit of self-reliance and the implementation of concrete schemes of economic co-operation among developing countries could be seriously hampered by the absence of institutional structures specially geared to existing possibilities.

Unity of action among developing countries is reinforced by their advantage in population and in the natural resources which they possess. These favourable conditions, apart from opening new opportunities for development, enhance the collective bargaining power of the developing countries vis-à-vis the developed world. Besides the points raised in this report, there are other specific issues, dealt with separately, in which an increased bargaining power would be of benefit to developing countries, particularly those relating to the integrated programme for commodities, the transfer of technology and international monetary arrangements. The consolidation and effective use of the developing countries' combined bargaining strength in international economic relations, therefore, is to be seen as a major objective of economic co-operation among themselves.

The development of an integrated global system for economic co-operation among developing countries would help to avoid inconsistencies and fragmentation in the pursuit of collective self-reliance. Apart from being open to the developing countries of all regions, such a system should encompass in a harmonious manner several measures and elements designed to secure the greatest advantage from multinational action. Accordingly, the system should include the following:

a. The strengthening and broadening of sub-regional and regional economic co-operation in a manner consistent with global co-operation among developing countries as a whole; and
b. A set of inter-related policies, mechanisms and institutions designed to implement new forms of joint action within a wide framework of third world co-operation, with special provisions included in favour of the relatively less advanced countries.

The elements which could form the core of this system of economic co-operation among developing countries are outlined in the remainder of this report, which is intended to initiate the process of consideration of this aspect of a new global development strategy.

Strengthening Economic Integration

The strengthening of regional and sub-regional economic groupings would necessarily assume different forms according to the pecularities of the existing or emerging schemes. At the same time, it should be emphasized that in spite of the difficulties which several of the integration groupings have faced, the countries participating in them may be best placed to initiate some of the newly suggested forms of economic co-operation either among their present members or through a process of outward expansion.

The accumulated experience of economic integration schemes of developing countries points to a few areas where improvement and new initiatives require priority attention. First, intergovernmental machinery and community institutions need, in many instances, to be improved in ways which would better harmonize national and common interests and better reflect the agreed goals of economic integration of the grouping concerned. Their technical capacity needs to be strengthened so as to make the most effective use of the existing instruments of economic integration.

Secondly, the existing instruments themselves need in many cases to be revised so as to make them more effective. This is particularly true in regard to trade liberalization regimes, systems of common external protection and common fiscal incentive schemes.

Thirdly, the measures which have been adopted to secure greater benefits for the least developed member countries of economic groupings need, in many cases, to be revised and endowed with an element of automaticity with the aim of making them more effective. Considerable emphasis should be placed on this, since the failure of the existing devices for benefiting the least developed countries has been one of the most important obstacles in the path towards fully fledged economic integration among developing countries.

Fourthly and most important, emphasis should be shifted decisively from trade matters toward joint endeavours in the development of regional industrial and agricultural resources and of a common transportation infrastructure. The transitional preoccupation with reliance on market mechanisms through trade liberalization and external protection have had only a limited impact on growth, virtually none on structural development and, through the imbalances they create, have raised political obstacles to co-operation even before substantial economic gains could be secured for the co-operating countries. Although the importance of co-operation in production is recognized and provided for in some economic integration treaties, in practice this form of co-operation has been relegated to a secondary order of priority in most integration groupings. The new suggested emphasis on production should also embrace common approaches to the transfer of technology and the development of indigenous technological capacity, and to foreign capital and transnational corporations.

The promotion of economic co-operation in the developing world as a whole could be fostered through the strengthening and outward expansion of regional groupings. Existing schemes could conceivably attract new full-scale members whenever it is politically and economically feasible. In some instances this could be initiated through participation by non-member countries in the implementation of pilot projects of those groupings in fields not so far covered by co-operation arrangements. The outward expansion of existing integration schemes could also proceed on the basis of limited and selective exchanges of concessions and other forms of mutual support between groupings and prospective partner countries or between groupings themselves. This could lead to a more comprehensive involvement of neighbouring states within a system of concentric circles with different degrees of economic integration.

The Main Elements of a System of Economic Co-operation Among Developing Countries Outside the Framework of Integration Groupings

Alongside the measures adopted to strengthen and broaden regional and sub-regional economic integration, a global system of economic co-operation among developing countries would require the adoption of policies and mechanisms necessary for new forms of joint action outside the framework of integration groupings consistent with regional and third world objectives, and providing for special benefits for the least advanced countries. The fields which could be covered are many. It would seem advisable, however, that as a first approach such coverage be confined to the most critical areas. In this connexion it should be pointed out that although the importance of multinational co-operation for the creation of physical infrastructure cannot be minimized, this facet of co-operation has already been largely explored and implemented in several parts of the world, both within and outside integration schemes, so that it might not be necessary to emphasize it as one of the fields in which new mechanisms and devices should be adopted. On the other hand, there are several fields in which it seems fundamental to adopt measures to facilitate and promote co-operation among developing countries outside the framework of integration groupings: (a) trade and (b) production.[4]

Trade Expansion

Trade expansion among developing countries should be viewed as part of a system of economic co-operation rather than as an end in itself to be brought about by a set of isolated measures. Consequently, it should be necessarily conditioned by the particular objectives of co-operation schemes. It could not in any sense be the automatic result of traditional measures of trade liberalization and the free play of market forces, but would rather be the outcome of a set of programmed actions related to those taken in the field of production. In accordance with this conception, trade expansion could be promoted by three major and complementary sets of instruments: first, a system of preferences among developing countries which would set in motion the process of liberalizing access to markets; second, a system of devices to promote trade actively and to improve the trading position of the developing countries, including the establishment of multinational import and export enterprises, the multinational pooling of imports on a selective basis together with the aggregation of marine cargoes, co-operation among state-trading mechanisms and the application, where appropriate, of multinational purchase and supply commitments under medium- and long-term contracts; third, a system of payments, including clearing arrangements, interregional payments schemes and reciprocal credit support and joint reserve management.

The System of Preferences

Although the principle of trade preferences has proved relatively successful in various sub-regional groupings among developing countries, at the regional and interregional levels preferential arrangements among those countries are still at an incipient stage. Together with measures of a more active nature, therefore, the emerging strategy for economic co-operation could consider a more vigorous development of preferential trading relationships at all levels with a view to ultimately establishing a comprehensive and well structured system of preferences for the third world as a whole.

The basic objectives of a third world preference scheme would be (a) to provide a limited advantage in favour of developing country suppliers vis-à-vis imports from developed countries, and (b) to ensure an equitable distribution of the costs and benefits of the scheme among the individual participating countries. To achieve these goals in a meaningful manner the scheme would need to consider the basic interests and widely different economic situations of the developing countries, their distinct export product patterns and the existing disparity in their reliance on different trade policy instruments. In fact, the frequency of such disparities requires that tariff preferences be complemented by greater flexibility of non-tariff barriers in cases in which these preclude access to markets. Otherwise, the countries that rely mainly upon tariffs to protect their industries and safeguard their payments position would be at a disadvantage vis-à-vis those which apply other import restrictions.

As a consequence of these objectives, and in keeping with the spirit of the new international economic order, a third world preference scheme should emphasize participation and solidarity rather than the principles of strict reciprocity. Although it should be sufficiently simple in its application, it should also provide for adequate possibilities to permit the participation of sub-regional and regional groupings and consider the special situation of the least developed countries. Consequently, a comprehensive system of preferences among developing countries could be based on the following major elements:

a. Coverage of traditional as well as non-traditional exports of developing countries, including manufactures, agricultural and processed agricultural products and other commodities.
b. The inclusion of tariff as well as non-tariff barriers which preclude or severely limit access to markets, such as quantitative restrictions,

licensing, import prohibitions and foreign exchange restrictions.

c. Multilateral negotiations leading to concessions for groups of products at the sub-regional, regional and third world levels. Such concessions should not necessarily aim at full trade liberalization but could be restricted to intermediate and realistic targets.
d. The possible inclusion of contractual commitments regarding supplies and purchases at mutually agreed price ranges as a technique for balancing concessions within multilateral agreements, mainly in connexion with public sector purchases and commodities handled by State trading agencies.
e. Special preferential concessions for the exports of the relatively less advanced countries taking into account the special circumstances of each particular case and linking these concessions to more active measures in the fields of production and finance.

The third world preference system could follow three interrelated approaches. One would consist of negotiations within existing and emerging sub-regional co-operation or integration groupings. Another would involve the formation of regional schemes covering the main geographical areas, which would not only ensure the outward-oriented development of integration groupings but also permit their harmonious co-operation with non-member countries of the same region. Over and above these two approaches a third world scheme could be applied; thus, inter-regional preferences would form part of regional preferences and both would be included as part of sub-regional co-operation or integration schemes.

Once the main elements of the structures of the scheme are defined, the question arises as to the best way to implement it. This would require a basic negotiation of the comprehensive approach at a third world level, but once the wide framework is defined, a pragmatic approach could be the step-by-step building of the system on the basis of existing or emerging sub-regional, regional and inter-regional schemes, including the General Agreement on Tariffs and Trade (GATT) Protocol relating to Trade Negotiations among Developing Countries. In a progressive way it would be possible to integrate into them the basic features of the third world system. Besides, such a procedure could have the advantage of linking preferential arrangements to payments schemes which should form part of the global system of economic co-operation among developing countries.

Active Measures of Trade Co-operation

Co-operation among developing countries in the field of trade should aim not only to facilitate commercial transactions among them, but also to promote their trade relations through special agreements and to improve their trading position vis-à-vis the developed countries in regard to both exports and imports.

Trade agreements among developing countries. Medium and long-term contractual agreements are an effective means of directly expanding trade and creating new trade flows among developing countries, particularly in the initial phases of co-operation. These arrangements should involve commitments to supply and purchase specific commodities within mutually agreed price ranges over given periods of time. Apart from introducing into trade relations a degree of stability consistent with the overall plans of both the exporting and importing countries, they would open up the possibility of compensating disequilibria in trade flows or in the distribution of benefits deriving from joint projects. Furthermore, they would help to avoid the need to direct exports mainly to markets where they are paid for in convertible currencies. Possibilities for contractual agreements of this kind may be generated in the context of negotiations on preferences among developing countries or as a by-product of close co-ordination of the operations of public sector institutions and state trading organizations.

Measures for improving the developing countries' trading position in regard to exports. The export trade of developing countries is characterized by dependence on the marketing systems and distribution channels of the developed countries, especially those organized through the intra-firm transactions of transnational corporations and through commodity markets or exchanges located in and controlled by developed countries. This helps to explain why the share of value-added retained by developing countries in most primary commodities is a minor proportion of the final selling price (in certain cases no more than 10-15 percent). Since many developing countries, often in the same region, export the same product to the same markets or transit points in developed countries, various types of joint action could be organized to increase the net proceeds accruing to the developing countries from their export products:

a. Producers' associations. Co-operation in this field should aim at the strengthening of existing producer organizations—particularly through expanded developing country membership—and at the formation of associations for commodities which are not currently covered by such arrangements. While in many cases these associations may undertake joint action aimed at improving and stabilizing prices they may also promote other measures intended to increase the returns to producers, such as co-operative efforts in processing, product improvement, technical support, and direct marketing, distribution and shipping. One of the tasks of such associations, therefore, should be to identify the particular measures or combination of measures which would be most effective in securing the best results for developing producer countries. The effectiveness of unified action in international markets could be further improved by some institutional linkage among the various producer associations. This could provide a permanent forum in which regular consultations could take place regarding developments in the world economy and international trade policy as they affect commodity markets, and regarding the support which might be needed within the framework of collective action by producers of specific raw materials.

In this connexion it may be noted that the Conference of the Ministers of Foreign Affairs of Non-Aligned Countries held in Lima in 1975 called on developing countries to consider the possibility of joining existing producer associations or to establish new ones as a means of increasing their effectiveness in international markets. The Conference also approved, in conformity with a resolution of the Dakar Conference of Developing Countries on Raw Materials, a resolution establishing a Council of Associations of Developing Countries Producers-Exporters of Raw Materials. A group of experts is in the process of preparing the draft statutes for its establishment.

b. The creation of multinational marketing corporations. The concentration of the developing countries' trade, geographically and by commodity, provides a ready-made opportunity for them to increase their earnings by participating jointly in some of the marketing and distribution functions currently performed by developed countries' institutions. Such benefits would be especially important in the case of commodities for which producers cannot easily achieve substantial price increases through collective action, except over long periods. In addition, multinational marketing corporations may serve to eliminate uneconomic intermediation of developed countries' institutions in trade among developing countries themselves and to expand more vigorously exports to non-traditional markets, particularly to the socialist countries of Eastern Europe. Similarly, they may promote a greater participation of developing countries in the shipping of their exports, since the pooling of marine cargoes would be an important step towards the creation of more economic conditions for the operation of co-operative ventures in this field.

c. The creation of commodity markets in developing countries. Geographic and commodity concentration of the principal exports of developing countries gives rise to the possibility of jointly organizing commodity markets or exchanges controlled by and located in these countries. The existing system, evolved historically out of circumstances which are very different from those of the present time, bears little or no relation to the economic interests of the developing countries. A collective approach on this front would be indispensable to effective action, since these markets are characterized by a situation of competing sellers and oligopolistically organized buyers, often operating with speculative motives.

d. Organization of joint market intelligence services. These services may be more efficiently and effectively organized on a joint basis by groups of developing countries and could be located in the major purchasing centres, including the socialist countries of Eastern Europe. The development of such a network of services should make it possible eventually to collate information quickly on a world-wide basis.

Measures for improving the developing countries' trading position as regards imports. The import trade of developing countries is also characterized by an asymmetrical situation. The procurements of over 130 developing countries, of which about 120 can be categorized as small-scale in terms of the size of their import sectors, are concentrated in less than a dozen major industrial countries and their transnational corporations. Multinational import co-operation may therefore be a useful instrument to improve the developing countries' trading position vis-à-vis the developed ones while at the same time it may be used to stimulate trade among the developing countries themselves.

a. Joint public sector purchasing. This should be an immediate possibility for effective co-operation among developing countries, since even where no general state trading system operates, most governments import, on their own account, materials for state-owned enterprises, public institutions and services, and for infrastructure projects.

b. Joint operations by state trading corporations. State trading institutions exist in many countries and are spreading to others. They provide an immediate vehicle for co-ordinating information and, to the extent convenient, for joint operations in at least a few imports of high unit value or critical importance in terms of their aggregate value.

c. The use of joint invitations to tender. Since the execution of infrastructure and other construction projects is subject to international bidding in many countries and these bids are likely to be more competitive for large than for small tenders, substantial savings could result from multinational co-operation, not only at the public sector level but among private institutions. The potential importance of this is illustrated by the fact that between 1969 and 1972 the developing countries imported $107.8 billion worth of machinery and equipment.

d. Joint import agreements. These agreements could be used for single commodities or for several commodities together. Their aim would be to secure the best available terms in purchasing imports and technology through effective competition and the economies associated with large-scale, long-term contracts.

e. Organization of information exchange services. This might begin immediately with regular exchanges among regionally grouped countries on the terms prevailing in markets for a limited number of commodities of special interest to them—in many cases relatively homogeneous products of high import value. Such services may later be expanded on an inter-regional basis.

The System of Payments

The flow of trade among developing countries is impeded in many cases by payments difficulties. In anticipation of such constraints and in order to facilitate the liberalization of trade regimes a scheme of payments facilitation must be envisaged as part of a system of economic co-operation. Indeed it should be considered that even where no payments restrictions exist, the use of national currencies to finance trade, including invisibles, tends to reduce the overall costs and risks of mutual transactions.

Clearing arrangements. Co-operation in the field of payments could be approached initially by a network of clearing arrangements at the sub-regional level, the creation of linkages between those arrangements on a regional basis and the further extension of such linkages to schemes among different regions in order to create ultimately a system of payments covering the third world. Furthermore, the system of linkages could also be extended to the settlements scheme of the socialist countries members of the International Bank for Economic Co-operation (IBEC).

In some cases, the clearing schemes could be built up through bilateral arrangements linked together in a multilateral framework, as is done by the Latin American Free Trade Association (LAFTA) countries, where each pair of central banks is free to work out its mutual credit lines, but where the clearing is calculated simultaneously and multilaterally by a single agent, which simply directs debtor central banks to make specified payments to specified creditor central banks without participating in the settlement process itself. Alternatively, a multilateral clearing system with a centralized clearing house is possible. Under such a scheme credit lines are established between each participant and the clearing house, and payments are made to and received from the clearing house. This is the system operating in Central America and envisaged by the Asian and West African schemes.

Fluctuating exchange rates for several of the major world currencies could have repercussions on clearing arrangements in those developing regions where different intervention currencies are used by the various countries, e.g. West Africa and Asia. The problems involved could be reduced through the use of a non-national unit of account such as the SDR or one independently determined by the member central banks, which would result in the distribution of the exchange risks among the two central banks involved in a particular trading transaction within the region.

The linkage of clearing arrangements. While amalgamation of two or more sub-regional clearing systems might be administratively cumbersome and unjustified in terms of the volume of transactions between the groups in question, a group-to-group link may well prove mutually rewarding, particularly where bilateral payments agreements between countries belonging to the two groups tend to depress actual trade flows below their potential levels for the sake of bilateral balancing. Such a series of links might provide the basis for inter-regional monetary arrangements and institutions spanning the entire third world. Thus, a counterpart to the Bank for International Settlements (BIS), serving as a central bank for central banks of developing countries, might be envisaged. Other proposals could also be considered, such as the creation of international liquidity units acceptable throughout the developing countries.

In order to initiate the linkage between the several sub-regional or regional clearing arrangements three practical alternatives could be considered:

1. A country which is a member of a clearing arrangement could participate in another such arrangement which is not incompatible and provides the country involved the advantages of multilateral compensation in both systems (e.g. a member of LAFTA participating in the Central American Clearing House).
2. A member country of a clearing arrangement could sign bilateral agreements with countries members of another clearing arrangement based on a network of bilateral agreements (e.g. a member of the Central American Clearing House entering into agreements with one or several members of the LAFTA clearing scheme).
3. Agreement could be reached among two or more clearing arrangements.

Reciprocal payments support and joint reserve management. The credit element in the existing clearing arrangements is only minor and is not viewed as one of their main objectives. However, the fact that the two Latin American clearing arrangements have preceded mutual support agreements covering roughly the same group of countries is no mere coincidence, because the spirit of mutual trust among the respective central banks built up through closer working contacts in connexion with the clearing arrangements was an indispensable element in the subsequent agreements involving mutual balance-of-payments support. These agreements, therefore, could be a second step in the establishment of a system of payments co-operation.

One objective of reciprocal payments support arrangements is to provide member countries with a third line of reserves over and above (a) those held nationally and (b) those available unconditionally or conditionally from the IMF. Another objective of such arrangements is the visible implementation of the principle of collective self-reliance together with independence from constraints on national economic policies that borrowing from foreign national or international agencies may imply.

In practice, a multilateral system of mutual support could encompass bilateral agreements. Bilateral forms of mutual support have in fact been successfully attempted in recent years on the basis of deposits made by a central bank of a surplus developing country with the central bank of a deficit developing country, thereby strengthening the latter, but also diversifying the financial and political risks of the former. Bilateral swap agreements, which have constituted such an important feature of co-operation among central banks of developed countries, could be envisaged by developing countries as well.

Bilateral forms of support can be co-ordinated in a multilateral framework without losing their essentially bilateral legal form. This is what has been achieved by the LAFTA countries and the Dominican Republic within the framework of mutual support arrangements limited at this stage by three conditions, namely that a country asking for support (a) should have insufficient reserves in its own judgment; (b) should have a global balance-of-payments deficit; and (c) should have experienced a deterioration in its net balance of trade vis-à-vis its regional trading partners participating in these support arrangements, as reflected in the multilateral clearing mechanism.

A fully multilateralized form of mutual support has been devised in Central America by means of a sub-regional monetary stabilization fund functioning along lines similar to those of the IMF, where the country's global deficit and its adjustment policies are the prime criteria for obtaining support from its partners. Although the regional trade balance does not figure as one of the criteria, it is evident that the partners wish to prevent payments restrictions stemming from global balance-of-payments difficulties from being imposed on their mutual trade. A regional fund can be strengthened by external support from non-members, which has been true of the Central American Monetary Stabilization Fund.

The Central American scheme can serve as a prelude to an actual reserve pooling scheme implying joint management of a certain portion of national monetary reserves, an idea actively being pursued in the Andean Group and in Asia under the auspices of the Economic and Social Commission for Asia and the Pacific (ESCAP). To the extent that such reserve pooling is achieved, the combined weight of such pools will give their member central banks added bargaining strength for better deposit conditions vis-à-vis the large financial reserve centres, as well as additional capacity to float loans in the capital markets. Moreover, the pooling of information and know-how of these reserve pools would give their managers a potentially better opportunity for minimizing exchange risks and optimizing exchange profits in a world of fluctuating exchange rates. Finally, the creation of reserve pools covering a sufficiently large number of countries would permit at least a portion of the combined exchange reserves to be repatriated to that region without affecting individual member countries' international liquidity positions.

Co-operation in Production

Co-operation in production among developing countries is still at an incipient stage and has not yet given rise to a significant expansion of complementary production structures in the third world. However, the development of such complementary productive capacity constitutes a major precondition for the expansion and diversification of trade among developing countries. In the past, scarcity of entrepreneurial, financial and technological resources, as well as the small size of most national markets, have been serious obstacles to the development of multinational enterprises. A global system of co-operation among developing countries should therefore include, as a basic element, the necessary incentives and mechanisms to support parallel efforts at the national level.

Until now, joint ventures have been mainly the result of ad hoc arrangements, and, with the single exception of the Andean Group's sectoral agreements, do not involve broad programmes of a multinational character. Several of these ventures, moreover, have only limited objectives, such as production for the host-country market or securing assured sources of raw materials by relatively more advanced countries.

On the other hand, the number of projects and proposals for joint ventures in many developing countries has substantially increased in recent years, covering a variety of activities. For particular industries, especially in the export sector, it may continue to be necessary for some time to come to purchase technology from developed countries. However, the prospects for co-operation in production among developing countries are very favourable in view of their growing technological capabilities, the relative scarcity of certain raw materials and the availability of financial resources in the developing countries themselves.

These opportunities would appear to call for organized collaboration and negotiations within a framework designed to identify and exploit multinational combinations of natural resources, technology, management, finance and markets, promoted through joint enterprises. The various possibilities for combining these factors provide a powerful incentive and rationale for multinational co-operation among developing countries in the productive sectors. Such co-operation, if based on mutually equitable contractual arrangements, could benefit fully from the economies of scale which certain enterprises require in order to become economically viable.

At present, however, a number of joint ventures between different developing countries differ little from those established by developed country enterprises in individual developing countries. The traditional character of all of these ventures arises from the combination of both equity participation and the supply of technology by developed country enterprises. However, under certain circumstances, the availability of equity financing from a developing country could facilitate the disaggregation by the host country of the elements of technology from the capital.

A variant of the latter type of joint venture referred to above would be the provision of both equity and technology from a co-operating developing country. The advantage in both of these cases would be the opening up of possibilities for the application of developing countries' technologies and the creation of an alternative for the host country to the exclusive reliance upon similar arrangements with developed countries.

To balance the interests of participating countries and to enhance the prospects for development, less emphasis should be placed on equity financing than on factor complementarity in joint enterprises. In fact, in some cases it may be desirable to replace equity participation by long-term loan financing combined with commitments for the supply of inputs or the purchase of part of the output.

Factor complementarity would lead to a better use of resources, diversification of production, economies of scale and specialization, an improvement in market positions in third countries, or a combination of all or several of these effects. The complementarity of resources on a global basis would widen the economic options of co-operating countries beyond those offered by narrowly confined geographical spheres and would expand the possibilities for integrated production structures of individual countries as well as of those sub-regional economic groupings with a limited range of primary materials. Undoubtedly, such complementarity serves to make the enterprises based upon them economically viable and of mutual interest to the participants. It permits the setting up of individual or joint enterprises or cross-participation in enterprises covering a limited number of sequential production stages within a productive sector, without requiring special compensation mechanisms and multinational institutional structures to back them up. Consequently, joint productive enterprises based on factor complementarity are easier to negotiate than projects forming part of large multinational planning schemes for industry as a whole or a major sector thereof, objectives that can only be pursued with some chances of success within a dense system of integration arrangements and close political collaboration.

In many instances, co-operation in production may require parallel efforts for the development of infrastructure and common services. In this connexion, it appears that co-operation among developing countries in these fields has already made substantial progress, whether or not the co-operating countries participate in particular economic integration groupings. In the area of infrastructure, common objectives and the distribution of benefits can be identified relatively clearly in advance of the establishment of the project, and this may have facilitated decisions on multinational collaboration in such projects as the construction of hydro-electric plants, road networks, telecommunications and the development of water basins. In addition, co-operation in the field of infrastructure can be, and in some cases has been, an effective means of securing additional benefits for the relatively less advanced or land-locked neighbouring countries.

A number of multinational enterprises also exist in the field of services, such as multinational airlines, joint shipping services, reinsurance pools and bilateral and multilateral finance and banking institutions. However, the need for sustained co-operation among developing countries in technological and research services is becoming a matter of greater urgency.

Although the existence of different possibilities regarding multinational enterprises makes it difficult, at this stage, to elaborate common detailed guidelines for their organization, it is nevertheless necessary to establish a framework of measures and mechanisms, for application at both the international and the national level in order to facilitate their establishment and operation.

International Instruments

An institutional structure for the promotion of co-operation in the productive sectors is an open question, but one for which an answer must be found. Among the alternatives, one preliminary formula could be for the United Nations system to provide for the technical apparatus needed to identify and evaluate possibilities and to convene the intergovernmental working or negotiating groups which might be necessary to reach agreements on specific proposals. Regional and sub-regional development banks might participate actively in these efforts.

As one of the first steps in determining appropriate multinational enterprises it might be advisable to draw up inventories of possible multinational projects within each region, in co-operation with regional and sub-regional financial institutions—and if possible with national development banks—such as the one to be carried out by UNCTAD in the Arab countries under the programme financed by UNDP (the United Nations Development Programme) and the Arab Fund for Economic and Social Development or the one for infrastructure projects carried out for Latin America by the Inter-American Development Bank.

Apart from the problem of identification, the implementation of multinational projects presents a problem of proper planning and evaluation, mainly in regard to securing the economies of scale. But the planning and evaluation of multinational projects are hampered by the fact that such data as exist in developing countries to meet the needs of project planning are usually collected and organized on a national basis and are often statistically incompatible with those of neighbouring countries. There is a need, therefore, to gather the technical data to carry out the analysis of regional projects. For each particular sector of production, data on both the specific area involved and the standard elements of the activity under consideration are essential. Although much data might be available in United Nations agencies and financial institutions such as the World Bank, they obviously need to be organized, completed and updated. To meet the most pressing needs in regard to the thorough preparation and evaluation of multinational projects in the productive sectors, the United Nations agencies involved and the multinational financial institutions could be requested to organize one or several data banks.

To facilitate the preparation of projects and the financing of multinational enterprises, regional and sub-regional development banks should give special preference to, and earmark non-reimbursable funds for, pre-investment activities related to co-operation in the productive sectors. They could also make use of the possibilities provided for in their charters for equity participation in productive ventures and, where such provisions are not included, establish specialized subsidiaries for that purpose. The activities of the International Finance Corporation (IFC) could also be intensified and geared towards multinational enterprises among developing countries. Equity financing by such institutions, even if small, could act as a catalyst for other commitments and could make for increased confidence in multinational enterprises. The financial institutions might also take the initiative in establishing regional technology facilities and institutions for project preparation and implementation.

An essential element for co-operation in production is the improvement of the scientific and technological infrastructure of developing countries. Important progress has been achieved by some developing countries in the development of an indigenous technological base, training facilities and negotiating capacity with respect to foreign technology transfer. The dissemination and exchange of experience and of their technological knowledge would prove useful for other developing countries. Intensive efforts need to be made to establish transfer and development of technology centres at sub-regional and regional levels, with appropriate links among them. Such centres, if established in sectors of particular interest to the developing countries concerned and provided they are closely linked to institutions directly responsible for development in the productive sectors, may become important instruments through which possibilities for co-operation in production among developing countries can be identified and implemented. The centres could *inter alia* draw up and assess inventories of technologies available in developing countries and help to define them and negotiate their transfer among such countries. They could actively promote new projects for multinational enterprises and carry out specific technological research projects of direct interest to production in various developing countries, including the adjustment of foreign technologies to their own specific conditions and requirements.

The feasibility of establishing specialized technology trading enterprises in developing countries for the commercialization and dissemination of technology to and among developing countries might also be explored on a national, sub-regional or regional basis. Close co-operation among a group of developing countries, whether institutionalized in this manner or of a more general type, could substantially improve their negotiating positions with respect to the terms and conditions of the transfer of technology from developed countries and assist in identifying sources of technology supply.

Another possibility for collective action in order to facilitate co-operation in production concerns the field of training, with respect to both technical capabilities and management. Joint action on a sub-regional or regional scale can provide a useful alternative to national facilities where the latter would not appear feasible. The co-ordination of training programmes, the organization of seminars and the exchange of personnel in the technical, economic or juridical fields open up a wide area for joint action by developing countries at the bilateral, sub-regional, regional and inter-regional levels.

Measures at the National Level

In addition to international action, consistent policy measures at the national level need to be adopted in the developing countries themselves to promote initiatives, pursue negotiations and organize the actual establishment of multinational enterprises. Public sector involvement can be of major importance in determining the success of multinational enterprises and a number of specific measures can substantially facilitate the smooth operation of such enterprises once established. Most of these facilitating measures can be implemented autonomously by the countries concerned, but they may also become elements of bilateral or multilateral agreements aimed at ensuring that the operations of multinational enterprises comply with the development objectives of the co-operating countries. These measures could include the following:

Provisions regarding tariffs and import restrictions. The access of inputs from partner countries for joint processing would have to be fully liberalized. In regard to output, if markets are shared, the importing countries would have to grant free access to their own markets. This provision could be reinforced either by an agreed margin of protection vis-à-vis competing third countries or by a quantitative import guarantee by the importing countries. In both cases, it would be necessary to have a clear understanding in advance concerning price clauses, quality and standards.

Foreign exchange provisions. Equity participation and trade may call for certain adjustments in foreign exchange regimes so as to enable regular transfers of export receipts, interest, dividends, salaries and capital between the participating countries.

Fiscal incentives. Multinational enterprises consistent with national development objectives should benefit on an equal footing from fiscal incentives enjoyed by national enterprises in the host country. A case might also be made for granting special preferential status for high priority industries.

In order to secure the harmonious operation of multinational enterprises and the application of necessary measures at the national level a clear definition of the main long-term characteristics of each particular enterprise, as well as of its operating principles, would be necessary. This should include rules regarding management and an understanding as to the manner in which decisions would be adopted and policy formulated.

Notes

1. *International Development Strategy for the Second United Nations Development Decade,* para. 39.
2. General Assembly resolution 3202 (S-VI), section 1, 1(b).
3. General Assembly resolution 3362 (S-VII), section VI, 1, reprinted as Chapter 2 above.
4. For measures to facilitate and promote coordination among developing countries in the area of development finance, see UNCTAD, *Economic Co-operation among Developing Countries: Report by the UNCTAD Secretariat* (TD/192), 2 December 1975, pp. 23-27.

24 *Economic Development and the Mexico Conference on Women: Development, Equality and Peace*

Barbara Rogers

The key objective of the New International Economic Order (NIEO) is development, the development of the Third World. The NIEO program itself deals with the external component of development. This reflects the recognition that the international environment is a crucial determinant of the development process.

Development also has, of course, many internal components. One of the most important ones—and to date one of the most neglected ones—is the role of women in economic processes. The importance of this role is based on two facts. One, women constitute a substantial percentage of the economically active in many developing countries. And two, they play a central role in the rural sector—the most important one in developing countries. The relatively recent reevaluation of the role of agriculture for development and the recent food crisis have highlighted the importance of this sector. Thus, without proper consideration of the role of women in economic processes—and especially their crucial importance in agriculture and food processing—national development planning is very incomplete. To the extent, therefore, to which the NIEO discussion has drawn attention to the economic role of women, it has not only contributed to a more adequate understanding of the development process, but it has also contributed to the establishment of the new order itself.

This chapter will briefly review the importance of women's work in developing countries and especially the impact of their low status on the critical areas of population growth and food production. It will then consider the impact of the NIEO on the Conference of Mexico on Women and on United Nations (UN) debates on the status of women. Finally, it will

---

The author wishes to thank Ms. Rasil S. Basu of the United Nations Secretariat for her help in preparing this chapter. The responsibility, of course, rests with the author.

examine the interrelationship of the NIEO and women's role in development.

Background

It is impossible in this presentation to review adequately the role of women in development.[1] Their work and the consequences of their low and often declining status affect the entire development process. For example, perhaps one-quarter to one-third of all families are headed by women. Yet, this is never taken into account by development planners, although these families generally suffer the most acute poverty.[2] Women are in many areas important in commerce and a failure to recognize this can lead to a monopolization of the modern commercial sector by foreigners.[3] The increasing number of illiterates worldwide are predominantly female.[4] Discrimination against women in urban employment exacerbates the rural-urban migration, overloading the facilities of cities, and seriously disrupting economic and social life both in cities and in rural areas.[5]

In all areas, common characteristics can be perceived with regard to the contribution of women: (1) women's role in development is important; (2) this importance is not only ignored, but women are actively or subtly discriminated against; and (3) this is economically counterproductive and obstructs the development process. This can be demonstrated by examining two critical and related areas that have only fairly recently become the focus of serious debate among development planners: population growth and food production.

The failure even to maintain current standards of nutrition and general welfare has received particularly dramatic attention in India, where drastic measures to promote sterilization are under discussion. There are many other countries, particularly in Asia but also in Africa and Latin America, where the dual issues of food and population are beginning to be seen as the key to development and, in fact, to any rational approach to the domestic component of development within the framework of the NIEO.

Women bear children, raise them, and in many cases support them by their own labor. Women have a particularly strong interest in controlling their own fertility, and where they have the means to do so, they can be highly motivated. Whether their motivation is allowed to prevail, however, depends on their relative status and authority within the family unit. Their status, as measured by a variety of indices, is positively correlated with their use of contraceptives. Other important factors are their level of education and employment.[6]

Indications are numerous that women tend to want fewer children than they have—the most obvious one being the extremely high incidence of abortion world-wide (estimated at some 55 million a year).[7] The link

Table 1. "Economically active" women, by continent (Percent)

	Europe	North America	Africa	Asia	Latin America
Percentage of women economically active	29.4	25.o	26.3	21.5	17.1
Percentage of economically active women employed in agriculture	23.o	2.5	49.o	52.o	12.o

Source: Commitment (United Nations Development Programme, Division of Information, 1974), No. 4 (1974), p. 2.

between population planning and the status of women was stated at the Conference on Population at Bucharest in 1974 but taken much further at Mexico the following year. Many developing countries spoke in favor of strengthening the draft World Plan of Action on this point at Mexico, including such surprizing newcomers to the issue as Brazil, Guatemala, Lesotho, and Tanzania. These countries had previously taken a very critical line on population policy. There is a difference in emphasis between these countries and the developed market economies, which have tended to emphasize "population control" and various numerical targets. The Declaration of Mexico, on the other hand, which is essentially a Third World document, formulates the issue as the right of every couple and individual to decide the number and spacing of their children and to have the information to do so.[8]

The central role of women in agriculture and food production is an equally basic fact for the Third World. The Economic Commission for Africa has estimated that between 60 percent and 80 percent of agricultural labor in Africa is done by women.[9] Tables 1, 2 and 3 give an indication of women's work in agriculture. It is particularly evident from Table 3 that women constitute a substantial proportion of the family labor on small farms and also of the agricultural wage labor on larger ones. The figures, however, must be treated with some caution since very little research has so far been done on this issue. Furthermore, the figures probably do not reflect important items, such as, for example, the importance of animal husbandry performed by women in the region of Arab influence.

Work done by women in agriculture suffers from the low priority hitherto allocated to this sector by development planners. Where attention is paid to agriculture, changes—e.g., the introduction of "improved farming techniques"—often disregard the role of women and, as a consequence, are not effective or may even be counterproductive. When little or no attempts are made to improve the productivity of women, the upgrading

Table 2. Participation by African Women in the rural economy (Percent)

Responsibility	Women's contribution
A. Production supply distribution	
Food production	70
Domestic food storage	50
Food processing	100
Animal husbandry	50
Marketing	60
Brewing	90
Water supply	90
Fuel supply	80
B. Household, community	
Bearing, rearing, initial education of children	100
Cooking for husband, children, elders	100
Cleaning, washing, etc.	100
Housebuilding	30
House repair	50
Community self-help projects	70

Source: Adapted from Economic Commission for Africa, "The Role of Woman in African Development." Background Paper for the Conference of Mexico, (E/CONF.66/BP/8), 10 April 1975, p. 10.

of other components of the production system does little to improve the productivity of the system as a whole. In the Central African Republic, for example, women performed 55 percent of the agricultural labor in a "traditional" village and 68 percent in one subject to "improved farming techniques."[10] Clearly, the failure to upgrade women's productivity limits the amount of work that will be done under the new system. In fact, it handicaps it by improving productivity in one area (e.g., mechanization of the work done by men, such as preparation of the soil for sowing) while actually reducing it in related areas (by increasing the area to be weeded by women). This approach can lead to the complete failure of a project, as has been seen, for example, in some attempts in West Africa to boost rice production: without realizing that rice is grown by the women of the area, the instructors attempted to teach their methods to the men—who showed no interest. The result was complete failure, with the women subdividing the carefully improved fields into small traditional plots.[11]

Rural women are just beginning to be recognized as the "neglected resource in development."[12] As stated in a recent Food and Agricultural Organization (FAO) publication, "in the rural sector . . . the efficient use of women working together with men is one of the primary means by which improvements in many fields can be brought about. Food production, animal husbandry and the land tenure system are a few."[13] The Declaration of Mexico, adopted by the conference on the initiative of the Third World group of states, is unequivocal on this point:

Table 3. Women in the agricultural labor force (Percent)

Country	Female family labor as percentage of total family labor	Percentage of women among own-account farmers	Percentage of women among agricultural wage laborers
Africa south of the Sahara			
Ghana	39.6	37	6
Kenya	-	-	27
Liberia	46.2	18	4
Mauritius	13.3	11	20
Sierra Leone	42.4	10	5
Region of Arab influence			
Algeria	48.1	2	-
Egypt	3.2	1	4
Iran	5.6	2	4
Libya	2.5	-	-
Pakistan	15.1	4	6
Sudan	10.3	-	4
Syria	0.2	1	8
Tunisia	47.5	-	2
Turkey	51.0	-	23
South and East Asia			
Hong Kong	42.5	-	25
India	33.3	-	44
Malaysia	28.1	19	39
Philippines	14.6	4	12
South Korea	46.4	13	10
Sri Lanka	6.5	3	40
Thailand	51.5	14	35
Latin America			
Brazil	10.7	5	5
Chile	6.5	6	2
Colombia	5.3	5	3
Ecuador	5.0	5	4
Honduras	1.4	1	6
Jamaica	15.3	13	17
Mexico	4.3	5	16

Source: Based on Ester Boserup, *Woman's Role*, Tables 3, 8 and 9.

Modernization of the agricultural sector of vast areas of the world is an indispensable element for progress, particularly as it creates opportunities for millions of rural women to participate in development. Governments, the United Nations, its specialized agencies and other competent regional and international organizations should support projects designed to utilize the maximum potential and to develop the self-reliance of rural women.[14]

The Impact of the New International Economic Order on the Issue of Women

As outlined in the previous section, it is becoming evident to planners in governments and in international agencies that the role of women's work in economic development is important; that it has too often been ignored; and that this has been harmful to the development process. In the two key areas of population and agriculture (and particularly in food production), women play a key role in finding workable solutions. It must be emphasized, however, that awareness of this issue is at an early stage, and there are many traditional-minded planners at all levels who have never adequately considered the role of women and the importance of their work. This failure to connect the issues of women's economic and social status and the whole development process is partly the fault of those who were primarily concerned with the sociopolitical status of women, although a much more important reason is the general indifference to their work, even where attention was given to women in development.

In the UN, the main body concerned with women—and, until recently, the only one with any continuing mandate in this regard—is the Commission on the Status of Women, which has been meeting regularly since 1946. A major instrument produced by the Commission was the Declaration on the Elimination of Discrimination Against Women, called for by the General Assembly in 1963 and finally adopted by it on 7 November 1967. This document illustrates the approach of the Commission during the 1950s and most of the 1960s, an approach that was primarily concerned with human rights, as set forth in the Universal Declaration of Human Rights and the International Covenants on Human Rights. Thus, there is only one brief reference to development in the entire Declaration on the Elimination of Discrimination, which is in the preamble:

> *Convinced* that the full and complete development of a country, the welfare of the world and the cause of peace require the maximum participation of women as well as men in all fields. . . .

The rest of the document is concerned with women's access to equal rights and the elimination of discrimination.[15]

Unfortunately, human rights have the lowest possible priority of any issue—unless they are related to some issue of political importance, such as southern Africa or the Middle East. As a human rights issue, the question of discrimination against women has been given minimal attention in the UN, although it has to be recognized that the various International Conventions on the Status of Women[16] have had a substantial impact in their own right.[17]

It was partly the realization of this lack of priority that prompted the commission to concentrate, since the beginning of the 1970s, on women in developing countries. More important, however, was the changing character of the delegates to the commission. More high-powered women from Third World countries began to participate in its work, balancing the well-meaning but perhaps amateur approach of the women nominated by industrialized countries. Many of these earlier generations of women were not professionals, although they were often involved in non-governmental work on behalf of women in their own countries, in political, social, and legislative areas. It was not that the Commission ignored the question of women's work. However, the emphasis was overwhelmingly on women in industrialized countries. In general, relatively low priority was given to women's work as opposed to their political, social, and legal problems, although these areas are of course interconnected and cannot be discussed in isolation. Job discrimination in employment or wage levels, for example, are political and legal problems.

An important part of the impetus for considering women's role in development came from the regional commissions of the UN, where women's work was seen as the most important issue. In this respect, pioneering work was done by the Economic Commission for Africa (ECA) which, since 1970, has produced more research material on this subject matter and has more integrated projects under way than any other agency. The other regional commissions are beginning to pay serious attention to raising women's productivity, largely as a result of ECA's example and the changing climate of opinion that crystallized at Mexico.

Although a number of important initiatives regarding such problems as work opportunities for women have been undertaken in industrialized countries—and have been gathering momentum since the beginning of the 1970s—the UN, as such, has played little part in them; it is national and regional bodies, such as the European Community (EC), that are involved in this effort. But the public debate on the issue of women, as reflected in the international media, has clearly had some impact on debates in the UN, helping to bring it into focus perhaps for the first time for many delegates. However, media distortions of what the issues are, and the real importance of them for the long-term prospects of society and the economy, have meant that the publicity is somewhat counter-productive as far as Third World male delegates are concerned. Feminism can easily be dismissed as an American phenomenon which is irrelevant to the women of developing countries. The fact that there are strong women's movements in many of these countries is easily ignored by men anxious to preserve the status quo.

The major influence on the work of the Commission on the Status of Women, causing it to emphasize women's role in development much more strongly, has, in fact, been the mounting influence of Third World economic issues in the UN generally. This was expressed first in General Assembly resolution 2626 (XXV), which launched the Second UN Development Decade in 1970. Since then, there have been, at each session of the General Assembly, resolutions on women in development, and this has also been the pattern for the regional commissions and the specialized agencies of the UN. As indicated by a UN Secretariat study on the treatment of the issue of women in the various UN bodies:

> More and more United Nations bodies have become aware that the neglect of women in development plans and programmes constitutes the wastage of a valuable human resource with serious implications for the development effort itself.[18]

However, the major stimulus for this new emphasis on women in development has been the spirit as well as the letter of the NIEO. This became particularly obvious at the World Conference of the International Women's Year in Mexico, 19 June-2 July 1975. Although the resolutions of the Sixth and Seventh Special Sessions actually did not mention women as a separate issue, they were largely responsible for the heavy emphasis placed on the topic of women in development in the preparation of the background papers and the draft Plan of Action for the Mexico Conference. This was the first time that UN body had produced a collection of material on this issue—much of it drawing on recent studies done sporadically in various parts of the UN system and elsewhere. The preliminary material gathered for Mexico laid the basis for a much more coherent consideration of the issue of women in development by the UN system.

The declaration, plan of action, and resolutions passed by the Mexico Conference give the predominant place to the question of women in development, together with other issues related to it such as education, family planning, employment, health and nutrition, and the family in modern society. The declaration highlights such principles as equality between men and women; equal opportunity for women; and the right of women to work, to receive equal pay for work of equal value, and to equal conditions and opportunities for advancement. The right of women to decide freely whether or not to marry, and the right of every couple and individual to decide the number and spacing of their children, are mentioned expressly. Much of the Declaration, however, expands on the following theme:

> The issue of inequality, as it affects the vast majority of the women of the world, is closely linked with the problem of under-development, which exists as a result not only of unsuitable internal structures, but also of a profoundly unjust world economic system.[19]

There is both a negative and a positive reason for the stress on development at Mexico. On the negative side was a failure of the U.S. and the USSR to agree on the "peace" theme. The confrontation had already come to a head at the meetings of the preparatory committee in New York, which was charged with drafting the Plan of Action. Despite strong statements on the part of the Soviet Union and allied delegations to make disarmament a major theme, the United States resisted, arguing that disarmament was not a "suitable" issue for a conference on women. Nevertheless, the Soviet Union had a strong delegation at Mexico, primarily to press the disarmament issue. However, the conflict over this matter produced a virtual stalemate. In this situation, the more constructive action went to the Third World countries. They benefited from the economic development momentum that built up subsequent to the Sixth Special Session and, of course, they had numerical superiority, as well as the very strong backing of Mexico, whose president, Luis Echeverria, had a strong personal interest in exercising leadership in this conference.[20] The most direct influence of the Third World manifested itself in the Declaration of Mexico, a document that was in fact produced by the Group of 77 at Mexico itself, drawing on documents prepared at preparatory conferences in Somalia, Zaire, and Venezuela. It was co-sponsored by 74 developing countries and adopted by a vote of 89 to 3, with 18 abstentions.[21] The Plan of Action, however, was adopted by consensus.

Inadequately reconciled with the theme of integrating women into development was a strong move to give priority to a mere reaffirmation of the NIEO, which some delegates even saw as an alternative to integrating women into development. Battles on this issue were fought largely within the individual delegations and drafting committees of the Third World group at Mexico, where the small number of women delegates were instrumental in reaching some kind of rational combination of the two issues within the very limited time available. The Declaration of Mexico contains elements of the two approaches—namely, priority on the integration of women into development on the one hand, and the achievement of the NIEO as an essential precondition on the other—in a reasonably coherent way.[22] Its paragraph 18 expresses the general approach quite well:

> The present state of international economic relations poses serious obstacles to a more efficient utilization of all human and material potential for accelerated development and for the improvement of living standards in developing countries aimed at the elimination of hunger, child mortality, unemployment, illiteracy, ignorance and backwardness, which concern all of humanity and women in particular. It is therefore essential to establish and implement with urgency the New International Economic Order of which the Charter of Economic Rights and Duties of States constitutes a basic element. . . .

Implementation

A crucial question related to the Mexico Conference and the whole of the International Women's Year of 1975 concerns the implementation of the decisions adopted by it. Many nongovernmental delegates were extremely angry at the tokenism they perceived in the management of the conference and dubbed the International Women's Year "one long Mother's Day." The problem of implementation of the resolutions was pointed out by Ashraf Pahlavi of Iran, a leading figure in the events of the Year, who observed that:

> If even 10 percent of these [documents] were to be implemented, then there would be a major improvement in the condition of millions of women. . . . The question is how to carry on from here in the face of chronic apathy on the part of most governments. . . . It is clear that the condition of women has not been noticeably changed by the Year. It is equally clear, however, that their problems received attention of an unprecedented scale. By providing a world forum, the Year helped the realization that in a global perspective the problems of women had far broader scope and graver dimensions than had generally been realized.[23]

As already mentioned, the Special Sessions did not make specific mention of the role of women in development. However, decisions made at the Mexico Conference ensure that in the future this issue will be a regular item on the agenda of debates on development and the NIEO in the UN and other forums. The World Plan of Action contains ambitious plans for review and appraisal to be undertaken at regular intervals by the UN system. In addition, the regional economic commissions are given special responsibility for monitoring "progress towards the greater and more effective participation of women in all aspects of development efforts."[24] It is indicative of the growing awareness of women's role in development that the General Assembly, at its 30th Session and acting on a proposal contained in one of the resolutions adopted in Mexico, declared that the decade 1976-85 should be the United Nations Decade for Women and Development, under the same slogan as the Mexico Conference: "Equality, Development and Peace."

Perhaps the most immediate boost to changes in development policies and programs, however, may come, at least initially, from the United States. A major early landmark was the passage in 1973 of the "Percy Amendment" to the Foreign Assistance Act of 1973. The amendment specified that all future U.S. development assistance should

> . . . give particular attention to those programs, projects, and activities which tend to integrate women into the national economy of foreign countries, thus improving their status and assisting the total development effort.[25]

This amendment and the changing climate of opinion on women in development are beginning to influence some of the UN agencies, where steps are being taken to evaluate programs and projects in terms of their impact on women as well as men. At the same time, however, a few countries in the Third World are far ahead in putting theory into practice. China is, of course, a widely publicized and important example, but equally interesting are such countries as Angola, Mozambique, and Guinea-Bissau, who involved women in governmental decision-making, as well as fighting, well before independence. Regardless of whether or not governments actively support the integration of women in development, drastic changes are taking place throughout the Third World which involve a complex network of factors, usually including strong women's organizations in many countries.

Summary and Conclusions

As outlined in this chapter, the issue of women in development is being increasingly recognized as an issue that has been seriously neglected by development planners and which, as a result, has led to many projects and programs that failed to reach their objective. This is particularly important in the context of population growth and food production, where the status and the productivity of women are key factors in any attempt to raise the living standard in the developing countries.

Until the late 1960s, very little attention had been paid to women's economic and social roles in developing countries. Beginning in 1970, this changed with the adoption of a number of pertinent General Assembly resolutions and, on a more profound level, with the collection of a useful body of material for the Mexico Conference. Partly because of the overall change in emphasis in UN debates to the needs of the Third World—epitomized in the Sixth and Seventh Special Sessions—and partly because of a recognition that an approach to the issue on a basis of human rights had failed to achieve satisfactory results, increasing stress was placed on women and their role in development. The conference itself, and the documents emerging from it, represent only a beginning: a program of action to be implemented in the course of the UN Decade on Women and Development, and involving the whole UN system, is the major positive result of the Mexico Conference.

There is a tendency in debates on the NIEO to concentrate on commodities, rather than people, and international, rather than national, redistribution of income. The issue of women is a unique one in that it stresses the mobilization of human resources rather than capital and technology alone. The point is well put in a statement by Bradford Morse, the UN Development Programme Administrator:

> Last year the international community took great strides forward in putting economic and social development into proper focus. Perhaps more than at any earlier time, humanity *per se* overshadowed such abstractions as gross national

> product, terms of trade and balance of payments. International Women's Year compelled us to think about development at every step in terms of men and women. We were once again talking about people. . . . the equality and integration of women in development is a *sine qua non* for the establishment of an internationally equitable economic order, one that offers a better life for all men, women and children.[26]

The international and national components of development are interrelated. The international trade, financial, and other issues that figured so prominently in the resolutions adopted by the Sixth and Seventh Special Sessions are important in terms of the resources to be made available through the NIEO to the developing countries. But for these resources to be fully effective, they have to be complemented by a number of domestic changes. The NIEO discussion has contributed significantly to focusing attention on one aspect of the domestic changes required: the role of women in development. It has, thereby, set in motion a train of events that may well lead to a complete and conscious integration of women in the development process and, therefore, to the full realization of the human potential of the entire population in each developing country. This, in turn, is an important contribution to the establishment of the New International Economic Order.

Notes

1. For an outline of the issue, see Barbara Rogers, "Women's Contribution to Development" (New York: United Nations Development Programme, Division of Information, Development Issue Paper, 1976).
2. Estimate by Elise Boulding, quoted in June Nash, "Certain Aspects of the Integration of Women in the Development Process: A Point of View." Background Paper to the Conference of Mexico (E/CONF.66/BP/5), 9 June 1975, p. 8. See also Elise Boulding, "Women, Bread and Babies: Directing Aid to Fifth World Farmers," mimeographed. Background Paper to the Conference on the World Food and Population Crisis: A Role for the Private Sector (Dallas, Texas), 3 April 1975.
3. Ester Boserup, *Woman's Role in Economic Development* (London: George Allen and Unwin, 1970), pp. 87-99.
4. UNESCO, *Literacy, 1969-1971* (Paris: UNESCO, 1972), table 5.
5. Boserup, *Woman's Role,* Parts II and III; see also Ester Boserup and Christina Liljencrantz, *Integration of Women in Development: Why, When, How* (New York: United Nations Development Programme, May 1975), pp. 16-17.
6. See United Nations, *The Status of Women and Family Planning* (E/CN.6/575/Rev.1), 19 February 1974.

7. Worldwatch Institute and National Academy of Sciences, cited in *New York Times,* 22 February 1976.
8. For fuller discussion of the population issue at Mexico, see Adrienne Germaine, "Women: A Powerful Pressure Group for Family Planning?," *Populi* 2 (1975): 3-5.
9. Economic Commission for Africa, *The Changing and Contemporary Role of Women in African Development* (Addis Ababa: Economic Commission for Africa, 1974).
10. Boserup, *Woman's Role,* p. 21.
11. Philippe Delalande, *L'aide etrangère a la vulgarisation agricole au Senegal,* mimeographed (Dakar: Université de Dakar, 1966), p. 61.
12. FAO, "The Role of Women in Rural Development." Background Paper to the Conference of Mexico (E/CONF.66/BP/11), 24 March 1975, p. 2. See also Ford Foundation Task Force on Women, *Women and National Development in African Countries: Some Profound Contradictions* (New York: Ford Foundation, 1973).
13. FAO, "The Role of Women in Rural Development," p. v; see also Boserup, *Woman's Role*, Part I.
14. "Declaration of Mexico on the Equality of Women and their Contribution to Development and Peace, 1975," paragraph 25, in United Nations, *Report of the World Conference of the International Women's Year, Mexico City, 19 June-2 July 1975* (New York: United Nations, 1976). See also "Plans of Action," ibid.
15. See United Nations, Office of Public Information (OPI), *Declaration on the Elimination of Discrimination against Women* (New York: United Nations, OPI, 1973); Article 1, for example, which states: "Discrimination against women, denying or limiting as it does their equality of rights with men, is fundamentally unjust and constitutes an offence against human dignity."
16. A number of conventions have been adopted on such issues as political rights, suppression of prostitution and slavery, rights with regard to marriage, equal pay, abolition of discrimination in employment and education, and others. For a listing, see United Nations, *Meeting in Mexico* (New York: United Nations, 1975), pp. 101-3.
17. The conventions have been embodied in the national legislation of a number of countries, particularly recently independent ones of the Third World. A number of these countries are, at least on paper, far ahead of the industrialized countries in that their constitutions guarantee equal rights to all, regardless of sex.
18. United Nations, Secretary-General, *United Nations System and the Elimination of Discrimination against Women.* Background Paper to the Conference of Mexico (E/CONF.66/BP/1), 6 June 1975, p. 6.
19. Paragraph 4 of the Declaration of Mexico.
20. At that time, President Echeverria was campaigning for the post of

Secretary-General of the United Nations.
21. The declaration was adopted under great pressure of time and an alternative draft offered by the United States and the Federal Republic of Germany was never officially considered. This led to some reluctance by some developed countries to vote for it, particularly as the Group of 77's draft contained a number of references to which they were opposed (e.g., the condemnation of Zionism as a form of racism) or to which they had already registered opposition on earlier occasions (e.g., the Charter of Economic Rights and Duties of States). For a presentation of these arguments, see the discussion by Ambassador Barbara White of the United States, cited in United Nations, *Meeting in Mexico,* p. 27. Denmark, Israel, and the United States voted against the Declaration.
22. See in particular the preamble, and paragraphs 14-18 of the Declaration.
23. *New York Times,* 5 January 1976.
24. United Nations, *Declaration of Mexico: Plans of Action* (New York: United Nations, 1975), p. 54.
25. United States Government, *Foreign Assistance Act of 1973,* PL 93-189 (December 1973).
26. "Message by the UNDP Administrator, Mr. Bradford Morse, to the United Nations Seminar on Participation of Women in Economic, Social and Political Development: Obstacles that Hinder Their Integration," Buenos Aires, 22-30 March 1976, mimeographed, pp. 1, 4.

Index